LEY FINANCE EDITIONS

McMillan on Option

McMillan on Options

Lawrence G. McMillan

John Wiley & Sons, Inc.

New York • Chichester • Brisbane • Toronto • Singapore

Copyright © 1996 by Lawrence G. McMillan.
Published by John Wiley & Sons, Inc.

Library of Congress Cataloging-in-Publication Data

McMillan, L. G. (Lawrence G.)
    McMillan on options / Lawrence G. McMillan.
      p. cm. — (Wiley finance editions)
    Includes index.
    ISBN 0-471-11960-1 (cloth: alk. paper)
    1. Options (Finance) I. Title. II. Series.
  HG6042.M348 1996
  332.63'228—dc20   96-27174

Printed in the United States of America

10 9 8 7 6 5 4 3 2 1

Preface

When people learn that I have written another book, they usually ask one of two questions: "Is this an update of your other book?" or "What's the difference between this one and your other one?" First of all, this is most assuredly *not* an update of *Options as a Strategic Investment* (OSI). This is a completely different, stand-alone book that relates option trading in actual examples. Second, there is a substantial difference between this book and OSI. This book is not intended to be a comprehensive definition of strategies—that is better derived from OSI, which is a reference work. This is a book in which the application of options to actual trading situations is discussed. There are plenty of actual trading examples, many of them derived from my own trading experience. In addition, there are a number of stories—some humorous, some more on the tragic side—that illustrate the rewards and pitfalls of trading, especially trading options. In addition, the *content* of this book covers ground that one does not normally find in books on options; that content will be discussed shortly.

There is a continuous discussion of futures trading, as well as stock and index trading, herein. The futures markets offer many interesting situations for option trading and strategies. To that end, the basic definitions of futures options—and how they compare to, and differ from, stock options—are included in Chapter 1.

While the book is not really meant for beginners, it contains all the necessary definitions. Thus, serious traders will have no trouble at all in getting up to speed. In fact, many of the techniques described in this book do not require familiarity with option strategies at all. The more elementary option strategy definitions are not expanded upon at great length here, however, as my objective is to describe practical applications. For example, it is not my intention to detail the explicit calculations of break-even points and explain follow-up actions for these basic strategies. Readers who feel a need to better understand the basics should refer to the aforementioned work, OSI, which describes virtually all conceivable strategies in a rather large amount of detail.

As for content, the book is basically divided into five major sections, spread out over seven rather lengthy chapters. The first part—Chapters 1 and 2—lays out the basic definitions and reviews option strategies, so that the framework is in place to understand and utilize the material in succeeding chapters. Even seasoned option professionals should enjoy reading these introductory chapters, for the trading tales that accompany many of the strategies are sure to elicit some nodding of heads. Graphs and charts are liberally used. Since things are more easily seen in graphs than in tables, over 120 such graphs and charts are included in this book.

The next three chapters—3 through 5—are intensive discussions of some very important trading tactics, based on options. However, they are more of a basic nature and don't require a theoretical approach to option trading. In fact, a stock or futures trader should be able to absorb this information rather quickly, even if he doesn't have a clue as to what the delta of an option is. Don't get me wrong—I encourage every option trader to use a model via a computer program in order to evaluate an option before he actually buys or sells it. However, these chapters don't require anything more theoretical than that.

Chapter 3 contains material that is extremely important to all traders—particularly stock traders, although futures traders will certainly benefit as well. I like to think of the information in this chapter as demonstrating how versatile options can be—they don't have to be merely a speculative vehicle. A basic understanding of the concepts involving using options to construct positions that are equivalent to owning stock or futures contracts is shown to be necessary for many applications. For example, it allows a futures trader to extract himself from a position, even though the futures may be locked limit against him.

Later in the same chapter, there is an extremely detailed discussion of how the expiration of options and futures affect the stock market. Several trading systems are laid out that have good track records, and that can be used month after month. Finally, the use of options or futures to protect a portfolio of stocks is also discussed in some detail. If we ever go into another bear market, these strategies will certainly become very popular.

Chapter 4 is my favorite—"The Predictive Power of Options." Since options offer leverage, they are a popular trading vehicle for all manner of speculators. By observing both option prices and option volume, you can draw many important conclusions regarding the forthcoming direction of stocks and futures. A large part of the chapter describes how to use option volume to buy stock (or sometimes sell it) in advance of major corporate news items, such as takeovers or earnings surprises. However, another lengthy discussion involves the put–call ratio—a contrary indicator—as it applies to a wide variety of indices and futures. The work on futures' put–call ratios is, I believe, unique in the annals of technical analysis in that the techniques are applied to and rated on a vast array of futures markets.

Several trading systems—from day-trading to seasonal patterns—with profitable track records are described in Chapter 5. Many traders, even those who are technically inclined, often overlook the power of seasonality. Moreover, the use of options in intermarket spreads is explained. Options give intermarket spreaders an additional chance to make money, if applied in the ways shown.

For those with a theoretical bent, Chapter 6 may be your favorite. The use of neutral option strategies is discussed, especially with respect to predicting and trading volatility. One of my pet peeves is that the term "neutral" is thrown around with such ease and, as a result, is often applied to positions that have considerable risk. The intent of Chapter 6 is to not only set the record straight, but to demonstrate that—while neutral trading can certainly be profitable—it is not the easy-money, no-work technique that some proponents seem to be extolling. I am often asked how I base my decisions on taking a position, rolling, and so forth, so the backspread example in Chapter 6 is intended to be almost a diary of what I was thinking and how I traded the position over the course of six months.

The book winds up with a discussion of money management, trading philosophy, and some trading guidelines—all in Chapter 7. Some of my favorite trading stories and sayings are related in this chapter. I hope you enjoy them as well.

My hope is that this book will bring more traders into the option markets, as they realize that options can be used in many ways.

Options don't merely have to be treated as a speculative vehicle. In fact, you might be strictly a stock or futures trader, but find that options can give you valuable buy and sell signals. Those with a more theoretical bent will find that volatility trading can be lucrative as well.

There is no doubt that options and other derivatives now hold a major place in the investment landscape, but it is disconcerting to see how many people still don't seem to understand options. In fact, they are quick to place blame on derivatives when things go wrong. Only by dissemination of information, such as that in this book, can we hope to overcome such negative and uneducated attitudes. When we have another bear market, option traders will probably do very well—whether they use options as a protective device or as a speculative one. Some have even gone so far as to predict that angry investors, who do not understand derivatives, will attempt to blame that bear market and its concomitant losses on options and other derivatives. That would be ludicrous, of course, but if we can convince more and more people of the viability of option trading, then affixing any future blame will be a moot point.

I've been in this business so long now that there are literally hundreds of people I could thank for helping me get to this point. However, in the interest of space and time, I will limit my kudos to those who specifically helped with this book, and with the concepts behind it: Shelley Kaufman, who did all the graphics work in this book and who is an invaluable confidant on all matters; Peter Bricken, who first came up with the idea of monitoring option volume as a precursor of corporate news events; Van Hemphill, Mike Gallagher, and Jeff Kaufman, who provided information on expiration activity that is nonpareil and who have helped me to clarify my thinking on strategies regarding expiration; Chris Myers, who convinced me to write this book; Peter Kopple, off whom I can constantly bounce ideas; and Art Kaufman, who convinced me that I could go into business for myself. Finally, a special thanks to my wife, Janet, who puts up with my crazy hours, and to my children, Karen and Glenn.

LAWRENCE G. MCMILLAN

Randolph, New Jersey
September 1996

Contents

List of Figures

McMillan on Options

1 Option History, Definitions, and Terms

There are many types of listed options trading today: stock options, index options, and futures options are the major ones. The object of this book is to explore some of the many ways in which options can be used, and to give practical demonstrations that will help the reader make money.

Options are useful in a wide array of applications. They can be used to establish self-contained strategies, they can be used as substitutes for other instruments, or they can be used to enhance or protect one's position in the underlying instrument, whether that is stock, index, or futures. In the course of this book, the reader may discover that there are more useful applications of options than he ever imagined. As stated in the Preface, this book is not really meant for novices, but contains all definitions to serve as a platform for the larger discussion.

UNDERLYING INSTRUMENTS

Let's begin with the definitions of the simplest terms, as a means of establishing the basic building blocks. Before even getting into what an option *is*, we should have some idea of the kinds of things that have options. That is, what are the underlying instruments that provide the groundwork for the various listed derivative securities (options, warrants, etc.)? The simplest underlying instrument is common stock. Options that give the investor the right to buy or sell common stock are called *stock options* or *equity options*.

Another very popular type of underlying instrument is an *index*. An index is created when prices of a group of financial instruments—stocks, for example—are grouped together and "averaged" in some manner so that the resulting number is an index that supposedly is representative of how that particular group of financial instruments is performing. The best-known index is the Dow-Jones Industrial Average, but there are indices of many other groups of stocks; indices with a large number of stocks in them are the S&P 500 and the Value Line Index, for example. There are also many stock indices that track various groups of stocks that are in the same industry: Utility Index, Oil Index, Gold and Silver Index, for example. There are even indices on foreign stock markets, but they have options listed in the United States; these include the Japan Index, Hong Kong Index, and Mexico Index, as well as several others. Indices are not restricted to stocks, however. There are indices of commodities, such as the Commodity Research Bureau Index. Moreover, there are indices of bonds and rates; these include such things as the Short-Term Rate Index, the Muni Bond Index, and the 30-Year Bond Rate Index. Options on these indices are called *index options*. Appendix A contains a list of available index options.

Finally, the third broad category of underlying instrument is *futures*. This is probably the least understood type of underlying instrument, but as you will see when we get into strategies, futures options are extremely useful and very important. Some people mistakenly think options and futures are nearly the same thing. Nothing could be further from the truth. The "dry" definition is *a futures contract is a standardized contract calling for the delivery of a specified quantity of a certain commodity, or delivery of cash, at some future time*. In reality, owning a futures contract is very much like owning stock, except that the futures' price is related to the cash price of the underlying commodity, and the futures contract has a fixed expiration date. Thus, futures contracts can climb in price infinitely, just as stocks can, and they could theoretically trade all the way down to zero, just as stocks can. Moreover, futures can generally be traded on very small percentages of margin, so that the risk of owning futures is quite large, as are the potential rewards. We discuss futures contracts in more detail later, but this brief description should suffice to lay the groundwork for the following discussion of options terms. As might be suspected, options on futures contracts are called *futures options*.

OPTION TERMS

An *option* is the right to buy or sell a particular underlying security at a specific price, and that right is only good for a certain period of time. The specific items in that definition of an option are as follows:

- **Type.** Type describes whether we are talking about a call option or a put option. If we are talking about stock options, then a call option gives its owner the right to *buy* stock, while a put option gives him the right to *sell* stock. While it is possible to use options in many ways, if we are merely talking about buying options, then a call option purchase is bullish—we want the underlying stock to increase in price—and a put option purchase is bearish—we want the stock to decline.
- **Underlying Security.** Underlying security is what *specifically* can be bought or sold by the option holder. In the case of stock options, it's the actual stock that can be bought or sold (IBM, for example).
- **Strike Price.** The strike price is the price at which the underlying security can be bought (call option) or sold (put option). Listed options have some standardization as far as striking prices are concerned. For example, stock and index options have striking prices spaced five points apart. Moreover stock options also have strikes spaced 2½ points apart if the strike is below 25. Futures option striking prices are more complex, because of the differing natures of the underlying futures, but they are still standardized for each commodity (one point apart for bonds, for example, or 10 points apart for a more volatile commodity like corn).
- **Expiration Date.** The expiration date is the date by which the option must either be liquidated (i.e., sold in the open market) or exercised (converted into the physical instrument

that underlies the option contract—stock, index, or futures). Again, expiration dates were standardized with the listing of options on exchanges. For stock options and most index options, this date is the Saturday following the third Friday of the expiration month (which, by default, makes the third Friday of the month the last trading day). However, for futures options, these dates vary widely. More about that later. The most heavily traded listed options usually have less than nine months of life remaining, but there are longer-term options—called LEAPS options when one is referring to stock options or index options—that can extend out to two years or more.

These four terms combine to uniquely describe any option contract. It is common to describe the option by stating these terms in this order: underlying, expiration date, strike, and type. For example, an option described as an *IBM July 50 call* completely describes the fact that this option gives you the right to buy IBM at a price of 50, up until the expiration date in July. Similarly, a futures option described as the *U.S. Bond Dec 98 put* gives you the right to sell the underlying 30-year U.S. Government Bond futures contract at a price of 98, up until the expiration of the December options.

THE COST OF AN OPTION

The cost of an option is, of course, called the *price*, but it is also referred to as the *premium*. You may notice that we have not yet described *how much* of the underlying instrument can be bought or sold via the option contract. Listed options generally standardize this quantity. For example, stock options give the owner the right to buy (call) or sell (put) 100 shares of the underlying stock. If the stock splits or declares a stock dividend, then that quantity is adjusted to reflect the split. But, in general, stock options are spoken of as being options on 100 shares of stock. Index options, too, are generally for 100 "shares" of the underlying index, but since the index is not usually a physical entity (i.e., it does not really have *shares*), index options often convert into cash. We will describe that process shortly. Finally, futures options are exercisable into *one* futures contract, regardless of how many bushels, pounds, bales, or bonds that futures contract represents in terms of the actual commodity.

Only by knowing this quantity can you tell how many actual dollars an option contract will cost, since option prices are quoted in units. For example, if someone tells you that the IBM July 50 call is trading at 3 (and we know that the option is for 100 shares of IBM), then the actual cost of the option is $300. Thus, one option trading at 3 costs $300 and "controls" 100 shares of IBM until the expiration date.

It is a fairly common mistake for a beginner to say "I want to buy 100 options" when what he really means is he wants to buy one option (this mistake derives from the fact that if a stock investor wants to control 100 shares of IBM, then he tells his broker to buy 100 IBM common stock). This can result in some big errors for customers and/or their brokerage firms, or possibly even worse. You can see that if you told your broker to buy 500 of the above IBM options, you would have to pay $150,000 for those options (500 × $300), but if you really meant to buy 5 options (to "control" 500 shares of IBM), you thought you were making a $1,500 investment (5 × $300). Quite a difference.

Of course these sorts of things tend to balloon out of control at the worst times (Murphy's Law is what they call it). When the market crashed 190 points on one Friday in October of 1990 as the UAL deal fell apart, people were genuinely concerned. On Monday morning, a rather large stockholder had been reading about buying puts as protection for his stocks, so he put in a market order to buy something like 1,500 puts at the market. His broker was a little taken aback, but since this was a large stockholder, he put the order in. Of course, that morning, the puts were extremely expensive as people were fearful of another 1987-style crash. Even though the options had been quoted at a price of 5 on Friday night, the order was filled on Monday morning at the extremely high price of 12 because of fear that prices would crash further. Two days later, the customer received his confirm, requesting payment of $1.8 million. The customer called his broker and said that he had meant to buy puts on 1,500 shares, not 1,500 puts— a difference of roughly $1,782,000! Of course, by this time, the market had rallied and the puts were trading at only a dollar or two (1 or 2 points, that is). I'm not sure how the lawsuit turned out.

The cost—in U.S. dollars—of any particular futures option depends, of course, on how much of the commodity the futures control. We have already said that a futures option "controls" one futures contract. But each futures contract is somewhat different. For example, soybean futures and options are worth $50 per point. So if someone says that a soybean July 600 put is selling for 12, then it would cost $600 (12 × $50) to buy that option. However, Eurodollar futures and options are worth $2,500 per point, so if a Eurodollar Dec 98 call is selling for 0.70, then you have to pay $1,750 (0.70 × $2,500) to buy it. We specify the terms for most of the larger futures contracts later in Appendix B.

THE HISTORY OF LISTED OPTIONS

On April 26, 1973, the Chicago Board Option Exchange (CBOE) opened its doors and began trading listed call options on 16 stocks. From that humble beginning, option trading has evolved to today's broad and active markets. We thought it might be interesting to review how option trading got to where it is today (nostalgic might be a better word for "old-timers" who have been around since the beginning). In addition, a review of the history of listed option trading might provide some insight for newer traders as to how and why the markets have developed the way they have.

The Over-the-Counter Market

Prior to listed option trading, puts and calls traded over the counter. In this form, there were several dealers of options who found both a buyer and a seller (writer) of a contract, got them to agree on terms, and executed a trade between them. The term "writer" arose from the fact that an actual contract was being "written" and the issuing party was the seller of the option. The dealer generally took a commission out of the middle of this trade: for example, the buyer might have paid 3¼ and the seller received 3. The remaining ¼ point was kept by the dealer as payment for lining up the trade.

Options of this type were generally struck at the current stock price; thus if the stock was selling at 46⅜ when the contract was agreed upon, then that would be the striking price of the calls (or puts). This made for some very awkward calculations. Moreover, these over-the-counter options normally had expiration dates that were fixed time periods when they were issued: the choices were time periods of 6 months + 10 days, 95 days, 65 days, or 35 days. One other term that was unusual: dividends went to the holder of the call upon exercise. Thus, upon exercise, the striking price would actually be adjusted for the dividends paid over the life of the option.

Besides the relatively arduous task of finding two parties who wanted to take opposite sides of a particular trade, the greatest hindrance to development of the over-the-counter market was that there was virtually no secondary market at all. Suppose you bought a call on a stock with these terms: strike price 46⅜, expiration date 35 days from trade date. Later, if the stock went up a couple of points quickly, you might theoretically have wanted to sell your over-the-counter call. However, who were you going to sell it to? The dealer might try to find another buyer, but the terms would be the same as the original call. Thus, if the stock had risen to 48¾ after 10 calendar days had passed, the dealer would be trying to find someone to buy a call that was 2⅜ points in-the-money that had 25 days of life remaining. Needless to say, it would be virtually impossible for a buyer to be found. Thus, option holders were often forced to hold on until expiration or to trade stock against their option in order to lock in some profit. Since this was in the days of fixed commission rates, it was a relatively expensive matter to be trading stock against an option holding. Altogether, this was a small option market, trading less than 1,000 contracts daily in total.

The CBOE Beginning

This over-the-counter arrangement was onerous for all parties. So it was decided to put into practice the idea of standardizing things by having fixed striking prices and fixed expiration dates, and having all trades clear through a central clearing corporation. These solutions all came from the Chicago Board of Trade (CBOT), since standardization of futures contracts had proved to be workable there. The first president of the CBOE was Joe Sullivan, who had headed the research project for the CBOT.

However, since over-the-counter option trading was "the way it had always been," the idea of standardizing things was met with heavy skepticism. The extent of this skepticism was most evident in one interesting story: the major over-the-counter dealers were offered seats on the fledgling CBOE for the nominal cost of $10,000 apiece. A seat today is worth over $450,000. Few of them took the opportunity to buy those seats for what turned out to be a paltry amount; many were convinced that the new exchange was little more than a joke. In addition, since these new options were traded on an exchange, the Securities and Exchange Commission (SEC) had to approve them and issue regulations.

Nevertheless, the Chicago Board Options Exchange opened its doors on April 26, 1973, with first-day volume of 911 calls being traded on 16 stocks. Surprisingly—and even some traders who were around at the beginning may find this hard to remember—IBM was not one of the original 16. It was listed in the second group of 16 stocks, which were added in the fall of 1973. Given the fact that IBM has been, by far, the most active equity option stock, it is hard to remember that it wasn't one of the originals. In fact, the original group was a rather odd array of stocks. If you were around at the beginning, test your memory. How many of them can you remember? They are listed three paragraphs below.

Besides standardizing the terms of options, the CBOE introduced the market maker system to listed equity markets and also was responsible for the Option Clearing Corporation (OCC), the guarantor of all options trades. Both of these concepts were important in giving the new exchange viability from the viewpoints of depth of markets and reliability of the exercise process. If you exercised your call, the OCC stood ready to make delivery even if the writer of the call somehow defaulted (margin rules, of course, generally prevented such a default, but the existence of the OCC was an important concept).

The second group of 16 stocks that were listed contained some of the most active traders over the years, in addition to IBM: RCA,

Avon, Exxon, Kerr-McGee, Kresge (now K-Mart), and Sears to name a few. Another group of eight stocks was added in November 1974, and the growth of the listed option market was off and running. The AMEX listed options in January 1975, while the Philadelphia Stock Exchange added their options in June of 1975. Furthermore, the success of this listed market eventually spurred the listing of futures options that we have today (agricultural options trading had been banned since the 1920s due to excesses within the industry, and there was no such thing as a financial future at the time). The continued issuance of new products—such as index futures and options, and financial futures—and the subsequent growth and revitalization of the exchanges that listed them can be traced to the success of the CBOE. The old over-the-counter market was virtually eliminated, except for options on stocks that weren't listed on the option exchanges.

The original sixteen stocks whose options were initially listed on the CBOE were: AT&T, Atlantic Richfield, Brunswick, Eastman Kodak, Ford, Gulf & Western, Loews, McDonalds, Merck, Northwest Airlines, Pennzoil, Polaroid, Sperry Rand, Texas Instruments, Upjohn, and Xerox.

Index Options

The next large innovation in the equity markets was the introduction of index trading. This historic type of trading began when the Kansas City Board of Trade listed futures on the Value Line Index in 1982. The CBOE invented the OEX index (composed of 100 fairly large stocks, all of which had options listed on the CBOE), and listed the first index options on it on March 11, 1983. Today the OEX index is known as the Standard & Poor's 100 Index, but it still trades with the symbol "OEX." This has been by far the single most successful equity or index option product ever listed. Meanwhile, the Chicago Mercantile Exchange started trading in S&P 500 futures, whose success and power extended far beyond the arena of futures and option trading—eventually becoming the "king" of all index trading and subsequently being the instrument that was blamed for the crash of 1987 and numerous other nervous days in the market.

The reason that these index products were so successful was that for the first time it was possible for an investor to have a view on the market itself and to be able to act on that view directly. Prior to the existence of index products, the investor—whether an individual or a large institutional money manager—had to implement his market view by buying stock. As we all know, it is often possible to be right on the market but to be wrong on a particular stock. Being able to trade indices directly took care of that problem.

Futures Options

The initial listing of financial futures contracts depends on how you define financial futures. If you include currencies, then the 1972 listing of currency futures on the Chicago Merc marked the beginning. If, however, you mean interest rate futures, the initial listing was GNMA futures on the CBOT in 1975. T-bill futures followed in 1976. However, the most popular contracts, the 30-year U.S. Bond contract and the Eurodollar futures were listed in 1977 and 1981, respectively. Options on these products didn't appear until several years after the futures were listed (1982 for the bonds, 1986 for Eurodollars). The first agricultural options were listed on soybeans in 1984.

Today's Over-the-Counter Market

According to the CBOE, there are several hundred million option contracts traded annually in the United States today. There are, of course, many foreign exchanges that trade listed options as well, having patterned themselves after the success of the U.S. markets. Ironically, there is a large volume of option contracts trading that is not counted in these figures, for there is an active over-the-counter market in derivative products again today!

We seem to have come full circle. While today's over-the-counter market is much more sophisticated than its predecessor, it has certain similarities. The greatest similarity is that contracts are not standardized. Today's large institutions that utilize options prefer to have them customized to their portfolios and positions (for it is unlikely that they own the exact composition of the S&P 500 or S&P 100, and therefore can't hedge completely with futures and options on those listed products); moreover, they may want expiration dates that are other than the standard ones.

A very large difference between the over-the-counter market of today and yesteryear is that the contracts today are generally issued by the larger securities firms (Salomon Brothers, Morgan Stanley, Banker's Trust, etc.). These firms then employ strategists and traders to hedge their resulting portfolio. This is a far cry from the old days where the brokerage firm merely located both a buyer and a seller and got them together for the option transaction. If history repeats itself, the exchanges will make attempts to move the current over-the-counter trading onto the listed marketplace. The CBOE has already listed FLEX options (which allow for varying expiration dates and striking prices) as the beginning of the inroad into this market.

Thus, option strategies and option trading are an ever-evolving story. Those who make the effort to understand and use options will certainly have more alternatives available to themselves than those who don't.

OPTION TRADING PROCEDURES

Listed options can be bought and sold whenever the exchange is open. This is the biggest advantage to trading listed options (as opposed to trading the older style over-the-counter options), and it is the reason why the option exchanges have enjoyed their success. Thus, if you buy an option in the morning, expecting the market to go higher, but then change your mind in the afternoon, you are perfectly free to go back into the market and sell your option.

The concepts of open interest are familiar to futures traders, but not necessarily to stock traders. When a trader first transacts a particular option in his account, he is said to be executing an *opening trade*. This is true whether he initially buys or sells the option. Such a trade adds to the *open interest* of that particular option series. Later, when he executes a trade that removes the option from his account, he is said to be executing a *closing trade*. A closing trade decreases the open interest. Some technicians keep an eye on open interest as a possible predictor of futures price movements by the underlying security. The reason that we mention this is that you must specify whether the trade is opening or closing when you place an option order.

An option order must specify the following:

1. Buy or sell.
2. Quantity.
3. The description of the option (e.g., IBM July 50 call).
4. Price.
5. Type of order (see the next paragraph).
6. Whether the trade is opening or closing.
7. Whether the account is "customer" or "firm."

Order types (item 5) for options are just like they are for stocks or futures. You can use *market orders* (dangerous in illiquid options), *limit orders* (probably a good idea most of the time), *stop orders* (not a good idea with options), and *good-until-canceled orders*. If you are trading directly through professional traders on the floor, you will probably want to use *market not held* orders (which gives the broker in the crowd the ability to make a decision of his own, for your account). Only use "market not held" if you know the floor broker and trust his judgment; it is not a good idea to use this type of order if you're entering your order through one of the large brokerage firms (they probably wouldn't accept a "not held" order anyway). Other, more exotic order types such as *market on close* are not available for most options, but you can always check with your broker to be sure.

Regarding item number 6: if you don't know the difference between "customer" and "firm," then you're a "customer." For the record, a firm trader is one who is trading the account of a member of the exchange (these are professional traders, many of whom trade from trading desks—you don't necessarily have to be on the trading floor in order to trade for a member firm's own account). A customer is everyone else—all the traders who are not members of the exchange or trading for the account of an exchange member. This distinction is placed on the order because a "customer" order has priority over a "firm" order in many situations on the trading floor.

A typical option order, then, might be: "Buy 5 IBM July 50 calls at 3, open customer," or if you are trading through a brokerage firm, they will assume you are a customer so you might need only to say "Buy 5 IBM July 50 calls at 3 to open." In either case, this is a limit order because you have specified a price, indicating that you are not willing to pay more than 3 for this option. If you are trading in a very liquid option (the most liquid options are IBM for stocks, OEX for indices, and Eurodollars for futures), you might use a market order: "Buy 10 Eurodollar Dec 98 calls at the market to open." If you get in the habit of stating your orders correctly and making your broker (or floor trader) repeat them back to you, you will eliminate almost all mistakes, or "errors" as they are officially called. I'd bet that more than 75 percent of all errors are caused by confusing buy and sell: the person stating the order says buy, but the person writing it down on the other end of the phone circles "sell" on the order ticket for some reason; sometimes, even if it's repeated back, the person giving the order isn't listening too carefully and the order goes in incorrectly.

One of the most embarrassing errors in history didn't involve options. In 1994, Bell Atlantic and Telecommunications Inc., a large cable TV operator, announced a merger that would have been very beneficial to Telecommunications Inc.'s stock price. The stock symbol for Telecommunications Inc. is TCOMA (its class A stock is the primary trading vehicle), but among "techies" the stock is known as TCI (this is something akin to Texas Instruments being known as TI to all the research labs guys, but its stock symbol is TXN). Well, as you might guess, the television financial news reporters— who often like to appear as if they are one of the "inside" guys—repeatedly stated that Bell Atlantic was buying TCI. As it turns out, there is a stock whose symbol is TCI—Transcontinental Realty Inc, a real estate trust, or REIT! Transcontinental Realty was up 3 points in fairly heavy trading before people started to realize their mistake. As soon as they did, it collapsed back to where it was. I have yet to meet anyone who actually admits that they bought TCI when they should have bought TCOMA, but they're out there somewhere, and some of them are probably "professional" arbs (or were).

The point is that each aspect of a trade should be handled in a professional manner—state the order properly, demand that it be repeated back, listen to the repeat. That's all you can do; if an order clerk subsequently types the wrong information into a computer, or mistakenly circles the wrong information on the floor ticket, you can't control that. But you can demand that restitution be made if you handle your end of things correctly. Most brokerage firm office managers have no problem refunding a customer the amount of an error that is clearly the brokerage firm's fault—you just don't want to be in the gray area where there is some dispute over what was said and never repeated.

EXERCISE AND ASSIGNMENT

An option is said to have *intrinsic value* when the stock price is above the strike price of a call or below the strike price of a put. Another term that describes the situation where an option has intrinsic value is to say that the option is *in-the-money*. If the option has no intrinsic value, it is said to be *out-of-the-money*. For calls, this would mean that the underlying's price is currently *below* the striking price of the call, and for puts it would mean that the underlying's price is *above* the strike price of the put.

Another related definition that is important is that of *parity*. Any derivative security that is trading with no time value premium is said to be trading *at parity*. Sometimes parity is used as a sort of measuring stick. One may say that an option is trading at a half-point or a quarter-point above parity.

Example: XYZ is 53.

July 40 call: $12\frac{3}{4}$	$\frac{1}{4}$ point below parity
July 45 call: 8	At parity
July 50 call: $3\frac{1}{4}$	$\frac{1}{4}$ point above parity

---

Ultimately, one of two things happens to an option as it reaches expiration: it is exercised or it expires worthless. The owner (also called the *holder*) of an out-of-the-money option will let it expire worthless. This is any call where the stock, index, or futures price is *below* the strike price at expiration. In the same manner, he will let a put expire worthless if the underlying price is *higher* than the strike price at expiration. For example, if one owned the IBM July 50 call and IBM was trading at 45 at expiration, why would you want to exercise your call to buy 100 shares of IBM at 50 when you can just go to the stock market and buy 100 shares of IBM for 45? You wouldn't, of course. Believe it or not, though, in the early days of option trading, things like that did happen occasionally.

In the movie, "Brewster's Millions," starring Richard Pryor, a minor league baseball player stands to inherit a large amount of money—something like $300 million—providing that he fulfill the terms of a rather crazy will: he must spend (or lose) something like $30 million in a short period of time. Of course, he goes through all kinds of crazy maneuvers to barely accomplish his appointed task by the given date. It's an intriguing movie, as it gets you thinking about how much money you could spend quickly. I've often thought that he could have simplified his life considerably by just buying some options that were about to expire, whose strike price was way above the current market price, and exercising them. He could have squandered the $30 million in an instant!

Of course, if the option is in-the-money—that is, the price of the underlying is higher than the strike price of a call—then the owner of the call will exercise it because it has value. In an example similar to the previous one, if you own the IBM July 50 call and IBM is selling at 55, then you would exercise the call because you can buy IBM at 50 via your call exercise, whereas you would have to pay 55 to buy IBM in the open market. Conversely a put holder would exercise his put if it is in-the-money, that is, if the underlying's current price were below the strike price, because the put gives him the right to sell at the higher price, the strike.

At the end of an option's life, there is a good chance that it ends up in the hands of a market maker, or other "firm" trader, if it has intrinsic value. This is because most "customers" sell their options in the open market rather than exercise them. They do this for two reasons: (1) they are required to come up with substantially more cash to buy the stock than it takes to buy the option, and (2) the commission on one option trade is smaller than two stock trades (if you exercise a call and buy stock, for example, you're going to have to sell the stock someday and pay another commission). Firm traders don't pay commissions (so that's why those seats cost so much!), and as expiration nears, they buy options from customers who are selling them in closing transactions. There is nothing particularly good or bad about this phenomenon, it's just the most efficient way for everybody to act as expiration approaches. The firm traders then exercise the options at expiration; they are not as concerned about capital requirements as most customers would be. In all probability, the firm traders have already "squared up" their positions by the time they exercise, so they don't end up being long or short much stock or futures at all.

Many people have heard and even repeated the statement that "90 percent of all options expire worthless." It's unclear where that got started—some say from a study done back in the 1940s regarding the illiquid over-the-counter market at that time. This statement is patent nonsense with respect to listed options, and one only has to think about it to realize the fact. Consider this scenario: when options are initially listed, they have striking prices that surround the current price of the underlying (if IBM is trading at 50, then there will be strikes of 40, 45, 50, 55, and 60, etc.). Now, puts and calls are traded at all strikes—not necessarily in equal quantities, but there will be some open interest in all series. As the stock fluctuates during the life of the options, various strikes will become more liquid as IBM's stock price nears that particular strike. As a result, open interest will build up at various strikes.

By expiration, if IBM has risen in price, nearly all the calls will be in-the-money and therefore will *not* be worthless; if IBM falls in price, nearly all the puts will be in-the-money at expiration. Since options are listed at least nine months in advance of expiration, there is a significant chance that the stock or futures contract will have a serious price change by the time expiration rolls around. In either case, I can assure you that far less than 90 percent of the options are expiring worthless. About the only time that a very large percentage of options would expire worthless would be when the underlying winds up right where it started. In the preceding example, if IBM was at exactly 50 at expiration (and all the calls and puts with a strike of 50 were considered worthless), then I would agree that you could say a large percentage expired worthless. But that is an extremely rare case.

I personally began trading options in 1973 when my broker, Ron Dilks, first pointed out a *Business Week* article to me that talked about listed options on Kresge. Since then, through my various endeavors as individual trader, risk arbitrageur, and money manager, I have had several *hundred thousand* contracts that were held until expiration. I have no exact way of knowing how many were exercised or assigned and how many expired worthless, but my general feeling is that the count is about 50-50. That is, about half were in-the-money at expiration, and half were not. I *do* know, with a certainty born of 20 years of experience, that nowhere near 90 percent expired worthless.

Mechanics of Exercise and Assignment

The control of exercise is at the behest of the owner of the option. He is the one that determines when to exercise. To exercise a stock or index option, he must notify his broker by 4 P.M. Eastern time (or 5 P.M. on expiration Friday) that he wants to exercise his option. His broker then notifies the OCC, which is the central clearing house for all listed stock options. The OCC only deals with member firms (your brokerage firm, for example), so it does not "know" individual customers or individual accounts. The OCC then gathers all exercise notices that it received that night and randomly assigns them to member firms who are short the option series that have been exercised. The next morning, the member firm who was assigned then randomly picks out customer accounts that are short that particular option series and notifies those option writers that they have been assigned. This assignment notice should be received by the option writer well in advance of the opening of trading, so he can plan any necessary trading action that the assignment notice might necessitate. The trades are deemed to have taken place on the *day of the exercise*; thus the person who is assigned doesn't find out until a day after the trade has actually taken place.

Futures option exercises work in a similar manner, although times may vary slightly, and the exchange is the clearing center, not the OCC.

Figure 1.1 summarizes what transaction takes place in the underlying security when a put or call option is exercised or assigned. For example, if you exercise a put, you sell the underlying and the seller of the put, who is then assigned, buys the underlying. This illustration is not correct for cash-based options (see Figure 1.2).

Most novice investors understand that you may first buy a security and then later sell it to take a profit or a loss. There are only two rules you need to know about making money in any market.

The first is: Buy low and sell high, not necessarily in that order.

The second is: He who sells what isn't his'n, must buy it back or go to prison.

That is, you may sometimes be better able to profit by selling a security first and buying back later. This is apropos to stocks, options, futures, bonds, or just about anything. The second rule, though, indicates that if this is a physical security—stocks or bonds— then you can't sell it without first borrowing it from an existing holder, or you could have a problem on your hands. However, futures and options may be sold short without any searching for existing physical securities since they are contracts.

Figure 1.1
EXERCISE AND ASSIGNMENT OF STOCK OR
FUTURES OPTIONS

	Call Option	**Put Option**
Exercise	Buy Underlying	Sell Underlying
Assigned	Sell Underlying	Buy Underlying

This is a good place to define what the term *cover* means. In the context of stock trading, when you first buy stock and then later sell it, you are said to liquidate your position. However, if you had first sold it short, then when you later buy it to close out your position, you are said to cover your position. Thus, it is common nomenclature to describe the closing out of a short position as covering. The term also applies to options. If you initially sell an option as the first transaction, that is called an *opening sell transaction*. This leaves you short the option, and you may someday be assigned on that option, if you do not first buy it back (cover it).

An extremely important point should be noted here: *if you are an option seller, you can't always tell if you're going to be assigned at expiration merely by observing the closing price of the underlying stock; you really need to wait until Monday morning to check your assignment notices.* There are two reasons for this. One is that if a stock holder has a large position that he can't sell in the open market, he might decide to exercise puts (if he owns them) to "blow out" his position. This may be easier than holding onto the stock and trying to rehedge it, or trying to sell it in the open market.

When I managed the arbitrage department for a major brokerage firm, we were long a lot of Dayton Hudson stock on Friday, October 16, 1987, the trading day before the crash. The stock had closed at about 50 on October 15th. We also owned the Oct 45 puts as a hedge. Friday, October 16th, was expiration day for the October options. As the day progressed, the market dropped over 100 points (the first time in history that that had happened) and Dayton Hudson was being smashed. It closed at 45½, but with very little stock being bid for. It appeared that there was no way we could sell our stock in the open market on Monday since the market was weak and there weren't many bids for the stock (of course, we didn't realize that on Monday there was going to be a crash). In addition, the longer-term options in Dayton Hudson were quite expensive and also rather illiquid. So, we exercised our Oct 45 puts and sold our entire position at 45—below the last sale price. Thus, whoever was short those Dayton Hudson puts was assigned, even though they were out-of-the-money, and he found out on Monday morning that he had bought stock at 45. I believe the stock opened around 42 and traded down from there.

The other reason that an option seller can't be sure about assignments until Monday morning after expiration is that corporate news may be released after the 4 P.M. Friday close. Since options may be exercised up until 5 P.M. on expiration Friday, it is possible for news to come out after the market closes that would make holders of the options want to exercise. This, by the way, is the reason your brokerage firm considers you to have written a naked option if you sell another option on expiration Friday without bothering to cover a deeply out-of-the-money option for a 16th.

Major news has come out between 4 P.M. and 5 P.M. on expiration Friday many times. Some of these have involved takeovers and some earnings news, or other corporate news. A rather famous one occurred in 1994. Gerber Products was the subject of takeover rumors for quite a while. On Friday, May 20th (expiration day), the stock closed at 34⅝. After the close, a takeover bid was announced, and the stock opened at 51 on Monday, May 23rd. Many sellers of the May 35 calls received assignment notices on that Monday morning and were rather upset; some had gone home Friday night assuming that their short May 35 calls were expiring worthless. There were even lawsuits filed, claiming that exercise notices were not delivered to the OCC on time. That is a very difficult allegation to prove, however.

Exercises Prior to Expiration.   Futures options are rarely exercised prior to expiration, except when they are deeply in-the-money. In that case, an option holder may exercise in order to reduce his carrying costs for holding an expensive option. Stock options, however, are exercised prior to expiration fairly often. The most common time is on the day before the stock goes ex-dividend. An equity call holder is not entitled to the dividend, so an in-the-money call that has no time value premium will drop in price by the ex-dividend amount.

Example: XYZ is trading at 55 and is going to go ex-dividend by 50 cents tomorrow. The July 50 call, which has only a short time remaining until expiration, is trading at 5. Tomorrow, the stock will open at 54½ (after going ex-dividend the 50 cents). Thus, the call will be trading for 4½ the next morning. The call holder will exercise (or sell his call to a market maker, who will exercise) rather than squander a half point.

Hence if an in-the-money call has no time value premium on the day before the stock goes ex-dividend, the call holder will generally exercise in order to preserve his value. The call seller, who is assigned, doesn't find out until the next day (the morning that the stock is going ex-dividend). Thus, the seller finds out that he actually sold the stock on the previous day, and thus he does not get the stock dividend. For this reason, it is often the case that when a stock declares a large cash dividend, the terms of the option are adjusted. Such an adjustment protects the call holder.

Cash Option Exercise.   We mentioned earlier that index options convert into cash, rather than stock. This is a convenient arrangement that avoids having to deliver hundreds of stocks for one option exercise. For example, there are options on the S&P 500 index. Suppose that the index is trading at a price of 453.47. Then, if an S&P call option is exercised, rather than receive a few shares of each of 500 stocks—which would be a back-office nightmare—the person who exercises receives cash in the amount of $45,347 (100 "shares" at 453.47) less the value of the strike price. If a Dec 400 call was being exercised, the call holder would thus receive a net of $5,347 ($45,347 – $40,000), less commission. The person who is assigned is *debited* a like amount of cash, plus commission. Figure 1.2 illustrates the exercise and assignment for cash-based options.

American-style options can be exercised at any time during their life. All stock options and futures options are of this type, as are OEX

Figure 1.2
EXERCISE AND ASSIGNMENT OF CASH-BASED
INDEX OPTIONS

	Call Option	**Put Option**
Exercise	Receive Cash	Receive Cash
Assigned	Pay Cash	Pay Cash

Index options. *European-style* options can only be exercised at the end of their life. Most index options are European exercise. In Chapter 5, accompanying the discussion of intermarket spread strategies, you will find an in-depth description of how European options behave.

Sellers of American-style options can be "surprised" by an assignment notice, because it can come at any time during the life of the option (there is usually one huge clue as to when such an assignment may happen, and it is that *the option no longer has any time value premium*). Writers of European-style options, however, know that they can only be assigned at expiration, so they can't get called out of their position early. This is an important difference where index options are concerned because all index options are cash-based, and American-style index options can create rather nasty scenarios when assigned.

Example: Suppose that you own a spread in OEX options (which are cash-based and American style): you are long the December 410 call and short the Dec 420 call, with the index trading at 440. Your spread is probably trading near its maximum value of 10 points (the differences of the strike prices). Then, you come to work one morning and find that your Dec 420 calls have been assigned. Your account is debited 20 points cash (440 − 420) and you are now left with the Dec 410 calls long, all by themselves. You have gone from a hedged position with very little market exposure to complete market exposure from the long side. If the stock market, as measured by OEX, were to open down substantially on the morning that you receive your assignment notice, you could lose a lot of money very quickly.

For the reason described in the example, most index options were designed to be European-style so that these problems wouldn't occur. However, OEX options remain American-style, a sort of outlaw venue, where macho traders don't fear to tread. Since OEX options are the most heavily traded—and therefore the most liquid—index options, these situations arise quite often, especially shortly before expiration. In fact, it has become rather commonplace for arbitrageurs with large stock and OEX positions to attempt to influence the market so that they can favorably exit their positions via early exercise. These machinations are discussed in Chapter 3.

FUTURES AND FUTURES OPTIONS

Since futures and especially futures options are less well-known to most investors, some time will be taken to describe them. First, let's discuss futures contracts; then we'll get to the options. As noted earlier, futures contracts are standardized, calling for the delivery of a specific amount of a commodity at some set time in the future. That "commodity" may be a physical commodity, such as corn or orange juice, or it may be cash, typically the case for index futures. Notice that there is no mention of anything like a "striking price" such as we have with options. Thus, futures contracts can rise infinitely and fall all the way to zero—owning one does not have limited risk like owning an option does. The margin required for a position in futures is generally much smaller than the actual value of the physical commodity underlying the futures contract—perhaps only 5 percent or 10 percent of the value. This makes the leverage in futures trading quite large, and consequently makes them a rather risky trading vehicle.

One of the things that makes futures so confusing to many is that there is no real standardization between the various commodities. What one might think of as the "expiration date" of a futures contract is typically referred to as the *last trading day*. The last trading day can vary widely within the expiration month, depending on which futures contract you are talking about. For example, March grain futures (corn, wheat, soybean) don't necessarily expire on the same day of the month as March pork belly futures or March S&P 500 futures.

First Notice Day

A more important date for a futures trader is actually the *first notice day*. For futures with a physical delivery, the first notice day is usually several weeks before the last trading day. *After the first notice day, the holder of a futures contract may be called upon to take delivery of the underlying physical commodity.* Thus, if a futures contract on gold calls for delivery of 100 ounces of a certain grade of gold, and you are long gold futures past the first notice day, you may have to accept delivery of 100 ounces of gold at the current market price. If the current price of gold were $400 an ounce, that would require an investment of $40,000. It was mentioned earlier that futures can be traded for only a small amount of margin, thereby creating huge leverage. However, after first notice day, many brokerage firms will require a much larger margin deposit because you are at risk of having to take delivery.

Normally, individual traders in the futures market are speculators who are not interested in taking or making delivery of physical commodities. They close out their positions in advance of first notice day. However, there is always the possibility that you could forget about the date and wind up being called upon to take delivery of some commodity. There are any number of false horror stories about someone having to take delivery of 5,000 bushels of soybeans and having them dumped in their front yard. These are patently false, but they make for good story telling, of course. In reality, your brokerage firm will make arrangements for a physical storage facility to take delivery in your name. You will then be charged fees for use of the storage facility, and any other related charges.

One trader that I knew had a position in gold futures that he rolled from month to month as each contract expired (that is, he sold the near-term month future that he owned and replaced it by buying the gold futures contract that expired in the next month). He figured it was cheaper to own gold in this manner than to actually buy gold and store it in a safe deposit box. He was very careful about rolling the futures out before the first notice day of the contract that he owned, but once he forgot and received a delivery notice.

His brokerage firm told him that they were taking delivery of the requisite amount of gold, in his name, in a depository in Philadelphia. He was assessed a fee of $190 per contract for this service. Of course, since he didn't really want to take delivery of the gold, his broker had to sell out the physical gold and then replace it with futures in his account. This type of transaction is rather common and is called *exchanging physical for futures*. Selling the gold cost another commission, of course, but the net result was rather painless for him. He never actually had to take possession of the gold, he merely had to pay the handling fees for delivery and sale of the physical gold.

"First notice day" does not apply to cash-based futures, such as S&P 500 Index futures. In the case of that type of futures contract, there is no delivery; a cash settlement takes place on the last day of trading of the contract. Therefore, since there is no physical delivery taking place, there is no need for a first notice day.

Futures Options Terms

Expiration Dates.   Futures *options* expire in advance of the first notice day, so that all option contracts are out of the way before physical delivery of the underlying commodity begins taking place. This is the reason that some futures options—those on physical commodities, such as soybeans, corn, orange juice, coffee—actually expire the month *before* the expiration month of the futures contract. Thus, March soybean futures options actually expire in February. Ask your broker, or check *Futures Magazine* monthly, for the specific expiration dates of the various futures option contracts. Also, many futures chart books carry the expiration dates of the options as well. For those who prefer to see the nitty gritty details themselves, Appendix B has a list of when the futures options on most of the major contracts expire. For example, coffee options expire on the first Friday of the month *preceding* the expiration month of the futures contract. Thus, May coffee options would expire on the first Friday of April.

Striking Prices.   As mentioned earlier, each different type of futures contract has its own set of striking prices for listed options. For example, soybean option strike prices are 25 points (cents) apart, corn options are 10 points apart, pork belly options are 2 points apart, and so on. When first beginning to familiarize yourself with futures options, you are best served by obtaining an inexpensive source, such as *Investors Business Daily* newspaper, that lists all the current options on one page. It is then an easy manner to observe where the strike prices are located for various futures contracts. For those traders with more sophisticated quote machines, an option "chain" is usually available that will display all currently traded options on a specific type of futures. For example, SIGNAL—a popular quote service that can be run on any computer—is one such source.

Unit of Trading.   Every futures option has *one* futures contract underlying it; that is, if you exercise your futures option, it will convert into one futures contract. That is a simple concept; what is more complicated is remembering how many dollars are represented by a one-point movement of either the underlying future or the futures option. With stock and index options, a one-point move is normally worth $100 (except in the case of stock splits, possibly). Futures options are less standardized. For example, a point (cent) move in grain options is worth $50, while a one-point move in the S&P 500 Index futures is worth $500. In *every* case, a one-point move in futures options is worth exactly the same number of dollars as a one-point move in the underlying futures contract.

Appendix B lists these dollar amounts for most of the major futures contracts. However, you can often determine this information from the newspaper listings of futures option prices. The newspaper normally lists the size of the underlying futures contract, in physical terms. The "dollars per point" can normally be determined by dividing the physical contract size by 100. For example, a soybean futures contract is for 5,000 bushels of soybeans, and that information will be listed in the newspaper right along with the prices. Dividing by 100, you arrive at the fact that a one-point (cent) move in soybeans is worth $50.

Price Quotes.   Traders of stocks are accustomed to being able to quote a bid and asked price for any stock or option they trade. In addition, any broker can obtain that information on his quote machine. Such is not the case with futures contracts nor with most futures option contracts. Rarely are you able to obtain a bid or offer quote for a futures contract on a quote machine. They can be obtained from the trading floor, but unless you are trading directly with the floor, in most cases it is too time-consuming to have your broker request a quote, for there would be several phone calls involved in getting it.

The trading floors do supply quotes to the major quote vendors. However, they are often "stale" quotes, and one cannot really rely on them much of the time. Where options are concerned, I don't recommend trading with market orders, so you need to know the option's quote. One way to speed up the quote and order entry process is to place an order at a price you would accept and to ask your broker to relay the *actual* market to you. In this way, your order is effective right away, and you get a quote back, too. If the actual market is far away from your order, then you can adjust the price on your order.

Commissions.   In the futures market, commissions are generally figured as a constant dollar amount per contract. For futures contracts, commissions are charged only when your position is closed out. Thus, if you buy a futures contract on wheat, for example, you are not charged any commission at that point. Later, when you sell the futures contract, you will then be charged the commission. The nomenclature to describe this process is *round turn*. If your commission rate is $20 per futures contract, it is usually stated as $20 per round turn.

Futures option commissions are normally a fixed amount as well, but they are charged on both the buy and sell, just as stock commissions are. In some cases, brokers attempt to charge a percentage of the option's price, but that is not the norm.

The fact that futures and futures option commissions are normally fixed amounts means that they are more or less onerous depending on the contract being traded. For example, if you are paying $20 per round turn and you are trading wheat (which is worth $50 per point), then the commission represents a move of 0.40 point in wheat, which is a rather large commission in terms of the distance wheat must move to make the commission back. However, if you are trading S&P 500 futures, which are worth $500 per point, then the commission only represents 0.04 point, which is less than one tick in the futures, and is almost a trivial amount in terms of the future's price movement.

Serial Options.   Futures contracts on the same commodity do not normally expire in every month of the year. For example, S&P 500 futures expire only in March, June, September, and December. Others may have five or six futures contract months per year. Experienced option traders know that most option trading takes place in the near-term contracts, especially as the options near their expiration dates.

   The futures exchanges realized that activity would be lessened if the nearest term option had as much as two or three months of life remaining. So they decided to introduce options that expire in the months between the actual expiration months of the futures contract itself. These options are called *serial options*. They generally are only listed for the one- or two-month expirations preceding an actual futures expiration month. The futures contract that underlies a serial option is the actual futures contract expiring in the next actual month.

Example: S&P 500 futures expire in March, June, September, and December of each year. There are also futures options expiring in those months. Both the futures and the options are cash-settled, and expire on the third Friday of the month. Suppose that the current date is April 1. Then the nearest future expires two and a half months in the future, in the middle of June.

   Since the S&P 500 futures contract is a very active one, there is naturally going to be great demand for trading of short-term options. Thus, the Chicago Merc (the exchange where these options are listed) began listing serial options. For example, the April S&P 500 futures options would expire on the third Friday of April, but instead of receiving cash when you exercise these options, you would instead receive a concomitant position in June S&P 500 futures. Assume you are long an S&P 500 April 460 call. If you exercise it, you would be long one June S&P 500 futures contract at a price of 460 in your account.

   Serial options exist on the S&Ps, all the currencies, all the bond and note contracts, gold, silver, platinum, live cattle, pork bellies, sugar, and orange juice. It should be noted that not every futures contract will have serial options. Some don't need them; for example, crude oil and its related products and natural gas all have futures that expire each month of the calendar year, so serial options are not necessary for those futures. However, many of the others have serial options, although not all. Grain futures don't have serial options—apparently the CBOT feels that the existing options are active enough and provide enough hedging opportunity without adding serial options.

Remember, the easiest way to tell if serial options exist is to see if there are options with expiration dates that *don't* match the expiration dates of the corresponding futures contracts. If there are, then those options are serial options. This can easily be determined from the newspaper or from your quote machine, if you have access to one.

There are many other nuances of futures options that are different from stock or index options, but they are addressed in the specific chapters on strategy and trading that follow.

INFLUENCES ON AN OPTION'S PRICE

As listed, but *not* in order of importance, there are six factors that influence the price of an option:

1. Price of the underlying instrument.
2. Striking price of the option.
3. Amount of time remaining until expiration.
4. Volatility of the underlying instrument.
5. Short-term interest rates, generally defined as the 90-day T-bill rate.
6. Dividends (if applicable).

Each of these six factors has an influence on the price of an option. In fact, each has a *direct* effect, causing the option to become more or less expensive as the factor itself increases. An easy one to discern is that the more *time remaining* until expiration, the more expensive the options will be. Conversely, as time decreases, so do option prices. Thus, option prices are directly related to the time remaining, as one factor. *Interest rates* also work in a more complicated manner, although that is not quite as obvious. When interest rates are high, arbitrageurs can pay more for calls since they will be earning more money on their credit balances, which are invested at current short-term interest rates. However, they will pay less for puts.

Sometimes the factors affect calls differently than puts. For example, as the *underlying's price* increases, calls get more expensive while puts get cheaper. *Dividends*, also, have opposite effects on puts and calls. If a company increases its dividend, calls will be cheaper, and puts will get more expensive. This is because the listed options do not have any right to the dividend. The options' prices merely reflect what the stock price will do, and if the dividend is increased, it will drop farther when it goes ex-dividend; thus puts increase in value, to account for the expected ex-dividend drop in stock price, and calls get cheaper.

Volatility

We discuss volatility at length in this book, so we want you to be clear about what it is. *Volatility is a measure of how fast the underlying changes in price.* If the underlying stock or future has the potential to change in price by a great deal in a short amount of time, then we say that the underlying is volatile. For example, over-the-counter biotech stocks are volatile stocks; orange juice futures in winter or soybean futures in summer are volatile as well.

There are two types of volatility that are pertinent to the discussion of option pricing. One is *historical* volatility, which is a statistical measure of how fast the underlying security has been changing in price. Historical volatility is quantifiable, that is, it's calculated by a standard formula, although some mathematicians disagree as to the best exact formula for calculating historical volatility. The other type of volatility is *implied volatility*. This is the volatility that is "implied" for future time periods, and the things that are doing the implying are the *listed options*.

The most startling example of implied volatility that I know of occurred during the crash of 1987. When implied volatility increases, the prices of all options increase as well. Thus, this trader received a pleasant surprise, one of the few pleasant surprise stories that relate to the crash of 1987.

On the Wednesday before the crash (10/14/87), OEX was trading at 295. A customer paid 1⅛ for the Dec 320 calls. These calls were trading with an implied volatility of about 15 percent, which was actually quite low for that era.

On the following Monday (10/19/87), the market crashed, and OEX was trading at 230. The customer figured he had lost his entire investment and, considering the large losses that others had taken, he was actually glad to have only lost a point and an eighth. He didn't even bother getting a quote on these options until Tuesday, the day after the crash, because he figured there wouldn't be any bid for them if he wanted to sell them.

What he didn't realize was that implied volatility had skyrocketed to nearly 50 percent for OEX options in the wake of the crash. The Dec 320 calls—now 90 points out of the money with less than two months until expiration—were trading at 1! Thus he had only lost an eighth. The power of implied volatility is great; it can even bail out losing trades sometimes.

Of course, most stories relating to the crash of 1987 were not so pleasant. In fact, one dogma circulating on the "street" was that "the crash of 1987 was so bad that even the liars lost money."

Another example of the difference between implied and historical volatility occurred in the following litigation situation, where the possible outcome of a lawsuit caused implied volatility to inflate, while the actual volatility of the underlying was quite stable.

An example from early 1994 dramatically shows the difference between historical and implied volatility. Advanced Micro Devices is a maker of semiconductor chips. So is Intel, the leader in the field. Intel had filed a lawsuit against Advanced Micro, claiming patent violations, and the case went to trial. The news caused Advanced Micro stock to drop in price and then stabilize in the low 20s.

The resulting court decision was sure to have a large effect on the price of Advanced Micro. If the courts decided in favor of Intel, Advanced Micro's stock was destined to drop a lot; however, if the decision went against Intel, then Advanced Micro stock was destined to rise back into the 30s, where it had been trading prior to the lawsuit.

As the decision approached, the historical (or actual) volatility of Advanced Micro Devices stock was rather normal: the stock was trading back and forth from about 19 to 22. Thus, the stock was not acting very volatile. This was quite normal because no one knew what the odds were of the stock moving up or down when the court handed down its decision; buyers and sellers were about in equilibrium. However, since the option prices were based on where the stock was going to be in the future, they were extremely expensive. For example, with the stock at 20, the calls expiring in one month were selling for over four points! This is extremely expensive for a one-month option on a $20 stock. The puts were similarly expensive. Thus, the options were implying that there was going to be a big change in price by Advanced Micro Devices; or, alternatively stated, the options were trading with a high implied volatility. As it turned out, the court decided in favor of Advanced Micro, and the stock jumped six points higher in one day. After that, the option prices settled back down and historical volatility and implied volatility were once again in line.

It is often the case that historical and implied volatility on a certain underlying issue are very nearly the same. Even when they differ, the reason is not normally as obvious as in the preceding example. We discuss how to measure these volatilities, how to interpret them, and what strategies to use when they differ, in later chapters.

You might think that it should be a fairly easy matter to determine the "fair" value of an option, given that the price is only dependent on the six factors listed earlier. Five of the six factors are known for certain at any one time. We certainly know the *price* of the underlying, and of course we know what the *strike price* is. We also know how much *time* is left until expiration of the option. Moreover, it is a simple matter to find out where short-term *interest rates* are. And, if there are any *dividends*, it is an easy task to find the amount and timing of the dividend. The one factor that we can't quantify with any certainty is volatility, especially the volatility in future time periods. This, then, is the "rub" in determining the fair—or theoretical—value of an option. If we don't know how volatile the underlying security is going to be—that is, we don't know how much the underlying is going to change in price and how fast it's going to do it—then how can we possibly decide how much to pay for the option?

The answer to this question is not an easy one, and we spend a great deal of time in this book trying to shed light on it.

How the Factors Affect the Option Price

It was shown earlier that each of the six factors has its own effect on option prices. The following table, which shows what happens as each factor *decreases* (if the factor were to *increase*, the result would be the opposite of that shown in the table, in each case):

Factor	Time	Underlying	Interest	Dividends	Volatility
Call price	Decreases	Decreases	Decreases	Increases	Decreases
Put price	Decreases	Increases	Increases	Decreases	Decreases

Moreover, some of these factors are interrelated so that it is not necessarily easy to tell which is exerting more power at any time. For example, if a stock or futures contract rallies, we can't say for certain that a call will necessarily increase in value. If the strike price is too far above the current price of the underlying, even a rather large short-term rally may not help out the call much at all. This would be especially true if there were very little time remaining.

Example: Suppose a stock has been in a long bear market, and is trading at 20. Then a rally sets in, and the stock jumps by 5 points to 25 in a day or two. Furthermore, suppose this happens with only a week or so remaining until the nearest expiration. The following data summarize this situation.

	February 7	February 9
Stock price	20	25
Feb 35 call	$1/16$	$1/16$
Aug 35 Call	$1/2$	$1 1/4$

The Feb 35 call, which is going to expire in a little more than a week, was not helped out by the stock's jump in price, but the longer-term Aug 35 call *was* because there is more time remaining for the August option. So stock price, strike price, and time are all related in determining whether the value of an option would increase or not when the stock makes a favorable move.

DELTA

Much more is said about the interdependence of these factors later, but first let's define some terms that are common among option traders. These terms describe just how much of an effect each factor has on the stock price. The best known such term is the *delta* of an option. *The delta of an option measures how much the option changes in price when the underlying moves one point.*

Example: XYZ is trading at 80, and the March 80 call is selling for 4. We observe that, when XYZ rises one point to 81, the March 80 call now sells for 4½. Thus, the option increased by a half point when the stock rose by one point. This option is said to have a delta of one-half, or 0.50.

The delta of a call option is a number that ranges between 0.00 and 1.00. To verify this for yourself, note that if a call is way out-of-the-money, it will not move at all, even if the stock rises by one point—the Feb 35 call in the prior example. Thus, the delta of a very deeply out-of-the-money call is 0.00. On the other hand, if the stock is trading far in excess of the striking price—that is, the option is way in-the-money—then the option and the stock move in concert. Thus, if the stock rises by one point, so will the option; hence the delta of such a deeply in-the-money option is 1.00. The delta of a *put* ranges between 0.00 and −1.00, reflecting the fact that the put moves in the opposite direction from the underlying security.

In between these two extremes (deeply out-of-the-money and deeply in-the-money), the delta of a call option ranges between zero and one. That is, call options that are out-of-the-money have small deltas, such as 0.25 or 0.30, meaning that they will only increase by about ¼ or ⅜ of a point when the underlying stock rises by a point.

In a similar manner, call options that are somewhat in-the-money will have higher deltas, such as 0.70 or 0.80, indicating that they will move much more like the common stock, but not *quite* as fast as the stock moves.

Example: The following table is an example of the deltas you might expect to see for various call options on a particular stock. As you will find out later, there are other factors that affect delta, but for now we will just observe how delta behaves when we view the relationship of the underlying price and the strike price.

Underlying Price: 80   Date: February 1

Call Option	Call Delta	Put Delta
May 70 call	0.94	−0.06
May 75 call	0.79	−0.21
May 80 call	0.58	−0.42
May 90 call	0.36	−0.64
May 100 call	0.20	−0.80*
May 110 call	0.10	−0.90*

The delta of a put and call at the same striking price, with the same expiration date, are related by the general formula:

$$\text{Put delta} = \text{call delta} - 1$$

There is an exception to this formula when the put is deeply in-the-money (the two asterisks in the preceding table). The deltas of stock or index puts, but *not* futures puts, may go to their maximum (−1.00) well in advance of expiration, even when the corresponding call option still has a positive, nonzero, delta. This has to do with the effects of conversion arbitrage. Thus, in the preceding table, the May 100 put and May 110 put would probably have deltas of nearly −1.00, rather than −0.80 and −0.90, respectively, as shown.

Did you notice that the delta of the at-the-money option is *not* 0.50? In fact, it is generally higher than that, for any type of *call* option—stock, index, or futures (while it is lower for the put option).

The reason for this is that stocks or futures can move farther to the upside (they can rise infinitely, in theory) than they can to the downside (they can only fall to zero). This means there is more than a 50-50 chance of prices rising over any extended time period, and thus the delta of the at-the-money call reflects this fact.

Some traders also think of the delta as a simple way of telling whether the option will be in-the-money at expiration. While this is not mathematically correct, it is sometimes useful. Thus, in the table, under this interpretation, we can say that there is a 20 percent chance that the stock will rise and be over 100 at May expiration, because the May call has a delta of 0.20. You may prefer to think of delta in this way, if it makes it clearer to you. There is really nothing wrong with this interpretation.

Understanding the concept of delta is mandatory for option traders, for it helps them to envision just how the option is going to move when the stock price moves. Since most traders have a feeling for what they expect of a stock when they buy it, or even when they buy the options, the understanding of delta can help them decide which option to buy.

What Affects Delta?

Anyone who has traded options, or even thought seriously about them, realizes that an out-of-the-money option does not gain much value when the stock rises slightly; the at- or in-the-money option will rise faster than the out-of-the-money call option. This is true for both puts and calls. Delta gives us a way to measure these relative movements.

For example, suppose a trader were going to buy the stock in the previous example, and he was looking for a quick move of 3 points, from 80 to 83. How much will the May 100 call appreciate? The delta tells us that the May 100 will increase by about 20 cents for each point that XYZ rises. The increase will then be 3×0.20, or 60 cents. Between commissions and the bid-asked spread in the option, there might not be much profit left if that option were bought; it just won't appreciate enough for a three-point stock move. However, buying the at-the-money May 80 call should work just fine: it will appreciate by 3×0.58, or 1.74 points (1¾), which is a good move and should leave a good profit even after commissions and the bid-asked spread are taken into consideration.

Of course, if this trader were looking for a move of 20 points by the stock over the next three months, then the purchase of the out-of-the-money calls is more feasible. The trader must therefore adjust his option purchase with respect to his outlook for the underlying security, and the delta helps him do just that.

The previous several examples demonstrate the relationship between the delta and the stock's price. However, other factors can influence the delta as well. One important factor is time. The delta of an option is affected by the passage of time. *An out-of-the-money option's delta will trend toward zero as time passes.* This merely means that an out-of-the-money option will respond less and less to short-term price changes in the underlying stock as the amount of life remaining in the option grows shorter and shorter. Sometimes it helps to envision things by looking at the extreme, or "end," points. For example, on the last day of trading, any option that is more than one strike out-of-the-money will probably have no delta at all—it is going to expire worthless and a one-point rise by the underlying stock will not result in *any* price change in the option. On the other hand, if an out-of-the-money option has a *long* time remaining (three years, say), then it *will* be responsive to movements by the underlying stock. *Thus, the more time value that an out-of-the-money option has, the farther its delta will be from zero.*

Just the opposite is true for in-the-money options: *the delta of an in-the-money option will increase to its maximum as time passes.* Again, thinking in the extreme may help. Any option that is more than just slightly in-the-money behaves just like the underlying on its last trading day. Thus, such a call would have a delta of 1.00 and a put would have a delta of −1.00. However, if there is a great deal of time remaining in the option (e.g., 3 years), even though it is in-the-money, it will have *some* time value premium. Consequently, while its movement may reflect *most* of the price change of the underlying security, it won't reflect all of it, so its delta will be less than the maximum. *Thus, the more time value premium that an in-the-money option has, the smaller its delta will be.*

The delta of an option can change swiftly, sometimes apparently defying the elementary mathematical definition. These concepts are discussed in great detail in Chapter 6, but an example at this time may be sufficient to illustrate the point.

H. J. Heinz stock was the subject of takeover rumors in January of 1995. Another food company had recently been acquired, and gossip swirled about the same thing happening to Heinz. As a result, options on Heinz had gained quite a bit of implied volatility. Takeover rumors often "heat up" on Fridays, as traders seemingly feel that there is a greater chance of a deal being announced over a weekend. Thus, it was not unusual that on a Friday, implied volatility reached a peak of about 50 percent. The accompanying table lists some of the option prices on that Friday, and then also shows where the same options were trading on the following Monday, when the stock closed off only $3/8$ of a point.

	Closing Price Friday	Closing Price Following Monday	Change
Stock	$39\frac{1}{4}$	$38\frac{7}{8}$	$-\frac{3}{8}$
Jan 40 call	$\frac{15}{16}$	$\frac{3}{8}$	$-\frac{9}{16}$
Feb 40 call	$1\frac{3}{4}$	$1\frac{5}{16}$	$-\frac{7}{16}$
March 40 call	$2\frac{3}{8}$	$1\frac{3}{4}$	$-\frac{5}{8}$

What was going on here? Each of these slightly out-the-money options was down *more* than the underlying stock. That is, each of these three options had a delta of more than 1.00! Normally, a slightly out-of-the-money option would have a delta of about 0.50 or less.

The actual delta of an option after any stock move can be computed by dividing the option's price change by the stock's price change. This simple calculation yields the following deltas for the preceding options:

Option	*Actual Delta*
Jan 40 call	1.50
Feb 40 call	1.17
March 40 call	1.67

In fact, what had happened was that a negative newspaper article appeared over the weekend. The article basically denigrated the takeover rumors and gave evidence that the company was *not* "in play." Thus, even though the stock itself only traded off three-eighths of a point, the options were crushed as implied volatility fell to about 35 percent from the 50 percent level of Friday. That is a huge change in implied volatility in one day, and it had a very harmful effect on the call prices. This is a vivid example of how a change in implied volatility can affect the price and delta of an option.

Thus, there is a relationship between price and volatility. It is a well-known fact that a change in one of these factors can affect an option's price. What is sometimes forgotten is that these factors can work together to dramatically affect an option's price, as in the Heinz example. Both volatility and stock price can change dramatically in a short period of time. The other three factors that determine an option's price—short-term interest rates, striking price, and dividend—have little or no effect most of the time, for they don't change much, and certainly not over a short time period.

TECHNICAL ANALYSIS

There are two major approaches to analyzing markets—technical and fundamental. Most investors are familiar with fundamental analysis. That is the process by which analysts attempt to forecast the future profits of a company by analyzing their market penetration, pricing structure, and other things having to do with the actual operation of the company's business. *Technical analysis*, on the other hand, has nothing at all to do with the tangible operations of the company. Rather it is an analysis of the *price* of the company's stock. Technicians (practitioners of technical analysis) feel that past price patterns leave valuable clues as to the future direction of prices. Technical analysis can be applied to any price pattern—stock, bonds, futures, and so on.

There is merit in both camps, although each camp tends to view the other as being somewhat inferior. This is a classic example of how each camp was "right" and yet each thought the other was wrong.

In 1991, the market was beginning to roll to the upside after the Gulf War was "won." Many brokerage firm analysts were predicting great things for basic American companies, such as Coca-Cola. Earnings were projected to increase for each of the next few years.

Technicians, however, were more interested in what the *market* was saying about Coke. The market's opinion is, of course, registered in the price of stock on a day-to-day basis. In this instance, Coke had traded up to a price of 44 several times, but had never been able to go higher. Thus, a technician would have said that, while he might believe the fundamental analysts' prediction of good fortune for the future earnings of the company, he would not buy the stock until it's price could actually go higher than 44.

That would have been a good strategy, for it wasn't until over two years later that Coke actually traded higher than 44—after repeatedly trying to exceed that level, but failing. A technician would thus have saved his investment capital until the stock price had some momentum.

Technical analysis is more apropos to short-term trading, since it attempts to give some timing on when to buy and when to sell. Fundamental analysis is a good long-range tool, but on the short run it is often woefully late (or way too early) in predicting the actual movement of stock prices; it is therefore a poor technique for timing. Fundamental analysts attempt to predict whether the tangible business operations of a company will make money. However, that information is only vaguely related to the price of a stock in the short term. Most option trading strategies are of a short-term nature, so fundamental analysis is almost useless, and technical analysis is a better approach.

Fundamental reports, however, can and do have an effect on the short-term trading of a stock (in Chapter 4, we examine ways to take advantage of this phenomenon). This usually happens when a company announces quarterly earnings that are significantly different from what the analysts have been expecting. A worse-than-expected earnings report will inevitably cause a stock to drop as soon as the information is made public, while better-than-expected earnings will normally cause the stock to rise in price immediately.

Don't confuse the market's short-term reaction to these fundamental reports with fundamental analysis itself. In fact, had the analysts been able to correctly predict the earnings, there would have been no "surprise." This is particularly true when the earnings are bad. Usually, by the time that Wall Street analysts change their opinions from positive to negative on a stock, it is too late to benefit stockholders. How many times have you seen a company report surprisingly bad earnings, which causes the stock price to immediately drop, and *then* all the brokerage firms downgrade the stock? Or how about a stock falling from lofty levels—perhaps as much as 50 percent—and then a brokerage firm downgrades it from "buy" to "hold"? Of what use is that to a short- or intermediate-term trader?

Thus, fundamental analysis may be more appropriate for the long-term picture, but is not useful for short-term decision making. The following story shows the difference between fundamental and technical analysis quite clearly.

Recently, I read an article that was originally published in 1948, regarding the price of Coca-Cola. The article stated that the price of Coke—which had rallied strongly following the end of World War II—was discounting all of the good fortune in the foreseeable future. Fundamental analysts disagreed, arguing that Coke was on its way to becoming a world leader in soft drinks (at the time, Coke was sold mostly in the United States).

In fact, the inflation-induced recession of 1948 *did* harm the price of Coke and it dropped 30 percent, but today it is many, many times its 1948 price. So, for the long term, fundamental analysts were right, but on the short term, technicians were correct.

Since many of the strategies presented in this book are of a short-to-intermediate-term nature, we favor technical analysis for that purpose. Technical analysis bases its price projections for the future on past prices, moving averages, or volume considerations. These are valuable tools in many cases, and we discuss them in detail as they arise in the context of the option strategies that we are presenting.

This chapter has covered a lot of ground in a short amount of space. Definitions, price behavior, and relationships of the variables affecting option prices have all been described. This has laid the groundwork for most of the later discussions in this book. In the next chapter, we take a look at various option strategies.

2 An Overview of Option Strategies

Even though the main thrust of this book is modern option trading applications, we want to cover the basics in terms of strategies. The purpose of this chapter is twofold: one, it will serve as a foundation of definitions for terms used later in the book, and two, it may serve as a learning or reference section, depending on the reader's previous knowledge of option strategies. Each of the major strategies is briefly described, with an example and a graph showing the strategy's profit and loss potential.

PROFIT GRAPHS

Some traders prefer to see columns of numbers, and others—myself included—prefer to look at graphs or charts. A "profit graph" is a graph of the potential profits and losses from a position. With options, it is possible to describe most the of major strategies by the shape of their profit graphs. A simple example should be sufficient to demonstrate the concept.

Example: Suppose that XYZ common stock is trading at 50, and the XYZ July 50 call is selling for 3, or $300. The profit *table* shown here details the potential profits and losses at various XYZ prices at July expiration. The same information is shown in the profit *graph*, Figure 2.1, which shows that this position has a limited loss on the downside, and can make theoretically unlimited profits on the upside.

At July Expiration

Stock Net Price	Call	
	Price	Result ($)
40	0	−300
45	0	−300
50	0	−300
53	3	0
55	5	+200
60	10	+700
70	20	+1700

Figure 2.1
CALL PURCHASE

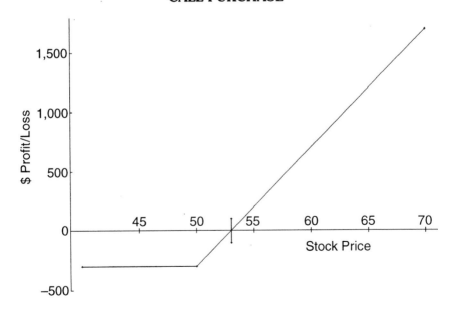

A quick look at the graph is all that is needed to understand the nature of this strategy. When the graph is labeled with the dollar amounts of risk and profit, and the break-even point, then we have a specific graph of this particular call option purchase. Thus, the profit graph can be generic or specific, depending on whether or not the axes are significant profit and loss points.

OUTRIGHT OPTION BUYING

The outright purchase of an option is the simplest type of option trade for most traders to understand, and some prefer to go no further. When we say "outright," we are referring to an option purchase that is not hedged by anything else, such as the sale of a similar option or the sale of stock. In the preceding example, the purchase of the XYZ July 50 call for 3 has several definable qualities that are fairly easily understood by most traders. First, the cost of one option is $300, and that is the most that can be lost. Second, the break-even point at expiration is 53 (plus commissions), for a call option is always worth at least the difference between the stock price (53) and the striking price (50). Third, nearly unlimited profits are available, for the option will appreciate in price as long as the underlying stock, XYZ, continues to rise in price.

This is typically felt to be an aggressive strategy, because the leverage is so high. You can lose all your money in a fairly short amount of time if the option expires worthless. In the preceding example, if the stock drops at all from the price of 50 (where it was trading when the option was purchased) by expiration, the option will expire worthless and the trader will lose the $300 he paid for the call. Leverage works both ways, of course, and thus huge percentages are possible as well. For example, if the stock were to advance by only 20 percent (from 50 to 60), then the option would be worth $1,000. So the stock trader would make 20 percent, while the option trader would make 233 percent ($300 becomes $1,000) from the same stock movement.

Before discussing option buying in more detail, let's look at an example of a put purchase. Since the put gives the holder the right to *sell* the underlying strike at the striking price (up until the expiration date), this is a bearishly oriented strategy. The put option will appreciate in value if the stock falls, and will lose value if the underlying stock rises in price.

Example: Suppose that XYZ common stock is trading at 50, and the XYZ July 50 put is selling for 2, or $200. The profit table and profit graph (Figure 2.2) are shown below.

At July Expiration

Stock Net Price	Put Price	Net Result ($)
30	20	+1800
35	15	+1300
40	10	+800
45	5	+300
50	0	−200
55	0	−200

Figure 2.2
PUT PURCHASE

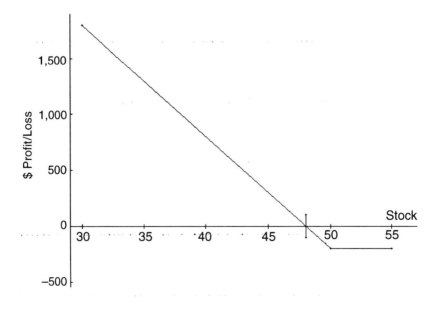

Figure 2.2 shows that this position has a limited loss on the upside, and can make very large profits on the downside.

Many experienced traders prefer option purchases to stock purchases, however, because they feel that if they can pick a reasonable percentage of trading winners—perhaps only 30 percent or 40 percent—the leverage provided by the winning trades will outweigh the more frequent, but limited losses incurred by the losing trades. The key in such a strategy is to be able to let profits run when they occur.

Buying options is often regarded as one of the most speculative trading activities. However, there are often differing ways in which to establish a strategy. These different ways may change the speculative to the conservative, or at least moderate things somewhat.

Before actually discussing the type of option you should purchase, it must be stated that the outlook for the performance of the stock is of utmost importance. *If the underlying stock drops in price, you are not going to profit from a call option purchase, no matter which call you buy.*

The main attraction for buying options—at least to the average or novice trader—is the leverage that is available. You can put up a fairly small amount of money (a couple of thousand dollars) and make returns in the 200 percent or 300 percent area. Of course, you can lose 100 percent fairly quickly as well.

In this regard, many novice traders buy out-of-the-money options in order to keep their cost down. They then dream of huge potential returns, but these returns are usually attainable only if the stock can make a rather large percentage move. To make matters worse, the typical buyer of out-of-the-money options buys options that have too short a life span—he does not give the stock enough time to make the large move that is required.

Over the years, I have spoken to numerous stock traders who have given up on options. They feel that they can make money trading stock, but always seem to lose when options are concerned. Their problems generally result from one mistake: buying too far out-of-the-money.

Professional stock traders often use options for one purpose only: to reduce their required investment in a position. They are not attempting to capture huge leveraged returns; rather they are merely using the option as a substitute for the stock itself. *In order to create an option position that is virtually the same as a stock position, you should buy in-the-money options, probably with little time remaining.* Moreover, if a professional normally trades 2,000 shares of stock, then he would probably buy 20 in-the-money calls; he does not usually attempt to leverage the quantity—the leverage is in the price.

By buying in-the-money options, you are minimizing the amount of money spent for time value premium. Time value premium is the part of an option that wastes away as time passes. Out-of-the-money options are *entirely* composed of time value premium. In-the-money options may have little, or sometimes even no time value premium.

Also, the in-the-money option will most closely match the performance of the underlying stock on a day-to-day basis. If the stock is up a point, the in-the-money call option will probably rise in price by at least three-quarters of a point or more. The out-of-the-money option may not move much at all. Of course, this fact could work against the call option holder if the stock moves *down* in price. That is why we originally stated that stock selection is of the utmost importance. An example may be helpful.

Example: Suppose that you have decided that XYZ is a good stock to buy for a short-term trade, and the stock is selling for 19 per share. If today were the first trading day of the year, which option would you buy?

Call Option	Offering Price
Jan 15	4
Jan 17½	2
Jan 20	½
March 17½	2½
March 20	1⅛
March 22½	½

The professional stock trader would buy either the Jan 15 call (which has no time value expense at all), or the Jan 17½ call, which has a half point of time value, but is 1½ points in-the-money and will move upward quickly if the stock advances.

The novice would be more inclined to buy the cheapest options (either the Jan 20 or the March 22½, both trading at ½) or maybe the March 20s.

In the preceding example, suppose the stock makes a quick move to 21—a 10 percent increase. The professional will make 2 points on the purchase of a Jan 15 call or 1½ points on the purchase of a Jan 17½ call—returns of 50 percent or 75 percent. The novice might have a larger percentage return, but he might actually make less money because it is unlikely that he would buy such a large quantity of out-of-the-money options that he would make more money than the trader who bought, for example, 20 in-the-money calls.

In order to quantify these concepts, you can judge how aggressive your option purchase is merely by looking at the delta of the call being bought. *The lower the delta, the more aggressive the option purchase.* If you think of the delta as being the probability of the option being in-the-money at expiration—which is an alternative, but still correct, way of viewing delta—you can see how speculative an out-of-the-money option purchase is.

Even if you do correctly predict the direction of the stock and your option purchase is profitable, you must be prepared to take follow-up action to lock in your profits where applicable. One of the easiest ways to lock in some profits while still retaining potential, is to sell out part of your position after gains have been made. This works for any type of investment—stock, options, futures, bonds, and so on. The biggest problem with doing that is that if really large gains occur, you have reduced the quantity of shares or contracts that you own and you therefore don't participate as much as you could have on the upside.

However, options actually sometimes provide a fairly easy means of having your cake and eating it too. That is, you can nail down some nice profits, but still preserve your "presence" in the stock. All that is required is to so sell the options you already own (and that are profitable) and buy the same number of options at the next strike. This is best accomplished when the stock has already reached the next strike, so that you are selling an in-the-money option and buying an at-the-money one.

Example: Suppose that you bought 10 XYZ June 20 calls for 2 each, when the stock was 21. This costs $2,000 before commissions. XYZ subsequently rallies to 25, and your calls are now worth 5 (at least). Upon investigation, you see that the July 25s are selling for 1½. You could therefore do the following:

> Sell 10 June 20 calls at 5: $5,000 credit
> Buy 10 July 25 calls at 1½: $1,500 debit

You therefore take a nice healthy $3,500 credit out of the position, less commissions—which more than covers your $2,000 initial cost—and you still have 10 long calls in case the stock explodes on the upside. The worst that can now happen is that the July 25s expire worthless, if the stock takes a dive. However, you have locked in a profit already, so that needn't overly concern you.

USING LONG OPTIONS
TO PROTECT STOCK

Another advantage of owning options is that they can be combined with stock or futures to produce a position that has much less risk than that of the underlying. Long puts can be bought as a hedge against the downside risk or owning stock, or long calls can be bought as a hedge against the risk of selling stock short.

Buying Puts as an Insurance Policy
for Long Stock

If a trader wants to protect against the downside risk of owning stock, he can buy a put against that stock. The ownership of the put will eliminate much of the downside risk, while still leaving room for plenty of gains on the upside.

Example: Suppose XYZ is selling for 51 and the July 50 put is selling for 2. If you buy 100 shares of stock and also buy the July 50 put, your profit potential at expiration would be the figures depicted in Table 2.1, or shown in the profit graph in Figure 2.3. Note that the position has limited risk, equal to the initial cost of the put (2 points) plus the amount by which the put was out-of-the-money (1 point). Moreover, it has unlimited upside profit potential, which is almost as large as that of owning the stock itself.

Table 2.1
LONG STOCK, LONG PUT PROFIT POTENTIAL

Stock Price	Long Stock Profit ($)	Option Price	Long Put Profit ($)	Net Profit ($)
30	−2100	20	+1800	−300
35	−1600	15	+1300	−300
40	−1100	10	+800	−300
45	−600	5	+300	−300
50	−100	0	−200	−300
55	+400	0	−200	+200
60	+900	0	−200	+700
70	+1900	0	−200	+1700

Figure 2.3
LONG STOCK, LONG PUT

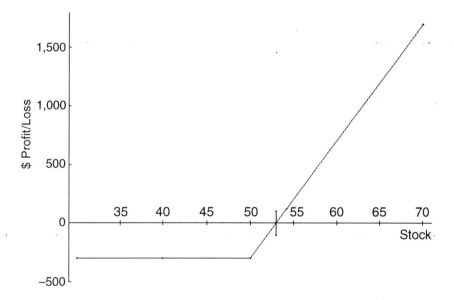

One other item is important: note that the *shape* of the profit graph of this position is exactly the same as the shape of the profit graph for owning a call. When two strategies' profit graphs have the same shape—as do call buying and this strategy of protecting long stock with a long put—then the two strategies are considered to be *equivalent*; which means they have the same profit and loss potential. We discuss equivalences repeatedly in this chapter. Note that just because two strategies are equivalent doesn't mean they have the same rates of return. For example, the cost of buying a call is far less than the cost of buying both 100 shares of stock and buying a put.

When you consider buying a put to protect a holding in your stock, you have several things to consider, just as you do with another form of "insurance." How much coverage do you want, how long a time period does the insurance cover, and how much are you willing to pay? Since options have varying expirations—even going out to two years or more with LEAPS options—as well as several striking prices, usually there are many choices. You might consider the amount by which the put is out-of-the-money as the "deductible" portion of your insurance policy.

A very short-term insurance policy that has a large deductible is not very expensive. Thus, if XYZ were at 51 in April, then the purchase of a July 45 put would represent a rather short-term, large deductible insurance policy. However, a 2-year LEAPS put with a striking price of 50 would be a much more expensive form of insurance because (1) it is long-term and (2) there isn't much of a deductible (only one point).

This strategy was employed, but rather rarely, back in the days of over-the-counter options, prior to the 1973 introduction of listed options. The first listed options were only calls (puts weren't listed until 1976, and then only on 25 stocks). Thus, in the early days of listed options, investors were forced to use covered calls as their only real means of lessening the downside risk of stock ownership.

The introduction of listed options coincided fairly closely with the last long-term bear market, which was the 1973–1974 bear market that saw the Dow-Jones Industrials decline from 1,000 to about 580 in a matter of approximately one year. The havoc wreaked on some of the "high-flying" stocks was even worse than the more than 40 percent loss suffered by the averages. The "nifty 50" stocks were supposed to be a group that would outperform the regular market, regardless of bull or bear markets. These stocks were very overpriced and eventually suffered some of the worst declines of that bear market.

One trader owned Polaroid at about 150 a share at the beginning of that market and wrote covered calls against it all the way down to its eventual low of 15! He claimed that he was able to protect nearly 75 percent of the loss with covered calls, a figure that may be a *slight* exaggeration—all trading stories grow in stature as the years pass—but is probably not a gross exaggeration. This shows just how expensive call options were in those early years (recall, there were no listed puts). It also reflects how large the volatility of that 1973–1974 market became as the months wore on.

In today's market, of course, option premiums are much smaller, and investors do not view covered call writing as providing much more than a modicum of downside protection. Today's strategy of insuring your stock holding by buying puts has become more and more popular since the crash of 1987. The main problem is that the protection is static. That is, if the underlying stock were to rally by a substantial amount after the insurance was purchased, the "deductible" portion of the policy becomes huge. For example, with XYZ at 51, if the stockholder initially bought the LEAPS put with a striking price of 50, his deductible was one point. If the stock then proceeds to rally 20 points to 71 over the next year, his policy is still in force, except that the deductible is now 21 points since the put *still* has a striking price of 50. The only way to "upgrade" the insurance would be to sell the original put and then to buy another put with a striking price closer to the current stock price.

Some money managers and individuals with large holdings have found that it is easier to buy index puts on a sector or broad-based index whose characteristics more or less match those of their stock portfolios. Then, they can buy all of their insurance at once—puts don't have to bought individually for each stock in the portfolio. This subject is covered in more detail in the next chapter.

Buying Calls to Protect Short Stock

Selling stock short is often considered a somewhat sophisticated strategy because theoretically there are unlimited risks involved. The stock could soar in price and cause large losses. While it is usually the case that a trader can limit his risk with stop-loss orders, or by paying attention to the market on a constant basis, it is sometimes easier for the short seller to know for certain that he has a limited loss even if the stock soars mightily. He can accomplish the task of limiting his loss by merely buying a call—probably an out-of-the-money one—against his short stock. Then, even if there were a high-priced takeover bid for the company, his loss would be limited on the upside. Thus a long call acts as insurance against large loss for a short seller, much in the same way that the stock*holder's* loss was limited by the ownership of a put in the previous section.

The profit graph of the long call/short stock position is presented in Figure 2.4. Note that its shape is the same as that of merely owning a put. Thus, long put is equivalent to long call/short stock. As a result, the strategy is also known as a *synthetic put*.

In fact, when options were first listed—and for the ensuing three years—there were only listed *calls*. Thus, the only way that you could have large downside profit potential with limited risk was to utilize this long call/short stock strategy. Even when puts first were listed in

Figure 2.4
LONG CALL, SHORT STOCK

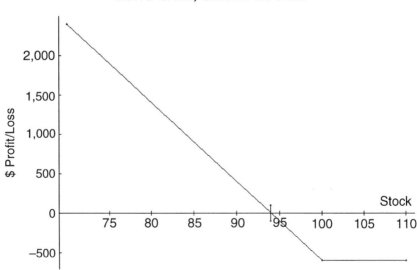

1976, there were only 25 stocks that had listed puts trading. If you wanted a position that was similar to owning a long put in any of the other optionable stocks, you still had to short the stock and buy a call.

The strategy was widely used, especially by professionals and arbitrageurs, and its name was shortened merely to "synthetic." If you were "doing synthetics," you were setting up a sizable position of short stock and long calls, either for the purpose of making an arbitrage profit via the interest earned on the short sale, and/or for the purpose of capitalizing on the collapse of the stock price. Today, since all stocks with listed options have both a listed put and a listed call, this strategy is no longer as widely used as it once was.

BUYING BOTH A PUT *AND* A CALL

In some cases, a trader may feel that there is the potential for explosive movement by an underling instrument, but he is uncertain of the direction that that movement might take. In such a case, he might consider buying *both* a put and a call with the same strike—a straddle. Then, if there is a large move—either up or down—he will make money. The drawback, of course, is that nothing much happens and time decay eats away at both the put and the call. This strategy has profit potential as shown in Figure 2.5; the maximum loss, which is equal to the initial premium paid, would be realized if the stock were exactly at the striking price at expiration. However, the possible rewards are large if the stock rises or falls far enough by expiration.

As a general rule of thumb, this is a strategy that should only be undertaken if two conditions are met: (1) the options are inexpensive on a historical basis (we have more to say about how to judge this condition in later chapters), and (2) the underlying has a history of being able to move distances large enough to make the straddle profitable.

Markets have a tendency to trade in small increments most of the time, and then to make most of their ground in a very short period of time. Studies have been done that show that 90 percent of the gains are made in only 10 percent of the trading days (other studies show similar figures for downside moves as well). It is often the case that options get very cheap just before large moves. This is especially true if the market has been rather trendless for a while just before a big

Figure 2.5
STRADDLE PURCHASE

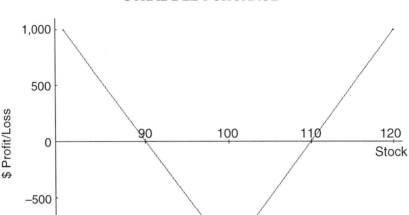

move occurs; option buyers are losing money to time decay and therefore are less aggressive in their bids for options, while option sellers become more aggressive as their profits build up. There have been many examples of options getting "cheap" just prior to large market explosions. One of the most famous was the cheapness of index options just prior to the crash of 1987, but there are many other instances as well, both in stocks and in futures. In fact, you might think that buying straddles works best just before big market declines because option prices tend to expand very quickly during declines (in stocks and indices). However, two of the swiftest rallies we have had since index options were listed were both preceded by very cheap options—one was in August 1983, and the other in the first half of 1995; therefore straddle buyers profited handsomely.

When the put and the call that are purchased have the same striking price and expiration month, you are buying a straddle. If they have different striking prices, you are buying a strangle or combination. The straddle purchase usually involves more risk in the worst case; however, it has better profit potential. The two profit graphs, Figures 2.5 and 2.6, compare the profitability of straddle buying and

Figure 2.6
COMBINATION (STRANGLE) PURCHASE

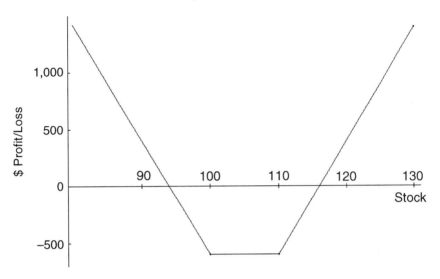

combination buying. It has been my experience that, if you have determined that you want to buy options in advance of what you perceive to be a potential price explosion by the underlying, you are better off buying straddles than buying combinations (strangles).

SELLING OPTIONS

Just as with any other type of security, the initial, or opening, transaction may be a sale rather than a purchase. When you do that with a stock, you must first borrow the shares before you can sell them "short." However, with options or futures, that is not necessary. The mere option transaction itself creates a contract, so that the buyer of the option is *long* the contract and the seller of the option is *short* the contract. The common term to describe the sale of an option as an opening transaction is to say the option has been *written*. This term comes from the old days when a physical contract was issued by the seller and delivered to the buyer. In today's paperless trading world, there is no longer any physical contract, but the term remains.

Covered Call Writing

When you write a *covered call*, you own the underlying *and* have sold a call option against it.

Example: Assume that XYZ is trading at 51 and a July 50 call is selling for 4. If you bought 100 shares of XYZ and sold one July 50 call, you would have a covered write with the following profit potential *at July expiration*:

Stock Price	Stock Profit ($)	Option Price	Option Profit ($)	Total Profit ($)
40	−1100	0	+400	−700
45	−600	0	+400	−200
50	−100	0	+400	+300
55	+400	5	−100	+300
60	+900	10	−600	+300

Figure 2.7 shows the same results as in the example profit table. Covered call writing is considered to be a conservative strategy. There is limited upside profit potential and rather large downside risk. The profit potential is limited because the trader has written the call and therefore has assumed the obligation to sell his stock at the striking price should he be assigned on the call. The risk of covered writing is less than that of owning the common stock, although that risk can still be considerable if the stock falls by a great distance. It is this reduction in risk that has made covered writing a "conservative" option strategy in the eyes of not only institutional money managers, but in the eyes of the courts as well.

Covered call writers are usually interested in two numbers: what kind of return would be made if the underlying stock were called away at expiration (called the *return if exercised*), and what kind of return would be made if the underlying stock were unchanged at expiration (called the *return if unchanged*). Of course, opinions of what is an acceptable return would probably differ depending on whether the stock were being bought specifically for the purpose of writing calls

Figure 2.7
COVERED CALL WRITE

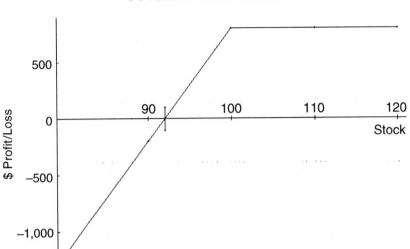

against it, or if an existing stockholder was writing calls against his long stock. The former probably represents the operation of the entire position as a strategy, while the latter may just be looking for a little additional income without really wanting to sell his stock.

There is an inherent attraction in selling options since an option is a wasting asset, and the writer enjoys the benefit of the time decay. This seems especially true to those who have suffered substantial losses due to time decay from owning options. As we pointed out earlier, option buyers who lose too much due to time decay are probably buying options that are too far out-of-the-money. Unfortunately, writing a deeply out-of-the-money option, while it will probably expire worthless, is not really a very conservative way to approach covered call writing. The minimal amount of premium brought in by such an approach does not provide much in the way of downside protection. As with any strategy, covered writing can be operated in a conservative or aggressive manner; the writing of deeply out-of-the-money calls is an aggressive approach.

A quite conservative covered write can be constructed by selling an in-the-money call against long stock. In such a case, there is downside protection all the way down to the striking price of the written option, which can be a considerable distance below the current stock price. Of course, the return from such a strategy is not going to be huge on the upside, but it is sometimes surprisingly large when you consider that the hefty call premium you receive can be used to reduce the cost of buying the stock.

Overall, covered writing is usually employed as a moderately bullish strategy, so that one can make money if the stock rises or remains relatively unchanged until expiration. What is sometimes forgotten is that this is *not* a very good strategy for bear markets, for stocks will normally fall faster than the protection provided by the limited amount of premium from the written call. Advocates of the strategy will say that, even in a bearish scenario, all you have to do is keep writing calls at lower strikes and eventually you will collect enough premium to recoup your losses. However, if after a stock falls quickly, you write a call with a lower strike, and then the stock rallies back quickly, you will surely have locked yourself into a loss no matter how large the premium you took in.

In summary, then, covered writing is a strategy designed to do best when stock prices are stable or moderately rising. If the underlying stock is, or becomes, volatile, this is not an attractive strategy because you cannot participate in large moves on the upside, but you *will* suffer the results of any large move to the downside.

Naked Option Writing

When an option is written without any offsetting position in the underlying stock, or without being hedged by a similar long option, that option is considered to be written *naked*. In general, naked option writing is considered to be risky because you can only make a limited amount of money, yet could lose large sums if the underlying stock or futures contract moved so far that you were forced to buy the option back for a great deal of money. In general, larger margin and equity requirements are required by most brokerage firms before they will allow a customer to participate in the sale of naked options as a strategy. Yet, in the next few sections we see that naked option writing may not be all that risky if approached in a reasonable manner.

The "investment" required to write a naked option is somewhat different from that required for buying stock or options. You must have collateral of a sufficient amount to cover your risk, in the eyes of your broker. Currently, if you are writing naked *stock* options, you must have collateral equal to 20 percent of the stock price, plus the premium of the option, less any out-of-the-money amount.

Example: Suppose XYZ were a $100 stock and you wanted to write one July 110 call naked for a premium of 4 points. You would need to have the following collateral:

$2,000	(20 percent of the value of 100 shares of XYZ)
−1,000	(the amount by which the call is out-of-the-money)
+400	(the premium of the option)
$1,400	

There is a minimum collateral requirement that you must meet (usually something like $250), no matter how far out-of-the-money the option is when initially written. Since the option premium is credited to your account when you sell the option, you can apply it toward your initial collateral requirement.

What is collateral? It's any type of equity in your account that is not already borrowed against; it could be cash, or any marginable security such as stock, bonds, or government or municipal debt securities. Note that you are not charged any interest for the naked option collateral requirement, as you would be if you were buying stocks on margin, for you are *not* borrowing any money from your broker. In fact, if you use government securities as collateral, you are allowed to earn interest on the credit balance that is generated from the sale of the naked options. Thus, in the preceding example, the $400 call premium could be invested in a money market fund and allowed to earn interest as long as you had $1,400 worth of equity in your T-bills.

The collateral requirement changes as the underlying stock moves up and down, to reflect the risk your broker envisions that you have in the position. For example, if XYZ rose to 120, the July 120 call might then be selling at 13. Your requirement would be $2,400

(20 percent of $12,000) plus $1300 for the option premium, for a total requirement of $3,700—considerably larger than it was when the option was first written.

For index options, the calculation is similar, except that only 15 percent of the index value is required, as opposed to the 20 percent required for stock options. This is because indices are less volatile than individual stocks.

For futures options, if you are using SPAN margin, the requirement is based on the volatility of the underlying futures contract. This is a sophisticated and enlightened way of approaching the matter, and hopefully one day will be employed for stock options. Thus, SPAN margin might require more collateral for pork belly options than it would for heating oil options, even though both futures might be trading at the same price (most of the time, pork bellies are more volatile than heating oil). If you are *not* using SPAN margin, then the requirement for writing a naked futures option is usually equal to the futures margin plus the option premium less one-half the out-of-the-money amount, if the option is out-of-the-money.

As with naked options, naked index or futures options require a minimum amount of margin. This is normally in the neighborhood of $200 to $300 per option, so that even an extremely out-of-the-money option will still require some collateral in order to write it naked.

Naked Put Writing

The sale of a put, without any accompanying position in the underlying stock, is termed naked put writing. It is a popular strategy among moderately sophisticated investors. The profit potential is a limited one; if the underlying security rises in price, the put that was sold will expire worthless, and you will profit by the amount of the original premium that was collected. The following example and Figure 2.8 define the strategy.

Example: Suppose XYZ is selling for 51 and the July 50 put is selling for 2. If you sell the July 50 put naked, your profit potential *at expiration* would be:

Stock Naked Put Price	Option	
	Price	Profit ($)
30	20	−1,800
35	15	−1,300
40	10	−800
45	5	−300
50	0	+200
55	0	+200
60	0	+200

Figure 2.8 shows the shape of the profits and losses associated with naked put writing. The profit is limited to the premium collected. On the other hand, if the underlying security falls in price, large risks could materialize. You would be forced to either buy back the put at a much higher price in that case, or you would have to

Figure 2.8
NAKED PUT WRITE

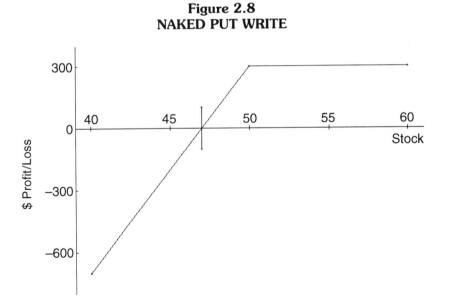

accept assignment of the stock at expiration. That is, the sale of a put obliges you to buy the stock if you are assigned at some later date. The purchase of this stock could require considerable money.

One of the worst put writing debacles of all time occurred in the crash of 1987. In the years and, particularly the months, leading up to the crash, many investors had been writing naked puts on the "stock market." In this case, the stock market was generally represented by the OEX Index, although some other broad-based indices were being used as well. One of the great attractions was that you only had to have collateral of 5 percent (!) of the value of the index at that time.

As the stock market inexorably ground its way higher and higher through 1986 and 1987, more and more investors became enamored with the idea of putting up about $3,000 in collateral to collect $100 or $200 in profits every month, month in and month out. Of course, when the crash came, OEX fell almost 100 points in two days. Thus, puts that had been sold for $100 were suddenly worth $8,000 to $10,000. To make matters worse, volatility had increased so dramatically that the puts were even more expensive than they normally should have been.

Needless to say, many investors were wiped out, some brokerage firms were wiped out, and lawsuits flew back and forth. In the aftermath, margin requirements were raised, brokers required more sophistication from their customers who wanted to write naked options, and limits were placed on stock market movement.

It is stories like this that make many traders leery of writing naked options. However, before turning the page to look for the next strategy, stop for a minute and look at the preceding profit graph of the naked put write (Figure 2.8) and compare that profit graph with the one of the covered call write in the last section (Figure 2.7). They are the same! That is, the profit and loss potential of a covered call write (which is considered to be a conservative strategy) is exactly the same as the profit and loss potential of a naked put write (which seems, by the previous example, to be a very risky strategy).

What is going on here? Is there some trick? No, there isn't. In fact, the two strategies *do* have the same profit and loss potential. The *investment* required for the two is slightly different, but the dollars of profit and loss are the same. But, you may ask, what about the

disaster scenario in the preceding example? Well, owning stocks during the crash was pretty risky, too, you may remember. In fact, any
time you own stock you have large risk to the downside—whether or
not you take in some call premium as a hedge—just as you have
downside risk from selling naked puts. In reality, covered call writing
probably isn't as conservative as some would have you believe, and
naked put selling isn't as dangerous, either.

The conventional wisdom is that covered call writing is the safest
form of option trading because it has less risk than owning stock. I've
always had some trouble with this argument because a stock can fall a
long way, and even if you sell calls against it several times on the way
down, you can still suffer some rather large losses in bear markets.
Moreover, no matter what kind of market you're in, the sale of a call
against your stock deprives you of the potential for large gains on the
upside, since you are obligated to sell your stock at the striking price.

More realistically, it could be said that covered call writing *can* be a
conservative strategy. As with all option strategies, it depends upon
how they're implemented as to whether or not they are conservative.
If you're selling "expensive" calls against a stock that is oversold (or
cheap by some other measure), then I would agree that that is probably a conservative method of covered call writing. However, if you're
selling out-of-the-money calls against a volatile, overpriced stock, that's
not very conservative because you are taking too much downside risk.

Recall that when two strategies' profit graphs have the same
shape—as do covered call writing and naked put selling—then the
two strategies are considered to be *equivalent*.

I generally prefer naked put selling strategy for two reasons: first,
you are only dealing with one security's bid–asked spread rather than
two, and second, the margin requirement is considerably smaller.
The stock owner receives dividends (if any are paid), but the naked
put seller can use T-bills as his collateral and earn interest that way.
Moreover, the price of the put has the dividend factored in (i.e., puts
are more expensive on high-dividend-paying stocks, all other things
being equal).

Put Writing Philosophy.   The naked put writing strategy is often
approached in this manner: if you sell an out-of-the-money put on a

stock that you like—and wouldn't mind owning—then you are in a "no-lose" situation. If the stock goes up, you profit by the amount of the premium received from selling the put. On the other hand, if the stock goes down below the striking price of the put you sold, you buy the stock at a low price, which is theoretically good since you don't mind owning the stock. At that point, you can just hold the stock or maybe even write some calls against it. This philosophy is quite widespread among naked put sellers. That is, they choose the puts they sell by looking at the qualities of the underlying stock. They are not overly concerned with whether the puts are "cheap" or "expensive" by statistical measures. In this manner, if you do eventually wind up being put the stock, you are thus buying a stock that you have confidence in and which is fundamentally attractive to you.

Unfortunately, the theory and the practice of it are sometimes at odds. It's all well and good to say that you wouldn't mind owning a stock if it dropped to the striking price of the puts you sold. However, what it if dropped to that level and kept on dropping? Then, it's not so much fun.

When LEAPS options (options with expirations extending out to two years) were introduced, they were generally only listed on some of the biggest and best stocks. One of the reasons this was done, as opposed to listing them on volatile highfliers with big option premiums, was to attract put writers who adhere to the philosophy just described. One of these stocks was IBM, which at the time was selling between 105 and 100. Long-term puts with a striking price of 90 were listed and many investors sold them naked, figuring that if they had a chance to own IBM at 90, they wouldn't mind. Well, they all got their chance as the stock began to drop rather precipitously and fell all the way to 45. It didn't recover right away, either. When the puts got so deeply in the money, most of them were assigned, even though there was over a year of life remaining in the puts. Many of those put writers, in the final analysis, were not really ready to buy IBM and hold it through a plunge like that. Some of them didn't have the money required to take on the debit necessary to buy the stock, so they tried to roll their puts to even longer-term puts, but those too were assigned. The moral is that even the best of stocks can go through its own bear market and, if it does, it will hurt covered call writers and naked put sellers.

Protecting Your Positions.   Regardless whether you use covered call writing or naked put selling, you have downside risk, as the previous story shows. Moreover, if you have a whole portfolio utilizing this strategy, you are especially subject to the risk of a market correction (or worse, a bear market). When markets get overextended, you should start thinking about protecting your covered writes or naked puts.

"How?" you ask. Well, there are several ways, assuming you want to continue to operate the strategy. One way would be to make your portfolio more conservative, utilizing underlying stocks that are less volatile and perhaps "cheap." Another way would be to buy some (other) puts to protect yourself. The easiest thing to do would be to buy some out-of-the-money OEX LEAPS puts, but they may be quite expensive in terms of implied volatility.

A less costly approach would be to buy (deeply) out-of-the-money puts on the individual issues that you own or have written naked puts on. If you are a covered call writer, you would then have a strategy that the professionals term a *collar*: long stock, short out-of-the-money call, long out-of-the-money put. If you are a naked put seller, then your resultant position would be a bullish put spread. In either case, you have limited your downside risk at the expense of some of your option writing profits.

Thus, a covered call writer or naked put seller should attempt to limit his losses, for if he sustains large losses in this limited-profit strategy, it will take a long time to make them back.

Naked Call Writing

The writing of naked calls is considered to be an extremely risky strategy, and many brokerage firms require their customers to demonstrate a certain amount of experience and/or sophistication before embarking on the strategy. In reality, it is really not much more risky than writing naked puts—and therefore, by equivalence, doing covered writes—for all those strategies can incur large losses if an unfavorable movement occurs in the underlying. The fact that a stock can rise more than 100 percent and it can only fall 100 percent, makes the ultimate risk larger with naked calls than with naked puts, but it can be very large in either case. An example of a naked call write follows.

Example: Suppose XYZ is selling for 51 and the July 50 call is selling for 3. If you sell the July 50 call naked, your profit potential at expiration would be:

Stock Price	Option Price	Naked Call Profit ($)
40	0	+300
45	0	+300
50	0	+300
55	5	−200
60	10	−700
70	20	−1,700

Figure 2.9 shows the shape of the profits and losses associated with naked call writing: limited profit potential to the downside and large risk if the underlying stock should rise dramatically. Most writers of naked calls are intrigued by the relentless effects of time decay and want to be on the side of a trade that benefits from that decay. This is generally the main impetus for the strategy. It is *not* primarily used as a way to profit if you expect the underlying to decline in price—long puts or synthetic puts and bear spreads would be more appropriate for that bearish scenario.

Writers of naked calls usually sell out-of-the-money calls that, in the call writer's opinion, are too expensive; he often feels that there is not enough time for the stock to climb to the striking price of the written call before expiration, or that the call is just selling for too high of a price. These are reasonable approaches, but even reasonable men can lose money.

Every option that is worthless at expiration had some value sometime during its life. However, if the option is out-of-the-money (perhaps by a relatively large amount), its value will begin to slip away, until, one day, the option will have the smallest possible bid: one-sixteenth of a point for stock

Figure 2.9
NAKED CALL WRITE

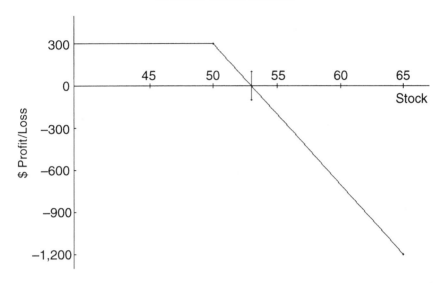

options, and similarly tiny amounts for futures options. This bid sometimes lingers for a while as traders who are short the option—either naked writers or covered writers—often attempt to cover their position and move on to the next trade. These option writers sometimes are therefore bidding for an option that is, by all statistical measures, doomed to be worthless. However, they are interested in closing out their trade.

In the early to mid-1980s there was a tendency among market makers and professional firms to "sell the teenies." That is, they would look for these situations where there was a sixteenth bid for options that had no statistical value and sell them. This sale normally took place quite close to expiration—within a week or so. Therefore, there was a very large probability that these professionals would collect the $6.25 for each sale. Moreover the collateral requirements were quite low; $250 at the most for the public and much less for market makers. Thus, the annualized rate of return was over 100 percent for this strategy (and much higher for floor traders).

The only problem was that there was the occasional gap up or down by a stock that would turn one of the "worthless" options into something with value. However, these were rare and the strategy was highly profitable for a long time. As with any profitable strategy, word gets around and more and more people start utilizing it. Such was the case with "selling teenies" on calls of Amax Corp., a metals stocks. It was trading under 30 with only a few days left until expiration. Moreover, the stock had been in a severe downtrend and there were striking prices all the way up to 50 and above. It appeared that the calls at all those strikes would expire worthless. Since the stock had at one time or another traded near each of those higher strikes, there was decent open interest at each one. Consequently, when each one eventually became bid at a sixteenth, the teenies were sold. Then, the unthinkable happened: an $80 per share bid was made for the company right before expiration. Small firms went out of business and even large ones suffered more than they had bargained for.

The resulting havoc pretty much ended "selling teenies" as a widely practiced strategy. However, the practice continues today in similar form, with the same results upon occasion. Now, option writers are more apt to cover their short options at fractional prices of a quarter or so, because too many times they sold an option at 2 or 3 dollars, only to see it fall to a fractional price, and then spring back to life once again as the stock reversed direction. This is the reality of the postcrash market, whose volatility still lingers in the memory of every option writer. When these writers cover, there are surely others out there attempting to use a strategy similar to "selling the teenies," only now they can get a quarter of a point for that sale. Even with only a week to go, this strategy produces its share of naked writing disasters every so often. Thus, naked option writers should not attempt to sell these extremely low-priced options just before expiration. Eventually, the large loss can and probably will wipe out all the "teeny" profits that were made.

Many futures traders also sell very low-priced options with a short time remaining until expiration. At least with futures, you can't have a takeover, but that still doesn't prevent the option owner from exercising if something changes with respect to the fundamentals.

In the spring of 1995, a large client was long a substantial number of calls on silver. The striking price of these calls was 550, but silver had drifted down over the life of the contract and was settling around 535 on the day that the calls expired. This client, however, was not a speculator, but was intensely interested in actually owning silver futures (and perhaps eventually, the metal itself). He owned a very large quantity of calls, and he looked at what would happen to the futures market if he let those calls expire and instead bought the same number of silver futures. He realized that his buying pressure would most likely push the price of silver futures back up over the 550 level and that his average price to buy all the futures he wanted might actually be higher than 550 by the time he was done. Therefore, he exercised the calls! Traders who were short the 550 calls had obviously gone home expecting to ring up some realized profits that expiration night, but instead found themselves in a nightmare situation as silver gapped open at 560 and traded even higher the next day. Not only did this gap opening cause panicky short covering by regular futures traders, but, after assignment, all of the naked options writers were now short futures as well and fed the frenzy even more. This proves that even futures option sellers should be extremely careful about operating a strategy of selling extremely low-priced options right before expiration.

Straddle and Combination Selling

One of the ways in which naked option writers attempt to hedge their positions is by selling both a naked put and naked call. The losses on one may be more than offset by the profits on the other, for they cannot both lose money at the same time unless volatility increases. The put and the call may have the *same* striking price (which is a straddle), or they may have *different* striking prices (a combination, or strangle as it is sometimes called). In either case, one still has unlimited risks—and by selling both the put and the call, the risks exist in either direction, up *or* down—but there is more profit potential if the stock is relatively unchanged, which is what stock or futures prices *are* most of the time over a short period. Figures 2.10 and 2.11 show the short combination and the short straddle.

Earlier, the collateral requirements for writing naked options were spelled out: 20 percent of the stock price, 15 percent for an index, and the futures margin for futures option. When you are writing both a naked put *and* a naked call, the collateral requirement is the *greater* of the put requirement or the call requirement; the other side does not require any additional collateral. In the case of a naked straddle, this means that you are forced to collateralize the in-the-

Figure 2.10
SHORT COMBINATION

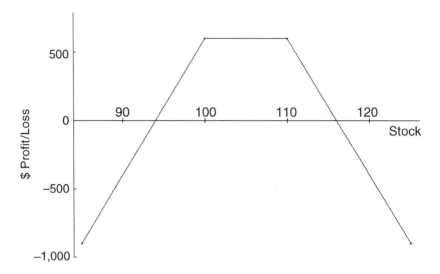

Figure 2.11
SHORT STRADDLE

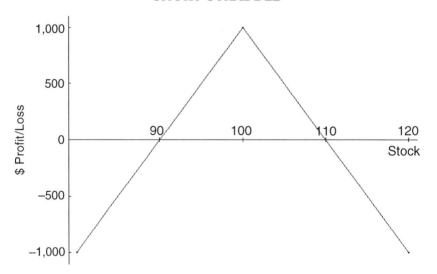

money option, while the other one is "free." In the case of a combination or strangle, the "greater" collateral requirement normally is applied to whichever option is nearer to the money (if both are out-of-the-money). Generally, it seems that combination selling is better than straddle selling, because there is a better chance that both options could expire worthless; moreover, if one option becomes an in-the-money option, it would generally take a major reversal for the underlying to swing back far enough to make the *other* option go in-the-money. Of course, when you are dealing with unlimited risk positions, you are constantly at risk of a volatile and sudden move by the underlying stock, index, or futures.

When puts were first listed, straddle trading was the de rigueur strategy. Even though only 25 stocks had listed puts, there was plenty of interest in trading straddles on them. In particular, since this was 1977 and there was a bear market of sorts going on, straddle *selling* was more popular than straddle buying; in those days, markets declined slowly instead of all at once as is the custom now, so that a strategy involving time decay worked well. As profits were built up over time, there was a general feeling that a long-term strategy of straddle selling would be the best approach to the market. Since most stocks wandered in trading ranges most of the time, according to computers, if you were to merely diversify and sell straddles in nearly all of the 25 issues available, you would have a nicely hedged portfolio. Of course, there were stopgap measures designed to limit losses should big moves occur, but they generally consisted of something like recentering the straddle at new strikes if the stock moved too far away from the current striking price of the straddle. Since IBM was by far the most liquid stock on which puts were trading, there were a large number of straddles sold on IBM.

The strategy was working rather well up until the second week of April 1978. It was on that Friday that a sleepy market awoke and bolted upward 20 points (up 3 percent on the Dow) and volume reached the previously unheard of levels of 52 million shares! What caused this was a discussion in Congress regarding lowering the capital gains tax; that same piece of news can still rally the market dramatically even today. What was even more noteworthy for straddle sellers, however, was the fact that IBM shot up over 14 points in one week—from 239 to 254. Most straddle sellers had long since covered their naked puts or rolled them to lower strikes as IBM had fallen farther and farther during the spring of 1978. What was left were a lot of naked calls that were going to expire worthless, or so the thinking went.

Instead, the rally by IBM through several strikes brought ruin to many a straddle seller that day. Similar, but smaller, moves in many other stocks pretty much ended the diversified straddle selling approach to trading as a popular strategy.

Of course, someone *made* money that was being lost by the straddle sellers—mostly owners of calls. The following story really doesn't apply to straddle selling per se, but since it involves the same set of events that were just described, it belongs here nevertheless.

The bearish market of late 1977 and early 1978 had been rough on many bulls, and one bullish professional trader was about wiped out. He was down to his last few positions—a rather sizable amount of deeply out-of-the-money calls on IBM, plus some calls on Avon, and a few other stocks. When the Aprils expired, he was destined to be out of business, for he had no further source of funds. So he was just waiting around for April expiration—not exactly anticipating the word from his clearing firm that his trading account was worthless. Then, only a week before April expiration came the big market rally, exploding the price of IBM dramatically higher. As it turned out, the trader made all his losses back in that one day and in the subsequent trading the next week.

Today, straddle and combination writers are much more apt to buy out-of-the-money options to protect themselves against disaster. This strategy is discussed in a later section, entitled "Credit Spreads."

Covered Straddle Writing.   In the wake of the 1978 debacle that naked straddle writers suffered, another approach to straddle writing became a little more popular, but it has never really captured the fancy of large quantities of option traders. It is the *covered straddle*, in which one buys 100 shares of the underlying stock and also sells a straddle at the same time. The call from the straddle sale is covered by the ownership of the stock, so what the trader really has is a covered call write plus a naked put. This is a fairly bullish position because, if the price of the underlying falls dramatically, he will lose money on both the long stock and the short put. It has limited upside profit potential, although if the stock remains relatively unchanged, the covered straddle writer would capture a fair amount of decaying time value premium.

If you recall our discussion of naked put selling and covered call writing, you may recall that we said the two strategies are equivalent. So a covered straddle—which is a covered write and a naked put—is *equivalent* to selling two naked puts. Therefore, it would be more efficient to just sell two naked puts rather than bother with the covered straddle write. It is more efficient not only in terms of collateral requirements, but also from the viewpoint that a covered straddle involves three separate securities (underlying, call, and put), while the naked put involves only one. So, merely selling two naked puts would lower commission costs and would also avoid having to deal with three bid–asked spreads.

SPREADS

Spreads are constructed by being both long an option and short another option on the same underlying, where both options are calls or both options are puts. Spreads are designed to limit risk, and they often limit profit potential as well, although not always. The risk-limiting nature is probably the more important aspect of a spread. If you are normally a naked call seller, you could limit your risk by buying another call that is *more* out-of-the-money than the one you sold. If the underlying rises dramatically, the call that you own will limit losses; therefore, you no longer have unlimited risk from the option sale. Of course, buying that call will cost you some of your profit if both options expire worthless, but many traders feel that the peace of mind that the spread provides is worth the small amount of money that is spent on the long, protective call.

We first describe the strategies in which the spreads are linear— that is, where the same number of options is bought as is sold.

Vertical Spreads

A spread is a *vertical* spread if both options have the same expiration month, but they have different striking prices. There are two main types of vertical spreads, the *bull spread* and the *bear spread*. Either one may be constructed with puts *or* with calls. In fact, it is even possible to construct them using the underlying and options as well.

Bull Spread.   A bull spread is a vertical spread that is typically constructed by buying a call at one strike and selling another call at a higher strike (both calls typically expire at the same time). The resulting position has profitability as shown in Figure 2.12. Since the profit potential is on the upside, you need to have a somewhat bullish outlook for this spread to work, hence the name. There is both limited risk and limited profit potential, although the risk is equal to 100 percent of the capital required—the same percentage risk as owning a call option.

If the underlying is near or below the lower strike when the spread is established, the profit potential can be several times the loss potential. If the underlying is initially midway between the two strikes, then the profit and loss potential will be approximately equal. Finally, if you establish bull spreads with the underlying at or above

Figure 2.12
BULL SPREAD

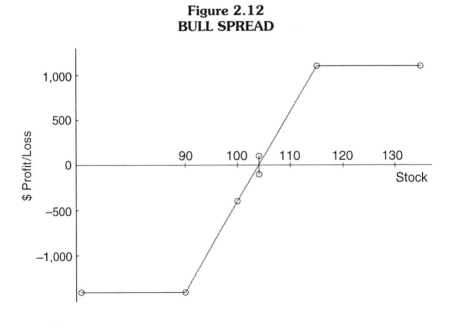

the higher strike, the risk is great in comparison to the potential rewards, but the probability of gain is high since both options are in-the-money to begin with.

One of the main reasons that traders use bull spreads instead of just buying calls outright is that they want to hedge their bets somewhat. This is particularly true if the options are "expensive"; the trader feels that he is at least selling something expensive against the expensive call that he is buying. However, he should not always use the bull spread approach just because the options have a lot of time value premium, for he is giving up a lot of upside profit potential in order to have a hedged position. If the underlying is volatile, then he should not be queasy about having to pay for time value premium on an in-the-money option—it is probably worth it, as the implied and historical volatilities most likely are closely in line.

Once the bull spread is established, it might not perform exactly as you expect. Figure 2.13 shows a typical bull spread using the 80 and 90 striking prices, bought when the underlying was 85—midway

Figure 2.13
BULL SPREAD COMPARISON

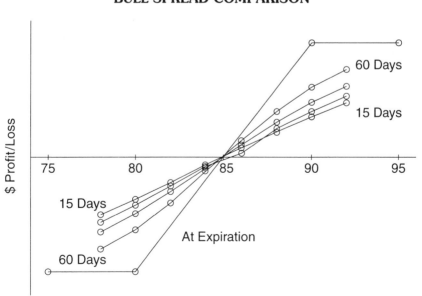

between the two strikes. The profit potential at several intermediate points in time is shown: at 15 days from inception, 30 days, 45 days, and 60 days. Notice that there is very little difference in the results as time passes (until you get very close to expiration, when the profit potential approaches the final shape of the bull spread). This phenomenon can sometimes be frustrating: if the underlying has a nice upward move shortly after you establish the spread, you will probably be disappointed in your profits at that time. This fact often causes bull spread holders to "overstay their welcome," as they figure they will continue to hold on for better results closer to expiration, only to see the underlying slip back and their profits dissipate.

Thus the bull spread is a low-risk and low-profit potential strategy—particularly if you remove it prior to expiration—but that is not what many traders intend when they establish it. To get a larger profit potential, you must establish the spread with the underlying close to the lower strike, or merely buy the call and not use the bull spread at all.

The preceding bull spread using calls always requires a *debit* to establish, since the call with a lower striking price will always cost more than the call with the higher strike that is being sold. However, an equivalent position can be established using puts, and the put spread is a credit spread. The following example illustrates this fact.

Example: XYZ is 55.

| July 50 call: 7 | July 50 put: 1½ |
| July 60 call: 2 | July 60 put: 6½ |

Call bull spread: buy July 50 call and sell July 60 call = 5 point debit.
Put bull spread: buy July 50 put and sell July 60 put = 5 point credit.

With either spread, you would make 5 points at expiration if XYZ is over 60, and you would lose 5 points if XYZ were below 50 at expiration.

The advantage to credit spreads is this: in the credit spread, the brokerage firm requires the difference in the strikes to be margined with collateral; then you can use the credit generated to reduce the requirement, if you want. We have already described collateral as any type of security that you own, stocks or bonds. Most brokerage firms will allow you to put up T-bills as collateral for the difference in the strikes, *and then they will let you put the credit from the spread in a money market fund and earn interest on it.* This additional feature makes the credit form of the spread more attractive to many investors.

There is actually one more way to construct a position that has the same profit potential as a bull spread: buy the underlying stock, buy an out-of-the-money put (which limits downside risk), and sell an out-of-the-money call (which limits upside profit potential). This position, known as a *collar*, is a rather popular form of protecting a stock position. It is discussed in more detail in the section on protecting a portfolio in Chapter 3. Thus, all three ways of constructing a bull spread are considered to be equivalent positions.

Bear Spread. The bear spread (Figure 2.14) is also a vertical spread, but it is constructed by taking the opposite actions of the bull

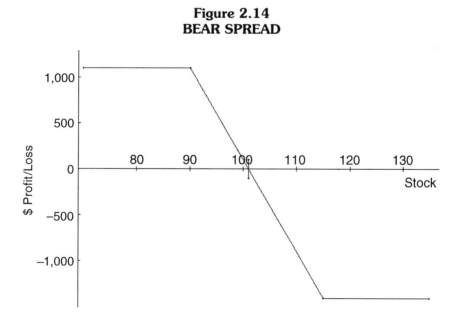

Figure 2.14
BEAR SPREAD

spread: if you are using calls, you buy the call with the *higher* strike and sell the call with the *lower* strike. This creates a spread that has its profit potential to the downside (hence, the name *bear* spread). Like the other vertical spreads, it has limited profit and risk potential.

When you establish a bear spread with calls, you take in a credit, so it has the advantages outlined earlier in terms of earning interest from the credit. The bear spread may also be constructed with puts, in which case you would have a debit spread: you would buy the put at the *higher* strike and sell a put at a *lower* strike as a hedge.

As with the bull spread, you may use the spread because the options are expensive. This helps reduce the risk if things go awry, but may severely limit the profit potential over the short term if the underlying moves in a favorable direction.

Sybase, a technology stock, was trading near 45 in the spring of 1995 and the options had become very expensive in advance of the company's earnings report. Since technology stocks were "in favor," there was a contingent that thought the stock would soar if the earnings were merely "in line." On the other hand, there were rumors that the earnings were going to be terrible. These two facts combined to make the options very expensive.

I knew a trader who felt that earnings were going to be bad and therefore wanted to buy puts. His initial reaction was to buy the April 45 puts, or perhaps the April 40 puts, but they were extremely expensive. With Sybase at 45, the April 40 puts were 2½ with only a month remaining until expiration. Figuring that these were just *too* expensive, he decided that it would be better to pay 4½ for the April 45s and then offset some of that cost by selling an out-of-the-money put. Thus, he created a bear spread—he bought the April 45s and sold the April 35s for a net debit of 3½.

Less than a week later, Sybase let the Street know that earnings would not only be bad, they would be terrible. The stock plunged 20 points to 23. The bear spread widened to its maximum potential—10 points (the difference in the two strikes, 45 – 35)—and the trader made 6½ points on his 3½ investment. Not a bad trade, but nowhere near the return that he could have made had he merely bought the "overpriced" April 45 puts in the first place. They rose from 4½ to 22. Using the spread cost a lot of money.

Thus, while it is sometimes attractive to use a spread to offset the cost of an expensive option, you should evaluate *why* the option is expensive and how far the underlying might move. If it's expensive because there is a potential for a short-term, explosive move in the stock, then a spread is probably ill-advised because the options *deserve* to be expensive. If, on the other hand, the options seem expensive only because the underlying has been stagnant, or if a move might be only a modest one, then a spread may be a viable strategy.

For example, gold sometimes goes into tight trading ranges for extended periods, during which time the options don't really get correspondingly cheaper. The options retain their premium because traders know that gold could once again become volatile at any time. The result of all this is that the options appear to be expensive (and they are, in comparison to the movement in the underlying gold futures). At times like that, bull or bear spreads are viable strategies. This same sort of relative option pricing can occur in any stock, index, or futures contract, whenever the underlying price becomes sluggish while the options retain their former premium levels.

Credit Spread.   We have already described the two basic credit spreads—the bull spread constructed with puts and the bear spread constructed with calls. However, "credit spreading" has taken on a wider meaning in the wake of the crash of 1987 and other stock market gaps, which have caused ruin for many a naked option writer. Such trading gaps are also common in futures, so the credit spread strategy, as it is applied today, is fairly widely practiced in futures option trading, also.

A look at the philosophy behind the credit spread, plus some historical evidence, will help to explain the current popularity of the strategy. Most option traders "know" that selling options is the more profitable way to approach option trading, because (1) time decay works in their favor, and (2) everyone says option buyers lose a lot of money. These are popular misconceptions that aren't always true. Many novice traders are convinced that professionals sell options almost exclusively, so they want to do what the "pros" do (it is *my* personal experience, however, that most professional traders attempt to establish a net long option position if they can).

The main problem with selling naked options is that there is unlimited risk—or at least, very large risk—if the underlying experiences a sudden move or gap opening. After the crash of 1987, when many naked put sellers were carried out on their shields, the limited risk nature of the credit spread caused it to gain tremendously in popularity.

Another problem with selling naked options is that brokers—assuming you pass the suitability tests and have enough equity in your account—want collateral of 20 percent of the value of a stock or 15 percent of the value of an index in order to allow you to sell a naked option. With OEX at 600, this is a requirement of $9,000 to write the 600 call or put naked (15 times $600). The higher that OEX rises, the greater will be the requirement, as it is recalculated each day by your brokerage firm. However, the requirement for a credit spread is only the difference in the strikes, less any credit received; thus a 10-point credit spread in OEX would require less than $1,000 apiece to establish—quite a savings over the $9,000 for a naked option.

Of course, the profitability of the sale of an option is reduced by buying the other option that creates the credit spread. This is a negative to some traders, but considering the reduction of capital required and the lessening of ultimate risk, it is often seen as a worthwhile cost.

Do credit spreads really win 90 percent of the time? I have seen proponents of the credit spread advise establishing the spread with extremely far out-of-the-money options, so that there is a very large chance of making money. For example, with OEX at 475 at the beginning of April, they might recommend the April 450-460 put spread for a half credit ($50). The probability of OEX falling 15 points in two weeks is small. Therefore, they reason, there is a good chance of making money. In fact, this type of spread has been very consistently profitable since the crash—the length of the current bull market.

But what's the *real* risk of the spread? It's that OEX could fall to 450 or lower, thereby causing a loss of $950. So you're risking $950 to make $50, but the probability of making the $50 is far greater than that of losing the $950. Let's just say that there's a 95 percent chance that the options will expire worthless, and a 5 percent chance that the maximum loss is realized. These are not the true mathematical numbers, and we haven't allowed for any possibility of OEX being *between* 450 and 460 at expiration, but they will suffice for this simple example. So we have a 95 percent chance of making

$50, which means our expected gain is $47.50 ($50 × 0.95), and a 5 percent chance of losing $950—a $47.50 loss! Therefore, our expected result is that we would make nothing and lose our commissions if we operated the strategy long enough.

Proponents of the strategy usually counter by saying that they would never let the spread lose its maximum amount—that they would close it out if OEX fell to some predetermined level, usually before either option gets to be an in-the-money option. This tactic means that they might only lose a point or less on the spread if they had to buy it back prematurely.

Mathematics would then tell us that they have greatly reduced the probability of both options expiring worthless, because there is a much greater chance that OEX could fall to 460 at any time before expiration than there is that it would be *below* 450 *at* expiration. So now, maybe there's a 70 percent chance of making $50, and a 30 percent chance of losing $100—again, not much better than an even-money proposition after commissions are included.

Why does the math seem to belie actual fact? The math says "don't waste your time with these spreads," while in actual fact, they have been very profitable. For one thing, the math is assuming a random market, and we have been in a mostly bullish market for the past several years. However, this doesn't mean the math is wrong. If you were to flip a coin 100 times and got 90 heads, would you say that the probability of getting heads on the next toss was greater than 50 percent? You might, but you would be wrong—it's still 50 percent.

In much the same manner, the credit spread strategy can be summed up. It doesn't have any theoretical edge, even though many people will tell you that it does, but if you want the reduced risk feature and the increased leverage offered by the lower collateral requirements, then it is an attractive, but not necessarily statistically superior, alternative to naked option writing. At the end of this section on linear spreads, we discuss when a spread *is* statistically attractive.

Calendar Spreads

A calendar spread is also called a *time spread*, because one is theoretically attempting to spread *time* and not *price* (although price is still a factor in how the spread behaves). A calendar spread in stock options consists of buying an option that expires in a certain future month and selling an option, with the same striking price, that expires in a closer month. For example, if the current month is April, then buying an IBM July 80 call and selling an IBM May 80 call would be a calendar spread. As time passes and May expiration approaches, time decay will begin to weigh more heavily against the May 80 call that is short than it does on the July call that is held long. As that happens, *the spread will make money if the underlying is near the striking price.*

Sometimes calendar spreads are also called *horizontal* spreads, to indicate that spread is across various expiration months, to differential from vertical spreads, where the spread is across various strikes.

The true spread trader will remove the position at or *before* May expiration, as he is interested in the characteristics of the spread itself—it will widen if the underlying remains near the striking price, and it will shrink if the underlying moves too far away from the striking price. This profitability, at near-term expiration, is shown in Figure 2.15. The spread has both limited profit potential and limited risk, with the risk being limited to the amount initially paid for the spread (a feature similar to the vertical spreads described earlier).

A more aggressive tack would be to continue to hold the long calls after the short calls have expired. This is not a recommended method of approaching the calendar spread strategy.

One of the biggest differences between stock (or index) options and futures options is that the expiration months are not necessarily directly related in futures options. Therefore, you must be careful when constructing calendar spreads with futures options. For example, there may be options on March Swiss Franc futures and on June Swiss Franc Futures. If you buy a June option and sell a March option, you do not necessarily have a calendar spread in the same sense that you do in the IBM example. The reason that this is true is that there are two distinct futures underlying the two Swiss Franc options—the June contract and the March contract. Whereas in the IBM example, only IBM stock underlies both of the options in the calendar spread.

While it is true that the March Swiss Franc futures and the June Swiss Franc futures are related, they do not necessarily move in con-

Figure 2.15
CALENDAR SPREAD

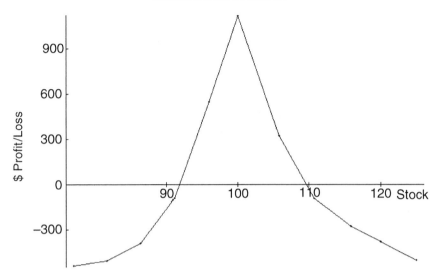

cert. In fact, in some futures—particularly those with actual commodities underlying them, such as grains and oil—the spread between the two futures contracts can vary substantially. This variation in the spread will cause the related options to behave in a manner that is not what one is used to seeing in calendar spreads on stocks or indices. It can even cause the option values to invert to the point where the near-term option sells for a higher price than the longer-term option. An example may be useful.

Example: Assume it is currently February, and that you notice that March Swiss Franc (SF) options are expensive with respect to June Swiss Franc options. Therefore, you want to establish a calendar spread. The following prices might exist:

March SF futures: 77.00	June SF futures: 78.00
March 78 call: 1.00	June 78 call: 3.00
	June 79 call: 2.00

Your initial reaction might be to try to establish a calendar spread by buying the June 78 call and selling the March 78 call. However, even though the strikes are the same for each call—78.00—the March call is one point out-of-the-money, while the June call is at-the-money. This increases the debit that you must initially pay for the spread and actually makes it a bullish position. A more neutral calendar spread would be to use calls that are equally out-of-the-money to begin with: buy the June 79 call and sell the March 78 call. Both options are one point out-of-the-money.

Even in that case, though, the spreader is subject to the vagaries of the relative movements of the March and June SF futures. For example, if interest rates in the United States or in Switzerland were to change, then the price differential between the two futures contracts themselves would surely change as well.

Currency futures have serial options. Therefore there would also be SF options that expire in both April and May. Moreover, the actual futures contract that underlies those serial options would be the June futures contract. Thus, you could construct a true calendar spread if you were to buy June SF calls and sell April or May SF calls. In that case, the only variable involved in the option spread would be time, for the same contract—the June SF futures contract—underlies both options.

Diagonal Spreads

Diagonal spreads are a combination of vertical and calendar spreads. The long and the short option in a diagonal spread have *both* different strikes and different expiration months. Usually, the diagonal spread is used in lieu of the vertical spread if you feel that it may take some time before the underlying makes its ultimate move.

Suppose that you're interested in establishing a bull spread. However, you also notice that the near-term options are quite expensive in comparison to the longer-term options. This type of situation often occurs in a fast-moving stock, or in rumor situations. So, instead of merely buying a bull spread, the trader might decide to diagonalize the spread in order to still have some bullish potential, but also to have the benefit of the time decay of the short-term option.

NCR Corp., a computer company, was the recipient of a takeover bid from AT&T in December 1990. Several factors were at work after the bid was made. First, the stock didn't advance to its full potential because of antitrust concerns. In addition, there were indications that the bid might be raised, so the near-term options were more expensive—on a relative basis. This presented an excellent opportunity for a diagonal spread. The following prices existed at the time:

NCR: 90

| NCR Jan 90 call: 3½ | NCR March 90 call: 5 |
| NCR Jan 95 call: 2 | NCR March 95 call: 3 |

Many risk arb traders who understood options were fairly certain that the deal would go through, but they thought there might be some delay. So they chose the diagonal spread: buying March 90 calls and selling Jan 95 calls. Indeed, there was a delay and NCR was still trading at 88 when the Jan 95 calls expired worthless. The arbs then were able to sell Feb 95 calls to further reduce the cost of the March 90 calls that they held. Those, too, expired worthless, and many arbs then just held onto their long calls. Eventually, the government acquiesced, and the stock moved up to 100 in early March, bringing good profits to both bull spreads and outright long positions.

Things got even better, as there were more delays and the arbs repeated the whole process with long June 100 calls and short April 105 calls (and then May 105 calls when those expired). In this entire situation, the diagonal spread was best.

This example also demonstrates the second step in a diagonal spread if things work out right: if the underlying remains fairly stable until the short-term call expires worthless, then you can sell an out-of-the-money call expiring in the next month to further reduce the cost of the option that you continue to hold. If there is initially only one month between the expirations of the calls in the spread (as in the NCR example), then there is only one additional opportunity to sell an out-of-the-money call against the one you already own. However, if there were several months between the two options' expirations when the spread is first established, then there can be numerous opportunities to continue to sell premium against the call that continues to be held long. Of course, once the stock makes a large move in either direction, the spread will more or less reach its maximum potential or maximum loss, and there will be no further opportunities to sell short-term premium.

In summary, diagonal spreads can be an attractive alternative to vertical spreads, especially if the near-term options are expensive with respect to the longer-term options. This applies to any underlying—stock, index, or futures contract.

When Spreads Are Attractive

At the beginning of the section on spreads, we stated that one of the main reasons traders enter into spreads is to reduce the risk of a single-sided position. This is especially true for naked option sellers; the large risk that naked option writing entails can be tempered by using a credit spread instead.

There is another consideration in any spread, and that is the relative pricing of the two options involved in the spread. If the option being purchased is "underpriced" with respect to the one being sold, then the spread has a statistical "edge" to it. When viewed from this perspective, spread trading becomes a strategy unto itself, and is one that has a mathematical advantage.

Grain futures call options—particularly corn and soybeans—have a natural tendency to be more expensive, on a relative basis, the farther they are out-of-the-money. Thus, if you buy an at-the-money soybean call and sell an out-of-the-money soybean call, which is a simple bull spread, you have a nice statistical advantage. You're buying something that is "cheaper" than the thing you're selling. Of course, you could still lose money if soybeans declined in price, since the initial spread's debit would be lost. Thus, an "edge" doesn't guarantee a profit, but it does mean that you have a better than even chance of making money if you pursue the same situation many times.

This soybean situation described how a debit spread might have an advantage. This advantage can sometimes exist with credit spreads as well, and would increase their attractiveness in those cases. For example, ever since the crash, out-of-the-money OEX calls have been less expensive than at-the-money OEX calls, so a credit call spread (which is a bear spread) has had a built-in edge, statistically. However, since the market has been going up for so long, the bear spread has not been particularly profitable.

In fact, many statistically oriented traders recognize the problem with applying statistics to spreads that have a price bias, such as vertical spreads do. For, no matter how favorably priced the options are in a vertical spread, you still need the underlying to move in a favorable direction in order to make money. Other spread strategies were born from this, many of which involve ratio writes or ratio spreads. We discuss those as the last section in this chapter. Their application as neutral spreads is reserved for a later chapter.

RATIO STRATEGIES

Ratio Writing

The most basic form of "ratio" strategy is the *call ratio write*. In this strategy, you buy or own a certain quantity of the underlying, and then sell a number of calls representing a *greater* number of shares than you own. Thus, you have naked call options in this strategy. As such, it is considered a relatively sophisticated strategy, as it has theoretically unlimited upside risk.

The strategy has a profit graph as shown in Figure 2.16. It has both an upside and downside breakeven point, and can make money anywhere in between, with the point of greatest profit at expiration being at the striking price of the written options. You may recognize this as the same shape as a naked straddle write, and since the two strategies have the same shape to their profit graph, they are equivalent.

Ratio call writing was the predecessor strategy to naked straddle selling—at least as far as listed option markets go—because there were listed calls for several years before there were listed puts. The strategy is considered to be a "neutral" strategy because you make money if the stock stays in a trading range.

You can also construct a ratio write by *shorting* the underlying and selling two puts. This is a rarely practiced form of the ratio write,

Figure 2.16
RATIO CALL WRITE

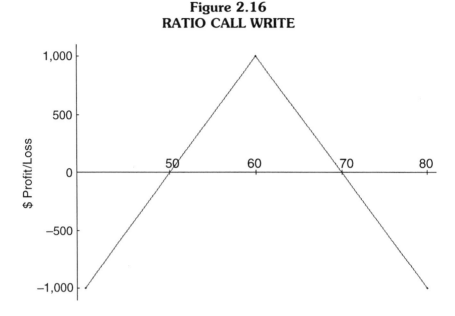

but if you think about the shape of the profit graph, you will realize it is the same as the one shown earlier. For stock options, the put ratio write is inferior to the call ratio write unless you are a professional and are able to earn interest on the credit balance generated by your short sale. For futures options, the call ratio write and the put ratio write should produce identical profit potential, although calls are often more liquid than puts, so this fact may also favor the call ratio write in any market.

Ratio Spreads

When the number of options that you buy in a spread differs from the number of options that you sell, you have a ratio spread of one form or another. As with other option strategies, the various types of ratio spreads have acquired their own names in order for traders and strategists to be able to quickly identify the profitability of the strategy merely by hearing its name.

Call Ratio Spreads. In a call ratio spread, one typically buys calls at a lower strike and then sells a greater number of calls at a higher strike. The credit brought in from the sale of the extra calls generally covers all, or nearly all, of the cost of the calls being purchased.

This strategy has little if any downside risk—equal only to the initial debit of the spread plus commissions. If the spread was initially established for a credit, then there is no downside risk. As with the ratio write, the point of maximum profitability at expiration is at the striking price of the written options, and a profit can be had all the way up to the upside breakeven point. Beyond that point, there are theoretically unlimited losses if the underlying were to rise too far, too fast, because there are naked calls involved in this strategy. These points are all shown in Figure 2.17.

This strategy is one that is favored by many traders over the ratio write because there is only risk on one side of the spread (the upside). Thus, it is easier to monitor. Moreover, if the underlying is initially at or below the *lower* strike in the spread, you often have a profit by

Figure 2.17
CALL RATIO SPREAD

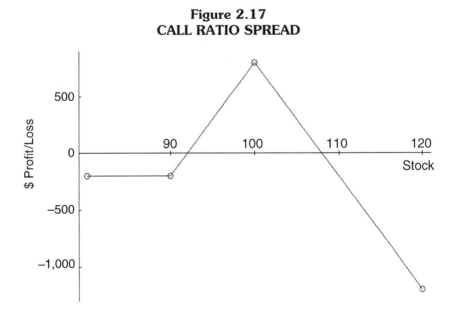

the time it rises to the higher strike. In that case, many traders prefer to take their profit at that time rather than waiting until expiration.

Ratio spreads are often attractive in futures options due to the fact that out-of-the-money calls are more expensive than at-the-money calls. This gives a built-in edge to the strategist who is using a call ratio spread. In the spring of 1993, gold futures were languishing in the $330-an-ounce neighborhood. However, professionals were amassing call ratio spreads by buying gold June 340 calls and selling enough June 360 calls to cover their costs. They were essentially buying one June 340 call for every two June 360s they sold. Thus, they had positions with no risk unless gold rose to nearly 380 before June expiration. In the spring and summer of that year, gold had an impressive rally that eventually carried to $400 an ounce. The rally was methodical, however, and not too explosive—the perfect scenario for the ratio spread. For, as gold rose to 360, the long calls were worth over $20 apiece since they were 20 points in the money, while the short calls were only worth $5 or $6. Thus, the traders were able to remove their entire position for a nice profit—selling their longs for 20 and buying back the two short for 6 each, leaving them with an $8 credit for each spread. Even though gold eventually traded higher, the traders had taken their profits and moved on to other situations.

This tale illustrates the real beauty of the call ratio spread: you can lay back with little or no downside risk (although capital is tied up, but that capital can be in the form of T-bills, so it at least earns interest). Then, if the underlying makes a move, you have a nice opportunity to exit with a profit. The danger is that the upward move by the underlying will be an explosive one and that you will not have a chance to remove your spread when it trades through the higher strike. This is especially true if there are gap or limit moves that occur when the underlying nears the point where you intended to take profits. Even in that less-than-desirable case, however, the ratio spreader is not in terrible straits. As long as you protect against unlimited upside losses, which would occur if the underlying rose through the upside *breakeven* point of the spread, this strategy should produce profits over the course of time. In one sense, this is an even more favorable strategy with futures options than it is with stock or index options, because of SPAN margin computations that are available for futures traders.

Put Ratio Spreads.   A similar strategy can be constructed with put options, only with puts you buy a put with a *higher* strike and sell a greater number of puts with a *lower* strike. Again, the sales offset most or all of the cost of the purchases.

As shown in Figure 2.18, the put ratio spread has little or no risk to the *upside*. It makes its maximum profit at expiration if the underlying is near the strike of the written options, and it has theoretically large downside risk if the underlying should plunge too far prior to expiration.

Similar theories apply to ratio put spreads as to ratio call spreads. It is generally best to establish the spread for no debit or a credit, and normally to initiate the position when the underlying is trading at a price above the higher strike in the spread. Then, if the underlying declines, there may be a chance to remove it as it passes through the lower strike—the point of eventual maximum profitability.

The main difference between ratio call spreads and ratio put spreads, especially for stock and index options, is that stocks tend to fall faster than they rise, so you may find yourself with something of

Figure 2.18
PUT RATIO SPREAD

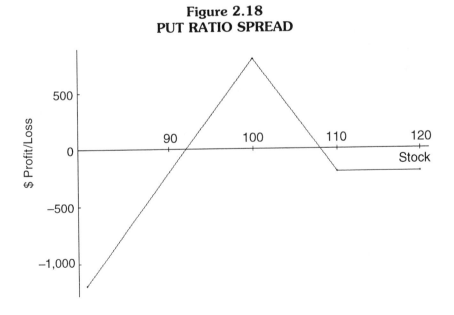

a "tiger by the tail" if a sudden downward move develops. Overall, though, this is also a reasonable approach to trading spreads.

Backspreads.   Strategies in which you own more options than you sell, and that therefore have theoretically large or unlimited *profit* potential are known as *backspreads*. In essence, they are just the opposite of ratio call spreads or ratio put spreads. In a larger sense, however, any strategy with unlimited profit potential and limited risk is called a backspread by some traders. In this broader definition, even a long straddle would be considered a backspread. For the purposes of this discussion, we are just going to concentrate on the backspread strategy that is the opposite of the ratio spreads described earlier.

Let's start with a call backspread. In this situation, we sell a call with a lower striking price and buy more calls at a higher striking price. Thus, we have extra long calls in this position and that provides us with unlimited profit potential (see Figure 2.19). Moreover, if the entire position was established for a credit, we have profit poten-

Figure 2.19
CALL BACKSPREAD

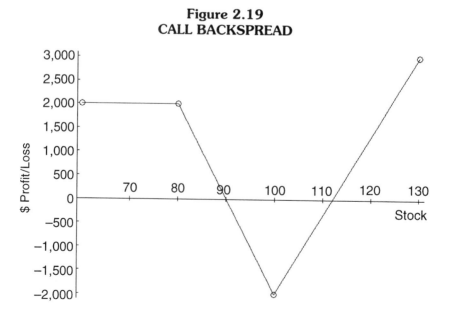

tial on the downside as well. If the underlying were to collapse and all the calls expired worthless, then we would keep the initial credit as our profit. The risk occurs near the higher striking price in the spread. The worst result occurs if the underlying is exactly at the higher strike at expiration. Thus, the entire profit picture looks something like a long straddle, with the downside profit flattening off at prices lower than the lower strike.

Normally, a call backspread is established when the underlying is somewhere in the near vicinity of the upper strike. When established in this manner, the strategist is looking for the underlying to make a move in either direction in order to give him some profitability. Another factor that experienced backspreaders look for when they establish these types of spreads is cheapness in the options. If the options are somewhat "underpriced," then there is an additional possibility that the preponderance of long calls in the spread will benefit from an increase in overall premium levels if, in the future, the options become more expensive. Moreover, if by some good fortune, the options being sold were relatively expensive in comparison to those being bought, then the spread has another built-in edge to it.

All of these factors came into play in what turned out to be one of the best backspreading opportunities of all time: the big upward move in the market from December of 1994 through all of 1995. That rally began with the OEX Index at a level of about 420 in December of 1994. By February, it had already reached 450 and many market seers were predicting a top after such an extensive run. Conversely, many bulls were predicting even higher prices because of the improving economy and the lack of inflation. Both arguments seemed to make some sense, so there appeared to be the possibility for a large move in either direction. This satisfied the first criterion in deciding when to use backspreads—that the underlying has the ability to move by a good deal in either direction.

Second, OEX options had become rather inexpensive, which is typical of index options' action in a bullish trend. So, with the options being cheap, backspreads were a good strategy because, if the options eventually became more expensive at a later date, the preponderance of long options in the backspread would benefit. Third, out-of-the-money OEX calls were selling at much cheaper relative prices than their in-the-money call counterparts. So all three of the main criteria for establishing a backspread were in place in the late winter of 1994–1995.

Backspreads established at that time became wildly profitable as OEX roared its way to levels above 600. Even traders who kept their backspreads neutral, by rolling the long calls to successively higher strikes as OEX rose in price, managed to make very large returns. All of this while continuing to remain in a position to benefit from a market drop if one had occurred. We examine this strategy thoroughly in Chapter 6.

This latter point—that the backspread trader was always in position to benefit from an unforeseen market drop (or even a crash)—is what, in my opinion, makes the backspread strategy superior to the long straddle strategy. For, in the backspread, you merely have to keep rolling your long calls up to higher strikes if the market rises. Your short calls remain where they were, and provide downside profit potential if the downward move ever comes. However, with a long straddle, if you merely roll your long calls up to higher strikes after a rally, you've done nothing for your downside profit because the puts that you own will then be quite far out-of-the-money. To gain downside potential, you would have to roll the puts to higher strikes as well. In essence, you have to move the *entire* straddle to a higher strike. The backspread trader has a much easier time adjusting and keeping neutral during a long rally.

Put Backspreads.   Put backspreads are just the opposite of put ratio spreads: you *sell* a put with a higher strike price and simultaneously buy a larger number of puts with a lower strike price. The position is normally established for a credit, with the underlying trading near the lower striking price.

The resultant position has profitability, as shown in Figure 2.20. There is limited upside profit potential, equal to the amount of the initial credit taken in when the spread is established. Downside profit potential is quite large, due to the excess long puts in the spread. The maximum risk occurs at the striking price of the long puts at expiration.

The ideal situation for put backspreads is to find cases where the puts with higher strikes (the ones you are going to sell) are relatively more expensive than puts with lower strikes (the ones you are going to buy). This would be the case in grain futures options and metals (gold and silver) futures options at almost any time. Thus, one of the

Figure 2.20
PUT BACKSPREAD

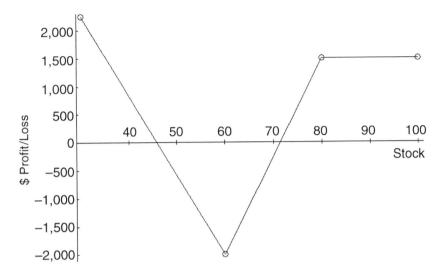

best ways to play for a downward move in those markets—if you are interested in a limited-risk strategy that can also make money if you are wrong and prices rise—is with a put backspread.

More Complex Constructions

Obviously, other strategies can be constructed by combining the strategies discussed in this chapter or modifying them. For example, the butterfly spread is a strategy that is the combination of both a bull spread and a bear spread, where both are credit spreads. Such a strategy is also the same as selling a straddle and protecting your risk by buying both an out-of-the-money call and an out-of-the-money put. The butterfly spread has profitability as shown in Figure 2.21. There are actually several ways to establish a butterfly spread; in addition to the two ways just mentioned, it can be established with all calls or with all puts (using three different strikes in either case). Many traders who protect their naked straddles with out-of-the-money options are using the butterfly spread, although they may not neces-

Figure 2.21
BUTTERFLY SPREAD

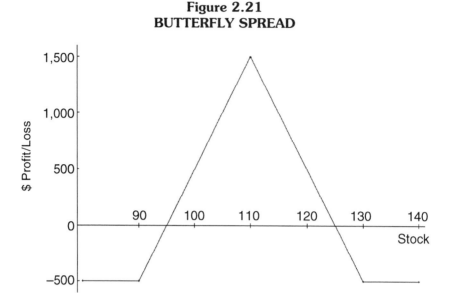

sarily call it by that name. Incidentally, if you sell a naked combination, or strangle (different strikes for the put and the call), and then protect *that* position with out-of-the-money options, your position involves *four* striking prices and is sometimes known as a *condor*.

It has become fashionable for underwriters and exchanges to create securities that are actually one of these option strategies, and then sell the security as a single unit to investors. For example, some of the larger investment banking houses created a security called PERCS (Preferred Equity Redemption Cumulative Stock). A PERCS is a preferred stock. These are issues on some of the largest corporations—General Motors, for example. A PERCS has a fixed life, such as three years. During that time, it yields far more than the underlying stock does. At the end of three years (or whatever time period is specified when the PERCS is initially issued), the PERCS becomes shares of the underlying stock itself, with one exception: if the underlying has risen too far, then the value of PERCS is limited to a fixed price. If the underlying is above that price, then the PERCS holder receives cash for his preferred shares at the end of the three years, rather than receiving shares of the underlying stock.

What you really have here is the equivalent of a covered write of a three-year option, but it's not sold that way, nor is the word "option" ever mentioned when PERCS are sold. Consider the premium received from writing a covered call that is a three-year, out-of-the-money option; it would be rather large. Suppose that the premium is distributed to the stockholder in quarterly amounts over the three-year period. Then, it would appear to the stockholder as if he were receiving an extra dividend. Furthermore, if the option expires worthless at the end of three years, then what is left is common stock. On the other hand, if the underlying climbs in price and rises above the striking price of the written call, then at the end of three years, the investor would be called out of his stock and he would receive cash. These qualities exactly describe the PERCS.

Other securities have been listed that resemble covered writing or other option strategies, and more of these securities are being listed all the time. Most are similar to PERCS, but have names like ELKS (Equity-Linked Securities) or SUNS (Stock Upside Note Securities).

Moreover, there are securities called Stock Index Securities that are guaranteed to return a specific amount, while allowing for the possibility of appreciation if the stock market rises during that time. These securities are the equivalent of taking some money and buying a zero-coupon bond with part of it, so that you are guaranteed return of principal, and then buying an option with the balance so you have substantial upside potential.

One of the most interesting of these securities has the symbol SIS (trading on the AMEX). It is based on the value of the Midcap 400 Index. The SIS value at expiration is calculated by the following formula:

$$\text{Cash value} = 10 + 11.5 * (\text{MID} / 166.10 - 1)$$

At a minimum, the security will be worth $10 at its expiration on 6/20/2000. However, if MID is above the "strike" of 166.10, the holder is entitled to the $10 plus 15 percent of the appreciation of MID above the strike.

The SIS securities were issued by Paine Webber, so in effect, they are debt of Paine Webber Corporation. So if Paine Webber were to be insolvent by that time, the "guaranteed" portion of the security could be in jeopardy.

Due partially to that fact, plus the fact that the IRS may tax this security as a zero-coupon bond, making holders pay taxes annually on their "discount" at which they bought it, if any, and due partially to the fact that not many people know about it, the SIS stock has traded at extreme discounts since inception.

For example, with MID trading at 185 in early 1995, SIS was selling for $9 per share. The cash settlement value of SIS with MID at 185 is 11.31 (= 10 + 11.5 * (185/166.1 − 1)). Thus, you could have bought the stock at 9 when it, in essence, had a net asset value of 11.31. Even with a tax consideration, this is a very attractive discount. Any closed-end mutual fund trading with that type of discount and having the quality of securities of the Midcap 400 would certainly be considered an attractive buy by many investors.

As the market rallied higher throughout 1995, MID rose to 220, but SIS only climbed to 11¼. The cash settlement value with MID at 220 is 13.73, so the deep discount still existed at that time. Only time will tell how the story turns out, but the point is that some of these "exotic" equity-related securities can present interesting investment opportunities.

There are other securities like the one just described. You can obtain their current terms by calling the exchange where they are listed—either the American Stock Exchange or the New York Stock Exchange.

Using an Option Model

Even the most experienced option traders check an option's theoretical value with a model before making a transaction. Thus, it should be even more mandatory for an inexperienced option trader to do the same. Without getting into the technical aspects of option modeling—the subject is discussed in Appendix C—traders should know that there are relatively easy and inexpensive ways to gain access to an option model.

There are six things required in order for an option's theoretical value to calculated: the stock price, the strike price, the expiration date, the short-term interest rate, the volatility of the underlying security, and the amount of the dividend (if there is one). These items can either be typed in by the user or they can be supplied from a larger computer somewhere.

A scientific calculator, such as the better ones manufactured by Texas Instruments or Hewlett-Packard are quite capable of calculating option theoretical values. You can buy the program that performs the calculations. Obviously, you have to enter the data items by hand if you choose this method.

Computers, of course, are a better alternative for evaluating options. Simple option calculation programs that calculate the implied volatility or theoretical value can be bought for $100 or less. The user is generally required to input the underlying price, the strike price, the expiration date, and so on. If implied volatility is desired, then the user has to type in the price of the option in question and the program will return implied volatility as an output.

More expensive calculation programs are available, and these are generally tied to a data source so that you don't have to enter anything other than the trading symbol of the underlying security. Not only are these types of programs more expensive to buy, but you must also pay for the data that is automatically being fed into them.

All of these approaches are valid, depending on your needs, and they are discussed in more detail in Chapter 7. Just make sure that you do indeed have access to a model and that you use it before making trades. Then you will know whether the option you are trading is expensive or cheap. We are *not* saying that you must only buy "cheap" options; we are saying, however, that you should know if the option you are buying is cheap or not. If it's expensive, that's okay, but you are at least aware that you are buying an option that might lose value if implied volatility decreases, even though the underlying security rises slightly in price.

SUMMARY

The broad overviews of the various strategies expressed in this chapter should be enough of a foundation for understanding the material in later chapters. As explained in the Preface to this book, it was not our intention to detail the explicit calculations of breakeven points and explain follow-up actions for these basic strategies.

3 The Versatile Option

In this chapter and in the two succeeding chapters, we are going to address the use of options in ways that don't require much in the way of theoretical evaluation of options (we are always in favor of an option trader using a model to evaluate an option before buying or selling it). These techniques, strategies, and trading methods are very useful and can be extremely profitable. It's just that they aren't so mathematical; they are of a more practical variety and, as such, may appeal to a broader audience of traders and short-term investors.

OPTIONS AS A DIRECT SUBSTITUTE FOR THE UNDERLYING

Options can be useful in a number of ways. Ways that go beyond the basic profit and loss of predefined strategies. Some of them depend on an understanding of basic equivalent positions. For example, in this segment we show you how to avoid ever having to worry about limit moves in futures contracts ever again. We also discuss ways in which using options can actually make your use of capital more efficient than merely trading stock.

Recall that two positions are *equivalent* if they have the same profitability, that is, their profit graphs have the same shape. One of the most important equivalences is the following: *a long position in the underlying security is equivalent to being both long a call and short a put with the same terms.* Conceptually, you can see that the long call gives you unlimited upside profit potential (just as being long the stock does), while being short the put gives you large downside risk (again, just as owning the stock would). An example may help to clarify this statement.

Example: With Microsoft trading at 92, in July 1995, the Aug 90 call was trading at 6 while the Aug 90 put was trading at 4. An option position that is equivalent to owning the common stock can be constructed by buying the Aug 90 call for 6 and selling the Aug 90 put at 4. We can verify this with a profit table.

Stock Price at August Expiration	Profit on Long Stock ($)	Profit on Long Call ($)	Profit on Short Put ($)	Total Option Profit ($)
70	−2,200	−600	−1,600	−2,200
80	−1,200	−600	−600	−1,200
90	−200	−600	+400	−200
100	+800	+400	+400	+800
110	+1,800	+1,400	+400	+1,800

Note that the totals in the second column (Profit on Long Stock) and the last column (Total Option Profit) are the same. This means that the option position and a long stock position are equivalent.

This is an important concept that should be routinely understood and used by all traders. First of all, it allows you to use options instead of the underlying. Using the Microsoft stock as an example again, note that if you bought 100 shares for cash, you would have to invest $9,200 plus a stock commission. However, the *collateral* requirement for the option position is this: first, the call option has to be paid for ($600) and then the naked put must be collateralized. The requirement for the naked put is 20 percent of the stock's price plus the put premium, less the out-of-the-money amount. So the naked put requires $1,840 (20 percent of $9,200), plus $400 (the price of the put), less $200 (the two points that the put is out-of-the-money), for a total collateral requirement of $2,040 for the naked put. The net collateral requirement for the option position is thus:

Position	Requirement
Long Call	$ 600
Naked Put	+2,040
Put Premium	−400
Total	$2,240

Therefore one can have nearly the same profitability as a stock trader for a much smaller collateral requirement. In the preceding Microsoft example, the profit was *exactly* the same whether you bought the stock or used the option strategy. However, if you look at most option prices, the option strategy will not generally have exactly the same profit and loss potential as the underlying stock, although it will be quite close. There are two reasons for this usually small differential: dividends and interest rates.

The stockholder receives the dividend (if there is one), while the option trader does not. The option trader can partially offset the loss of dividend if he uses T-bills as collateral for the position, since he can earn interest on the $2,000 or so of collateral while the position is in place.

The stock trader is tying up a lot more money. If the option trader invests the difference between the full cost of buying the stock and the collateral he needs for the option position—about $7,000 in the previous example—in certificates of deposit or in T-bills, he will earn a substantial amount of interest. Without going into detailed calculations to prove it, we state that the difference in the profitability of owning the stock or being in the option position can be offset by investing the $7,000 in short-term, interest-bearing instruments until the options' expiration date.

There is one other material comparison: the option trader is dealing with *two* bid–asked spreads and must pay two commissions to enter the position. The stock trader only has to be concerned with one of each of those items. In these days of discount commissions, the bid–asked spread is the more important consideration of the two and can be a serious one. Especially if you're dealing with relatively illiquid, or thinly traded, options, you may find that the option position becomes much more expensive than is necessary. In a situation such as this, it's often a good idea to use an option model to check what the theoretical difference between the call and the put price should be. Then you have some idea as to how to enter the order. A continuation of the same example illustrates this concept.

Example: Again assume that Microsoft is at 92, but this time you're interested in using the *Oct* 90 puts and calls in order to establish an option position that is equivalent to a long put position. The actual prices of the October options (in July) were:

Option	Bid–Offer
Oct 90 call	9¼–9¾
Oct 90 put	6–6½

Since there is a half point spread on each option, you might be in danger of "overpaying" for the option position if you merely buy the call and sell the put with a market order. At the market, buying the call and selling the put would cost a debit of 3¾ points (9¾ minus 6).

Here's where using an option model comes in handy. If we input 92 as the stock price, 90 as the striking price, October as the expiration date, and the current T-bill interest rate (it makes no difference what volatility we use), the model will tell us that, with the stock at 92, the call should sell for 3.27 more than the put. So, one might enter an option order as a spread: "Buy the Oct 90 call and sell the Oct 90 put for a debit of 3¼ points." Using the model in this way would prevent overpaying for the position (recall that it costs 3¾ at the "market" prices).

If the price of the underlying changes, the prices of the put and call would change in a relative manner also. For example, with Microsoft at 91, the call should then sell for 2.27 more than the put. The model is useful in showing you this information also. So, if you don't receive an execution right away, and then Microsoft changes in price, you'll know how to adjust your option order as well.

Equivalent Short Stock

Similarly, *a short position in the underlying security is equivalent to being both long a put and short a call with the same terms.* There are more benefits to the option equivalent position, when comparing it to a short sale of stock, than there were for long stock.

First, you're able to benefit from the reduced collateral requirements—you can "equivalently" short stock on just over 20 percent margin as opposed to the 50 percent required for shorting the actual stock itself. This benefit is quite similar to the same one for long stock.

When shorting stock, an uptick is required in order to establish the position, both in listed and NASDAQ stocks. However, an uptick is not required to enter into the option position, so it is easier to establish an "equivalent" short sale in a down market. This is especially useful in situations where a stock is breaking down quickly. This may involve a stock that has broken down through a major support level, or may involve a lot of stocks when the market goes into one of its famous nosedives. With the option equivalent strategy, you can always get "short" (or the equivalent thereof) right away. You may have to use market orders, which give up something in terms of price, but at least you can get the basic position established.

The final benefit for the option position as compared to a short sale is that you don't have to actually borrow the stock to enter into the option position; again, a time-saving and convenient benefit of the option position. It can sometimes take a long time to find stock to borrow, or your broker may not be able to find the stock at all. With the option equivalent strategy, you don't really need to worry about whether the stock is borrowable or not, with the exception pointed out in the next paragraph.

There is one possible complication with the equivalent short position: it *should* be noted, that if the stock is truly difficult to borrow, then you must be careful how you apply the option strategy. You may not be able to sell in-the-money calls as part of your strategy. This problem can be avoided by using a higher striking price—*if* one exists—so that the put is in-the-money and not the call. In the case of "unborrowable" stock, in-the-money calls may be so cheap that you would have to sell them at or below parity; if that happened, you might receive an early (perhaps immediate) assignment notice— thereby making you short the stock, which you could not fulfill since you can't find the stock to borrow. Your broker would then buy you in at the market and probably wouldn't be too happy with you, either. Your account might even be restricted if he feels you intentionally sold in-the-money calls on a stock that was clearly not borrowable.

Whenever a partial tender offer for stock is pending, there is a very high probability that all existing in-the-money calls will be assigned early. This situation has occurred many times over the years since listed options began trading, but there is always a story of someone who thinks he can make free money. He can't, and it sometimes becomes an expensive lesson.

Suppose that a partial tender for half of a company is in progress: $100 per share will be paid for 50 percent of the stock. The stock is trading at 80, though, because the remainder of the company is expected to trade at a price of 60 in the open market when the partial tender is completed. Thus, the stock will drop in price by $20 after the tender date is past.

A quick $20 could be made by any trader who shorted the stock. However, this stock cannot be borrowed because all stockholders want their shares in hand so they can tender them and receive $100 a share for half of them. So a trader cannot short it.

In-the-money calls on this stock will be selling at parity—for example, a Feb 60 call would be selling at 20 (the stock is at 80, so this is parity). Invariably, some fairly novice option trader, who knows that the stock will drop but can't find any stock to borrow, sells the Feb 60 call for 20 points, as an opening transaction. He can do this because one does not have to borrow an option in order to sell it short. He figures he will cover the option after the stock drops to 60 and make a fortune.

What *really* happens is that the call is exercised by the person who bought it (that person buys stock in this manner and tenders the stock to receive the partial tender price). This exercise results in the novice option trader being assigned on his short call. He normally doesn't find out about this until the day after the tender is over; that is, the stock is all set to begin trading at 60 when he receives the assignment notice. So, he quickly becomes short *stock*, and, since the stock can't be borrowed, his brokerage firm will not be happy. First, they will buy him in. But it won't be just a normal buy in the open market at 60. In fact, they will buy him in for *cash* because the stock is owed to someone who has already tendered and needs the stock immediately. The cash market price is going to be something higher than 80, so the novice trader ends up with a loss on the trade and perhaps restrictions on his trading account.

The point is that you can expect to be assigned on any call that is sold below parity. The call is trading there for a reason—whether that be an impending tender offer, an impending dividend, or the approach of expiration. If you sell a call at or below parity, you should be prepared to be short the stock by assignment in a very short time, probably as soon as the next day. If you have reason to expect that the stock is not borrowable, then don't sell an in-the-money call trading near parity, for you will only create problems for yourself.

Defending Against a Limit Move in Futures Contracts

All futures contracts are limited in the amount by which their price can change in any one day. The exchange where the future is traded determines the size of that daily limit. Limit moves usually occur as a result of an unexpected increase in supply or demand, perhaps caused by weather (storms or droughts), cartels (OPEC), or an unexpected government crop report. The greatest fear that any futures trader has is that he will get caught on the wrong side of a prolonged limit move and not be able to get out of his position. If this happens, huge losses could occur.

However, whenever there are listed futures options trading, the trader can extract himself from a limit move at any time. This strategy—using options as the equivalent of the underlying—is *mandatory* knowledge for every futures trader, for it can allow him to remove himself from a position that is locked limit against him. This knowledge can keep a loss small, preventing it from ballooning out of control to the point where the account might even be wiped out.

In late January of 1993, lumber had an extended move, trading up the limit several days in a row. March lumber futures were trading at 279 when housing starts were reported to be a very positive number. This expected increase in demand for lumber caused the futures to rise the five-point limit and lock there, limit up at 284, for the remainder of the day. The next seven(!) days, lumber was also up the five-point limit with virtually no trading taking place. Buyers were bidding, but there were very, very few willing sellers as more bullish statistics regarding housing sales and building projections were released by the government. As with many commodity futures, the limit increases if it is repeatedly hit. So after the eighth day of limit moves, the limit was increased to 10 points. Still, the demand was so great that the futures locked limit up for two more days! It now had risen to 339, and virtually no trades had taken place for 10 days. Short sellers were on the verge of being wiped out, since a one-point move in lumber is worth $160. So, the 55-point move from 284 to 339 was costing shorts $8,800 per contract.

Worse yet, the bull move was far from over, and the limit was raised to 15 points. After trading off the limit for a few hours on the 11th day, the futures contract locked limit up once again. Even the increased trading limit still couldn't stem the tide. Over the next nine days, lumber closed limit up eight times. Moreover, on five of those nine days, it was locked limit up all day. By this time March lumber was trading at 441. Thus, the loss on one short contract—if it was not covered during the few times that there had been free trading—had now reached 157 points, or $25,120!

This was a classic case where options could have saved the shorts a great deal of money. Lumber traders who understood options could have covered on that first day, when the futures locked limit up at 284. They would have paid a price of about 288 to cover their position. Thus, they could have taken a four-point loss, even after the series of limit moves had begun, as compared to the 55-point, or 157-point, losses that nonoption traders had to sustain. Moreover, option traders, if they didn't cover that first day, could have covered any day thereafter that they wanted to, although it got more expensive to do so each day.

Veteran futures traders can relate many horror stories of being caught on the wrong side of extended limit moves. A couple of others that come to mind are orange juice, in the fall of 1991, when it rose from 127 to 168 on a series of six limit moves without any chance to cover. Since orange juice is worth $150 per point, that translated into a $7,650 loss per contract. Also, in the spring of 1995, cotton futures sustained a series of limit moves *in both directions!* The wildest action came when the July contract was first limit *down* for five days in a row. Then, after a couple of days of free trading, it was *up* the limit for eight days in a row. In fact, cotton continued to be crazy all summer, with several others series of limit moves taking place.

In this section, we have talked about only two equivalences: long call plus short put is equivalent to being long the underlying, and short call plus long put is equivalent to being short the underlying. It is these two concepts that can save the skin of any futures trader. *If you are trading futures and you don't understand this concept, then stop trading futures or learn the concept.* You have no other choice, in my opinion. Let's use the lumber futures and their options, from the narrative, to look at just how this works.

Example: On the first day that November lumber locked limit up at 285, the Nov 285 call settled at 8 and the Nov 285 put settled at 5. Now, normally, a futures put and call with the same terms would trade for the same price when the underlying futures settle right at their striking price. However, that is not necessarily the case when limit moves are involved, because the options are "predicting" where the futures should be trading, were they allowed to trade freely.

Suppose that we are viewing this situation from the viewpoint of a trader who is short the November lumber futures contract, which is now locked limit up. He could have bought the Nov 285 call for 8 and sold the Nov 285 put for 5, a three-point debit. By executing this simple trade, he would have eliminated any further risk for himself. His option trades—long call and short put—are the equivalent of being long November lumber futures, and his futures position is short November lumber futures. Therefore, the sum of the two is a flattened position. Moreover, the price at which he has covered the futures is equal to the striking price plus the debit of the option position, or 285 + 3 = 288 in this case.

In order to verify this, note that if futures continue to rise, he will eventually be able to exercise his long call at expiration (or if it becomes very deep in-the-money and loses its time value premium). The call exercise means he buys lumber futures at 285, no matter how high they actually are at the time of the exercise. Since he also paid the three-point debit for the option position, he has a net cost of 288 (285 + 3) for covering his futures. Thus, he was able to cover his short futures at 288, saving himself countless heartaches as the ensuing bull move developed—a move which trapped the shorts who didn't understand this concept.

Note that if the lumber futures had suddenly plunged after the trader established his option position (long call and short put), it would have made no difference to him in terms of his exit price. Although, of course this didn't really happen, suppose that lumber futures had fallen to 225 or so. Eventually, he would be assigned on his short put. That assignment means he would buy the futures at 285, the striking price. Again, he must add the three-point debit that he originally paid for the option position, so his net cost for covering the futures would again be 288. Thus, no matter which way futures go after the option trade is established, he has locked himself into a buy at 288. He has no further risk or reward potential once the option trade is established; he has equivalently covered his short at 288.

Oftentimes, it's best to take the first loss—it may be the smallest one. In the case of lumber, that first loss would have involved using options to equivalently cover the short at 288. In the real-life lumber example, things got much worse as time passed. By the time lumber had risen the daily limit for six days in a row and had reached 335, the options were priced quite a bit higher than the market. In fact, the following prices were quoted at that time:

> November lumber: 335 (limit bid)
> Nov 335 calls: 30
> Nov 335 puts: 12

If the short seller had waited this long to attempt to cover, he would have to pay a greater premium over the settlement price. In fact, if he bought the calls at 30 and sold the puts at 12, this would entail an 18-point debit. Thus, his eventual buy price would be the striking price plus the debit, $335 + 18 = 353$. So, you can see that as more and more limit days piled up, the options began to get more and more expensive. Still, covering at 353 was a bargain compared to waiting until 460, when the bull move finally ended.

This strategy would have been a welcome one for cotton traders in the spring of 1995 when, as mentioned earlier, the futures traded limit down for five days and then shortly after traded limit *up* for eight days. Think how frustrating it would have been to be short the cotton futures and have a nice unrealized gain, only to get caught in the limit up moves and give it all back. Cotton traders who understood options wouldn't have worried, for on the first limit up day, they could have executed the long-call–short-put option strategy (equivalently covering their short position) and locked in their profits at that time.

Traders who are *long* and who get trapped in a series of down limit moves can use the companion option strategy to extract themselves. They would buy the put and sell the call in order to establish an option position that is the equivalent of a short futures contract.

This would then offset their long futures contract that they actually own, and the loss would be locked in. There would be no further risk (or reward either).

In summary, futures traders must understand this strategy. It does not prevent losses from ever occurring, but it does allow one to take his losses when he wants. He will never be "caught" by a series of limit moves and have to stand helplessly by while his equity dissipates. As to *when* you should use the option strategy, I would use it when the futures trade through your stop price. For example, if you were short November lumber that day and had a stop in to cover at 289.25, your stop was never executed because the futures jumped from 285 to 290 and no trades took place—not even at 290. I would *then* step in and execute the option strategy because the stop price had been exceeded.

OPTIONS AS A PROXY FOR THE UNDERLYING

In the first part of this chapter, we discussed how to use options to completely replicate a position in the underlying security. Another useful option tactic is to use options as a *proxy* for the underlying. Generally, this is done when you want more leverage or less risk, or both, than the underlying security itself possesses.

Option Buying as a Short-Term Stock Substitute

In Chapter 1, we dealt with buying calls as a substitute for buying stock or futures. The idea was to use an in-the-money call option for that purpose, for it provides leverage but also is not so subject to the ravages of time decay. The in-the-money option has very little time value premium to begin with.

The same philosophy can be applied to buying short-term, in-the-money puts as a proxy for shorting stock. This has the additional advantages that we described when we discussed fully equivalent positions: the short sale proxy can be obtained without needing an uptick, and, in the case of common stock, there is no borrowing necessary. Moreover, since in-the-money puts generally have even less time value premium than in-the-money calls do, it is usually quite easy to find an in-the-money put that has very little time value premium. In both cases, the in-the-money option will mirror almost all of the short-term movement of the underlying. This is an especially attractive feature for a short-term trader.

Option Buying as a Long-Term Stock Substitute

Short-term traders aren't the only ones who can benefit from the limited-risk nature of owning a call as opposed to owning the underlying security. Investors with a longer-term viewpoint can avail themselves of this feature as well; they could substitute a long in-the-money call for their long stock. As LEAPS have become more popular, brokers have been advising investors of the benefits of selling the stock they own and buying long-term calls (LEAPS) as a substitute, or buying LEAPS instead of making an initial purchase in a particular common stock. This strategy also increases in popularity during long bullish runs in the stock market.

If an investor sells his stock and buys a call option, he has removed quite a bit of money from the market. He should then take that money and buy a bank certificate of deposit (CD) or T-bill whose maturity more or less matches the expiration date of the option he purchased. The option gives him upside profit potential, while most of his money is safe in CDs or T-bills. Even if things go terribly awry and the stock collapses and the option expires worthless, he will still have his money in the bank, plus the interest earned by the CD or T-bill.

The costs to the stock owner who decides to use this strategy are commissions, the time value premium of the call, and the loss of dividends. The benefits are the interest that can be earned from freeing up a substantial portion of his funds, plus the fact that there is less downside risk in owning the call than in owning the stock. There generally is a *net cost of switching*, that is, the interest earned won't completely offset the loss of the dividend, the time premium, and the commissions. The investor must decide if it is worth that cost in order to have his downside risk limited over the life of the LEAPS options.

The cost to switch may seem like a reasonably small price to pay to remove a lot of downside risk. However, one detriment that might exist is that the underlying common stock might declare an increased dividend or, even worse, a special cash dividend. The LEAPS call owner would not be entitled to that dividend increase—in whatever form—while, obviously, the common stock owner would be. If the company declared a stock split or stock dividend, it would have no effect on this strategy since the call owner *is* entitled to a stock split or stock dividend.

There may be other mitigating circumstances involving tax considerations. If the stock is currently a profitable investment, the sale would generate a capital gain, and taxes might be owed. If the stock is currently being held at a loss, the purchase of the call would constitute a wash sale and the loss could not be taken at the current time.

Using LEAPS Puts Instead of Calls

In the preceding strategy, the stock owner paid some cost in order to limit the risk of his stock ownership to a fixed price. He might be able to accomplish the same thing at a lower cost to himself. If he buys a LEAPS put against the stock that he owns, he has a position that is *equivalent* to owning a LEAPS call. He would still have upside profit potential (now in the form of long stock), he would have downside protection (provided by the long put), he would have spent less in commissions (only the commission for the put), and he might not disturb the tax holding period of his stock.

The comparison between substituting a call or buying a put is a relatively simple one. Merely compare the cost of switching with the cost of the put. If arbitrageurs are doing their job, the put will most likely be the better way to go. Moreover, capital gains don't have to be realized with this method. The purchase of a put may suspend his holding period for tax purposes (if he is not already a long-term holder), but the LEAPS call strategy had its own tax complications as well. Moreover, he would remain fully represented for all dividends since he continues to own the common stock.

Whether one uses the put or the call, if the underlying stock rises in value, the strategist will want to sell the LEAPS option he owns and buy another one with a higher strike, in order to further protect the profits that built up as the stock rises.

In my opinion, the purchase of a LEAPS put is a more efficient way to protect long stock. However, the former strategy—selling the stock and replacing it with a long call—is usually preferred by broker-age firms.

THE EFFECT OF STOCK INDEX FUTURES ON THE STOCK MARKET

The strategy of buying puts on individual equities in order to protect them from downside loss is the simplest usage of a derivative security to hedge a position. Another simple strategy is to sell index futures against stock holdings. The main problem with doing that is that it removes the upside potential from one's portfolio, a distasteful alternative to almost all stockholders. There are more complex strategies, of course, most of which have to do with hedging an entire portfolio of stocks with derivatives.

The idea of using derivatives to insure a portfolio of stocks first achieved recognition in the mid-1980s when the term *portfolio insurance* became widespread. At that time, the theory involved selling S&P 500 futures contracts against a portfolio of stocks, in a particular manner. Since there are a couple of other strategies that also involve selling S&P 500 futures against a portfolio of stocks—index arbitrage and program trading—the various strategies are often confused with each other, especially by the media. There are also theories that involve the purchase of index *put* options to protects portfolios. We explore these various strategies in this section.

First, it may be useful to spend some time clarifying the three strategies involving futures before we actually approach the topic of how portfolio insurance is structured today. These futures strategies often have an effect on the movements of the overall stock market, so it is important for nearly all stock traders to understand these effects.

Index arbitrage is the easiest one to understand, for in this strategy the arbitrageur takes a position in a stock index futures contract and takes exactly the opposite position in the stocks themselves. For example, an arbitraguer might sell the S&P 500 futures and more or less simultaneously buy the correct amount of each of those 500 stocks, in order to set up a perfect hedge. With computerized trading, 500 stocks can be bought almost simultaneously with the push of a button.

Arbitrage, by the way, is merely the simultaneous buying and selling of the same thing in two different forms. For arbitrage to be profitable, the arbitrageur must have at least a small positive differential in price between what he buys and sells. One common example involves the strategy that we have spent a great deal of this chapter discussing—using options to establish a position that is equivalent to the underlying security. Thus if you buy a call and sell a put, you have a position that is equivalent to long stock. If you then short the underlying stock, you have an arbitrage, because you bought the stock in one form (the option equivalent form) and sold the stock itself. Most of the time, arbitrage produces a profit that is only a fraction of a point; however, when done repeatedly, these profits add up. There are countless ways in which arbitrage can be done, but usually only member firms can trade arbitrage profitably, because commissions would wipe out the profits for a public trader or customer.

Arbitrage is an ancient and widely practiced trading method. It is both useful and necessary, especially in the derivatives markets, in order to provide liquidity and depth to markets. If arbitrage is not possible in a derivative contract, or if arbitrage is extremely difficult, the contract often fails within a short period of time.

Now let's return to index arbitrage, specifically. If an index arbitrage is established at favorable prices, the arbitrageur locks in a guaranteed profit on the trade. It may behoove us to spend a minute explaining *why* and *when* index arbitrage is profitable, for that knowledge is necessary for any day trader of index futures contracts, particularly, the S&P 500 Index futures. On any day, the trader can calculate the *fair value* of the S&P 500 futures contract. This fair value is a function of only four things: (1) the price of the S&P 500 cash index, (2) interest rates, (3) the time until the contract expires, and (4) dividends on the S&P 500 stocks themselves. The actual formula is

$$\text{Fair value of S\&P futures} = \text{SPX} \times (1 + r)^t - \text{dividends}$$

where SPX = S&P 500 Cash Index, r = the risk-free interest rate, and t = time remaining in years.

Example: Suppose the S&P 500 Cash Index is trading at 561.00. Also, there are 51 days remaining until the contract expires, short-term T-bill rates are 6 percent, and the total of all dividends to be paid by the S&P 500 stocks during the next 51 days total $3.23. Note that 51 days is 0.1397 year.

$$\text{Fair value} = 561.00 \times (1.06)^{0.1397} - 3.23$$
$$= 561.00 \times 1.0082 - 3.23 = 562.36$$

Sometimes the fair value is stated strictly in terms of the premium of the futures contract, which in this case is $562.36 - 561.00 = 1.36$ premium.

The premium of the futures versus the cash index fluctuates during the trading day as supply and demand forces the market around. If the futures acquire too much premium (we'll define "too much" shortly), they are said to be expensive, and arbitrageurs will sell the futures and buy stocks. This action alone will force the stock market higher for a short while, until the excess premium is removed from the futures. Since the arbitrageurs are *selling* futures at the same that they are buying stocks, it usually only takes a short time before the arbitrage opportunity disappears. That is, the arbitrageurs' own actions force the premium of the futures versus the cash index to shrink.

In a similar manner, the futures may trade down below fair value; that is, they are said to be trading at a "discount" [to fair value]. If futures get too cheap, then arbitrage can be done in the opposite manner: futures are bought and stocks are sold. If the arbitrageur has no position prior to establishing this position, then he must sell the stocks *short*. Since selling stocks short requires that they be sold on upticks, this form of arbitrage is more difficult to enact. However, many arbitrage firms will initially buy stocks and sell futures at fair value—meaning they have no profit in the position—in order to have "ammunition" to be able to sell stocks (long) and buy futures when the futures go to extreme discounts.

Index arbitrage is available almost every trading day. All the arbitrageur needs in order to make money is for the futures premium to deviate from fair value by an amount large enough to cover the arb's transaction costs (which are low).

Example: Suppose again that the fair value for the S&P 500 futures premium is 1.36, as in the previous example. Arbitrageurs have quote machines that can display the S&P 500 Index in at least three ways: the last sale value (which is what is widely disseminated), the bid value, and the offer value. For example, the offer value would be the price that the arb would pay for the S&P 500 Cash Index if he were able to buy all 500 stocks on their current offering price.

An arb sees that the S&P 500 Cash Index is trading at 561.00 and the Index is offered at 561.50. That is, it would actually cost 561.50 for the arb to buy the Index in its correct composition (the proper amount of all 500 stocks). Furthermore, he notes that the futures are running to the upside, and they are currently selling at 563.75. So, if he could sell futures at 563.75 and buy the Cash Index on the offering at 561.50, he would have established the arbitrage at a 2.25 point differential. Since fair value is only 1.36, this means that he has 0.89 profit in his pocket (2.25 minus 1.36, less transaction costs, which will be quite small).

In reality, our mythical arbitrageur is not the only person in town who sees this opportunity. In fact, *every* index arbitrageur sees this opportunity on his quote machine. Therefore, they may all rush in at once to execute the arbitrage. This causes two things to happen: (1) the arbitrage opportunity usually disappears quickly, and (2) none of them actually get to buy the S&P 500 Cash Index at 561.50 because they are all forcing prices higher.

So, in reality, an index arbitrageur builds in a "fudge factor," or slippage, to account for the fact that he may have to buy the Cash Index at a higher price than is shown on his screen. Most arbitrageurs want to see the futures at least 0.70 to 0.90 overvalued or undervalued before they will attempt to execute the arbitrage. For this reason, we do not constantly see the stock market being buffeted by buying and selling from index arbitrageurs. The futures don't normally get that far away from fair value, but, as stated earlier, they *do* get far enough out of line at least once or twice a day, almost every day, for arbitrage to be profitably established.

I have noticed a very easy way to tell if buy or sell arbitrage is actively being done in the market: watch an indicator called TICKI. It can be quoted on all the major quote machines. It is the *net* upticks or downticks of the 30 stocks in the Dow Jones Industrials. Therefore its maximum value is +30 and its minimum value is −30. If TICKI rises to +22 or higher, you can be sure that computerized buy programs are being executed; if TICKI falls to −22 or lower, computerized sell programs are taking place. A trading system using this indicator is explained in Chapter 5.

So, the action of index arbitrage being established causes short-term movements in the stock market. However, it also causes the arbitrage opportunity to disappear (in theory), so index arbitrage does not have a lasting effect on the market. It may all be over within a matter of minutes, depending on what causes the futures to be mispriced in the first place. In fact, you may wonder why the futures ever get overpriced or underpriced to begin with. Usually, it is because someone who is not interested in arbitrage decides to take a relatively large position in the futures. What follows is one of history's classic examples.

In the winter of 1995, Barings Bank collapsed under the weight of a now-infamous trader who overextended the bank's resources. Many people still don't understand what happened there, but we can summarize the debacle: the trader sold naked straddles on the Japanese stock market, and then when the market suffered a rather severe and quick decline, he didn't cover the naked short straddles. Instead, he bought index futures in an attempt to force the entire Japanese stock market higher in order to bring his position back to profitability. Perhaps the first part of this story belongs in Chapter 2, along with the discussion of selling naked straddles, but we prefer it here because it relates to index arbitrage as well.

Once the market fell initially, it was at levels below the breakeven price of the straddles. The trader then decided to buy index futures on the Japanese stock market. He was able to buy these on small amounts of margin. As he bought enough of these futures, he created a large premium on the futures. This attracted index arbitrageurs, who actually bought Japanese stocks and sold the futures. Thus the arbitrageurs were in fact forcing the Japanese stock market higher, but only briefly. After each bout of arbitrage buying, the index futures returned to approximately fair value, and the Barings trader had to buy more futures and start the cycle all over again.

By the time that Barings ran out of money, the strategy had worked to a certain degree—open interest in the Japanese index futures was at its largest level in history, indicating that plenty of index arbitrageurs were loaded to the gills with positions. Unfortunately, the Japanese stock market dropped farther, due to natural market activity and Barings was wiped out, for they were not only short straddles but now were also long massive amounts of index futures. Add to that the fact that they had bought those futures at inflated prices, which added more to the losses, and you have the story of how a long-standing institution went out of business in a very short time. The *real* problem, of course, was that the trader—or his supervisors— should have covered some or all of the short puts when the naked straddles first got into trouble. This would have meant taking a loss, but they would have still been in business.

Now let's move on to the second of the three strategies that involve selling index futures against stocks that are owned, portfolio insurance. Many portfolio managers in the mid-1980s were attracted to the protective quality of owning puts against their stocks, but they didn't like the cost of the (expensive) puts. If the market continued to rise, the puts that the manager bought would expire worthless, and his performance would suffer in comparison to both his competitors who didn't buy puts and the overall stock market.

Despite this aversion to paying put premiums, the fast-rising markets of those years—which saw the Dow-Jones Industrials nearly triple between 1982 and 1987—were making stockholders nervous, and there was demand for a product that would offer downside protection without having the onerous cost of owning puts. In addition, the protection should still afford room for upside appreciation if the market continued to rise.

In response to this demand, a strategy was created that was termed *portfolio insurance*. In essence, it worked like this: initially, the stockholder did nothing to hedge his stock position. However, if the market dropped by a certain fixed amount, then the portfolio manager would sell futures against a portion of his holdings, perhaps 10 to 20 percent on this first sale. Then, if the market dropped further, more futures would be sold to provide more protection. Finally, if the market dropped far enough, enough futures would be sold so that the entire portfolio would be protected. This strategy had several attractive features. First, even though futures weren't sold until the market started to fall, if the strategy was executed properly, the only loss to the portfolio would be approximately the same as the time value premium if puts had been bought in the first place. Second, if the market rallied initially, then there was no expense at all since no futures were sold. Finally, the portfolio manager was getting the benefit of selling futures, which trade at a premium to the cash index, so he eventually would be making a small profit from that premium as well. On paper, the mathematics all worked out, and the strategy attracted several large institutions as practitioners.

Unfortunately, there was one flaw in the strategy, a flaw that is common to many theoretical attempts at trading in the market: it assumed a relatively stable and rational market environment in which to operate. This flaw led to disaster and was the main reason why the crash of 1987 became a crash rather than just a very nasty downturn in the market.

The stock market had peaked at just over 2,700 in late August of 1987 (the rally had begun from just below Dow 800 in August of 1982). It then fell back to about 2,500, but rallied again to 2,640 by the first week in October. Some portfolio insurance was sold on that drop and things seemed to be working fairly well, as intended.

The first sign that things might be getting dicey was a 92-point, one-day drop on October sixth. However, the market seemed to weather that and, although it slid some over the next week, there was actually a good rally on Tuesday, October 13th, when the market was up over 70 points at midday and managed to close nearly 40 points higher, at just over 2,500. Again, the decline was orderly enough for most of the portfolio insurance to be sold, although rumors were circulating that some portfolio managers were now becoming traders and hadn't sold all the futures that they were supposed to. They were waiting for a further rally back toward 2,600. That rally never came (not for a couple of years, anyway).

Trouble began on Wednesday, Thursday, and Friday, October 14th through 16th. The market was down 96, 57, and 109 points, respectively, on those three days. The swiftness of the decline left the portfolio insurance managers gasping for breath. They did not sell the required number of futures for two reasons: (1) the decline was so fast that it was almost impossible to sell that many futures in so short a time, and (2) the futures were trading at discounts to fair value, a fact not accounted for in the theory of the strategy. Thus, some of the portfolio managers did nothing (with the exception of praying, perhaps). To their dismay, their stocks were losing huge chunks of value and they were not getting the protection that they had theorized from their short futures, since they were not short nearly as many futures as they were supposed to be.

Monday, October 19th, only made the problem worse. The market gapped down 200 points right on the opening and the portfolio insurance crowd hoped against hope for a reflex rally. When that rally did not materialize by about noon, they decided that they had to catch up on their futures selling and at least hold the losses to their current levels (the Dow was now just over the 2,000 level). So they waded in and sold futures . . . and sold futures . . . and sold even more futures. They were selling futures at 15.00 points discount to parity (forget fair value; forget theory; just sell the required number of futures!). Many professionals who were long stock realized that they could sell their long stocks and buy futures and lock in 15 points, so they did that. This added more selling pressure to the market, which continued to collapse until it finished off 508 points on that fateful day.

Obviously, there was plenty of natural selling in the stock market on the days leading up to, and including, October 19th. But the portfolio insurance strategy exacerbated the decline to disastrous proportions. No one knows the exact extent to which portfolio insurance contributed to the debacle, but it was substantial. Not only that, the institutions practicing the strategy got hammered anyway, as they never did get their protection properly in place. In addition, they became the subject of derision from Wall Street, government investigations were initiated, and in general, things were very uncomfortable.

This fiasco pretty much ended the strategy of portfolio insurance as practiced with index futures. Two new measures that came out of the government investigation were that index futures trading limits be installed and that futures halt trading at various points if the Dow Jones Industrials should rise or fall too far, too fast. These rule changes effectively wiped out the portfolio insurance strategy using futures, for no money manager could ever trust that he would be able to sell his futures when he wanted to, even if he religiously followed the strategy to the letter. If the futures were locked limit down, or they weren't available for trading, then he would never be able to sell the required number of futures.

Today, portfolio insurance is conducted with put options, which brings its own brand of problems. We discuss that strategy using puts shortly. First, however, let's touch on the third use of futures as a hedge to a stock portfolio, program trading. This term is the catch-all for all forms of computer-generated buy or sell programs that enter the marketplace. You often hear the financial media blame a market decline on "sell programs," or credit "buy programs" for a market advance. In reality, many of those "programs" are index arbitrage, but the media don't make the distinction.

To professional traders who hedge stocks with futures, *program trading* has a distinctly different definition from index arbitrage. The name originally came from the functions provided by block desks to hedge themselves (or their customers) while large stock orders, or programs, were executed. A large customer might call one of the larger trading houses and give an order to buy millions of dollars worth of stock, say by the close of trading. Usually, there is some sort of price level at which the trading house attempts to fill the order; otherwise, the client could pay up wildly for the stocks. If the trading house actually has to pay more for the stocks, it still gives the execution to the client at the client's price and takes a loss for the difference in the house's error account.

Since these trading houses are not in the business of losing money, they will often hedge themselves by buying some futures while also buying the stocks. Then, if the stock buying forces the overall market too high, and they are looking at losses in order to satisfy the customer's prices, at least they will have some profit from the futures to offset those losses.

Suppose a large customer calls a major trading house and says that he has $30 million worth of stock to buy, and there are about 200 stocks that comprise the order. In order to get the order, the trading house may tell the customer that he can get the best execution through them, because they will guarantee the prices at the time that the order is received.

Now, obviously the trading firm can't really do that without taking some risk, but they will risk a little in order to get the customer's business. If they decide that the 200 stocks behave in a manner that is essentially the same as the S&P 500, they might buy S&P 500 futures as a hedge. Thirty million dollars is about 100 futures contracts if the futures are trading at a price near 600.

So the trading firm buys 100 futures and then sets about buying the stocks. If they have to pay more for the stock than the price they promised the customer, that will be a cost of doing business. However, that cost is offset by a similar profit in the futures. As the stocks are bought, the futures are sold out.

Note that the futures and stocks are *both* being bought in this case. The futures are sold out when their hedging function is no longer needed. When these programs are executed, the market jumps, the futures often get large premium, and index arbitrage may be a by-product. Also, the TICKI Indicator, which we mentioned earlier, usually registers a high number (over +22) as well.

Because analytic methods have become more sophisticated, it has become possible for clients and traders to determine how many index futures, and *which* index futures, are best used to simulate almost any diverse portfolio of common stocks. This has allowed trading houses to be very competitive in their business, for those with better hedging techniques can offer an institutional client better prices (whether buying *or* selling). Thus, the larger institutions will often show a program out for bids before deciding which trading house gets the order. The institution has to be rather secretive about the actual details of the portfolio, however, or else the information would be leaked all over Wall Street.

So, *program trading* is a more general term that describes the machinations involved in these institutional buy or sell orders. The entire process works in reverse when large quantities of stock are being sold; the trading houses will sell futures to hedge their risk while they execute the client's sell order. In some cases the trading house may be able to execute the order for the client (probably via loading it into a computer and letting the computer generate orders) without using futures at all. This would still qualify as a buy program or a sell program, even though the general public and the media associate futures with programs.

In summary, these three strategies—index arbitrage, portfolio insurance, and program trading—are ways in which large traders hedge portfolios of stocks with index futures. When the strategies are initially executed, there is a short-term effect on the stock market, as it accelerates up or down, depending on whether stocks are being bought or sold as part of the strategy. In general, however, this effect is short-lived and the market quickly returns to an equilibrium state.

THE EFFECT OF INDEX FUTURES AND INDEX OPTION EXPIRATION ON THE STOCK MARKET

As long as we're discussing the effect that futures have on the stock market, we might as well address a related topic: their effect at expiration. Sometimes, expiring options and futures have a rather large influence on the market. This effect used to be limited mostly to expiration day itself, but in recent years it has expanded to the point where there may be an effect at certain times preceding and following expiration also.

The reason that there is a noticeable expiration effect is related to the fact that the index futures and options settle for *cash*, while the common stocks that are used to hedge them settle for actual shares of stock. Thus, even if the position is a perfectly hedged arbitrage position, only the stock side is traded at expiration—the futures automatically settle for cash without any trade taking place.

Example: The final cash settlement price of the S&P 500 futures is determined, somewhat artificially, by using the opening price of each of the 500 stocks in the index on expiration day (the third Friday of the expiration month). Suppose that an index arbitrageur has a perfectly hedged position, in which he is long all 500 of the stocks in the S&P 500 Cash Index, in their proper proportions, and is simultaneously short enough S&P 500 futures in order to perfectly hedge the stocks.

If the arbitrageur decided to remove his position at expiration, all he would have to do would be to sell each stock at its opening price on expiration day (he uses "market on open" sell orders). By definition, if each stock were sold on the opening, the eventual price that he received for selling his stock portfolio would be exactly the same as the cash settlement price of the S&P 500 futures. Thus, he would remove his arbitrage at parity, receiving the same price for both his long side (stocks) and his short side (futures).

The by-product of having executed the removal of this completely hedged arbitrage position, however, is that a lot of stock is sold. Thus, the stock market would be down on the opening, for no reason other than index arbitrageurs were removing positions.

Where index options are concerned, the position is slightly different, but the result is the same. If you owned all 100 of the OEX stocks in their proper proportion, your hedge would be short OEX calls and long OEX puts, where both the puts and the calls have the same terms (same expiration date and striking price). From the discussion at the beginning of this chapter, you know that being short the calls and long the puts is equivalent to being short OEX itself. So, in effect, the OEX arbitrageur in this case is long the physical OEX stocks and is short the equivalent of OEX, or, as it is commonly called, an "equivalent futures position (EFP)."

The "artificial" effect that the index expiration has on the stock market has bothered (and still does bother) some investors, mostly those who don't trade derivatives, and they are usually only bothered if the market is driven *down* artificially. If the arbs are short stock and long futures, then they must *buy* stock to remove their positions, which forces the market higher at expiration and is normally okay with the critics.

Note that arbitrageurs don't *have* to remove their position at expiration. Instead, they might roll their futures or options out to the next month. If they do this, then of course, that has zero effect on the stock market because no physical stocks are bought or sold. The arbitrageurs make an economic determination, based on dividends, interest rates, and the prices of the respective futures or options, in order to decide whether or not to remove the position at expiration or to roll it out to an ensuing expiration month.

A little history of how the S&P futures expiration has evolved over the years might be useful. Initially, S&P 500 futures settled at the close of trading on that third Friday, expiration day. This created rather wide swings because the NYSE specialist was being bom-barded with large sell orders (for example) at what is generally an illiquid time—late Friday afternoon. Moreover, OEX arbitrage was also sizable and was being unwound at the same time, generally in the same direction.

In order to dampen the expiration effect, the S&P 500 contracts and many other futures and option contracts were switched to *opening settlement*. Opening settlement is what was described in the previous example, where the opening price of each stock is used to determine the actual cash settlement price. (*Note*: when a futures or option contract has opening settlement on Friday morning, then the last trades in the contracts themselves take place at the close of trad-ing on Thursday night—they do not trade on Friday morning.) By doing things this way, the specialist can attempt to round up large institutions and brokerage firms to help him with the trade; if a large quantity of stock is being sold by an arbitrageur, the specialist may be able to find several institutions willing to buy part of that block of stock. This might delay the opening of the stock, but it generally allows for less of a gap opening and therefore less of an effect on the overall stock market itself.

In reality, the perception for arbitrage to have a large effect on the stock market was always larger than any actual effect. The movements on the expiration Fridays during the mid- to late 1980s are listed below. You can see that there was never any huge effect on the quarterly expirations, when the S&P 500 futures expired:

Date	Dow Change	% Change	Date	Dow Change	% Change
9/83	+10	0.8	9/86	-12	-0.7
12/83	+6	0.5	12/86	+16	0.8
3/84	+17	1.4	3/87	+34	1.5
6/84	-11	-1.0	6/87	+12	0.5
9/84	-21	-1.7	9/87	+27	1.1
12/84	-5	-0.4	12/87	+51	2.6
3/85	-13	-1.0	3/88	+1	0.0
6/85	+25	1.9	6/88	+10	0.5
9/85	-9	-0.7	9/88	+6	0.3
12/85	0	0.0	12/88	+17	0.8
3/86	-36	-2.0	3/89	-48	-2.1
6/86	24	1.3	6/89	+6	0.2

The opening settlement went into effect for the December 1987 expiration. You can see that the two biggest moves on the chart occurred *after* the opening settlement was created, so it is debatable whether it helps much. In theory, however, it does, and it is certainly here to stay, at least as far as the S&P 500 futures are concerned. By the way, if you look at the monthly expirations between the quarterly expiration, which are predominantly influenced by OEX, you will find even less volatility in general (the one exception being October of 1987, of course—but what happened that day [down 109 points] was far greater than any expiration effect of OEX options).

Most other index futures and index options use an opening settlement as well. The main exception is the OEX Index options, which continue to use a closing settlement. This is mostly due to the fact that the CBOE (where the options trade) is reluctant to tamper with a highly successful contract, which is certainly a valid point.

Games People Play

If you were able to discern, in advance, what the intentions of the arbitrageurs were, and how much stock they had to buy or sell, then you could make a nice little trade for yourself. That is, if you knew that the OEX arbs were going to buy a lot of stock at the close of trading on expiration, then you could wait until about 3:30 P.M. Eastern time and buy OEX in- or at-the-money calls, expiring that day. When the arbs bought stock to unwind their positions and thereby forced OEX quickly higher, you would profit.

Since things are never that easy on Wall Street, you might correctly suspect that it is not an easy matter to find out what the arbs intend to do at any expiration. However, because of the fast potential rewards, it is an endeavor that many traders undertake, trying to predict the stock market's movement as affected by expiration unwinding of arbitrage positions. It is my opinion that the best index to use for this type of short-term trading is OEX, as the moves occur at the end of the day. On the other hand, if you attempt to play the S&P 500 expiration, you must hold a position overnight from Thursday night to the opening on Friday morning (recall that SPX is opening settlement on Friday morning, but there is no trading of SPX options or S&P 500 futures after Thursday's close). Too many things can happen overnight, especially since many government statistics are released prior to the opening on a Friday. Such nonexpiration factors can affect the expiration, so I feel you're better off trying to trade the OEX expiration.

If you're going to trade the expiration, but not as an arbitrageur, the three things you should attempt to determine are (1) whether the arbs are long or short stock coming into the expiration, (2) if they are going to unwind their positions or are going to roll them, and (3) what the open interest in in-the-money OEX calls looks like. It turns out that a good floor source can give you the best information on the first two. The reason that this is true is that the arbs will *always* attempt to roll their position out to the next expiration month if they can; it is a lot of work to establish these arbitrage positions (whether 100 or 500 stocks are involved), so it's a lot easier for the arbs if they can keep their stocks and merely roll their options. But they will only execute the roll at a price that is favorable to them; if they can't get their price, then they'll unwind the position at expiration and look to reestablish it at some later date.

The reason floor brokers are of great help is that spread brokers in the OEX pit can see how the arbs are bidding for the "rolls." That is, they can see if the arbs are attempting to roll a long call/short put position or are trying to do the opposite. If the arbs are attempting to roll a long call/short put position, then the arbs must be short stock. Therefore, there is potential buying power at expiration. In addition, spread brokers can tell whether or not the "rolls" are actually being traded or are just being bid for. If they are actually trading, that lessens the potential expiration effect.

In April of 1995, there was a large arbitrage position. The market had been in the midst of a strong bull run, and there was huge open interest in OEX calls, indicating a large OEX arbitrage position. Floor sources told us that the arbs were attempting to roll long calls out to May or June expiration, so it was apparent that the arbs held short stock positions hedged by long call/short put option positions. These facts were known more than a week prior to expiration, and seemed to be fairly common knowledge among professional traders.

Moreover, as expiration approached, there was very little actual trading of the rolls. Open interest was remaining fairly constant in the OEX April calls, and floor traders did not see many rolls being executed. This embold-ened traders and, by Thursday afternoon of expiration week, it was becom-ing obvious that there just wasn't enough time or supply for the arbs to be able to roll. Therefore, there was going to be rather massive buying of stocks in the OEX Index at the close of trading on Friday.

The buying actually started on Thursday (more about *that* strategy later), when the market reversed from a moderate down day to close up 23 on Thursday. Friday saw another 40 points tacked on, with the majority of it coming late as the buy programs were executed. Traders who had done the analysis of the arbs' position made very good profits in short-term OEX calls, as OEX rose over 7 points.

You can see from this example that a foreknowledge of the arbs' positions, and their subsequent handling of those positions as expira-tion approaches, can produce a profitable speculative trade. Don't be dismayed if you don't know floor sources—it may be possible to glean similar information from your brokerage firm's option depart-ment, as they talk to floor traders. Also, since the advent of CNBC's more advanced coverage of the day-to-day aspects of trading, you can often get the opinion, on TV, of some of the more "connected" floor traders.

Open Interest Implications

On the other hand, it is important to understand that it is not neces-sarily easy to discern this information regarding arbitrage positions. Some of the arbs even go so far as to leak *incorrect* information about their positions. The best that an outside observer can do is to put together enough information to make an educated guess; if the guess is good enough, the rewards will be ample. There are certain basic facts that are irrefutable and will help anyone determine what is going on. One important guide is open interest of OEX options. As expiration approaches, public customers tend to sell in-the-money options and hold at- or out-of-the-money options. Those in-the-money options are predominantly in the hands of arbitrageurs by expiration. Thus, if you observe the day-to-day changes of open interest of in-the-money options as expiration approaches, you can get a "feel" for how much buying or selling power remains in the market.

June 1995 expiration was a fairly good example of how open interest provided clues beyond the information that was generally available. It was fairly common knowledge that the arbs were once again short stock, hedged by long calls and short puts. Also, the market had rallied to new highs at 510 during the previous month, so most of the OEX calls were in-the-money as expiration drew near.

On Wednesday morning of expiration week, open interest in the calls with strikes from 440 (the lowest strike) through 505 totalled almost 130,000 contracts. On Wednesday night, at the close of trading, 40,000 contracts were exercised. This early exercise was announced on TV, and was pretty much common knowledge. Exercise figures are available on any given day from the Option Clearing Corporation in Chicago. On Thursday evening, another 46,000 contracts were exercised. Again, this early exercise was widely broadcast on TV.

At this point many analysts, having seen two days of early exercises, felt that there wasn't enough firepower left for expiration. They felt that expiration day itself would be a dull one. However, that was not the case at all. Most of the open interest had *not* been rolled out to later months, so there were still 44,000 in-the-money calls that represented buying power. In fact, it turned out to be good buying power as OEX meandered slightly higher most of expiration day and then spurted on the closing buy program to finish over three points higher on the day.

Although static numbers are subject to change, I find that an open interest of 40,000 to 50,000 in-the-money contracts is sufficient to cause a market move of at least 1.00 OEX or S&P points at expiration, or at the close of trading on one of the days immediately preceding expiration. Of course, at many expirations the open interest is far greater than that and larger moves can occur.

Open interest can therefore be a valuable guide to what is happening at expiration. Always check it as a backup to whatever "stories" you are hearing, for it is a reliable indicator. Unfortunately, it is only published once a day (before the market opens), so you can't tell if it is changing during the day. That is where floor sources can come in handy. For example, if you know open interest is large entering expiration day, but your floor sources tell you that the arbs are rolling their positions out to the next expiration month, then you would have to modify your plans, since the effect of the arbs on the closing would be reduced or eliminated. You should always expect a number of positions to be rolled on expiration day itself; some arbs would just rather keep their stock positions in place at almost any cost. However, as a rule of thumb, if there is an open interest of at least 40,000 in-the-money contracts as the day begins, you have a good shot at having enough program activity to be able to make a profitable trade.

A few other important points should be made. If there is 40,000 open interest in in-the-money puts, then sell programs are possible. So you should really net out the open interest between the in-the-money calls and the in-the-money puts. Over the years, buy programs at expiration have been far more prevalent than sell programs, but be mindful of the possibility of a sell. You need to monitor the in-the-money put open interest for that purpose.

As expiration day itself approaches, the largest open interest will probably be in the at-the-money strike (or perhaps two strikes, if OEX is right between two of them). This open interest can be critical, for it might tilt the balance between buys and sell, depending on the way the market moves, or it might add enough additional ammunition to push the open interest total from below 40,000 to over 40,000, thus creating a tradeable situation.

Suppose that OEX is trading at 579 as expiration Friday begins, and the total open interest of all in-the-money calls up through the 575 strike is 35,000 contracts. Moreover, the open interest of all in-the-money puts down through the 585 strike is 25,000 contracts. On the surface, it appears that this expiration will not offer much in the way of a trading opportunity, because there is only a net of 10,000 contracts on the buy side.

However, when we look at the expiring *580* calls, we see that open interest is 40,000 contracts. At the beginning of the day, most of that open interest is probably in the hands of customers. However, if OEX were to rise and be above 580 by the end of the day, a large portion of that open interest could pass from customers' hands into the hands of arbitrageurs. In turn, that would mean, also, that there was net of 50,000 in-the-money contracts on the call side, and therefore buy programs might be possible at the close of trading.

A Hedged Strategy

We're going to spend more time discussing the arbs' actions, but first we want to give you a strategy that is a hedge, but that can still make some nice money for you on expiration day. Obviously, if you have the arbs' intentions pegged exactly right, you can just buy some expiring OEX calls and make money. But there are a number of things that can go wrong, even if you have done your homework correctly. First of all, the market may have an interim adverse move *before* the arbs swing into action. *Just because there is going to be buying on the close, for example, it does not mean that the market will be up for the day.* Some speculators hear that there is going to a buy program on the close and they look for an entry point all day long in order to buy the market. This could mean that you have bought the wrong calls, or that you lose money on your call even though you had things figured out correctly.

In May 1995 there was a fairly large arbitrage position that once again consisted of the arbs being short stock, hedged by the long call/short put position. Expectations were high that the arbs were actually going to buy their stock a day early, on Thursday night. Speculators who had this figured out waited until about 3:30 P.M. on Thursday to buy calls on OEX, expecting the arbs to begin forcing the market higher shortly thereafter.

However, at the same time, the news media were interviewing a Fed governor who made some bearish comments regarding the future of interest rates. As a result, the bond market and then the stock market got slammed.

At the close, there *was* a small buy program, followed by a rather large exercise of OEX calls by the arbs, but it came too late for those who had bought calls *before* the Fed governor's remarks.

This example shows the frustrations that can accompany the unhedged OEX call buyer who is attempting to figure out what the arbs are going to do. He might be right, but he might not make money. There is another strategy—a hedged strategy—that can help prevent losses like that, while still allowing for profits to be made. For example, if you are approaching expiration as a *strategist*, and not as a *speculator*, then you would take the following position on expiration Friday, if you expected the arbs to execute buy programs on the close:

<blockquote>
Buy five in-the-money expiring OEX calls
and Sell one S&P 500 near-term futures contract as a hedge
</blockquote>

Note that the S&P 500 contract is never expiring that Friday (the *old* contract may have expired that morning, but the currently trading S&P 500 contract always has at least one month remaining until expiration, and sometimes as many as three months). The reason we use five OEX calls and only one S&P 500 future is that OEX options are worth $100 per point, while S&P 500 options are worth $500 per point. In essence, this is a complete hedge—all stock movements are accounted for, except for the difference in movement of OEX versus SPX (the S&P 500 Cash Index). That's what we're looking for—for OEX to outperform the S&P 500 on the close.

The *margin* required for this strategy is that both sides must be fully margined, even though they are obviously hedged. Until cross-margining becomes a reality, you must pay for the calls in full and also margin the S&P futures.

Example: The February 1992 expiration was a classic example of how this strategy worked well as a hedged vehicle. After the market opened and stabilized, these prices were available:

<blockquote>
OEX: 386.02
OEX Feb 380 call: 6½
S&P March future: 413.30
</blockquote>

The hedged strategy was established by buying five of the OEX Feb 380 in-the-money calls that were due to expire that evening, and they were hedged with the sale of an S&P March future (the nearest term futures contract). Note that the OEX calls have a slight premium, because traders are expecting a buy program. The premium on OEX calls, as expiration nears, is often a "tip" as to how OEX market makers view the upcoming expiration. If the in-the-money calls have a premium, as in the preceding prices, then market makers are expecting a buy program. If in-the-money puts have a premium, then market makers are looking for a sell program.

On that Friday, the market traded lower almost all day. Then, later in the day, as expiration approached, large buy imbalances were posted for "market on close" orders. These imbalances are released at 3:40 P.M. by the NYSE in order to advertise the blocks of stocks to be traded; this will draw in sellers (in theory) to help out the specialist in making a fair and reasonable market.

As the close of trading approached, and then as the "market on close" buy programs hit the tape, the relevant prices were as follows:

Time (P.M.)	OEX	SPX (S&P 500 Cash Index)	S&P March Futures
3:59	384.51	410.81	411.80
4:00	384.68	410.90	412.25
4:01	384.95	411.04	412.20
4:03	385.47	411.29	411.90
4:05	385.80	411.42	412.00
Final	385.82	411.43	412.15
Gain from 3:59 P.M. to final:	1.31	0.62	0.35

First, notice that OEX rose 1.31 after 4 P.M. on the buy programs—from 384.81 to 385.82—while SPX only rose 0.62 over the same six-minute time period. This confirms the fact that we stated earlier: that OEX will rise faster than SPX when the buy programs enter the market. Also, notice that the S&P March futures only rose 0.35—from 411.80 to 412.15. This means that the premium was shrinking on the futures as the end of trading neared.

The actual strategy would be unwound by exercising the Feb 380 calls, receiving 5.82 as the settlement price (OEX closed at 385.82), and buying the March futures back in the open market. The profits and losses would be:

Position	Buy Price	Sell Price	Net Gain ($)
5 OEX Feb 380 calls	6.50	5.82	–340
1 March S&P future	412.00	413.30	+650
Total Gain			+310

Of course, commissions would have to be subtracted from this figure, but they shouldn't be more than $100 or so. Therefore, a profit remains. The investment required would be the full cost of the OEX calls, $3,250, plus the futures margin, which is about $9,000.

The final point that should be made here is that this profit was made, even though OEX declined on the day (OEX was 386.02 in the morning when the position was established, but closed at 385.82). Almost certainly, a straight call purchase would have lost money, but the hedged strategy made money because it was only attempting to capture the differential between OEX and SPX, and not necessarily to predict the direction of the overall market on expiration Friday.

The idea behind this strategy is that the OEX Index will go up at the close of trading on expiration day, as the "market on close" buy orders are executed. The S&P Cash Index will not increase as much, nor will the futures contract, since the buy programs have a smaller effect on the broader-based SPX Index. Since it is expected that the buying will be concentrated in the stocks that make up the OEX Index, this strategy is a reasonable way to approach the problem of expiration in a hedged manner. The recommended hedged strategy is not concerned with the eventual market direction other than to attempt to predict the relationship between OEX and SPX at the close of trading.

The strategy is only intended as a day trade; keeping it as short-term as possible (less than one full trading day) will help keep losses small. The risk is that the SPX Index outperforms OEX on expiration day. This could happen if institutional sellers come into the market to meet the buy orders of the arbs, or if the arbs roll their positions after you, as a strategist, have established your hedged strategy, or if you have misjudged the arbs' position.

In any case, you, as strategist, are attempting a day trade. You should wait until the market opens and stabilizes on Friday, expiration day, before taking a position. Even then, you shouldn't establish your entire position; you might wait to see if better prices are available during the trading day. The extent of the buy programs, if any, should be known by about 4:05 P.M. Eastern time as the market on close orders hit the tape. The futures trade until 4:15 P.M. The position can easily be removed: merely exercise your OEX calls and buy your S&P futures back in the open market before 4:15 P.M. (*Note:*

Expiration day is the only day that you can wait until *after* the close of trading to exercise your OEX calls.)

There may be additional benefits as well. Sometimes, the premium *shrinks* in the S&P futures, giving the hedged position an additional profit. Also, if the market were to suffer a severe drop on expiration day, large profits could accrue since you have a limited loss on your calls, but are not limited on the potential downside profits from the short futures contract. This has happened twice in recent years.

Expiration day, October 1987, was a rather harrowing day for the market. The arbs *had* been short stocks and long futures coming into expiration week. There had not been much opportunity to remove the positions because the portfolio insurance practitioners pushed the futures to discounts on Wednesday and Thursday of the week. So, coming into Friday, it seemed as if there were going to be arbitrage buy programs. A strategy of long October in-the-money calls and short December S&P futures worked beautifully as the market plunged 107 points that day and the futures closed at a four-point discount as well!

It is a much lesser-known fact, but the November 1991 expiration was even worse for the market. Again, as Friday, November 15th, opened for trading, it was a fairly common assumption that the arbs were short stock and long calls. Thus, buy programs were expected on the close of trading. However, the market began to sell off in midafternoon, and the selling gathered momentum. Eventually the Dow closed down 110 points and finished on the low of the day (OEX was off 16 points). Moreover, by the close of trading, arbs had removed their positions and there were actually *sell* programs on the close! Again the futures closed at a discount, so our hedged expiration strategy position profit was even greater than anticipated.

A risk of this strategy is that the S&P futures might gain a lot of premium near the close, for some reason, forcing the strategist to buy back overpriced futures in order to close out his position. Finally, one other point should be made about the hedged strategy. It can be modified into an aggressive one if conditions are right. If the buying on the close is particularly heavy, there is almost always a downward opening to stock prices on the following Monday morning, as stocks return to levels near where they were trading before the artificial buying took place. That doesn't always happen, but it has occurred many times in the past. In that case, the aggressive strategist might want to keep (some of) his short S&P futures over the weekend with the intention of covering them on Monday morning after the opening of trading. This is obviously not part of the hedged strategy, but it often proves profitable as well. This aggressive addition to the strategy introduces extra risk into the position, because some news item might come out that forces the market higher on Monday morning, expiration forces notwithstanding.

The preceding discussions all assumed that the arbs were going to be executing buy programs on the close of trading. However, that is not always the case. Sometimes they have sell programs, in which case the hedged strategy would be to buy five OEX in-the-money puts, and buy one S&P 500 futures contract as a hedge. This hedge is similar in concept: the risk is limited by the two hedged positions, and in this case, a large market rally (which wouldn't normally be expected to occur if there are sell programs around) could result in very large profits.

Speculation Early in Expiration Week

There is sometimes arbitrage activity *prior to* expiration day itself. This has become more common in recent years, and the activity is predominantly concentrated in OEX programs, since the OEX options can be exercised early. In fact, if this pre-expiration activity is large enough, it can have the effect of reducing expiration Friday to a total non-event. That is, the arbs can actually remove their entire position in the last days prior to expiration. Thus, even if you have done your homework and were ready for expiration Friday, that may not be enough. You may have to be prepared to trade on Wednesday or Thursday preceding expiration as well, or be left with no trades at all. First, let's discuss this from an arbitrageur's perspective, and then later we'll see how interested outsiders, such as ourselves, could make money from the arbs' actions.

The examples in the last section showed how the arbitrageurs unwind their positions on expiration Friday. However, the phenomenon revolving around the surge in prices on a Wednesday or Thursday preceding the Friday expiration is less well known. Sometimes arbs will attempt to unwind their position early because, although they are not guaranteed a perfect closeout of their position as they would be on expiration Friday, they can often make more money this way. Once again, they unwind their position at or near the close of trading, but in this discussion, they are unwinding a day or two early. The early unwinding relies on the fact that OEX options can be exercised prior to expiration day (they are American style).

Let's assume that the arbs are short stock, hedged by the long call/short put option position. We know that an arbitrageur can unwind his position at exactly *parity* on expiration day by buying all his stocks back with market on close orders and also exercising his long, in-the-money calls (or allowing himself to be assigned on his short, in-the-money *puts*). In either case, he unwinds the position without risk. However, *what if he could remove the position at a discount to parity?* Then he could make even more money. In order to unwind at a discount, however, he would have to buy his stocks back *before* the market closed, and then exercise his calls *after* the market closed. If he had bought those stocks back at a lower price than the actual market close, this would in effect result in his removing his position at a discount to parity.

Example: suppose an arbitrageur is short all the component stocks of the OEX Index in the proper proportion and has them hedged by long, in-the-money OEX calls. Furthermore, suppose that he wants to attempt to remove this position at a discount to parity. At about 3:45 P.M. on the day *before* expiration, he begins to buy some of his stock back in the open market. This forces OEX a little higher, so he buys more stock back. Again, OEX is forced higher by his buying actions. Finally, he buys the remainder of his stock back, market on close, and exercises his calls. The following figures might be representative of the prices he received.

Time of Day (P.M.)	OEX Price	Action
3:45	525.00	Buy back one quarter of short stock position
3:50	525.50	Buy back another quarter of position
4:00	526.00	Buy back the remainder market on close and exercise the long calls

Thus, the arb has bought back one quarter of his short stock position at 525.00, one quarter at 525.50, and the balance at 526.00. His net OEX buyback price is 525.62. Meanwhile he exercises his calls, all at parity with the close—526.00. Thus, he has removed his position at a 0.38-point discount to parity. If his position were large enough, that could represent a lot of money.

Arbitrageurs are, by nature, rather risk-averse people; arbitrageurs like to make a little, mostly risk-free money, on each trade and do a lot of trades. However, the arbitrageur assumes a certain amount of risk by attempting this early unwinding of his position; so you won't see all the arbs trying this. *His major risk in the early unwinding strategy is that someone else—a natural seller, perhaps—will enter the market and force OEX to go down while the arb is in the midst of unwinding his position.* If that happens, the arb may end up removing his position at a premium to parity, an act that could cost him a good deal of money. Still, there are more and more arbs who will attempt this early unwinding *if conditions are right.* We'll define what that means shortly.

But first, there is one additional way that the arbitrageur can make money by an early unwinding, but it involves even more risk: he can wait until the following morning to cover some of his short stock. It should be understood what happens when a large OEX in-the-money option position is exercised: it often removes one side of another trader's hedged position. An example of this was given in Chapter 1, under "cash option exercise." Essentially, what happens is that some other trader (*not* the arb) has a spread in OEX in-the-money options, where one side is completely hedging the other. Then a call assignment removes the short side of this trader's spread, and he is left with a long position. Since he had no market exposure before the assignment, and now has great market exposure after the assignment, it is reasonable to assume that this trader will try to sell something in order to reduce his exposure.

Thus an early assignment of OEX calls produces selling pressure on the market the next morning; similarly, an early assignment of OEX puts produces buying pressure on the market the next morning. Consequently, an arbitrageur who was short stock and also exercised his calls on Thursday night, say, might wait until Friday morning to cover some of his short stock because he knows that it is likely that his large call exercise will force the market lower on Friday morning. Of course, the arb assumes additional risk by attempting to do this, for there could be some news items that come out overnight and make the market rally, which would force him to cover his short stock at *higher* prices.

In summary, then, the arbitrageur can remove his position in one of two ways:

1. The riskless way: on expiration Friday, buy stocks back with market on close orders and exercise his calls for cash.
2. The aggressive way: on Wednesday or Thursday preceding expiration day, buy stocks back aggressively during the last half hour of trading; exercise calls for cash after the close; and possibly cover some remaining short stock the following morning.

We mentioned earlier that the arbs will only attempt method 2—the aggressive early unwinding—if conditions are right. What we mean by that is that they won't try to force the market in the opposite direction from which it is naturally trending. Thus, if they were contemplating an early unwinding on Thursday's close, but late on Thursday afternoon the market was selling off sharply, they would not attempt to jump in the way with their buy programs. In that case, they would most likely just unwind their positions on Friday, via the riskless method. On the other hand, if the market were already rallying on Thursday afternoon, they might feel more certain that they could "pour fuel on the fire" and get a *really big* rally going by buying back their short stock as part of an early unwinding.

The September 1994 expiration saw one of the biggest market moves due to early unwinding. As expiration week approached, open interest was one of the largest ever. A persistent rally since late June had allowed arbitrageurs to establish large hedged positions of short stock and long calls/short puts. Moreover, that same rally had now placed almost all of those calls in-the-money, so the potential was great for arbitrage activity near the September expiration.

On Monday, Tuesday, and Wednesday of expiration week, OEX closed higher each day, although only by a point or two. OEX closed at 435.22 that Wednesday. Then, as Thursday's trading unfolded, another modest rally was under way. By Thursday afternoon, the rally had gathered a little steam and OEX was trading near 437 shortly after 3 P.M. At that point, the rally began to gather some steam and OEX was up to nearly 439 by 3:50 P.M. Then, a huge buying spree hit the market late in the day, driving OEX all the way up to 442.03 on the close. So, OEX closed up 6.81 and the Dow-Jones Industrials were up 58 points.

The arbs had had a field day, jumping on an already rising market and pushing it higher quickly. But the arbs weren't done yet: on Thursday night, they exercised all of their in-the-money calls. It was the largest call exercise ever in OEX (up to that date). All OEX in-the-money calls—even the September 440 calls, which were only slightly in-the-money—closed at parity, as market makers knew that the exercises were forthcoming (by the way, those Sep 440 calls rose from one quarter on Wednesday's close to a price of 2 on Thursday's close). Those call exercises represented over $6 billion worth of OEX stock; thus $6 billion of stock had been bought by arbs on Thursday afternoon.

The next morning (Friday), the market opened down substantially (OEX was off nearly three points in early trading), partly due to a reaction to the early exercise, and partly due to bond market jitters. Thus, arbs who had held any short stock overnight were able to cover it at better prices on Friday morning. Needless to say, there was no buy program on Friday: OEX closed down 3.82 on Friday. The close of trading on Friday was very dull.

Thus, September 1994 was perhaps the ultimate real-life example of how early unwinding takes place and how it can affect the market. In fact, the overall stock market declined for several weeks after that, with OEX reaching a low of 418 on October 6th. This is not to imply that the expiration activity caused the market to decline for several weeks, but it *does* demonstrate that expiration week can move entirely differently from the natural tendency of the stock market.

For those who understood the strategy, the events of that Thursday, September 15, 1994, seemed rather logical. But it was soon apparent how many people didn't really understand what had happened. The aftermath of that expiration produced some almost comical comments by the media. After Friday's down day, CNBC television reported that expiration was a "sell" and they figured the market should rebound on Monday morning as an opposite reaction to the expiration sell programs. Apparently, since Friday was expiration and was a down day, the television commentators figured that there had been sell programs (they seemed to have totally missed the buy programs on Thursday). In fact, there had been almost no expiration-related programs at all, and the market traded lower on Monday also. *Barron's* ran numerous articles trying to explain what had happened, and in those you could almost feel that certain arbitrage firms were feeding somewhat nonsensical information to the media, perhaps in an attempt to keep everyone from understanding what really took place. The gist of the *Barron's* summary was that OEX traders and arbs bought OEX calls and then went in and bought OEX stocks in order to increase the price of their calls, and then exercised their calls on the close. If *that* was true, how were these "OEX traders" supposed to have disposed of their long stock—at big losses on Friday? Nonsense, to be sure; but when it was printed in *Barron's*, a lot of people believed it. Not all public commentators were unaware of what had happened, of course. After the market was down 67 on Tuesday following expiration, Larry Wachtel of Prudential acknowledged that the market needed to work off the artificial *buy* program of the preceding week. So at least *he* got it right.

The arbs were able to make such a large impact that September because "conditions were right": the market was trading higher and there was ample knowledge that a large arbitration position existed. However, when conditions are not right, the arbs will stand aside. You might want to go back and look at the example of the May 1995 expiration, which was described earlier in this chapter. That time, a Fed governor's negative comments generated true sellers of stocks, and the arbs conveniently stepped aside late in the day, preferring not to fight the trend. Conditions were not right for the arbs in that case.

Trading with the Arbs

So now that we have spent all this time explaining what the arbs are doing, let's see how the individual trader or interested outsider can make some money from this knowledge. Again, you have two approaches: (1) you can buy calls and attempt to speculate on what the arbs will do, or (2) you can take a more hedged position, figuring that you might not make as much, but it won't hurt as bad if you're wrong, either.

If you are going to merely buy calls—a strategy that has been highly profitable whenever the arbs do indeed make their early move—I would recommend approaching it in this manner: try to think like the arbs do, for they will do their buying late in the day and they won't fight a declining market. So, you, too, should wait until fairly late in the trading day before buying in- or at-the-money OEX calls, *but only if the market is up on the day or has risen significantly from a much lower low.*

If those conditions are met, then buy your calls, *but you must sell them (or exercise them) at 4 P.M. that same day,* for you don't want to get stuck with them overnight. If the arbs exercise a massive quantity of OEX calls, that could force the market lower the next morning, and that would harm your long call position. So, in essence, you approach this like a very short-term day trade: buy your calls at 3 P.M. or 3:30 P.M. and get out at 4 P.M. As you can see from the example of September 1994 expiration, the market can move a great deal in the last hour or half-hour if the arbs are "operating."

A *hedged* position can also be taken, much like the one that was previously described for trading on expiration day itself. With the hedged position, you would once again buy five OEX in-the-money, short-term calls and hedge them by selling an S&P 500 futures contract.

If you are implementing this hedged strategy on Wednesday or Thursday before expiration, you should be careful not to use the S&P futures contract that expires on that Friday. Rather, you should use the "front-month" contract, which is the term that describes the active contract. For example, if it is currently September, one would buy OEX September calls, and sell the December futures contract. Experienced futures traders know that the fastest and best executions are only available in the "front-month" contract. As before, this hedged strategy should be removed at the close of trading.

However, there is another small difference between using either strategy on a Wednesday or Thursday rather than on expiration Friday itself. That difference involves exercising the OEX calls. Recall that, on expiration Friday, you can merely call your broker after the close and exercise the calls (or they will be automatically exercised for you if they are in-the-money). However, the same courtesies do *not* apply to early exercise of OEX calls. On a regular trading day, which would include the Wednesday and Thursday before expiration Friday, you must have your OEX exercise instructions in by 4 P.M. So while you may certainly have a good idea in advance of 4 P.M. (say, at 3:45 P.M. or so) whether or not you will exercise your calls, you might prefer to actually trade out of the calls after 4 P.M. rather than bother with the exercise.

The Postexpiration Effect of Futures on the Stock Market: A Trading System

Earlier, there were allusions to the fact that, in the week following expiration, the stock market often has an opposite reaction to the buy and sell programs of expiration week. In general, this is true, but as with all general statements of this kind, you must be careful if you intend to use them as a basis for trading.

Using OEX as the measure of market performance, we did some specific historical analyses of what happens to the market in the week following expiration. The results are quite interesting and have proven to be tradeable in the past.

In order to conduct this study, we needed to determine whether there were buy or sell programs during expiration week, and then determine if there was an opposite move during the week following expiration. First, we determined the largest *absolute* move that occurred the week prior to expiration, by observing the move from the second Friday of the month to either the *highest* closing price of Wednesday, Thursday, or Friday of expiration week, or to the *lowest* closing price of those three days. This gives us the information as to whether buy or sell programs occurred during the week prior to expiration.

Then, we looked at the resulting moves from expiration Friday's closing price to the minimum (maximum) closing price during the following week. So, if the market was up during the week prior to expiration, we looked for the lowest closing price of the following week to see if the market had a reverse reaction to the buy programs. Conversely, if the market was *down* during expiration week, we looked for the maximum close during the week following.

The data in Table 3.1 summarize the study (months in which there was no significant move prior to expiration were ignored). From this data, it can be seen that the market does, indeed, often have an opposite reaction to the movements of expiration week. Some traders seem to feel that this effect is more pronounced at the quarterly expirations, when S&P futures expire on the same day as OEX options. Thus, we have broken the data out for those quarterly expirations as well. In either case, the market appears to reverse about 80 percent of the time, or four months out of five.

The pertinent question, of course, is "Is there a system that can be devised to trade this phenomenon?" In order to answer that question, we ran several sets of data, with different entry points and different (or even no) stop levels. The first conclusion that we came to was that you need to use a stop of some sort. There were several expirations in which the market continued on in the same direction *after* expiration as it had been going *prior* to expiration. These are

Table 3-1
SUMMARY OF THE STUDY OF
FUTURES' POSTEXPIRATION EFFECT
ON THE STOCK MARKET

Time Period	Number of Expirations	Number of Times Market Reversed
Monthly Expirations		
All expirations	142	115 (81%)
After 1/1/85	120	97 (81%)
After 1/1/90	61	47 (77%)
Quarterly Expirations		
All quarterly	50	40 (80%)
After 1/1/85	42	34 (81%)
After 1/1/90	22	16 (73%)

losses, and some of them were quite large without using stops (interestingly, many of these came in December, a month that you might want to avoid if you are trading this system).

Surprisingly, it turns out that using an absolute stop is far superior to using a *trailing* stop. A trailing stop is one that you adjust to lock in profits as a trade moves in your favor.

Example: Suppose that you buy the S&P 500 futures at a price of 563.00 and want to use a trailing stop of 1.50 points. Initially, your stop would be 561.50. However, suppose the trade moves in your favor and the futures close at the following prices over the next few days following inception of the trade. The new trailing stop is shown for each day, as it would be recalculated after the close of trading.

S&P Futures Close	Trailing Stop	Comment
(1) 564.20	562.70	Market up, raise stop
(2) 566.10	564.60	Market up, raise stop
(3) 565.50	564.60	Market down, same stop
(4) 568.00	566.50	Market up, raise stop
(5) 566.00		Stopped out

Note that on day three, when the futures closed lower at 565.50, but not low enough to stop out the trade, the trailing stop was not lowered. It can only be raised, never lowered.

In our OEX trading system, we ran several scenarios, but these two seem to be representative: using a stop of 2.20 OEX points, or using a stop of 3.10 OEX points. In Tables 3.2 and 3.3, we break down the results by total number of trades, the number of profitable trades, OEX profit per trade, and total OEX profit over the life of the system.

The best average profit, in either table, is the more than three-point profit per trade attained by trading the quarterly expirations since 1990. However, all of the systems are reasonably good. Since 1990, the larger stop (3.10 OEX points) seems to work better, but that is probably related to the fact that OEX has been trading at a

Table 3.2
STOP = 2.20 OEX POINTS

Time Period	Number of Trades	Number of Profits	Total Profit	Average Profit
Monthly Expirations				
All expirations	133	61 (46%)	139.08	1.05
After 1/1/85	115	48 (42%)	111.02	0.97
After 1/1/90	59	25 (42%)	87.71	1.49
Quarterly Expirations				
All quarterly	48	25 (52%)	88.09	1.84
After 1/1/85	40	19 (48%)	74.48	1.86
After 1/1/90	22	12 (55%)	66.24	3.01

higher price in the 1990s than it was in the 1980s. You should also note that the studies encompassing monthly expiration summaries prior to 1990 were hurt by the October 1987 expiration that lost 27 OEX points (that is, if you bought OEX on Friday night, October 16th, you lost 27 points when it opened that much lower on Monday, October 19th).

Table 3.3
STOP = 3.10 OEX POINTS

Time Period	Number of Trades	Number of Profits	Total Profit	Average Profit
Monthly Expirations				
All expirations	133	69 (52%)	135.11	1.02
After 1/1/85	115	56 (49%)	108.10	0.94
After 1/1/90	59	30 (51%)	97.59	1.65
Quarterly Expirations				
All quarterly	48	27 (56%)	84.76	1.77
After 1/1/85	40	21 (53%)	70.92	1.77
After 1/1/90	22	14 (64%)	71.25	3.24

These results are good enough to trade, so here is the system.

Step 1. Using the OEX closes on Wednesday, Thursday, and Friday of expiration week, determine the largest change from the previous Friday's OEX close.

Example 1: Suppose OEX closes at 530 on the second Friday of the month. Then, during the ensuing week, the following closes are registered:

Day	OEX Close	Change from Second Friday
Wednesday	528.35	–1.65
Thursday	533.25	+3.25
Friday	529.50	–0.50

In this case, we would use +3.25 as the largest change, assuming buy programs on Thursday pushed the OEX to that closing high for the three-day period.

Example 2: Again, suppose OEX closed at 530 on the second Friday of another expiration month. Then, during the ensuing week, the following closes are registered:

Day	OEX Close	Change from Second Friday
Wednesday	532.05	+2.05
Thursday	529.00	–1.00
Friday	527.00	–3.00

In this case, we would use –3.00 as the largest change, indicating that sell programs on Friday pushed the OEX to that closing low.

If the absolute value of the largest change is less than 1.50 OEX points, then don't make a trade—there were apparently *no* buy or sell programs during expiration week, at least not enough to materially move the market.

Step 2. If the largest change was at least 1.50 points in one direction or the other, then do the following. If the largest change was positive (Example 1), then buy programs took place during expiration week, and *the system says to short the market*. If the largest change was negative (Example 2), then *sell programs* took place during expiration week, and the system says to *buy* the market. Given the statistics in the previous tables, you may want to take a larger position at quarterly expirations than you do at regular monthly expirations.

Step 3. Use an intraday stop of 3.10 OEX points if the market moves against you. Otherwise hold the trade until the following Friday (the Friday following expiration day) and close it down at that time. If any of the Fridays in the system are holidays, then use Thursday's close of that week instead of Friday for the appropriate calculation given earlier.

It might be better to implement this strategy by buying OEX puts or calls, rather than by buying or shorting S&P 500 futures. For example, in the debacle of 1987, your loss would have been limited had you owned OEX calls rather than S&P futures.

Finally, you should use some trading common sense. For example, if you have built up a very large profit in just a day or two of trading, it would probably be wise to realize at least a part of that profit. Even though the system says to hold on until Friday, you would be neglectful if you let the entire profit evaporate on a reverse move by OEX.

There does not seem to be any longer-term effect after expiration, as the market's results are mixed when measured one month after expiration. In fact, the percentage of months that gained ground the month after expiration are about 60 percent—approximately what one would expect to find in an ongoing bull market of such long duration.

To summarize this entire section, it is important to understand the effect of futures and options on the market at or near expiration. Moreover, this understanding can lead to profitable trades if you have correctly assessed the arbitrageurs' positions and intentions. Observing open interest can help determine the arbitrage position, as can receiving reliable reports from floor brokers. During expiration week, should you decide to trade along with the arbs, the safest way is to use the hedged strategy—buying OEX calls and selling S&P 500 futures against them, for example—but outright call buying can sometimes be attempted successfully, as well. Also, it was shown that expiration activity is often reversed to a certain extent in the week following expiration. That postexpiration phenomenon can be traded as well, using the trading system presented.

OPTIONS AS AN INSURANCE POLICY

We first entered the subject of how futures affect the market when we were discussing how derivatives can be used to hedge stocks. Examples of using *futures* as that hedge were 1980s-style portfolio insurance and program trading. Options can, of course, be used as protection for stocks as well, sometimes with greater efficiency.

We saw earlier that insurance for individual stocks can be most efficiently created by buying equity put options specifically against those stocks. This method—buying individual equity puts to protect each individual equity in your portfolio—is often the most efficient and cost-effective way of creating insurance for a portfolio of stocks. You merely buy slightly out-of-the-money puts against the individual issues that you own. For example, if you own 2,000 shares of Microsoft, selling at 93, then you might want to buy 20 Microsoft Oct 80 puts as protection. Or if you desire greater protection, then buy 20 Oct 85 puts or even Oct 90s.

You could buy puts individually for each stock in your portfolio (assuming that the stock has listed options trading). Then, when you were done, you would have a "perfect" hedge—perfect in the sense that the puts will increase in value at the same rate your stocks fall, if they fall far enough. Thus, no matter what happens to each stock individually, your puts will provide protection below their respective striking prices.

Money managers sometimes modify the insurance strategy so as to decrease the cost of the puts used as insurance: the stock owner not only buys an out-of-the-money put as insurance, but also sells an out-of-the-money call in order to pay for most or all of the cost of his put. The resultant position: long stock, long out-of-the-money put, and short out-of-the-money call, has a profit potential as shown in Figure 3.1. By using this strategy, which is called a *collar*, the stock owner is giving up some of his upside profit potential in order to lower the cost of his insurance. We'll talk more about the collar strategy shortly.

You can also protect an entire portfolio of stocks with index or sector options. This is an easier method, as you only need to place a single order and pay one commission in order to create the protection. The problems with using index options are twofold: first, there is almost certain to be tracking error. *Tracking error* is a term that describes the difference in performance between your portfolio and a broad-based index. Second, the index options often trade with an inflated implied volatility, meaning that you are "overpaying" for

Figure 3.1
THE COLLAR AS INSURANCE

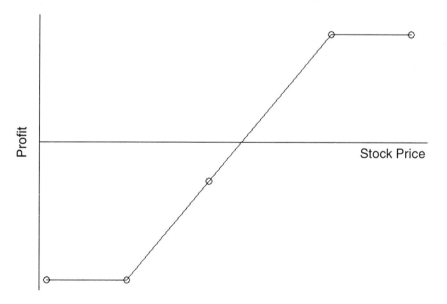

your protection. Individual equity puts often trade with an implied volatility that is very much in line with the stock's historical volatility. This means that you generally won't be overpaying for individual equity puts. In addition, there is no tracking error when you buy individual equity puts. Despite these drawbacks, many portfolio managers prefer to use index options for protection, simply because they can't physically buy options on the 300, 400, or 500 stocks that they own in their large portfolios.

Example: Suppose that a stockholder owns a rather diverse portfolio of stocks—worth $1.4 million—and he wants a temporary hedge because he feels the market is due for a sharp, short-term decline. He might decide to sell some S&P 500 futures against his portfolio. Recall that a one-point move in S&P futures is worth $500. Therefore, if the S&P 500 futures were trading at 560, then each futures contract represents $280,000 worth of protection (560 times $500 per point). He would thus sell 5 futures to hedge his $1.4 million portfolio, since $1.4 million ÷ $280,000 = 5.

Now suppose that the market does indeed drop and his portfolio loses almost 15 percent of its value, falling to $1.2 million, a loss of $200,000. Furthermore, during the market decline, the S&P 500 futures dropped by 30 points. Thus, the five S&P futures that he is short netted a profit of only $75,000.

Even though he sold an appropriate *dollar* amount of S&P 500 futures, his portfolio and the S&P 500 performed in a different manner. This difference in performance may be due to tracking error. However, it could be the Beta as well (we discuss Beta shortly). These two would account for the $125,000 net loss that he suffered in this example.

If you owned a portfolio of stocks that were the exact makeup of the S&P 500 or the OEX (S&P 100) indices, then you wouldn't have to worry about tracking error at all; you could easily compute the number of options or futures that would be required to hedge your position. However, no individual investors and few institutional investors are in this position. Rather, you usually have a portfolio of stocks that bear little resemblance to the indices themselves. However, in order to hedge this portfolio, you have to use the options or futures that are listed—ones that don't exactly match the makeup of your portfolio. So you must try to select an index that will perform more or less like your portfolio of stocks if you want to use index puts as protection. If the portfolio is broad-based, then OEX or SPX will suffice. If the portfolio is more specific, you may be better served by using puts on a Sector index.

It's a simple matter to calculate your portfolio's actual net worth, but when you are attempting to use index puts as protection— assuming you don't own *exactly* the stocks that make up the index— then you must first calculate the *adjusted* net worth of your portfolio. In order to do this, it is necessary to use a factor which we call *relative Beta*. We define relative Beta later, but for now suffice it to say that it is a measure of how each stock in the portfolio in question relates to the index that you are using as a hedge. Simply stated, if the relative Beta is 2.0, then the stock in question moves twice as fast as the index in question.

Example: To show how this calculation works, assume that a trader has a small portfolio that consists of 1,000 IBM, 2,000 General Motors, 300 Texas Instruments, and 500 AT&T. This is a rather diverse portfolio, so he might consider using a broad-based index such as the OEX Index for his hedge. In order to do so, he multiplies the actual net worth by the relative Beta in order to determine the *adjusted* net worth.

Stock	Quantity (a)	Price (b)	Net Worth (a × b = c)	Relative Beta (d)	Adjusted Net Worth (c × d)
IBM	1,000	110	110,000	1.1	121,000
GM	2,000	50	100,000	1.3	130,000
Texas Instruments	300	160	48,000	2.0	96,000
AT&T	500	50	25,000	1.0	25,000
Totals:			283,000		372,000

This portfolio's adjusted net worth is higher than its actual net worth, indicating that it is more volatile than the OEX Index. If he were comparing the portfolio to a *different* index or sector, then the relative Betas would change.

Assume that OEX is trading at 525. Then he would divide 372,000 by 525 to arrive at the number of "shares" of OEX he needs to hedge this portfolio. That division tells him that 708.57 shares of OEX would be required as a hedge. If he were going to buy OEX puts, which represent 100 shares of OEX, then he would buy seven puts as a hedge.

The preceding example is a simple one, since you would expect this portfolio to perform more or less like the stock market. Although, even *that* is a big assumption, since IBM was falling for quite some time, while the overall market was rising. The calculations become more perplexing when you have a portfolio that performs less like the broad market and more like one of the sector indices. The following examples illustrate this problem.

Example: Now suppose that we are discussing a more volatile, technology stock portfolio consisting of 2,000 Microsoft, 1,000 Intel, 500 Texas Instruments, and 500 IBM. This portfolio might perform extremely differently from the OEX Index. In fact, one of the technology sector indices might be a better hedge. First, let's see how the calculations relate to the OEX Index:

Hedging with OEX

Stock	Quantity (a)	Price (b)	Net Worth (a × b = c)	Relative Beta (d)	Adjusted Net Worth (c × d)
Microsoft	2,000	100	200,000	3.1	620,000
Intel	1,000	67	67,000	4.0	268,000
Texas Inst.	500	160	80,000	2.0	160,000
IBM	500	110	55,000	1.1	56,500
Totals:			402,000		1,104,500

This portfolio is almost three times as volatile as OEX (i.e., the adjusted net worth is almost three times the net worth). With OEX at 525, this would necessitate hedging with $1,104,500/525 = 2,103.81$ shares of OEX, or 21 OEX puts.

When the adjusted net worth is so disparate from actual net worth, you should consider using a sector index as a hedge instead. The large discrepancy between actual and adjusted net worth indicates that tracking error could be a large problem. There is a Semiconductor Sector Index (Symbol: SOX) that might be a better hedge for this high-tech portfolio. Each stock has a totally different relative Beta when the SOX Index is considered.

Hedging with SOX

Stock	Quantity (a)	Price (b)	Net Worth (a × b = c)	Relative Beta (d)	Adjusted Net Worth (c × d)
Microsoft	2,000	100	200,000	1.2	240,000
Intel	1,000	67	67,000	1.5	100,500
Texas Inst.	500	160	80,000	1.0	80,000
IBM	500	110	55,000	0.7	38,500
Totals:			402,000		458,500

Using the SOX Index gives us a much closer relationship between actual and adjusted net worth. Since the SOX Index is trading at about 300, you would need 458,400/300 = 1,528 shares of SOX to hedge this portfolio. Or you would need to buy about 15 SOX puts.

Note: The reason that the relative Betas are smaller for the SOX Index is that the index itself is quite volatile—as are these stocks—so on a *relative* basis, the index's volatility is much closer to the portfolio's volatility.

This might be a good time to describe how to compute the relative Beta. *Beta* is a statistical measure that is used by portfolio managers to correlate how well a certain stock "tracks" the broad stock market. There are two problems with using Beta: (1) the Betas that are published are generally for a long period of time, such as one or two years, and that is an awfully long time to be measuring how a stock performs, and (2) Beta is not really a measure of volatility, but of direction *and* volatility. Thus, a stock that goes up when the market goes down will have a small Beta, even though it might be a relatively volatile stock.

IBM is a classic example of a relatively volatile stock that has a low Beta—at least in the summer of 1995—because it has correlated poorly with the stock market in recent years. For example, IBM fell from 140 to 47 during 1991 and 1992, while the broad stock market was rising about 20 percent. Then, from the summer of 1994 through the summer of 1995, IBM doubled in price, while the broad stock market rose 31 percent. The Beta had fallen to 0.86 by the end of 1992, reflecting the negative correlation between IBM and the broad market. But, by the summer of 1995, it had risen to 1.52! So which one is correct? *Both*, but at different times; that's why it's sometimes difficult to use Beta as the *relative* Beta.

Other measures of volatility that option traders are familiar with are the historical volatility and implied volatility of the stock's options. Because you can also compute the historical and implied volatilities for an index or sector and its options, *you can construct another measure of relative Beta by dividing the stock's volatility by that of the index.* For example, in the summer of 1995, IBM's historical volatility was approximately 24 percent and OEX's historical volatility was about 12 percent, so the relative Beta would be $24/12 = 2.0$. Incidentally, the same calculation done for IBM at the end of 1992 would have yielded a very similar result. So, this method of computing relative Beta is more stable, as the volatility of a stock tends to remain fairly constant, even though its price may change.

Either using historical or implied volatility for computing relative Beta is acceptable, although my gut feeling is that the historical volatility method gives a better picture of how the stock is going to perform, and thus reduces tracking error.

The following fact, mentioned earlier, is worth repeating: *If, when you compute the adjusted net worth with respect to a certain index, there is a large difference between the actual net worth and the adjusted net worth, then you might be subjecting yourself to a rather large tracking error exposure by using that index.* Thus, you should be willing to use sector indices to hedge small portfolios and/or portfolios that do not correlate well with the broad market.

There are further nuances involved in hedging a portfolio of stocks, and we will touch on some of them now. The preceding examples involved calculating the number of "shares" of the index that were needed as a hedge. That number was then converted into "number of puts to buy" merely by dividing by 100. This assumes that you are buying at-the-money puts as protection. In reality, this protection won't be full protection until the index falls and the put's delta nears 1.0 (actually, *minus* 1.0).

If you were to buy out-of-the-money puts, their protective quality wouldn't kick in until the index fell below the striking price of those puts. So, to be correct, you should convert the *adjusted net worth* directly into "number of puts" to buy, by using the following formula, which is quite similar to what we did earlier:

$$\text{Number of puts to buy} = \frac{\text{adjusted net worth}}{100 \times \text{strike price of put}}$$

Example: returning to the first OEX example, in which the portfolio consisted of IBM, GM, Texas Instruments, and AT&T, recall that the adjusted net worth was $372,000 vis-à-vis the OEX Index. OEX was trading at 525 at the time. In order to determine how many puts to buy, according to the preceding formula, you would arrive at the following figures:

Insurance Put Strike Price	Formula Result	Number of Puts to Buy
525	7.0857	7
500	7.4400	7 or 8
475	7.8316	8

You can see that you would buy slightly more puts at lower strikes because you need them to provide "full" protection should the index fall to that lower level. Of course, the protective capability of these out-of-the-money puts doesn't take effect until the index drops in price. For example, with OEX at 525, if you buy the 475 puts, then you don't have any real protection until the index falls almost 10 percent (50/525 = 9.5%).

Buying out-of-the-money puts is a cheaper form of insurance—almost like disaster insurance. As with any type of insurance, whether it be fire, personal injury, etc.—it costs less if there is a smaller probability of actually being used. Thus, the total dollars spent on insurance will be far less if you buy out-of-the-money puts than if you buy at-the-money puts. You need to make a decision on two things: (1) the length of the insurance, and (2) the deductible portion that you are willing to assume. As always, the bigger the deductible that you assume, the lower your insurance premiums will be. For example, many self-employed individuals have opted for high-deductible health insurance; they are willing to pay a couple of thousand dollars of medical expenses themselves, but are insured for anything over that amount, in case a real medical crisis arises. The cost of that form of insurance is much lower than a normal individual policy.

The type of insurance you select for your stock portfolio can be structured in a similar manner. The "deductible" portion of portfolio insurance is the distance between the current index value and the striking price of the out-of-the-money put that you are purchasing. With OEX at 585, you might buy Dec 575 puts and have very little deductible—only 10 OEX points, or about 2 percent. This means that if your portfolio performs in line with OEX, your portfolio would be protected if OEX fell below 575. Your portfolio would lose money while OEX declined from 585 to 575, but below that level it would be protected.

This low-deductible policy would be fairly costly insurance—the puts would be rather expensive since they're not very far out-of-the-money. On the other hand, you might decide to buy the 550 strike, which has a much larger deductible of 35 OEX points, or 6 percent. That would be less costly because the puts are farther out-of-the-money.

So, in the final analysis of purchasing insurance, you must know what it costs and what kind of protection it provides. Thus, I would recommend making a table similar to the one shown in the next example.

Example: Suppose that a money manager has a portfolio that has an *adjusted* net worth of $1.7 million. He wants to use OEX as a hedge, but is uncertain about what strike price to use as well as what expiration date to use. He might make a spreadsheet similar to the following one in order to help him decide.

First, use the formula given earlier to decide how many puts to buy, depending on the striking price involved:

Number of OEX Puts to Buy

Striking Price of Protective Put	Number of Puts Needed as Protection
450	38
475	36
500	34
525	32

Now, assume that the following prices exist for puts of varying expirations at these striking prices. These prices conform closely with actual OEX put prices in effect during the late summer of 1995. The longer-term puts have higher implied volatilities than the short-term puts do; this is to be expected, and is a fact that buyers of insurance have to live with.

Prices of Various OEX Puts

| | Expiration | | |
Strike	Dec 1995	Dec 1996	Dec 1997
450	1	10	17
475	3	14	21
500	6	20	28
525	13	27	35

Now, using the "number of puts to buy" from the first table in this example, and the prices in this table, we can calculate the *actual cost* of insurance for these various striking prices and expiration dates. Obviously, longer-term insurance is going to cost more, and so is insurance with a higher striking price because it provides more immediate protection (i.e., it has a smaller deductible).

Actual Dollar Cost of Insurance

| | Expiration | | |
Strike	Dec 1995 ($)	Dec 1996 ($)	Dec 1997 ($)
450	3,800	38,000	64,600
475	10,800	50,400	75,600
500	20,400	68,000	95,200
525	41,600	86,400	112,000

Finally, convert these actual dollar amounts into percentages of the actual net worth in order to see how the purchase of this insurance might affect performance figures.

Cost of Insurance as a Percent of Net Worth

Strike	Dec 1995 (%)	Dec 1996 (%)	Dec 1997 (%)
	Expiration		
450	0.2	2.2	3.8
475	0.6	3.0	4.4
500	1.2	4.0	5.6
525	2.4	5.1	6.6

This portfolio manager can now see that if he buys the longest term protection, using at-the-money options (Dec 1997 expiration, 525 strike), he will have to pay 6.6 percent of the current value of his portfolio. If the market rallies over that time period, his performance will be 6.6 percent worse (about 3 percent annually, since there are more than two years of life in those puts) than some money manager who did not buy puts. If he wants cheaper protection, he can buy out-of-the-money puts, or shorter-term puts.

Earlier, we described the *collar*, a strategy in which the stockholder not only buys an out-of-the-money put, but also sells an out-of-the-money call as a means of financing the put. This has been a very popular strategy with index options in the past few years, and has been somewhat responsible for keeping OEX puts expensive and OEX calls cheap, relatively speaking.

THE COLLAR

Using options to protect your portfolio is, for most people, more of a theoretical exercise than a practical application. By that I mean that most people *think* about using puts to protect their stocks—and they might even look at a few prices in the newspaper and figure out how much it would cost to hedge themselves—but when it comes right down to it, most people consider the put cost too expensive and therefore don't bother buying the protection.

Especially in a bull market, an investor may feel that money spent buying puts was merely flushed down the drain. That laissez faire attitude could get you in trouble, however. Do you have that same perspective on your homeowner's insurance? It's something akin to feeling that fire insurance is unnecessary because the house hasn't burned down before (or recently). The comparison, admittedly, is not a direct one because a natural disaster can occur on a moment's notice, while a decline in stock prices is usually less sudden—unless another crash were to occur—so you would have some chance to buy insurance for your stocks as prices started to fall. However, if you are sitting on large stock profits, you should take a serious look at buying protection using options.

One approach that I like that limits the cost of insurance, although it may remove some or all of your upside profit potential, is the *collar*. In this protection strategy, you buy an out-of-the-money put as insurance and also sell an out-of-the-money call to help finance the cost of the insurance. Thus, you have placed a sort of collar on your stock—you have limited downside risk, but have limited upside profit potential as well. Often, with a collar, it is assumed that you sell calls and buy puts in equal quantity. However, there is a modification to the collar strategy that is useful because you don't necessarily have to eliminate all of your upside profit potential.

Example: Disney (DIS) was on a strong run in 1995, but suffered a setback in late November after earnings were announced. The stock was selling at about 61, and perhaps a holder of 1,000 shares would like to lock in some of the 50 percent-plus gains generated by the stock that year. Assume that he is willing to risk 10 percent (down to 55), but wants insurance if DIS falls farther than that. The following prices exist:

DIS: 61   April 55 put: 1⅛   April 65 call: 2¼

Since the call is selling for twice the price of the put, he can sell 5 April 65 calls and buy 10 April 55 puts without actually laying out any money. Then, not only is his entire 1,000-share position protected at exactly 55, but he will make profits up to 65 on all of his shares. Even if prices rise beyond 65, he still has 500 shares that are not covered by the calls that were sold, and those 500 shares can provide upside profit potential.

This form of the collar is often a more palatable type of insurance to many investors, since there is no actual cost (in the form of a debit) for the insurance. The cost comes in the form of reduced upside profit potential. With this form of collar, however, you don't even have to give up all of your upside profit potential, only a portion of it. This type of collar even works for highly volatile stocks. Try looking at the option prices on the most extended stock in your portfolio, and you may find a collar that fits like a glove.

HEDGING WITH OVER-THE-COUNTER OPTIONS

Another avenue that many large institutional stockholders use in order to hedge their stock portfolios is over-the-counter options. As described in Chapter 1, these over-the-counter options are transactions between two parties directly, not traded on an exchange. Typically, these over-the-counter transactions can be tailored exactly to what the portfolio manager wants, so he can buy puts and sell calls on his exact stock portfolio, and he can utilize nonstandard striking prices if he wants to. Tracking error can be completely eliminated in this manner, for the over-the-counter put can be constructed as a put on *exactly* the stocks in the money manager's portfolio at that time.

The ability to utilize nonstandard strikes can be advantageous. Suppose the stock owner says, "I want to protect my portfolio if the market declines by more than 8 percent. At what strike can I sell a call that will cover the cost of a put with that protection?" The over-the-counter option dealer (typically a large trading firm such as Goldman, Sachs or Morgan Stanley) will then return to him with an offer such as, "You can sell calls 10 percent out-of-the-money and buy puts 8 percent out-of-the-money for the same price on each." This strategy can be used for a single stock or for an entire portfolio; the trading firm will structure the options to fit the portfolio manager's wishes.

There are even more "complicated" options that are being used in the current markets in order to hedge portfolios. They fall in the category of *exotic options*. Exotic options are ones whose values may be dependent on a vast array of conditional parameters.

One simple type of exotic option is called a *down-and-out* option. This option behaves like a normal option, except that it has an additional feature: *if the stock drops to a preset price at any time prior to expiration, the option automatically becomes worthless.* For example, if IBM is currently at 110, then someone might buy a Dec 110 call that is down-and-out at 100. So, if IBM drops to 100 at any time before the December expiration of the option, the call becomes worthless at that time. Otherwise, if IBM never falls that far, then the option behaves just like a normal call and has value if IBM is over 110 at expiration.

You may wonder why anyone would want to buy an option that could "disappear" like that. The main reason is that it's cheaper than an ordinary listed IBM Dec 110 call. It's cheaper because there's a greater chance that the down-and-out option will be worthless. So, if the call buyer feels that IBM will *not* trade at 100 during the life of the call, he can buy a cheaper option initially by utilizing the exotic option as opposed to a listed option.

These exotic options can be structured in many different and imaginative ways. An entire book could probably be written just describing these exotic options. That is beyond the scope of what we are attempting to discuss here. However, there is one interesting exotic option that is being used today as a means of portfolio insurance: the *pay-later option*. This kind of exotic option is obtained for free, initially, and only has to be paid for if the option finishes in-the-money at expiration. Thus, a money manger who wants downside protection might contact an over-the-counter firm and buy a pay-later put option. If the market goes up, this money manager owes no money and his performance is the same as any of his competing money managers who did not own insurance. He only has to pay for the put if the market does indeed collapse. He doesn't get a completely free ride, of course, for if the market drops and the put has to be paid for, it will be far more expensive than an ordinary listed put would have been. This is just one example of the many ways that exotic options are being used by sophisticated money managers.

Whenever over-the-counter options are concerned, the Option Clearing Corporation is *not* involved. This could present a problem at some time in the future. Recall that most of these options represent a transaction between a customer (institution) and a large brokerage firm, which is creating these options. Thus, the large firm acquires a position that it eventually must hedge. For example, if money managers are repeatedly buying put options as protection—in whatever exotic form they may be—the brokerage firm is selling those puts. There is the possibility that eventually, the brokerage firm's position may become quite large: they could be short many puts.

The possibility that this might happen worries many regulators, for they realize that these large firms must hedge their positions. If the market falls and the firms are short a lot of puts, then they must either sell stocks or sell futures in order to hedge those short puts. Does that have a familiar ring to it? It's exactly what happened in the crash of 1987, when there was a rush by the portfolio insurance crowd to sell futures. Of course, no one wants to see that scenario repeated, and the large firms do their best to find over-the-counter sellers of puts to help offset their positions. The worrisome part of this scenario is that no one knows the total extent of the exposure. There are no open interest figures that need to be reported and no reports that are filed. Therefore, there always exists the possibility that a dramatic down market could turn into another crash if there is a rush to hedge the over-the-counter positions.

SUMMARY

In this chapter, we presented some basic option methodology that can be very profitable in a number of situations. An understanding of the option positions that are equivalent to being long or short the underlying is a useful tool, and a mandatory one for futures traders. Considerable time was spent explaining how great an effect S&P futures have on the stock market, and then strategies were laid out for profiting from that knowledge, especially at expiration of options and futures. Finally, techniques for protecting a portfolio of stocks with options were demonstrated.

4 The Predictive Power of Options

Options can sometimes be a very useful tool for predicting the movement of the underlying instrument. In certain cases, option statistics are sentiment indicators, indicating what the "public" is doing. In other cases, it pays to watch option volume and pricing levels because "smart money" might be buying options in preparation for a move by an underlying stock. In this chapter, we explore how to use and interpret option statistics for the purposes of trading the underlying.

USING STOCK OPTION VOLUME AS AN INDICATOR

Most traders have noticed, or at least have heard financial commentators mention, the fact that a takeover offer or other surprise corporate announcement was "tipped" off by heavy option trading on the day(s) preceding the actual announcement. Obviously, someone had advance knowledge of the corporate event, or at least rumors were strongly circulating among the "in crowd." Of course, most people only find out about this heavy volume *after* the fact.

A significant increase in the trading volume of a stock's options often is a precursor of movement by the underlying stock. This statement is only true if the volume is speculative in nature. If the increased volume is due to irrelevant factors, such as arbitrage or spread trading, then it is meaningless as far as predicting stock movement. Later, we discuss methods for screening out such irrelevant data.

The reason that the preceding statement is true is leverage. Those with inside knowledge will buy options because they can score highly leveraged gains when that knowledge becomes fact. For the same reason—leverage—they prefer to buy options rather than stock. Their "tracks" are visible to the entire investment community, in terms of increased option trading volume. Whether or not those insiders are acting legally is unimportant, for it is perfectly legal to monitor option volume and trade accordingly.

I've had some traders argue with the premise that those with inside information buy options rather than stock, and I usually ask them this question: If you had tomorrow's newspaper, what would you do, buy stock or options? Actually, the correct answer to that question is "play the lottery," but you get the point. If you know you have an almost sure thing, you would look to maximize your percentage returns as much as possible. By the way, if you ever *do* get a copy of tomorrow's paper and there isn't any lottery tomorrow, then head out to the race track.

It should be pointed out that stock volume often increases as well, prior to major corporate announcements. Some of the stock volume is spillover from the option pits as market makers rush to buy stock to cover some of the options they have been selling in the course of making markets. Also, the stock market is generally more liquid than the option market, so the insiders may be forced to buy stock in order to amass a large position. However, it is the option volume that provides the most reliable clues to the major corporate announcements that make stocks move: earnings reports, takeovers or mergers, and filings or settlements of major lawsuits.

How Much Is Too Much?

When looking for "increased option volume," don't be concerned with the most active options. These are two distinctly different things: *Increased option volume* refers to the amount of trading in a stock's options *compared to the average number of options traded on that stock*. The stocks with the heaviest option volume are likely to be IBM or Philip Morris, for example, but *any* stock can see its option volume shoot up to high levels when compared to its normal volume.

On a typical day in the summer of 1995, the most active optionable stocks and their average option volume were:

Stock	Total Option Volume	Average Option Volume
IBM	37,705	33,743
Intel	36,984	30,688
Micron Tech	25,539	21,569
Microsoft	22,455	21,371
Compaq	18,409	11,973

As you can see, the high-tech stocks dominated the trading volume. There is very little that is unusual in these figures when you compare the total volume for that particular day with the average volume. However, these volume figures were also traded on that same day:

Stock	Total Option Volume	Average Option Volume
Novell	24,410	8,489
Home Shopping	1,430	148
Integrated Silicon	1,158	368
Maxtor	1,670	557

You can see that the ratio of total option volume to average volume on each of these four stocks was at least 3-to-1, and was quite a bit larger for Home Shopping Network. On that particular day, Novell's option volume was due to news that was already out (bad earnings), but the other three were definitely ones to watch, as their option volume might be foretelling some significant corporate news. As it eventually turned out, not much happened in Home Shopping or Maxtor, but the Integrated Silicon volume was another story. The option volume shown here mostly consisted of puts, which was a bearish indication by the options. The stock fell 14 points within a week, an excellent trade produced by option volume.

It is situations of this latter variety that can alert you to stocks that are about to make significant moves. If there is excessive call option volume, then you would expect to see positive news announced soon and would look to buy the underlying stock. If there is excessive put option volume, then a short sale is possible because bad news may be just around the corner. If there is excessive volume in both the puts and the calls, it is my experience that the stock is generally leaning to the positive side, but not always, so you should be ready for a breakout in either direction and follow it in that case.

The Analysis

Now let's discuss, theoretically, the steps to follow after first spotting a potential true high-volume situation. After that, we discuss some of the specifics (and problems) involved with applying this theory. Experience has taught us that only situations in which today's total option volume is greater than *double* the "average" option volume are worth exploring, and where the options are normally very active, an even greater ratio is desirable. Once one of these high-volume situations has been identified, some additional work must be done.

First, you must screen out situations where the option volume is related to nonspeculative things, such as arbitrage. On a given day, you may find between 40 and 60 different stocks that have traded double their average option volume. As expiration approaches each month, that number can swell to well over 100 underlying issues. In reality, only a handful of these have true speculative volume; the others can be disregarded after careful analysis. This analysis can be time-consuming, but computers can help to a certain extent. Over the years, though, we have found that it can be a mistake to let the computers screen out too many situations. If you miss just one 20-point takeover because you were trying to save yourself a couple of minutes of analysis each day, you will rue your decision.

One screen is to see if too much of the total volume is concentrated in too few options. *If almost all of the option volume is concentrated in one series (that is, just one call or just one put), then it is unlikely that anything special is going on with that stock.* For example, if most of the total volume is in one call series, then it is quite likely that an institution executed a sale of calls against stock that they own. This sale of options would most likely be executed at one time and would appear on the tape as a block sale (if you have access to option time and sales, you would readily spot this fact). On the other hand, if most of the volume is in one put series, then an institution probably bought a block of puts to protect a holding in the underlying stock. In either case, the trade, no matter how large it is and how many times it exceeds the average volume, has nothing to do with supposed corporate developments. Thus, this situation should be rejected as not having any trading viability.

This situation is fairly common; ones like it occur almost every day. For example, assume that total option volume in XYZ options was 1,385 contracts, while average option volume at the time was only 250 total contracts per day. Thus, this situation would show up on the initial computer runs. Suppose the stock had closed at 35 that day. Upon further inspection, however, this is how that volume broke down:

Option	Volume
Sep 35 call	1,350 contracts
Sep 30 put	23 contracts
Oct 40 call	12 contracts

Thus, even though total volume of 1,385 contracts was significant in light of the fact that average volume is only 250 contracts, it appears that a block trade of 1,300 or more contracts took place. We say this is a block trade because there is only significant volume in the one series: the Sep 35 call. In fact, if you subtract out the block trade, you often have a situation where option volume was *below* average that day.

If the volume is predominantly concentrated in one series, but is not identifiable as a block trade from the time and sales tape, it is probably still not noteworthy. It is our feeling that if the public (which includes unknown inside traders) enters the marketplace and repeatedly buys one option series, the market makers end up selling them most of the options. The market makers are, by definition, risk averse. They attempt to make their money, if possible, by buying on the bid and selling on the offer. If they can do that repeatedly and go home "flat" every night, they would be quite satisfied. When there is large demand in one series, the market makers cannot get flat, so they must hedge themselves by buying other options to partially offset the ones they are selling to the public. When they do this, the heavy option volume propagates itself out from the series that the speculators are buying into other months and striking prices. This telltale "picture" is what we look for to define a true speculative situation. We show some examples of it shortly. For now, suffice it to say that if nearly all the option volume is concentrated in one series, then there is very little chance (note, we do not say *no* chance) that a true speculative position is at hand.

There is always an exception to any rule, and the exception to this concentration of volume screen may occur in a low-priced stock. If a stock is selling for less than $5 per share, it is possible that the only striking price for its options is 5. Moreover, since you can fairly assume that the stock has been declining for some time in order to be so low-priced, there is probably very little activity in the options. In such a case, there may be virtually no options offered in the midterm or long-term options. Thus, if "insiders" come in to buy options from the market makers, the market makers may have no place to go to buy other options (they can always buy stock, of course, but it would be in fragmented pieces so it would be hard to spot). Thus, at the end of the day, almost all of the option volume might be concentrated in one series because that is the only series that is virtually available for trading.

Suppose that XYZ is a $4 stock, and that it has been depressed at those levels for some time. The option exchange may even be considering delisting it. At one time there were striking prices of 15, 12½, 10, and 7½, but these are all now delisted because they have no open interest. Suppose it is June, and that the only options available for trading are the July 5s, August 5s, and October 5s.

An insider wants to buy options in XYZ because he knows that the company is going to announce the signing of a large contract that will spur the stock and make it rise in price. He first attempts to buy the July 5 calls, and the market makers sell him several hundred before they realize that this is such a large buyer. Since this is a rather illiquid issue, there are no offers to speak of in either the Aug 5 calls or the Oct 5 calls. In fact, these same market makers won't sell those calls, of course. Finally, they are forced to buy stock as a hedge. The insider is probably buying stock by now, too, since they won't sell him any more calls.

The end result is that we have a truly speculative situation, but at day's end almost all of the option volume is concentrated in the one series—the July 5 calls. This is a stock that option volume watchers should want to be in, but they will "screen" themselves out of it if they blindly apply the screen that discards all situations in which the option volume is mostly in one series.

Another reason that there may be a large increase in volume is because a spread trade has been executed. There are option strategists who control rather large sums of money and who sometimes execute large ratio spreads, vertical spreads, or combinations. Again, this type of trading has nothing to do with predicting forthcoming corporate announcements, and we must screen it out also. *Thus, if almost all of the option volume is concentrated in just two series, especially if the two series have approximately equal volume, then once again it is unlikely that a true speculative situation exists.*

Suppose XYZ is trading at 50, and we notice the following option activity at the end of a trading day.

Average volume: 100 contracts

Today's volume:

Option	Volume
Feb 50 call	400 contracts
Feb 55 call	425 contracts
March 50 call	40 contracts
Total volume:	865 contracts

On the surface, this looks like a huge option volume day, since 865 contracts traded as opposed to the average of a mere 100 contracts. However, most of the volume was in just two series—the Feb 50 and Feb 55 calls—so it looks like this was a spread positioned by a nonspeculative trader. We would discard this stock from further consideration as a trading candidate for that day.

Another screening "rule" will also get rid of arbitrage situations. In conversion or reversal arbitrage, the arbitrageur takes a position that is equivalent to the underlying stock. This is the type of trade that we discussed at length for some other applications, in Chapter 3: Buying the calls and selling the puts with the same terms is the same as being long the stock. If a large arbitrage has taken place, then we will notice increased volume in just those two series—the put and the call with the same terms. If that constitutes most of the option volume, then we can ignore the situation as having much validity in terms of a true prognostication.

This time, suppose XYZ is trading at 40, with the following option volume:

Average volume: 300 contracts

Today's volume:

Option	Volume
March 45 call	700 contracts
March 45 put	700 contracts
March 40 call	250 contracts

Total volume: 1,450 contracts

Once again, we would probably discard this situation as it appears that the volume in the March 45 calls and puts is part of an arbitrage (or a stock equivalent position, as described in Chapter 2).

Further screens can be applied. For example, a significant portion of the option volume will consist of at- or out-of-the-money options if insiders are doing the buying. Remember, they are attempting to use leverage, so they will normally attempt to buy the cheapest options possible. *Thus, if you see that a large amount of the daily volume is being contributed by deeply in-the-money options, then you can be reasonably assured that this situation can be discarded.*

Suppose XYZ is trading at 48 and option volume is heavy at 1,000 contracts as compared to the average volume of 250 contracts. However, the distribution of the option volume looks like this:

Option	Price	Volume
Oct 40 call	8½	400 contracts
Sep 35 call	13	400 contracts
Sep 45 call	4	150 contracts
Sep 50 call	1½	50 contracts

Here, 80 percent of the volume is in options that are 8 or 13 points in-the-money. If the call buying were being done by speculators with some sort of inside information, they would want leverage. They would buy the Sep 50 call and the Sep 45 call before they would buy the more expensive in-the-money calls.

Admittedly, you would get some leverage by owning an 8½ dollar call or a 13 dollar call as opposed to a 48 dollar stock, but that wouldn't be your first choice if you had inside information. Thus, we would have to conclude that this option volume is not predicting any corporate developments. It is more likely that a quasi arbitrage or deeply in-the-money spread or covered write was established by an institutional or arbitrage trader.

There is an exception to this screen also, and it involves put options. There is a strategy that some very large traders use in order to get short stock in a fairly easy manner. Suppose that you had a large amount of capital at your disposal, and you knew that a stock was about to get some bad news. Or perhaps it was already trading down some, and you were having trouble getting an uptick to short the stock. No problem. If you could just buy a block of stock and simultaneously buy some in-the-money puts at parity, your problem would be solved. Why? Because you could then just sell your stock, which is long, as sloppily and rapidly as you wanted in the open market. This would leave you with just the long puts, which would of course be increasing in value as you pummelled the stock. After you were done selling your long stock, you would probably have scared other stockholders into selling, so they would be pushing the stock down farther and increasing the value of your puts as well. Finally, you could exercise your puts to get short if you wanted to, but there wouldn't really be any necessity for that.

You might say that this all sounds well and good, but how could the trader just buy stock and buy puts in large size so easily? The answer is that an arbitrageur will take the other side of the trade, merely in order to earn interest on the credit balance generated by selling the stock and selling the puts. Eventually, when the speculative trader exercises the puts, the arbitrageur will be assigned and his position will disappear.

This example is in two parts. The first part shows the arbitrage, and the second shows how the situation looks to the trader who is monitoring option volume. Assume that it is early in July, and XYZ is selling at 22, and an insider knows bad earnings are on the way. He buys some out-of-the-money puts and a negative rumor circulates on the Street. A large, aggressive trader gets wind of the rumor and decides to capitalize on the situation also.

The large trader calls up an arbitrageur and asks if he would sell the stock (short) and sell the July 30 puts. The arbitrageur says that he will, subject to being able to borrow the stock. A check with the stock loan department shows that 60,000 shares of the stock are available for borrowing. Thus the following trade takes place as two block trades, the stock being executed probably on a regional stock exchange, and the options being executed on the option exchange.

Large Trader	Arbitrageur
Buys 60,000 XYZ at 22⅛ (an uptick)	Sells short 60,000 XYZ at 22⅛ (an uptick)
Buys 600 July 30 puts at 7⅞	Sells 600 July 30 puts at 7⅞
Net money: $1,800,000 debit	$1,800,000 credit

As long as the position is in place, the arbitrageur is earning interest on $1,800,000. The arbitrageur has risk that the stock could rise above 30, in which case it would cost him more than $1,800,000 to buy his position back. But, the large trader will tacitly assure the arbitrageur that the puts will be exercised before that happens. Note that when the puts are exercised, the arbitrageur's position is completely closed out: the put exercise causes him to be assigned—that is, the arb buys stock—60,000 shares at 30.

Meanwhile, the large trader begins to sell the 60,000 shares that he is long into the open market. He "pounds" the stock downward until he draws out other big sellers, at which point he buys back the stock for a nice profit, exercises his puts, and closes out both his and the arb's positions. This may take place in as short a period as one day, or it may stretch out a little. There are also slight variations on the order of events that the large trader transacts after the arbitrage position is established, but the end result is the same: the stock goes down.

Now, suppose that separate from all of this, you are monitoring the option volume of XYZ on that first day and you notice that 850 contracts traded, while average volume was only 250. Furthermore, these contracts are mostly puts, but they have this distribution:

Option	Volume
Sep 20 put	200 contracts (bought by the insider)
Sep 20 call	50 contracts (unknown origin)
Sep 30 put	600 contracts (described above)

If you blindly applied the screen against in-the-money options, you would ignore this situation, but since puts are involved, a closer look is required. If the stock starts to "tank," you should probably buy some puts yourself, as you can then be fairly certain that whoever bought those 600 in-the-money puts is hammering the stock, and you can ride his coattails profitably.

The last major screen that is usually applied is one concerning the expiration dates of the options that are most heavily traded: the near-terms or the far-terms. For reasons of leverage once again, the speculators with inside information will buy the near-term options (assuming that they are not too near-term), for these are cheaper in price and are generally the most liquid contracts. The one exception would be if the most near-term options are going to expire in a matter of just days, then the majority of volume might move out one month to the next contract. However, if a majority of the volume is concentrated in longer-term contracts, then you would have to suspect that institutions are writing covered calls; they often prefer to write call options with several months of life remaining or buy midterm puts as protection.

As mentioned earlier, the approach of an expiration Friday can cause option volume to increase in many issues. This is because many option traders either close out their positions or roll them out to the next month. These activities are again among those that are *not* indicative of speculative activity, but are just in the normal course of events. Of course, such activities will still show up in the initial test when you look for stocks whose daily option volume is at least double the average volume.

Most option traders who have positions in expiring options will wait until nearly the last trading day—the third Friday of the month—before closing out those positions, although some expiration-related activity begins on Wednesday and increases on Thursday. Thus, the observer of option volume must allow for this potential increase in activity when he is applying his screens. On expiration Friday itself, he can literally ignore all trading in the expiring options as having anything to do with speculation. In addition, some of the volume in the next month's options—whatever amount is related to positions being rolled out to later months—is irrelevant as speculation also.

On the Thursday before expiration, these same statements are *mostly* true, although there have been a few cases throughout the history of listed options where a takeover did occur on expiration Friday. One of those was Gerber, whose story was related in Chapter 1. Another occurred back in 1987.

Farmer's Group options had been extremely active all day on the Thursday prior to expiration; moreover, a substantial portion of that volume was in options that were expiring the next day. Option volume continued to be heavy on expiration day itself. Rumors were running rampant that a takeover of the insurance company was imminent. However, by the time the stock market closed, there was no news of the merger. Moreover, when the time had come to submit exercise notices, there was still no announcement. However, it was not long thereafter that news of a large takeover was announced. Thus, it was necessary to monitor the Thursday volume in expiring options in order to "catch" this takeover.

So, while you can ignore *most* of the volume in options that are going to expire in two or three days as being irrelevant due to expiration, it would be a mistake to be dogmatic and say that all such volume can be ignored. Thus, as expiration approaches, you will have a larger and larger universe to screen. The screening process itself thus becomes more of an art than a science as expiration approaches. My general guideline is that I will tend to eliminate any situation near expiration unless the option volume is truly dramatic, probably at least three or four times the average volume. And even

then, of course, that volume must pass all of the previously mentioned screens.

There is another "message" that stock options can give you at
expiration: they can often tell you *whether "old" rumors are still
alive*. This information can be gleaned by seeing what the option volume looks like in a stock that was recently a takeover rumor, perhaps
a month or so before expiration. At the time of the initial rumor,
traders buy call options. However, if the rumor dies down, they continue to hold many of these calls all the way to expiration, hoping for
the best. At expiration, they will sell these calls to recoup what they
can. Then, if the rumor is still alive, they will buy calls in the next
expiration month. So, as an observer of these option activities, if you
see that all of the volume in a recent rumor stock is concentrated in
the expiring options, then you can assume that the rumor is "dead."
However, if you see approximately equal volume in the expiring
options and the options of the next month, then you can assume that
the rumor is still alive. Knowing this, you can continue to monitor the
stock for signs of a breakout.

So, now that we have spent a great deal of time describing what
to screen out, we will show you what a real takeover- (or rumor-)
inspired option volume pattern looks like. This is one that we spotted
for the customers of our daily service.

On July 26, 1995, Southern Pacific Railroad (RSP) suddenly spurted a
point higher, from 19 to 20, in one day. Option volume was heavy. Nearly
2,600 contracts traded that day—almost all of which were calls—as
opposed to an average volume of less than 900 contracts daily. August
expiration was more than three weeks away, so there was plenty of trading
in the August options. The call option volume looked like this:

RSP: 20; July 26

Strike Price	Expiration		
	Aug	Sep	Nov
12½ calls			30
15 calls	25	50	
17½ calls	220	88	
20 calls	1,100	580	120

Only a few puts had traded: 140 of the Aug 17½ puts and 230 of the Nov 230 puts.

The strike price of 20 was the highest strike price available. Note the preponderance of call volume at that strike. That is good. Also, note how the August calls are the most active at the two highest strikes; that is also good. In addition, the put volume doesn't seem to indicate that much, if any, arbitrage was going on, since there is very little matching of call volume and put volume in the same series. Finally, there doesn't really seem to be much, if any, spread activity either; even if all of the in-the-money calls were related to spreads against the calls with a striking price of 20 (and they most assuredly are not *all* in that category), that would still leave a lot of speculative activity in both the Aug 20 and Sep 20 calls. In fact, it is more logical to assume that the Nov 20 calls and many of the in-the-money calls were bought by market makers as a hedge against the Aug 20 and Sep 20 calls they were selling to the public.

All in all, this is a "classic" volume pattern, and it was justified. Option volume remained high as the stock oscillated back and forth around 20 for the next five days. Then, on the sixth day, the stock received a takeover bid from Union Pacific Railroad.

Analysis in Real Time

You have surely noticed that all of analyses are based on closing option volume and closing prices. Most of the time, this is sufficient because option volume will generally begin to significantly increase at least two days or more in advance of a major corporate news announcement. In fact, I am often suspicious of option volume that "springs up" only on the day before an expected announcement, such as an earnings report. However, there have been cases where option volume is related to a takeover that occurs the next day. Thus, waiting for the market to close before doing the analysis may cost you some profit opportunities.

On December 16, 1994, Caesar's World options traded nearly 2,500 contracts and the stock jumped two points. Average option volume was just over 400 contracts, so this increase was significant. The stock had previously been rather dull, trading in a range between 40 and 46, and option volume had been quite low for some time. However, the next day, before the market opened, Caesar's received a takeover bid from ITT Corporation and subsequently opened 20 points higher!

Another significant and similar situation occurred on June 2, 1995. That was a Friday, and Lotus Corporation rallied 3½ points to 32½ on option volume of nearly 8,200 contracts. Average daily option volume was 2,500 contracts. Lotus *had* been trading down previous to that day, as it had reported bad earnings a few weeks earlier, and the stock was under selling pressure. Monday morning, before the market opened, IBM announced a $65 a share takeover, and Lotus opened up 29 points at 61½!

Those observers of option volume who only use closing prices were unable to capitalize on these situations because, even though option volume on the day in question had a significantly speculative look, the takeover bids were received before trading began the next day. Although there are only a few of these situations each year, they can be lucrative to spot if you have the wherewithal to do so.

In order to trade these latter situations, you must do your option volume analysis in real-time, *during* the trading day. Then, if your analysis reveals a truly speculative situation, you can buy stock or options during the same trading day. Some small adjustments need to be made to the volume screens when analyzing option volume in real-time, during the trading day. The amount by which total volume exceeds average volume should be lessened, depending on the time of day at which you are running the analysis. For example, if you are running the analysis at noon, you might want to see all situations in which the total daily volume is equal to or greater than average volume (rather than *double* average volume, which is what we look for at the close of trading).

Experience has shown that running a real-time analysis about an hour or an hour and a half before the close of trading is appropriate. This gives you enough time to do analysis and still be able to take a position if you feel one is warranted. The main problem with real-time analysis is that it can lead to buying overhyped late-day situations, especially on a Friday, when rumors are swirling very fast. Therefore, my advice is to be rather stringent on your criteria for taking on a position based on real-time analysis. Remember, *most* rumors don't turn into takeovers the next day, so you'll normally have plenty of time to take a position.

Examples

Now that we have gone over the methodology for selecting some of these stocks, let's look at some actual examples. The following ones are all taken from actual trading situations that we identified for customers of our daily fax service in 1994 or 1995.

The Southern Pacific Railroad example, whose option data were just shown, is a good place to start. Review the data printed in the previous table, showing the option volume on July 26, 1995. Figure 4.1 is a price chart of Southern Pacific at that time. Along the bottom of the graph, option volume is shown. The option volume line looks very "choppy" because on many days, Southern Pacific options were not trading at all.

Figure 4.1
SOUTHERN PACIFIC RAILROAD

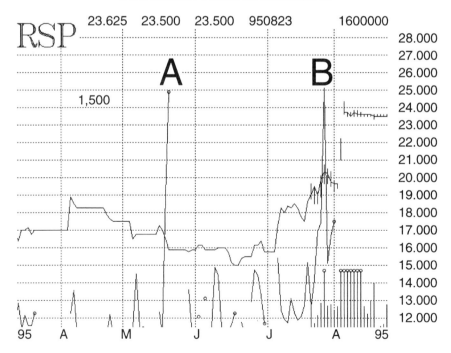

This graph of option volume only tells us the *total* volume, of course, and does not give us information on the detailed breakdown, which is necessary for the various screening activities that we have described so far in this chapter. Look at the graph of option volume in May 1995. Note the large volume spike (point A). That apparently was unrelated to speculative activity, as the stock not only traded sideways after that, but there was no option volume at all for the next several days. Now, look at the option volume on the graph in late July 1995 (point B). This time the volume spike *was* speculative in nature, with the actual peak coming on July 27, 1995 (one day after the volume that we first noticed in the preceding example). Not only that, but volume remained heavy for several successive days.

The stock traded between 19 and 20 for several days while this heavy option volume was occurring. Then, on August 3, 1995, Union Pacific made its takeover bid and the stock jumped to 24 the next day (the graph only shows the option volume *prior* to the takeover bid; there is always plenty of option volume on the day after the corporate news is announced). Thus, this Southern Pacific Railroad situation was a classic example of using option volume to spot a takeover just before it was announced. There was a good speculative look to the option volume for a full week before the actual announcement, so traders had plenty of time to get into the stock.

One of the most profitable takeovers of 1994 was the bid for American Cyanamid (ACY) made by American Home Products. This one, too, was able to be detected by observers of option volume. The graph of ACY during the pertinent period is shown in Figure 4.2.

The stock was trading modestly downward with little option volume in January and February of 1994. In fact, it made a low at 43 in March, and the first burst of option volume accompanied the initial rally off of that low (point A). The latter half of March had very heavy option volume, considering that average volume was running at very low levels in those days. All option volume statistics would increase as the spring and summer of 1994 passed.

ACY traded sideways during April, and option volume once again dropped off to nearly nothing. Then, on May 1st, another burst of option volume got the stock rolling to the upside. At that time, this was the heaviest option volume to date in ACY (point B). This burst

Figure 4.2
AMERICAN CYANAMID

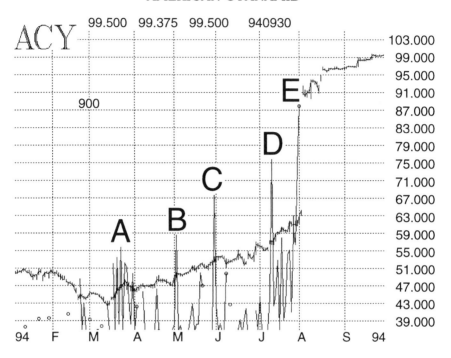

of option volume proved to be short-lived, but the stock continued higher for the month of May, climbing to 53 by month's end. Then, *another* day of heavy option trading was recorded (point C).

After this once-again short burst of option activity, the stock backed and filled a little before advancing again in late June and early July. Finally, on July 11th, the stock gapped two points higher accompanied by the heaviest option volume yet (point D). By this time, takeover rumors were circulating. You can see that the stock worked higher during the middle of July. But there was a major difference this time: while option volume backed off some from the point D peak, the option trading remained active, trading at levels about equal to where they had been at point A back in March.

By late July, the stock was trading near 60, and option volume then proceeded to reach the highest levels ever (point E). On July

Table 4.1
ACY: 63; JULY 29

Strike Price	Aug	Sep	Oct	Jan
		Expiration		
55 calls	100	33		
60 calls	542	315		
65 calls	1,189	369	45	29

29th (a Friday) and August 1st (the following Monday), the option volume accelerated to extreme levels. Table 4.1 shows the option trading data for July 29th, but a very similar pattern occurred on August 1st.

A total of 2,622 calls had traded. A total of 297 puts also traded, scattered among five different series. Average volume at the time was 697 total contracts. So option volume on this particular day was about four times the average. You can see that the "speculative" look that we have talked about existed in the distribution of the call volume: most of it was in the near-term, August, options, and most of it was in the highest strike (65).

Finally, late in the day on August 1st, American Home Products made their bid. ACY was halted on the NYSE at 63, and reopened at 91 in the third market. This was a successful culmination to the story for option volume observers. Since watching option volume is a short-term trading activity, these traders were probably in and out of the stock several times during the spring and summer of 1994, each time garnering small profits, until the big strike in early August.

Another 1994 takeover that was signaled by increased option trading volume was Gerber (GEB). In fact, the first signs of speculative activity in Gerber were increasing option prices, but that is a phenomenon that we discuss later in this chapter. Figure 4.3 shows the price history and option volume of Gerber during 1994.

Until early March 1994, Gerber was trading in a very tight range of 27 to 29 with no option volume on most days. Then, in March the stock broke out to 33, accompanied by heavy call volume (point A).

Figure 4.3
GERBER—OPTION VOLATILITY

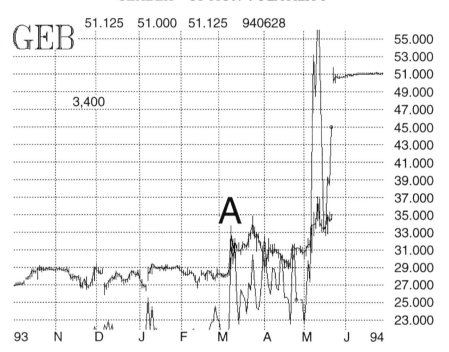

A couple of weeks later, the stock managed to move up to 35 intraday, and option volume remained relatively heavy on most days. Rumors of a takeover were rampant and, when nothing happened, traders began to exit the stock. So Gerber fell all the way back to 29 by mid-April.

Then, on May 6th, the stock jumped two points, from 31 to over 33, and option volume hit its highest levels ever. This was a clear-cut signal that the stock was "in play" once again. Table 4.2 shows what the option volume looked like on that day. It is another classic example of what speculative option volume looks like in advance of corporate news. Nearly 8,800 calls traded that day, and about 400 puts traded as well. At the time, average daily option volume was 2,770 contracts. This tripling of normal volume was an impressive sign that something was happening in Gerber.

Table 4.2
GEB: 33⅝; MAY 6

Strike Price	Expiration			
	May	June	July	Oct
25 calls	78	15	40	2
30 calls	1,909	414	268	29
35 calls	4,112	1,079	584	252

The stock continued to climb higher over the next two weeks, and option volume rose to even loftier levels. The peak price was 37, and by Friday, May 20th (option expiration day for the May options), Gerber had fallen back a little to close at 34⅝. As related in a story in Chapter 1, the takeover bid was received that night. On Monday, Gerber opened at 51. Much to their chagrin, some option writers were assigned on (out-of-the-money) May 35 calls.

Chipcom (CHPM) was a stock that was on the defensive for much of 1995, but then it turned—almost on a dime—and option volume observers picked up another takeover. From the Figure 4.4, you can see that option volume was moderately heavy in April 1995, when the stock was falling from 46 to 28. Then as it settled in a trading range of 32–34 in May, option volume almost disappeared. The company announced bad earnings on May 26th and fell 12 points in one day. This caused option volume to surge briefly (point A on graph).

However, the stock began an almost immediate recovery and got back up to 26 in June, before falling back some. It closed at 26 again on Friday, July 21st, and option volume surged. As shown in Table 4.3, option volume that day had a speculative look to it as well, although it wasn't as "classic" a pattern as some of the ones described earlier. A total of 2,014 calls had traded (and 562 puts traded also). This total volume of 2,576 was huge compared to the average volume of 280 total contracts per day—more than 9 times the average.

This volume pattern has some slight anomalies in it. First, the heaviest volume is in the September options, even though the

Figure 4.4
CHIPCOM

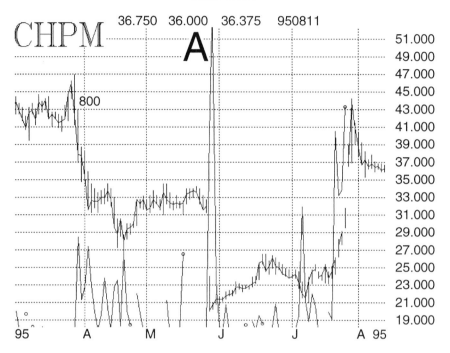

August options had four weeks of life remaining at the time. Second, the majority of the volume is in the *at-the-money* strike (25) instead of the out-of-the-money (30). Both of these facts are slightly different from what you would hope to observe in an ideal situation. Note that there were not any August 30 calls available for trading at the exchange.

Overall, this volume pattern was not "perfect," but was encouraging. Because of that, you might bring other factors in the decision making. At the time, I felt that since the stock had topped out previously at 26 back in June, I would want to see it break out over that level in July in order to confirm that the option volume pattern was a meaningful one.

The next trading day, Monday, CHPM did indeed break out over the 26 resistance, and on a small gap to boot. Option volume re-

Table 4.3
CHPM: 26; JULY 21

| | Expiration | | |
Strike Price	Aug	Sep	Oct
22½ calls	77	31	28
25 calls	338	1,482	59
30 calls	n/a	69	66

mained heavy, and the stock closed at 27½. This was a clear sign to buy the stock. It traded as high as 31¾ over the next three days, and option volume continued to be very heavy all during that time. Surprisingly, the volume never did develop the "classic" pattern, as more September and October options traded than did Augusts.

Nevertheless, a merger bid was received on July 27th from Three Com, and the stock jumped to 37. As an added bonus, after that there were rumors of a competing bid by Cabletron Systems, and the stock traded at 44 the next day! Although, the competing bid never developed, Chipcom rallied as the price of Three Com stock rallied. Again, a takeover situation was detected in advance by observers of option volume, although this time a little technical analysis had to be thrown in to complete the picture.

There is one other trait of the Chipcom situation that is interesting—a trait that occurs with some frequency in takeover situations: the stock, while trending down, becomes a takeover target because of its low stock price. It's sort of a catch-22 situation. The target company is doing poorly and its earnings are bad, so the stock sells off. However, if they have a good basic business, product, etc., the low stock price itself may raise the eyebrows of cash-rich companies in its field. These cash-rich companies can then step in and buy the relatively low-priced stock for what they feel is a reasonable price. In the case of Chipcom, the stock had traded as high as 51 in late 1994 (not shown on Figure 4.4), before plunging to a low of 20 in May 1995. This vast decrease in stock price obviously attracted the attention of Three Com, who apparently saw an opportunity to buy a (mismanaged?) company at a price well below its highs of the previous year. This theme of a stock becoming a takeover target after its stock hits new lows is repeated in several of the upcoming examples, including the next one—U.S. Shoe—to a certain extent.

U.S. Shoe (USR) had traded up to a high of 24 in the summer of 1994 before beginning an eight-month slide that took it to the 18–19 area. While this wasn't a large percentage drop, it was probably enough to help attract a buyer.

The chart of USR's stock price and option volume is in Figure 4.5. The first high-volume day for option trading saw the stock rise to 20½ (point A), as there were rumors that the company was going to sell its footwear business. The very next day, the company announced that those talks had broken off, and the stock plunged to 16 at one point before recovering a little to close at 17¼. Then, the day after that—February 21st—the stock jumped two points to 19¼

Figure 4.5
U.S. SHOE

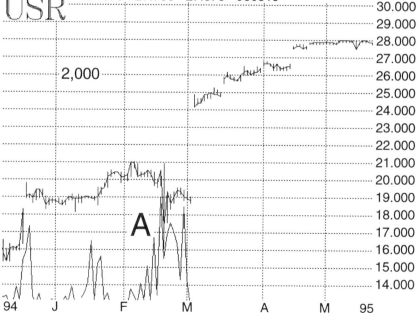

Table 4.4
USR: 19¼; FEB 21

Strike Price	Expiration			
	March	April	July	Oct
17½ calls	285	130	31	40
20 calls	654	603	105	
22½ calls	60	460	60	

as takeover rumors surfaced. Table 4.4 shows the pattern of option trading on that day, February 21st, when 2,428 calls had traded, plus 168 puts as well. Average volume was only 876 total contracts at that time, so that day was nearly triple the normal option volume, a wake-up call for option volume observers.

Option volume continued to run heavy during the rest of February as the stock hovered near 19. It is somewhat ironic that volume tailed off on March 1st to 970 total contracts and to a *very* low 209 contracts on March 2nd. The stock slumped to 18¾ as well, and it looked like the rumors had cooled off. Then, the next day—March 3rd—the company received a $25 per share takeover bid and the stock jumped six points. The takeover bid had come from an outside company, not the one that was originally discussing the sale of the footwear division.

Ordinarily, when you are trading based on increased option volume, we recommend that you take profits as soon as the news becomes public. You have established your position on the basis that "someone" knows something about future corporate news. If you are fortunate enough to have a position and then see that news actually announced, you should say "thank you" and take your profit, as a general rule.

However, as with all general rules, there can be exceptions, and U.S. Shoe was one of them. There is a postscript to the story of U.S. Shoe. Look at the graph in Figure 4.6. It is the same as the previous graph, except that the option volume is shown on through the rest of the stock's life. There was a huge surge in option volume on the day the stock rose six points, which is certainly to be expected. However,

Figure 4.6
U.S. SHOE—OPTION VOLUME

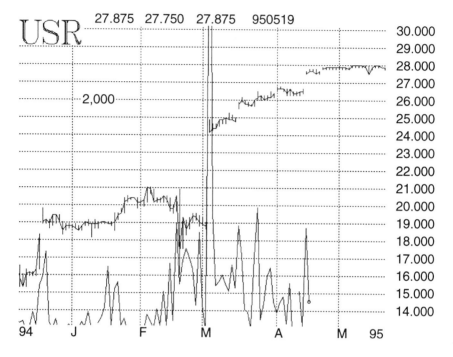

option volume normally abates after that, especially if the takeover bid is a "done deal." In the case of U.S. Shoe, though, option volume continued to be heavy (it technically wasn't more than twice normal because the heavy option volume on that one day had inflated the average volume figures). Sure enough, the company that had originally wanted the footwear division came back and bid a higher price for U.S. Shoe. You can see from the graph that the stock was eventually taken over at 28 in May, a nice premium to even the $25 offer of March.

Option volume doesn't just spot takeover situations. It is also very useful in catching corporate earnings surprises. It has been my experience that option trading activity will often pick up on the day before a company releases its quarterly earnings. This is such a frequent occurrence that option observers should probably *not* attempt to trade under those circumstances. However, if the option volume picks up several days before the earnings announcement—perhaps remaining heavy for several days prior—then there is a much better chance that a meaningful trade is being predicted by the options. The next two examples are cases in point.

Motorola (MOT) was due to release earnings on Tuesday, July 12, 1994. Motorola's options are generally quite active, but on Wednesday, July 6th, and for the next four trading days, the option activity picked up tremendously. Moreover, since the majority of that activity was in call options, it appeared that insiders had knowledge that the quarterly earnings were going to be better than expected.

Figure 4.7 shows Motorola's stock price and option volume during that time. Notice that the stock had been trading in a range of 43

Figure 4.7
MOTOROLA

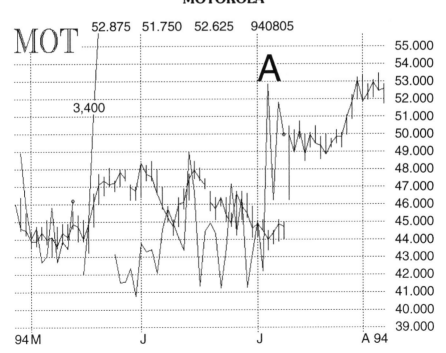

to 48 during most of May and June 1994. During that time, option volume was fairly active, but normal. However, with the stock near the low end of the range during the first week of July, option volume began to surge (point A). The following data are from the first day of increased option volume—July 6th—and is representative of the pattern that occurred during each of those four days prior to the actual release of earnings. Since a lot of puts traded that day, as well as calls, Table 4.5 details the trading in all options. Just over 7,500 calls traded that day, and almost 5,400 puts traded as well. Average total volume at the time was 5,624 contracts, so the total volume on that day (12,900 contracts) was over twice the average volume.

The volume pattern in Table 4.5 is not as clear-cut as one might like to see, but since the options were so active, it is worth analyzing. First, you must remember that Motorola options are always active to a certain extent. So, whatever normally causes that activity was probably taking place on July 6th in the normal course of events; then, on top of that activity, there was some speculative activity as well, in advance of the earnings report. If you only look at the striking prices of 45 and higher, the pattern looks fairly speculative in terms of call volume. There are a number of puts trading at those strikes, but

Table 4.5
MOT: 44½; JULY 6

Strike Price	Expiration			
	July	Aug	Oct	Jan
40 calls	1,980	52	30	50
puts	998	167	1,451	42
42½ calls	122	0	19	
puts	1,113		46	
45 calls	1,152	746	103	22
puts	399	220	125	49
47½ calls	1,363	504	244	
puts	322		125	
50 calls	804	299	122	
puts	0	290	31	

nothing unusual compared to the calls. So, from observing the activity at the three higher strikes, you would figure that the option volume was predicting a positive earnings surprise because of the heavy call volume.

However, at the two lower strikes, things get a little cloudy. There are a lot of puts traded at those strikes, and you might think that those puts were predicting bad earnings on the horizon. The July 42½ puts, which traded 1,113 contracts, certainly look like speculative volume. However, the Oct 40 puts, which traded 1,451 contracts, probably are not speculative because speculators would be buying July or August puts. Finally, the July 40 puts (998 contracts traded) might easily be part of an arbitrage with the July 40 calls, since so many of those calls traded too.

Sometimes, when both call volume and put volume are heavy, the stock can be ready to make a rather large move in either direction. It can be very difficult to determine that direction merely from observing the option volume, because of the balance in call volume and put volume. This phenomenon can arise, in part, because market makers are trading puts to hedge calls, or vice versa, thereby distorting the option volume patterns created by the speculators. Motorola calls were quite expensive since the speculators were buying them heavily. So, market makers, who were short calls by virtue of their market-making activity, might have sold stock and bought some of the puts to hedge their short call position.

In Motorola data just discussed, it *appears* that the call volume has a more speculative look than the put volume, because of the facts mentioned regarding the Oct 40 puts and the July 40 puts. However, rather than attempt to get too deep into analyzing *why* there was heavy option volume in specific series, I prefer to watch the stock price for a minor breakout in either direction in order to confirm the direction of the move. On July 6th, the day in question, MOT had had a high of 44½ and closed at 44. The stock traded higher over the next two days, which to me was a confirmation that the pending move was going to be to the upside.

This volume pattern continued pretty much the same way for the ensuing three days. Total volume was more than double normal volume, and, while call volume was dominant, there was a lot of put volume trading as well. Finally, on July 12th, the earnings were released and were a huge positive surprise. The stock gapped higher on the opening and closed over five points higher that day.

All in all, this example shows several typical things. First, if you are going to use option volume to predict an earnings surprise, you want to see the option volume reach high levels for several days prior to the actual earnings announcement itself. Second, when option activity increases in a stock where options are normally quite active, then you are going to have extraneous volume clouding the issue, so you must be a little more analytical in interpreting what the option volume is predicting. Third, whenever puts and calls are both active, you can use the stock price itself as a guide to the direction of the eventual move.

Another classic example of how option volume predicted an earnings surprise occurred in the spring of 1995 in Sybase (SYBS). This one, however, came on the downside and was predicted by heavy trading in Sybase puts for a significant period of time.

The graph of Sybase and the total option volume are shown in Figure 4.8. The stock had been under a little pressure in the fall of 1994, and then made a disappointing earnings announcement in January of 1995. The stock fell over six points on that day and option volume surged (point A on chart). That volume, however, was not predictive—it was reactive, as it came *after* the news was released.

SYBS continued to trade sideways at a lower level—42 to 46—until late February, when rumors began to circulate that the earnings were going to be bad again at the next earnings release. This caused another spike in option volume (point B), much of which was put volume. However, after a brief foray below 40 on the last trading day of February 1995, the stock climbed back into the trading range.

On March 21st, option volume surged again (point C), and it had the same pattern of heavier put volume than call volume. That came with the stock at 44¼. From that time on, the stock basically traded down. Since that day—March 21st—was the best day to buy puts, that is the day whose detailed trading is shown in Table 4.6. A total of 3,670 contracts traded that day, and 2,450 of them were puts, an unusually large percentage (67 percent). Note the volume in the deeply in-the-money puts, a very bearish sign. Average volume at the time

Figure 4.8
SYBASE

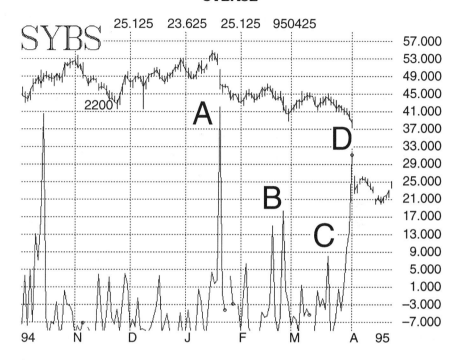

Table 4.6
SYBS: 44¼; MARCH 21

Strike Price	March	April	June
40 calls	150	0	
puts	0	280	
45 calls	180	270	
puts	420	450	
50 calls	0	620	0
puts	0	1,100	100
55 calls	0		
puts	100		

was 1,256, so the 3,670 contracts was almost three times normal—enough to bring this situation to the attention of option observers.

From that day on, Sybase traded lower, eventually breaking below 40 on April 3rd. There was heavy option volume on both March 31st (a Friday) and Monday, April 3rd (point D in Figure 4.8). On Friday, March 31, 3,638 contracts traded, of which 1,830 (or 50 percent) were puts. That wasn't quite as impressive as the option volume shown in Table 4.6, but the trading on Monday, April 3rd, left little doubt as to what the option volume was attempting to say (see Table 4.7). Option volume jumped to nearly 5,800 contracts on this day, and puts accounted for a staggering 4,120 contracts (71 percent of total volume). Look at the huge volume in the out-of-the-money puts with a striking price of 35. This was a sign that the bearish speculators were out in force and with confidence.

The next day, April 4th, the company made a pre-earnings announcement, indicating that earnings (which were not to be released until later in April) would fall short of expectations. The stock opened 14 points lower. A masterful coup for observers of option volume.

Table 4.7
SYBS: 38½; APRIL 3

Strike Price	Expiration		
	April	May	June
35 calls	0	0	0
puts	960	750	110
40 calls	890	220	
puts	940	630	150
45 calls	410	78	
puts	200		
50 calls	0	180	
puts	280		
55 calls	0		
puts	100		

The next example is one that is less clear-cut than some of those previously shown. It involves Syntex (SYN), which was a long-rumored takeover stock. Unfortunately for most of the people who had bought Syntex over the years, the takeover never actually materialized, and in fact the stock kept drifting down to lower and lower levels. As was mentioned earlier, if a company has a viable business, a low stock price may attract suitors. This fact is not lost on the Wall Street crowd, however, so the least little hint of a rumor was all it would take to get Syntex stock and options excited. We discuss this example in some detail, in order to show you that things don't always work out as planned.

The graph of Syntex and its option volume is shown in Figure 4.9. The time frame is late 1993 and the first half of 1994. Syntex stock had been as high as 54 in the past (1991), but by late 1993 was trending down toward 15. In mid-December 1993, option vol-

Figure 4.9
SYNTEX

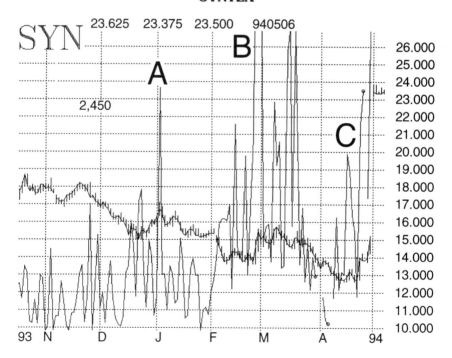

ume surged a little and the stock made a bottom, rallying to 17 by year-end. The big volume came on the first trading day of 1994, however (point A on the graph). On that day, January 4th, the option trading volume was as shown in Table 4.8.

Call option volume surged to 7,931 contracts that day, and 479 scattered puts traded as well. Since average volume was only 2,377 at the time, this was indeed a significant surge of option trading. Moreover, it had a very speculative look, although it might have been preferable if more trading had occurred in the January and February series and a little less in the March series.

As good as the option volume looked on January 4th, it proved to be a one-day wonder and—worse yet—it marked an intermediate-term top for the stock, exactly the opposite of what is "supposed" to happen. Instead, the stock fell to 14 by early February and option volume died down substantially.

The stock stabilized in mid-to-late February and option volume began to surge once again. This time, however, traders were more reluctant to chase the stock, and it didn't advance much until late February, when option volume surged so much that it went clear off the top of the graph in Figure 4.9 (point B). Somewhat ironically, the stock only rose by ⅝ to 14⅝, again demonstrating the skepticism with which stock traders viewed Syntex. However, those with inside information were becoming even more aggressive in buying the calls. Table 4.9 shows how the option volume looked on that day of heaviest volume, February 25th. Call volume was a massive 12,851 contracts, and an additional 6,500 puts traded as well. At the time, average daily volume was 3,383, so once again this was an opportunity for followers of option volume to buy the stock.

Table 4.8
SYN: 16⅞; JANUARY 4

Strike Price	Jan	Feb	March	June
	Expiration			
15 calls	350	544	214	185
17½ calls	2,924	529	993	83
20 calls	302		1,229	579

Table 4.9
SYN: 14⅝; FEBRUARY 25

Strike Price	Expiration			
	March	April	June	Sep
12½ calls	514	33	265	188
15 calls	8,081	1,154	3,964	379
17½ calls	1,168	177	2,744	253
20 calls	172		535	
22½ calls	30		414	

Option volume remained very heavy for the rest of February, and the first half of March (see Figure 4.9). Unfortunately, the stock did not make much headway. It *did* trade up to nearly 16, but that was in early March. Then, once again, it began another rather nasty descent, eventually falling to 12½ in mid-April. With the decline in the stock price, option volume had almost completely dried up by mid-April. At that time, however, option volume once again returned (point C in Figure 4.9). As had happened in February, the stock price did not really trade higher—again showing the skepticism amongst traders.

Then, in late April (April 23rd), both the stock and the options got "heated" together. First, the stock jumped from 12 to 13 in one day, and simultaneously option volume rose to the highest levels since March. Then on April 29th, Syntex traded over 15, and option volume once again had an extremely speculative look (see Table 4.10). Nearly 13,000 calls had traded, and, even though over 3,000

Table 4.10
SYN: 15⅛; APRIL 29

Strike Price	Expiration			
	May	June	Sep	Dec
12½ calls	56	85	71	
15 calls	2,453	3,922	693	34
17½ calls	436	3,596	370	32
20 calls	24	741	164	

puts traded (most of them with a strike of 10), this was a sign that the rumors were back in force.

Those traders who weren't gun-shy from having traded Syntex before were able to buy it and reap the rewards—which were huge in percentage terms—as the stock received a takeover bid and opened at 23½ the next day. In the minds of many traders, Syntex was a "good riddance" type of stock. This was true for short-term traders, who had been "burned" by many false takeover rumors in the past, as well as for long-term holders who saw the stock taken over at a price that was less than 90 percent of the daily closes over the previous several years. Only the observers of option volume felt somewhat redeemed, and even they had lost money a couple of times before the final takeover occurred.

This example not only shows that surges in option volume are not guarantees that a takeover or earnings surprise will happen every time, but it also stresses the need for money management. Since these are short-term trading situations, I strongly recommend that you use a tight stop on any purchase made using option volume as the catalyst for establishing the position. In my mind, that means *taking a loss of no greater than one point on any position* (unless, of course, the stock gaps open). Thus, if you had bought the stock in early January at 16⅞, you would have been stopped out within two days. Then, in late February, you would once again have been stopped out in late March or early April (although most short-term traders wouldn't hold a stock for a month if it wasn't going higher). Even though these were both losing trades, losses would have been small. That is an important fact, for you need to have your capital fairly intact because the next opportunity—in late April—was, in fact, the real thing. So, if you had limited your losses on the first two trades, you would have wound up with a nice overall profit on the third trade, which resulted in a big gain.

As an end to these examples, it should be pointed that *not every major corporate news event is leaked beforehand.* It is fairly common to see a takeover occur that had little or no advance notice. Mostly these unknown takeovers are in smaller stocks, but occasionally they occur in very large stocks as well. One large takeover that was kept quiet was Matsushita's takeover of MCA/United Artists in the early 1990s. MCA was in the midst of a very nasty decline, in connection with the bear market of that year; it traded down to 34, from a high of 71 earlier in the year. Suddenly, and without warning, Matsushita made a bid for $71 for the company, and it gapped up to $60 the next day.

In a similar manner, one of the biggest mergers of all time, in terms of dollar amount of stock purchased, was kept quiet and it was never rumored—even by analysts—because the combination didn't seem possible. That was Disney's takeover of Cap Cities ABC in the summer of 1995. Cap Cities had been trading quietly at 96 on a slow Friday in July. The total option volume in Cap Cities that day was 100 contracts, as compared to an average volume of 272—nothing unusual at all there. Moreover, Cap Cities had been in a downtrend with low stock volume. Disney made an astounding bid of $65 per share *plus* one share of Disney. Since Disney was trading at about 65 at the time, this equated to a $130 bid for Cap Cities.

This just goes to show that a takeover can be kept quiet, but it usually isn't if too many people know about it. In the Disney situation, the deal was originally proposed personally by the chairman of Disney to the chairman of Cap Cities. Then they brought in a few trusted confidantes to hammer out the details. However, as soon as you start involving investment bankers, printers, and the like, the chances of someone "spilling the beans" increases greatly. Once the information is in the hands of disinterested parties, those parties are probably going to buy options, and that's where we can profit.

Profitability

The preceding examples are certainly enough to demonstrate the worth of trading stocks based on increasing option volume. Large profits are possible, and if you limit your losses with fairly tight (mental) stops, then you can expect to achieve an excellent rate of return. In order to help you gauge what to expect, some general statistics can be offered.

First, no matter how careful you are with your screening of option activity, *you are probably going to have losers on slightly more than 50 percent of your trades.* Some of these are caused by picking up stock in which the option volume was due to extraneous factors rather than the option buying being caused by those with inside information. Second, with the use of tight stops, you may find that a stock backs off and stops you out, due to a large seller—who sells because of price considerations, having nothing to do with corporate news—or due to a cooling of somewhat widespread rumors. You may find yourself reentering these stocks (à la the Syntex example given earlier) if the rumors return. Personally, I prefer to take the small losses and then reenter the position if it becomes active again.

As for taking profits, there are at least three considerations. As mentioned before, one is to liquidate your position when the corporate news becomes public. Generally, this is a most pleasing task, for the announcement will make the stock move in your favor. Sometimes, however, the corporate announcement means taking a loss, and these losses can be some of the largest and most painful. For example, I have seen situations where call trading volume built up heavily for several days prior to a stock's earnings release. Then, the actual earnings, when announced, were only in-line, or perhaps the earnings were good but projections for the next quarter's sales didn't look so good, or something similarly negative was stated by the company along with the earnings release. In a sensitive market, such a stock can gap down, perhaps opening below your stop price, thereby causing a loss.

A second consideration for taking profits, or at least protecting them, is to use a trailing stop. If the stock begins to move in your favor, but no actual corporate announcement is forthcoming, then I would suggest that you raise your stop price. As these unrealized profits begin to accrue, you may want to give the stock a little more breathing room by setting the (mental) stop price somewhat *more* than a point below the stock's price. You would approach the profits in this manner because the objective of (short-term) trading is to let profits run.

A third point regarding profit-taking is this: I would recommend taking partial profits if you get a substantial, quick move in your favor, and no corporate news has been announced. This tactic allows you more freedom to hold the remainder of your position with a slightly wider stop. It also ensures that an unforeseen news development won't be as painful as it might have been.

A classic example of the usefulness of money management occurred in the trading of U.S. Surgical in July of 1995. The stock had, at times in the past, been the subject of takeover rumors and heavy option volume occasionally developed. This time, the stock was trading at about 24½ when the option volume shot up and option observers bought the stock in that price range. Two days later, better-than-expected earnings were reported, and in addition a major brokerage firm upgraded the stock on projected improved earnings. The stock traded above 27 in just three days. At the time, we recommended to our clients that they take partial profits and raise the stop to 25½ from its initial level of 23⅜.

The very next day, after opening near 27, the *same* analyst recanted his positive expectations. It doesn't really even matter what his reasoning was (although it certainly seemed specious), but the stock proceeded to fall over two points that day, stopping us out of the position. Fortunately, with the use of the trailing stop and the fact that we took a partial profit, we still had nearly a two-point gain in a very short period of time.

This tactic of taking some partial profits can even be applied to intraday trading, as sometimes you will already be in a position when rumors come into the market and make the stock go to extreme levels. At extremes, natural sellers may appear, based merely on price (or buyers, if you are short). For example, Integrated Silicon stock was mentioned in an earlier example as having had heavy put volume. We had our customers short the stock and it proceeded to fall seven points in three days, and then on the third day, it was down another six points before rallying nearly four points near the close. Natural buyers had appeared; they figured the stock had gotten so cheap that it was a buy regardless of what kind of bad news was coming out. The next day the stock rallied five points. Those traders able to watch the stock in real time were able to react when they saw it reverse direction as buyers stepped in. Covering at that time was superior to waiting until the closing, or until a buy stop was later elected.

Further Considerations

You can readily see that this analysis of option volume requires you to have access to "average option volume." We use the 20-day moving average of volume in our calculations. We also keep the 20-day moving average of both puts and calls separately. There are very few software systems that provide this information, and none of them do the screening that is necessary, for that is largely a human function. One service is Telescan, but there are severe limitations with how they implement their moving averages, for there is very little meaningful screening available. Another software vendor that provides this information is Option Vue, and through their Opscan service, you can customize your analysis significantly, but you may still be left with a large number of choices. On an average day, there will be 40 or more stocks whose option volume is more than double its average volume. However, after screening, only a handful are actually showing speculative option buying—the others are distorted by covered writes, spreads, and arbitrage. This means that the best, and only, way to accurately screen the volume is for a trader who understands what he is looking for to analyze the data. With practice, this can be you, if you have access to the data. Another way is through our Daily Volume Alert service, where we do the screening and report the few situations that represent true speculative volume each day to our subscribers.

I am often asked the question, "Do you personally buy the stock or buy the options, and, if options, which ones?" A lot of the time, the options in these rumor stocks are quite expensive because not only are the insiders buying them, but other traders and market makers are buying them as well. This makes the at-the-money and out-of-the-money options too expensive to buy in most cases. *I typically prefer buying the short-term, in-the-money option* because it has little or no time value premium and therefore behaves very much like the stock does.

While an in-the-money option doesn't have the extreme leverage capability of an out-of-the-money option, it still provides leverage, and it will generally make a profit whenever the stock makes a move in your favor, no matter how long it takes or how small the move, which cannot be said for owning out-of-the-money options. There is nothing worse than owning an expensive option out-of-the-money if a rumor that is supporting the stock is denied by the company. The stock drops, but the options absolutely collapse as implied volatility drops. Thus, you can have situations where the at-the-money option drops in price nearly as much as, or more than, the underlying stock does.

Even though I prefer using the in-the-money option, *I would never argue with someone who wanted to purchase the stock itself*. In a trading situation, it is often better to be in the stock, rather than in options. Stock is more liquid, the bid–asked spread is often tighter, and you can use stop orders if you want to. I do not recommend using stop orders with options—you will invariably be disappointed with the results over the long term. Also, you will find that, in a trading situation, you will be taking small profits fairly often, perhaps when the stock moves a point or two in your favor. Options, of course, will move in your favor when the stock does, but the liquidity of the stock often makes it a better trading vehicle.

Is there *ever* any purpose in using out-of-the-money options in these speculative situations? Yes, there is. When the options are expensive, then I often use a bull spread, even an out-of-the-money bull spread.

With Federal Paperboard (FBO) at about 41 in early November 1995, option volume was very strong, so that a purchase was in order. However, the options were extremely expensive:

FBO: 41

Nov 40 call: 4
Nov 45 call: 2
Nov 50 call: 1

These options had only a couple of weeks of life remaining, so you can see how heavy the speculation was. I recommended that our customers purchase the Nov 45–Nov 50 call bull spread. This cost a point, or perhaps 1¼, the next day.

Within a week, the stock was taken over, and it traded at 53. The spread was removed for 4⅞. This is a classic case of why a bull spread is sometimes useful.

For comparison purposes, let's say the spread was sold for 5, and any of the other options could have been sold at parity with the stock at 53. The following table compares the various returns that would have been available from various purchases:

Purchase	Cost	Sale Price	Return (%)
Bull Spread	1	5	400
Nov 40 call	4	13	225
Nov 45 call	2	8	300
Nov 50 call	1	3	200
Common stock	41	53	29

Thus, the spread was the best choice by far, in terms of returns realized. The reason that it was able to outperform the other calls was that each individual call was so expensive to begin with, that it hampered the overall returns. However, at least in the bull spread situation, we were both buying and selling an expensive option, and that balanced itself out somewhat. Of course, had the takeover been at a much higher price, the spread would not have been the best winner, but it would still have done very well, and its initial cost was small—only one point.

Using Stops

It was mentioned earlier that you should use protective stops, and fairly close ones at that, when operating a short-term trading strategy. This concept is not unique to stock trading (whether based on option volume or any other criteria), but to futures trading as well. With the use of stops (and letting your profits run), you can operate very profitably even if you only have 40 to 50 percent winners. Also favor the use of trailing stops: adjusting your stops to lock in profits if you are fortunate enough to have the stock make a move in your favor. You don't necessarily have to keep the trailing stops as tight as the initial stop; you may want to leave the stock a little more room if it is already moving in your favor.

A concept that I usually recommend, if you have access to real-time data, or if someone is watching your account for you, is to use *mental* stops instead of actual stops. An actual stop is a stop order that is actually placed with your broker and is therefore an order on the floor of the exchange. The advantage of the actual stop is that you don't have to monitor it—it's always working for you even when you're away doing something else. The *disadvantage* of the actual stop is that you don't get a chance to assess the situation when the stock gets to your stop price; you are automatically out. Moreover, you might not get a particularly good execution and, even though this sounds a little paranoid, it does happen; sometimes the specialists or market makers will drive the stock down only to "pick off" your stop and then the stock will go right back up again.

The *mental* stop allows you some flexibility when the stock hits your stop price. The way a mental stop is normally implemented is to set a limit minder on your quote machine at the price in question. Then, when the stock hits that price, your quote machine will "beep" or otherwise signal you that a limit has been reached. You can then look at the stock and perhaps watch its trading activity for a few minutes to see if this is actually a time to sell the stock. For example, if the stock hits your mental stop price, but you see that there is a large bid for the stock and that the selling has been rather light, you may decide that this would not be a good time to sell the stock, and you would continue to hold it. On the other hand, if you see that the selling has been aggressive and that bids are small in size, you would probably decide to go ahead and sell as it seems that the stock might drop even farther. The mental stop allows you this flexibility. It may sometimes cost you an extra eighth of a point versus the actual stop, but it will save you in those situations where it is fairly obvious that the stock is going to lift right back up. Of course, the mental stop can only be used if you are present when the stock reaches your stop price. If you have another job, or are often away from a quote machine, then you must use actual stops.

Another type of mental stop that I have found useful is the *closing stop*. That is, I won't stop myself out unless the stock is actually closing below my sell stop price (or above my *buy* stop price). This is an order that can be placed as an actual stop in the futures market, but not in the stock market ("Stop, close only"). I have found that, especially with rumor stocks and other short-term situations, the stock may trade down through what appears to be minor support, intraday, but then bounces back above it by the close of trading. If you were using an intraday stop, you would have stopped yourself out. However, with the closing stop, you retain your position. It's relatively easy to monitor, even if you don't have access to a quote machine; merely call your broker just before the close of trading, and if the stock appears that it's going to close lower than your stop price, sell it. The drawback, of course, occurs when the stock not only violates your stop level, intraday, but continues on down and closes *much* lower. That is why you may want to pay attention in real time if you are using this type of stop, because you may want to liquidate your position *before* the close if you see a nasty situation developing.

In any case, placing stops can be more of an art than a science. Some traders prefer to use money management stops. That is, they will only risk a certain amount of money on a trade, and will therefore determine their stop price based on a dollar amount of risk. This concept is discussed in Chapter 7. Other traders prefer to use technical analysis to aid them in placing their stops. I think both concepts can be used together in a short-term trading methodology. In this system of using option volume to select stocks, we want to keep our initial losses small, approximately three-quarters of a point to a point. That is the money management part of the stop. Then, if we can find a point in that range that is a technical support point, we can combine both philosophies.

For example, if there have been a couple of daily bottoms at the same price, that represents technical support. If that support is approximately at the distance where we want our stop, we would set the stop—actual or mental—at a point *below* those two daily bottoms. Figure 4.10, a chart of Bethlehem Steel (BS), illustrates this concept. If we bought BS at 14¼ (the last bar on the chart on the right), we might set our stop at 13¾, based on the fact that there had been double bottoms at 14 during the previous week.

Of course, you won't always be able to find such a convenient thing as a double bottom, but you may often be able to identify a support area which, if breached, would be a rather negative occurrence. This would be your stop point.

Figure 4.11 illustrates the concept. If you buy ADM at the last sale (on the right of the chart), you might feel that its price represents a nice breakout. However, if it fell back below the row of daily tops that had occurred over the last month at 17½, the breakout would be negated. So you might place your stop at 17, which is well below the row of intraday tops.

Finally, if there is no technical support area visible, then you would just have to rely on your money management stop. The money management part of the stop selection process is the most important, and should be the first consideration. If, for example, you

Figure 4.10
BETHLEHEM STEEL

are going to place your stops at one point below your entry price because of money management, you would not override that consideration because technical support is 2½ points below your entry price. To use a stop of 2½ points below your entry price is just too far and too much risk, if your normal money management stop is one point. The technical analysis portion of the stop selection process should only be used if it falls within the guidelines of your money management stop.

The preceding discussion was from the viewpoint of protecting a long position in a stock. Obviously, for a short position, things would be similar. A protective buy stop might be placed just *above* a couple of intraday *tops* on the bar chart. Or if the stock has broken down below a congestion area, then a buy stop might be placed just above the intraday bottoms that defined the breakdown.

Figure 4.11
ADM, 12/27/95

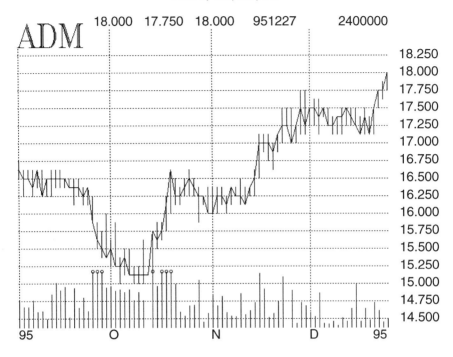

Stop orders can also sometimes be used for entering a position, as can limit orders. We spent a good deal of time going over the reasons and methods for screening out option volume that was not speculative in nature. However, we also stated that you may still end up with a stock whose increased option volume was due to something other than insiders buying options in advance of corporate news. As one further type of screen, I often wait until I see the stock trade above the high price it made on the day of the heavy option volume, before I actually buy the stock. The reasoning is: if the stock can't even penetrate the previous day's high, then maybe the option volume wasn't as good as I thought it was.

If you are waiting for the stock to reach a slightly higher price (i.e., above the previous day's high), you can use a *buy stop* order to get into the stock. Just place the buy stop an eighth of a point above the previous day's high. If it is elected, you know the stock has continued on from the previous day's action, and you are in a stock with momentum. If it is not elected, you may have avoided a stock whose option volume was extraneous. You can, of course, leave the stop in place for subsequent days if you continue to like the option activity.

The chart of Grupo Tribasa (GTR), Figure 4.12, is a good example of this philosophy. Option volume first picked up when the stock was trading near 8 (point A on chart). The high that day was 8⅜, and there had been several failures, intraday, at 8½ previously. Thus, even though there was good option volume, we wanted to see the stock break out to 8⅝ before actually buying it. It could not do so for nearly a month, and then there was heavy option volume again (point B). Again, it couldn't follow through on that volume the next day. But, finally, it did break out three days later.

Figure 4.12
GRUPO TRIBASA

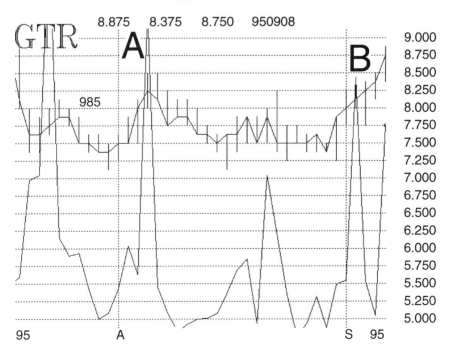

Limit orders can also be used to enter a position. Many traders don't like to "chase" stocks on breakouts, and I can agree with that philosophy, especially if you miss the actual breakout itself. In the Grupo Tribasa example, we were able to catch the breakout just as it was occurring. However, you may find that sometimes you won't have heavy option volume until the day a breakout occurs. This doesn't necessarily mean that you should avoid the stock, but you might wait for a pullback to buy it, depending on how the news reads.

Figure 4.13, the chart of U.S. Surgical (USS), illustrates this concept. In late July 1995, the stock was trading just above 23. There had been previous resistance at 24. On the day in question, USS bolted 1½ points higher on heavy option volume and closed at the high of the day, 24¾. This looked like an attractive situation, but not so spectacular that the stock had to be chased and bought at the daily

Figure 4.13
U.S. SURGICAL, 7/20/95

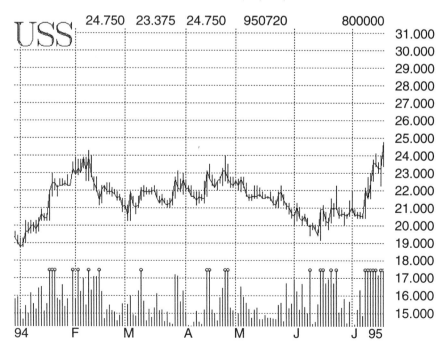

high after its breakout. In fact, we used a limit order to buy the stock at 24¼, which was just over the support area. It traded down to that level a couple of times over the next few days, before embarking on a move to 28.

When Option Volume Is Not a Good Predictor

Before concluding, it should be pointed out where equity option volume does *not* work as a predictor of a movement by the underlying. It seems to be able to work for almost all stocks, with the exception of gold stocks and foreign stocks. It has been my experience that heavy option volume in gold stocks is merely a reflection of speculation in the stocks themselves and is not a predictor of an upcoming corporate news item. Much the same is true of foreign stock ADRs, which have listed options trading. It seems that, if someone actually had inside information on one of those stocks, he would buy the stock in the foreign market and not risk SEC penalties by trading in the United States.

You may also be wondering if this same concept can be applied to index options or to futures options. After rather extensive research, I have concluded that option volume is *not* useful in predicting the movement of either indices or futures, as it is for stocks. At first, I thought there might be some logic involved in using option volume to predict the movement of indices, especially sector indices. For example, if a large brokerage house was doing a positive research piece on the oil stocks, then I thought the report might leak in advance and that leak would appear in the marketplace as call buying the Oil & Gas Index (symbol: $XOI). That sort of thing has just never materialized. Either the brokerage firms are extremely secretive with their reports (unlikely), or the sector options are just too illiquid for insiders to bother with (certainly possible). Since history has shown there to be almost no correlation between index option volume and the subsequent moves in the index, we have to conclude that index option volume is not a good predictor of index movement.

As for futures options, there also seems to be no relationship between an increase in option volume and a move by the underlying futures. This seems logical in the case of futures. There can't be a takeover of corn or soybeans, for example. The only news items that materially affect commodities are government reports of supply and demand. These reports are closely guarded and, while many analysts attempt to predict what the government report will be, the actual reports are never leaked. The only time they were leaked was in the movie *Trading Places* when Eddie Murphy and Dan Aykroyd got the best of the Duke Brothers. But in real life, it just doesn't happen. So, since there are no news events that can be obtained in advance by "insiders" in the futures markets, futures option volume cannot be used to predict the price of the underlying future in the way that we use equity options to predict stock prices.

This concludes a rather extensive section on using option volume to predict moves in stocks. This is a valid approach to short-term trading, as can be seen by the many examples shown. Admittedly, the system isn't simple and takes some work to apply, but the rewards can be quite beneficial.

USING OPTION PRICES AS AN INDICATOR

The actual price level of the options on a stock, index, or futures contract may sometimes also be useful in predicting the forthcoming movements of that underlying instrument. Option premiums are not only sometimes useful in identifying corporate news-related items, much as option volume is, but are also useful in other situations. We will look at several ways in which expensive options or cheap options are useful for predictive purposes.

Just as it was necessary to compare option *volume* to something meaningful (its 20-day moving average of volume), it is equally necessary to have a strict measure of option prices so that we can decide whether options are expensive or not. In order to judge the expensiveness or cheapness of options, we use *implied volatility*. Implied volatility was defined through examples in Chapter 1, but we will give a slightly more illustrative definition here, for those now familiar with the concept.

As stated earlier, an option's price is a function of:

> Stock Price
> Strike Price
> Time Remaining Until Expiration
> Interest Rates
> Volatility

(We'll omit dividends for now.) Now suppose IBM is trading at 99, and we are attempting to determine the implied volatility of an IBM Oct 100 call, trading at 7.

Of the factors that compose the option's price, four of them are known and fixed: we know the stock price (99), the strike price (100), the time remaining until expiration (however long it is until the third Friday in October), and the short-term interest rate. What we don't know is volatility.

Buy we *do* know that the Oct 100 call is trading at 7. So, what volatility would we have to plug into a mathematical option pricing model, given the values of the other four factors, to make the model say that the call was worth 7? Whatever volatility that is, is the *implied volatility*.

Each separate option on the same underlying security will have somewhat different implied volatilities. Therefore, you need to average them in some manner in order to arrive at a single daily number for implied volatility for the stock, index, or futures contract in question. I prefer to weight the individual implied volatilities by both their trading volume and the distance between the current strike price and the option's striking price. More heavily traded options get the most weight, and options that are at or close to the money get the most weight.

Finally, once the daily implied volatility is determined, it may oscillate rather crazily from day to day, so I prefer to use a moving average of implied volatilities in order to smooth things out. A 10- or 20-day moving average seems to work best. If you use too "long" of a moving average, then you may be including too much extraneous, "old" data in your moving average of implied volatility. We want to be able to spot sudden changes in implied volatility, but we want those changes to be meaningful. It is rather common for implied volatility to change by quite a bit over 50 days, but not so common for it to change significantly over 10 or 20 days' time.

Expensive Stock Options May Predict Corporate News

Just as heavy option volume can be a predictor of corporate news items, so can expensive options, but only in certain specific situations. In fact, you may often find that option volume and implied volatility are increasing *together* in rumored takeover situations or prior to other significant corporate news releases. This phenomenon is caused once again by traders who have inside information attempting to take positions with the most leverage. When both volume and volatility are increasing, it is usually most beneficial to apply the analyses of option volume that were discussed earlier in this chapter.

However, at times, you may find the implied volatility increasing without a concomitant increase in option volume. In many cases, this can be the first warning sign that someone is attempting to trade with inside information. This situation of increased volatility *without* option volume usually occurs in illiquid options.

Consider this scenario, in order to see why options might get expensive before they get active: aggressive traders want to buy options because they feel they have information that will make the stock move significantly. However, the options are illiquid, so the market makers only sell the traders a few options before raising the offering price. The traders then step up and buy a few more options at the higher price before the market makers once again raise their offerings. This may go on for a little while, but eventually the options will have gotten so expensive that the traders will stop chasing them higher. The traders may decide to buy stock instead, or they may just bid for the options. In any case, what has happened is that the options have gotten quite expensive, but with very little option volume actually having traded.

We mentioned earlier in this chapter that Gerber option volume signaled the eventual takeover in Gerber (GEB), but at that time we also mentioned that increasing option prices were the first warning sign. You may want to compare this discussion with that previous one.

Figure 4.14 shows Gerber's stock price history, and the "wiggly" line on the bottom of the chart is the *daily* implied volatility of the options (weighted in a manner as described previously).

Figure 4.14
GERBER—IMPLIED VOLATILITY

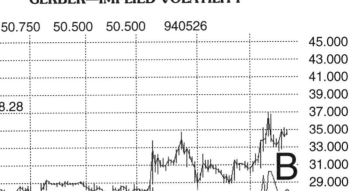

On the bottom left of the chart, there was so little option trading in general that there is no implied volatility line shown for many of those days. In fact, Gerber options were some of the most illiquid options listed. The stock was very dull and, as a result, traders had little interest in Gerber options. For example, GEB was locked in a narrow trading range between 27 and 29 from September of 1993 until March of 1994, an astoundingly narrow range for nine months!

However, note that in December and January implied volatility began to increase (point A). This was evidence that someone was trying to buy the options well in advance of the actual pickup in option volume. There wasn't really much option volume until early March, when the stock broke out of its trading range and rallied. At that time, you can see from Figure 4.14 that *implied volatility* jumped to new highs in March as well.

For the next two months—through April and May—the stock rallied, along with heavy option volume and steadily increasing implied volatility, culminating at point B on the chart, just before the takeover. This "double combination" was an important harbinger of the takeover to come. You will notice, however, that option *volume* players never really got "notified" until the stock had already broken out to 32 or 33. Even then, the stock suffered a pullback to 29 before eventually heading higher. However, those traders who were paying attention to implied volatility could easily have bought in the 27 to 29 range back in January or February of 1994.

Even casual observers of option premium levels understand that options often get expensive right before a takeover or other significant corporate news announcement. One group of such casual observers would be covered call writers; those covered writers may sometimes have access to lists such as "the best covered writes," which are generally the highest returns from selling covered options. Invariably, takeover and rumor stocks appear on such a list. This is not to say that you should write covered calls on rumor stocks, it's just an observation that the calls are often expensive prior to a takeover actually occurring.

A friend of mine, who is a professional trader, has often said that "the only option worth buying is an overpriced one." Now, while this is a mathematical non sequitur, it has a modicum of truth in it. Obviously, in the long run, you would hurt your statistical chances of making money if you constantly bought overpriced options. However, in certain situations—and this is of course what the trader was referring to—these overpriced options foretell profitable moves by the underlying stock.

Mathematicians will tell you that constantly overpaying for options is the road to ruin. If you constantly buy every rumor and every expensive option, you will be a loser in the long run. However, expensive options *can* be useful in helping to pinpoint potentially profitable stock movements. In fact, you might use that fact to actually buy stock rather than options.

Analyzing Implied Volatility for Speculative Trades

It is difficult to quantify exactly how to decide if the options are "expensive," but these are the guidelines that I use. First, the *daily* implied volatility—that is, the weighted average of the implied volatilities for each of the various options for today's trading—is what I use for the comparison. This is the most recent measure of the expensiveness of the options, and is therefore the most useful implied volatility to compare against other statistics. This daily implied volatility can then be compared to various other implieds: the 20-day moving average of *implied* volatility and various moving averages of *historical* volatility.

It seems best to compare the daily implied volatility with the various historical volatilities. If there is a significant differential between them, then that is a situation that should be examined. It is less important to compare the daily implied volatility with a moving average of implied volatility, because that is less likely to highlight interesting situations, especially if the implied volatility has been creeping higher for some time. This method, by the way, is different from the analysis that we use in Chapter 6, when we want to *trade* volatility.

The three following examples illustrate some of the considerations that take place. The first two examples involve the Gerber options depicted in the previous graph.

Example 1: In January 1994, with Gerber near 29 on one of the early days of Gerber's increased implied volatility (point A in Figure 4.14), the various measures stood at these levels:

> *Daily Implied Volatility: 51 percent*
>
> 10-day historical volatility: 23%
> 20-day historical volatility: 20%
> 50-day historical volatility: 28%
> 100-day historical volatility: 26%
>
> 20-day implied volatility average: 28%

You can see that the implied volatility has literally exploded as compared to any of the other measures of volatility. Look at the historical volatilities.

They are meandering around in the mid-20 percent range, indicating that the stock has been rather trendless. Not much has been going on. Moreover, the recent moving average of implied volatility is low, reflecting the fact that not much has been happening in the options either.

Obviously, this is a situation that demands some attention—perhaps not right away (because there is always the chance of a one-day fluke), but certainly if the implied volatility keeps registering at such high levels. It *did* persist (see previous graph), allowing the purchase of stock at low levels. (*Note*: Buying the options at this point would probably not have been profitable, for it is unlikely that you would have bought options that expired in June or later. However, a stock buyer would have been buying near the low and could have carried the position profitably all the way until the takeover.)

The next example is also of Gerber, but at a much later time: in May, right before the actual takeover occurred. Once again, implied volatility had taken a sudden jump, but from much different levels.

Example 2: By the middle of May, just a week or so before the takeover (point B in Figure 4.14), Gerber's stock had rallied to the 35 level and option implied volatility took another jump.

<u>*Daily Implied Volatility: 84%*</u>

10-day historical volatility: 67%
20-day historical volatility: 55%
50-day historical volatility: 57%
100-day historical volatility: 44%

20-day implied volatility average: 78%

All of these numbers are at vastly increased levels, when compared with Example 1. First, note that the daily implied volatility is still much higher than each of the historical volatilities.

The historical volatilities themselves tell an interesting tale, too. Note how much higher the short-term historical volatilities are as compared to the longer-term ones. This was caused by the fact that the stock broke higher, then fell, and then rallied (see Figure 4.14). The 100-day historical volatilities still contained some of the older, stodgy price movements, while the 10- and 20-day historical volatilities contained only the recent, volatile movements. Nevertheless, the daily implied volatility is still higher than any of the historical volatilities.

Finally, the daily implied volatility is not much higher than the 20-day average of implied volatility. Obviously, this means that implied volatility had been on the increase for some time.

What is important to recognize from this example is that the takeover occurred within a week, so we should treat the preceding data as significant. This means that a comparison of *daily* implied volatility and the 20-day *average* of implied volatility need not show a significant difference. It is more important for the various historical volatilities to differ from the daily volatility. When that happens, we have a situation that is worthy of note.

The previous example showed how implied and historical volatilities looks when a stock has just been getting hotter and hotter until a takeover occurs. The next example shows a slightly different situation: a stock *had* been the subject of a fairly hot and heavy takeover rumor, but the rumor then died out. Suddenly, the rumor recurred and shortly thereafter the takeover happened.

Example 3: In May 1995, there was a rumor that Banksouth (BKSO) was going to be taken over. At the time, implied volatility increased as did option volume. Moreover, the stock itself became rather volatile. However, nothing happened, and by the summer, the stock was down rather substantially from the May levels.

Then, in late August 1995, the rumors returned and implied volatility took a sudden leap. On September 1st, the volatilities were as follows:

Daily Implied Volatility: 46%

10-day historical volatility: 15%
20-day Historical volatility: 22%
50-day historical volatility: 26%
100-day historical volatility: 32%

20-day average of implied volatility: 34%

The trend of historical volatilities in this example is just the opposite of those in the previous example. Banksouth's actual (historical) volatility was on the wane at the time of this snapshot of volatility. It had been volatile earlier in the summer, but by September 1st it was becoming a very docile stock. The only remembrance of the earlier volatility was in the longer, 50-day and 100-day historical volatilities.

Note that the 20-day moving average of implied volatility is also higher than all of the historical volatilities, but is quite a bit lower than the daily implied volatility. Once again, the moving average of implied volatility does not seem to be that important.

The takeover occurred the next day and, while it was a modest one—only boosting the stock by about three points—it was still a takeover.

These examples show that implied volatility can be an important consideration. If it significantly exceeds the various historical volatilities, you should take a closer look at what is going on in the stock.

Here are the steps that I feel should be followed in order to identify situations such as those just described. The first two steps can be done with a computer: (1) compare the daily implied volatility with the 20-day moving average of implied volatility; if the daily is lower than the 20-day moving average, discard this stock; (2) compare the weighted daily implied volatility with the 10-, 20-, 50-, and 100-day historical volatilities. If it is at least 20 percent higher than three of those four historicals, the situation should be investigated further.

Further investigation necessitates taking a look at the individual option's implied volatilities that make up the weighted daily implied volatility for the stock. It is always possible that a "strange" occurrence has distorted the daily implied volatility, especially if you are using closing prices in your analysis. In that case, there is no speculative value to this stock and it can be culled from your list of prospects.

As an example of how individual options might distort the daily implied volatility, consider these data, collected in September.

XYZ: 25   Daily weighted implied volatility: 33%

Option	Price	Volume	Implied Volatility (%)
Jan 20 call	5.75	1,800	40
Oct 25 call	0.75	300	23
Dec 25 call	1.00	100	19
Jan 25 call	1.50	100	25
Oct 27½ call	0.13	150	26
Dec 27½ call	0.38	250	23

All of the options except the Jan 20 call have implied volatilities well below the weighted daily implied volatility of 33 percent. Thus, the Jan 20 call is dominant, but you can see that it was probably a covered write that caused the volume. Speculators would not be buying a January, in-the-money call with the stock at 25 in September. Thus, you would discard XYZ as a stock whose increased implied volatility was a potential precursor of corporate developments—at least for today.

Thus, the individual options' implied volatility must be examined, and, in doing so, the volume must be looked at as well. While there might not be enough volume to allow the stock to make the "high-volume" screens, there should at least be a speculative pattern to whatever volume there is. Obviously, in the preceding example, the volume did *not* have a speculative look to it. The following example depicts what we would expect to see in a typical low-volume situation with high implied volatility.

Equifax (EFX) is a small company whose options are not normally active—trading on average about 400 contracts per day. In addition, the 20-day moving average of implied volatility is 29 percent.

However, on a day in September, the daily weighted implied volatility shot up to 44 percent. This alerts us to look at the individual options. EFX closed at 40 on this day.

Option	Price	Volume	Implied Volatility (%)
Oct 40 call	2	110	42
Nov 40 call	2.875	120	44
Oct 45 call	0.75	160	50

In this case, while *volume* was small, it does have a potential speculative look to it. Moreover, each of the options is expensive when compared with the 20-day moving average of implied volatility (29 percent). So this is a stock that we would want to regard as a potential buy.

Before ending these examples, there is one other scenario involving increased implied volatility that occurs with some frequency. When a stock has been the subject of a rumor for some time, its options often get quite active, thereby inflating the 20-day volume average. Thus, it becomes harder and harder for the stock to appear on the high-volume list because it can't double the now-inflated volume. In a situation such as this, your only clue to the fact that the stock may still be "hot" is high implied volatility. The following example details such a situation.

Interdigital Communications (IDC) is a stock that had been "hot" a couple of times in 1995. Early in the year, it had roared from 3 to 13 on the back of increasing business, plus rumors that it was about to win a large lawsuit from Motorola. However, they eventually lost the lawsuit to Motorola and the stock collapsed to 5. Those events caused option volume, as well as volatility, to increase a lot.

However, after being calm for a couple of months, option volume picked up again as the stock gathered momentum once more, trading up to near 9. This once again caused option volume to increase. But nothing came of that move, and the stock slowly began to settle below 8 as speculators exited the stock, looking for more action in other places.

Then, in September 1995, Interdigital options got expensive and somewhat active. However, since the average *volume* was already inflated by the previous action, the only clue for traders was the increased volatility.

IDC: 7¾   20-day moving average of implied volatility: 60%

Average daily volume: 2,444 contracts

Daily Weighted Implied Volatility: 77%
10-day historical volatility: 36%
20-day historical volatility: 42%
50-day historical volatility: 46%
100-day historical volatility: 49%

Option	Price	Volume	Implied Volatility (%)
Oct 7½ call	0.81	700	76
Dec 7½ call	1.31	200	76
Mar 7½ call	1.81	200	78
Oct 10 call	0.19	500	85
Nov 10 call	0.38	200	81
Dec 10 call	0.50	200	75
Mar 10 call	1.00	200	76

Total volume was a healthy 2,200 contracts, but because the *average* volume was an inflated 2,444 contracts, this stock doesn't show up on the volume screens. However, the daily implied volatility is 78 percent, well above the 20-day moving average, and well above the historicals also. Since the individual options also look speculative in nature, we would want to take a look at IDC as a trading candidate. It quickly moved two points higher.

Thus, implied volatility was useful in even a situation where we had relatively active options, because it helped identify a potential trading candidate even though the volume screens would not.

As a final word on using implied volatility to select speculative stock trading candidates, let me stress that *volume is still important.* Without volume eventually appearing, I wouldn't get too excited about buying the stock. Thus, in the previous examples, the implied volatility is used to *identify* a potential trading situation, but I would usually want some confirmation from volume (which may not come for a few days) before taking too large a position in the stock. The reason that we want a volume confirmation is to avoid being in a stock that suffers a huge gap to the downside, for option implied volatility can be a predictor of such gaps also, as we see in the next section.

Implied Volatility Can Predict Trading Gaps

When a corporate event that is going to cause a large change in a stock's valuation is on the horizon—and it may be a publicly announced event—the options will become extremely expensive in advance of the actual event occurring. An example: the appearance of a small biotech company before the Food & Drug Administration (FDA) regarding approval of the company's only viable drug. Or possibly the pending culmination of a lawsuit whose outcome will cause a company's (or perhaps even two companys') stock to change in price dramatically.

What we are basically talking about here is an event that will dramatically change the fundamentals of a corporation. After the announcement of the event, the company's fortunes will have changed so much that its stock price will be drastically different.

These types of events can also be forewarned of by implied volatility increases in a stock's options. What *cannot* be foretold in these situations, however, is the *direction* in which the stock will move, only that the stock *will* move.

This can still be useful information, especially if you are already a stockholder or if you are considering making a purchase of the stock. If the options are foretelling a major price change in the stock—direction unknown—you may want to avoid the stock until the news event is released.

In these situations, we are not talking about a news event that is "leaked" in advance. In general, no one knows what these outcomes will be. Courts do not release their verdicts in advance to anyone (in fact, if it is a jury trial, no one even knows what the verdict will be until it is announced in court). Nor does the FDA leak any of its decisions in advance.

A few actual historical examples will best serve to illustrate this phenomenon. We have already alluded to a couple of these in previous chapters. One was the Intel Corporation patent-infringement lawsuit against Advanced Micro Devices (AMD).

As the date approached, in March 1994, for the court to reach a decision, the implied volatility of options in both stocks increased, but those of Advanced Micro, the smaller company, were most noticeable. Intel's normal daily implied volatility was about 30 percent, but just before the announcement of the verdict, it grew to nearly 40 percent, an increase, but not much of one as you shall see from these examples. On the other hand, the smaller Advanced Micro's normal daily implied volatility was in the 50 to 60 percent range. But, during February and early March 1994, its implied volatility rose first to 120 percent, and then to over 130 percent! Now *that's* an increase in implied volatility.

All of this increase in volatility was taking place without the stocks actually changing much in price, because no one knew which way the verdict was going to go. However, they did know that the stocks would react strongly when the verdict was eventually announced.

When the verdict was finally announced, Advanced Micro had won. The stock jumped six points higher. AMD's implied volatility immediately collapsed, dropping down to 58 percent after the verdict. Intel fell three points over a two-day period following the verdict.

Some trial outcomes are less difficult to predict. Obviously, the AMD/Intel trial was a "too close to call" situation. Large trading firms employ their own lawyers to give them guidance on how a trial might turn out, and they sometimes even send lawyers to the courtroom to observe the proceedings. If they can glean an indication of what the trial's outcome might be, they can act before most other investors. In general, though, there is little or no clue as to the outcome. As I wrote in my daily fax report, prior to a court verdict being released, "attempting to predict these outcomes is about as difficult as predicting an election (look in your encyclopedia under Clement Attlee, Harry Truman, or George Pataki if you think elections are predictable), which is why the premiums are so high."

Another patent suit is also a good example. It involved Interdigital Communications (IDC) and Motorola (MOT); we referred to it in the IDC example at the end of the last section.

As mentioned in that previous example, IDC rallied from 3 to 13 on the back of a plethora of new contracts being signed. Also, apparently, the stock was rallying partly on some investors' expectations that it would win its patent lawsuit with Motorola.

Since IDC was a low-priced stock to begin with, its normal daily implied volatilities were very high, in the 100 to 110 percent range. However, as the verdict drew near, in March of 1995, implied volatility in IDC began to skyrocket. It routinely registered levels of 150 to 170 percent at that time.

The stock was trading at 12 when the court decided in favor of Motorola. IDC opened down seven points the next day. Implied volatility followed its normal pattern then, by dropping to 85 percent. Once the news is out, implied volatility returns to a much lower level.

This IDC example is a good illustration of how the increase in implied volatility might have been a good warning sign for an investor. If you had bought IDC at a lower price, you were enjoying the ride from 3 to 13. During that time, the company was announcing the signing of new contracts with a great deal of frequency. If you were only interested in the fundamentals of the stock (or the technicals, for that matter), everything appeared to be quite rosy. However, if you noticed the option premium exploding, you were given advance notice that the stock was in a high-risk mode. It might gap either up or down, but *something* was going to happen. Thus, if you didn't want to risk your accumulated profits, you could have sold, exiting in advance of the court's decision.

Hearings by regulatory bodies can be as important to some stock's future as the outcomes of lawsuits are to others. This is especially true of small biotech or drug companies, because not only are the Food and Drug Administration (FDA) decisions not leaked in advance, they are often so arbitrary that no one can predict the outcome. Thus, the options of a small biotech or drug company will often expand to very expensive levels as the date nears for the FDA to release its findings. Readers are referred to the example of Gensia Pharmaceuticals in Chapter 1. The graph of Gensia and the implied volatility of the options are shown in Figure 4.15. Even though the stock was up a point to 10 on the day before the FDA announce-

Figure 4.15
GENSIA PHARMACEUTICALS

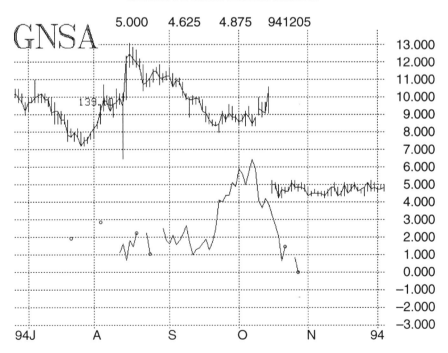

ment, it received an unfavorable ruling and dropped 50 percent to 5. Thus, it was evident that stock traders—at least those who pushed the stock up a point the day before—had no real clue as to the direction that the stock would take after the ruling. Neither did option traders, but at least the option premium was telling you as much. The following example is relevant as well.

United Bioscience (UBS) was a fledgling biotech company, trading at about $7 a share in late 1994 (the stock had been nearly twice that price about a year before, but delays in getting its drug approved by the FDA had weighed upon the stock price). On a normal day, the implied volatility of UBS options was in the 50 percent to 60 percent range.

In November, when traders learned that the FDA hearing was scheduled for early December, and that it could potentially decide the fate of the company, option implied volatility rose to 135 percent. By early December, it had reached an astounding 185 percent.

On December 12th, the FDA declined approval for the drug and the stock dropped to 2½. Essentially, the option's implied volatility dropped to 0 because the nearest strike price was 5, which was 100 percent above the stock price. In fact, the options were delisted when the stock didn't recover for several months. If the stock ever recovers, options will probably be relisted.

There can be other miscellaneous events that have similar effects on stock options. One that comes to mind occurred in 1995, and it involved Genetech and Roche, the large European drug company that owned warrants to buy all of Genetech. As those warrants neared their expiration date, the implied volatility of Genetech options doubled because, if Roche did exercise their warrants, Genetech was going to jump higher in price. However, if Roche decided not to pursue Genetech, the stock could have fallen a great deal. As it turned out, a middle ground was reached when Genetech allowed Roche to extend the expiration date of the warrants for four years, in return for raising the exercise price. In any case, holders of Genetech were alerted to the potential explosiveness of the warrant expiration (something the average stockholder may not have been aware of) by the increasing volatility in the options.

Sometimes, the consequences are less severe, but may be very important just the same. In the early fall of 1995, IBM had broken above 100 for the first time in years and was merrily trading up to 115 when it suddenly changed direction and began a fairly steady and rather quick decline to 103. Option implied volatility jumped dramatically (for IBM, that is—from about 30 to 40 percent). This was a warning sign that something more severe than a technical correction was happening. A few days later, the company indicated to analysts that sales figures (and, by inference, earnings) should be adjusted lower. The stock quickly dropped to 92 before stabilizing. The volatility and price swings in this example are smaller, but it shows that a sudden increase in implied volatility should be heeded as a possible precursor of important corporate news.

Thus, a sudden increase in implied volatility without an accompanying move by the underlying stock can be a warning sign that a price gap is about to occur. It behooves us to pay attention to the premium level of the options before entering a stock position and even after buying the stock. Whether or not you are an option trader, the options may give you fair warning of a catastrophic event on the horizon. As a stock owner, you may not notice anything unusual from watching the stock trade, but if the options are too excited, then you'd better do a little extra research to find out why.

IMPLIED VOLATILITY CAN PREDICT A CHANGE OF TREND

In the previous section, implied volatility was increasing while the underlying stock was fairly docile. In this section, we're going to see how the observance of extreme volatility levels—both high and low—might be useful in predicting the end of a trend in the price of the underlying security. In certain cases, this not only applies to stock options, but to index and futures options as well.

In general, for both stocks and indices, a declining market means increasing volatility, while a bullish market has decreasing volatility. This statement refers to both historical and implied volatility. Sometimes it helps to think in extremes to help visualize general statements like this (mathematicians call this "evaluating the boundary conditions"). In this case, the most extreme bearish case I can think of is the crash of 1987. Volatilities shot through the roof at that time. Other similar events that demonstrated this increasing volatility in down markets were the "crash" of 1989 (the day the UAL deal fell apart) or the collapse of 1990 (when Iraq invaded Kuwait). As for upside extremes, the long bull market of the 1990s is as good an example as any. Volatilities steadily decreased for the broad market indices as the market continued to push higher.

There are several factors at work in producing these volatility changes. One is that stocks tend to fall faster than they rise. Bull markets take years; bear markets, especially in recent times, may take only months. Eventually, we will have a longer bear market again, but even large ones like 1969 and 1974 only consumed a little over a year's time. Also contributing to these volatility differences is the fact that a low-priced stock can move by a larger percentage more easily than a high-priced stock can. For example, it's not unusual to see a $5 stock move by a half point in a day; it doesn't take that much buying or selling pressure to move any stock by a half point. However, that's a 10 percent move, and you rarely see a $100 stock move by 10 points, or even 5 points for that matter. Thus, we would *expect* to see volatility increase as prices fall, and likewise decrease as prices rise. Finally, since the indices are composed of stocks, they should, and do, display the same characteristics.

Futures, however, are different, and as a result it is difficult to make such a general statement regarding futures prices and volatility. Some futures and futures options behave like stocks do, but many behave in the opposite manner. That is, volatility shrinks as prices fall, and may explode if prices rise. Again, it may help to think of how commodity prices move in order to explain this phenomenon. There is an inherent demand for most commodities and therefore prices cannot fall too low (in fact, some commodities, like corn, even have a government price floor under them). However, given the vagaries of droughts and floods or other similar events, commodity prices can, and often do, explode to the upside. Thus, even though commodity markets can move with equal rapidity in both directions, they often move faster to the upside than the downside.

In reality, futures option volatilities will more often reflect the trend and how fast it is moving. Grain futures tend to fall relatively slowly, while they may rise dramatically (and many grain traders still remember the huge bull markets of 1973 and 1974, so every time prices start up, there is hope of a repeat of those bullish moves). As a result, you will find that implied volatility in grain options increases tremendously during bull moves and falls during bearish moves. However, another commodity will most likely react differently. For example, oil has had the potential for both big increases and big decreases over the years, and so whenever a trend seems to be accelerating in oil prices, the implied volatility of oil options will increase.

Given this general background, let's examine how these observations can be used to establish positions that might be profitable.

Covered Call Writing When Volatility Increases

We discussed the covered call writing strategy in Chapter 2. The conclusion was that it is best used when prices are stable or rising moderately; it is not such a great strategy in volatile markets. So what would make a covered write a great strategy would be not only stable stock prices, but expensive options that can be sold against that relatively stable stock.

We have just stated that implied volatility increases when stock prices fall, so if we could "catch" a stock right as its downtrend is ending, we would probably find that the options are about as expensive as they are going to get and, while the stock may not reverse into a bullish trend immediately, it will at least be stabilizing as it builds a bottom. So if we can find this situation, the covered writing strategy would be most appropriate.

Finally, a bit of contrarian theory can be thrown into this mix as well. If a stock has been falling for some time—perhaps rapidly—eventually put buyers will panic and start paying up to ridiculous levels for those puts. This causes the implied volatility of the options to inflate. Of course, contrarians would recognize everyone's desire to own puts as a sign of a bottom in the stock (if everyone wants to own puts, it must be the wrong thing to do since the majority is usually wrong; therefore the stock is nearing a buy zone, or at least will stop going down, and the large number of put buyers will lose money).

All of these thoughts can be summed up in this one statement: *when implied volatility reaches an extreme peak during a stock's*

downtrend, then the stock is ready to at least stabilize, and pos-
sibly even move higher. The same thought applies to index options
as well.

A classic example of this occurred in early 1993, involving IBM. IBM's stock
had peaked near 180 in 1987 and, after the crash, had never responded as
well as the overall market. It was able to rally back to about 140 in the
beginning of the 1991 bull market, but then began to stumble badly when it
was apparent that the company wasn't positioned for the computer boom
of the time. It fell slowly but steadily at first, eventually breaking 100 on the
downside in early 1992. A short rally brought it back up to 100 in June of
1992, and then the decline began to accelerate with a vengeance. Figure
4.16, which shows both the price of IBM and the implied volatility of its
options, encompasses the period from August of 1992 to October of 1994.
The sharp decline in price during the last half of 1992 is evident on the left

Figure 4.16
IBM, 8/92–10/94

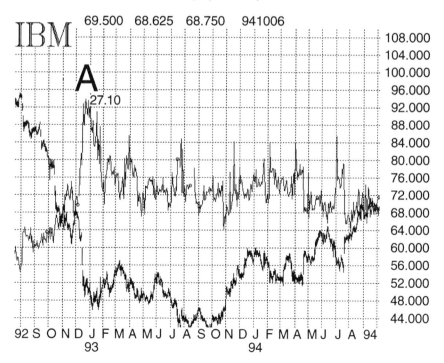

side of the chart. We mentioned this same time period back in Chapter 2 when we were using IBM as an example of naked put writing.

During the slow but steady part of the decline (March 1991 to July 1992), IBM's implied volatility had risen only modestly from the 20 percent area to about 25 percent. And, in fact, when the stock rallied back to 100 in June of 1992, implied volatility quickly settled back to the 20 percent range once again. However, when the more rapid decline of late 1992 began to unfold, implied volatility began to skyrocket. You can see from Figure 4.16 that it was increasing from August 1992 through November 1992, and then it literally exploded during December 1992 (point A on chart). Implied volatility had risen to nearly 50 percent by that time! This occurred with the stock near 50.

By early January, implied volatility was still high—near 40 percent—but it looked as if the peak volatilities had been seen. This then was a signal that the stock was going to stop going down. It was also a signal to begin establishing covered writes in IBM. These covered writes were very profitable, whether the strategy was followed for only a couple of months, or if it took a more intermediate-term view. Look at Figure 4.16 again. You can see that IBM stabilized and stayed near 50 through June of 1993. Thus a covered write of any (expensive) call with a striking price of 50 would have worked out very well.

If you had taken a longer-term view, things might have worked out even better. You can see from the chart that, even though IBM made a slightly lower low in the summer of 1993, it generally moved sideways for the entire year of 1993 and even into early 1994. However, option implied volatility remained relatively high during that time. Notice from the chart that the implied volatility during all of 1993 was higher than the implied volatility on the far left side of the chart (August, 1992). Thus, you could have repeatedly written covered calls and taken in expensive premiums while the stock price was more or less unchanged. Eventually, IBM *did* begin to rally and you would have been called away for a final time, but not before registering some very nice profits along the way. By late 1994, implied volatilities had dropped back into the low 20 percent neighborhood.

The additional advantage that the covered writer had during 1993, of course, was that he was selling options that were expensive and was therefore getting more downside protection than he was theoretically entitled to. This is when the covered write strategy is at its best.

Another similar example is found in the trading of Telefonos de Mexico (TMX), or Telmex as it is commonly called. When the peso was unexpectedly devalued in late 1994, Mexican financial investments collapsed in value. Since Telmex is the largest stock in Mexico (it's the telephone company), it was a focus of attention.

The chart of Telmex is shown as Figure 4.17, and includes the implied volatility of its options. Prior to what is shown on the chart, Telmex had peaked in price at around 75, fallen into the 50s, and then rallied back into the high 60s (point A on chart). As had been the case with the initial decline in IBM, the implied volatility of Telmex options did not really change much; it was near 30 percent the entire time.

In fact, except for a small spike in volatility in late August 1994, the implied volatility stayed pretty stable even while the stock was falling. In November and December the stock was falling to a price of 50, and implied volatility was increasing very gradually. Then, the peso devaluation came and the stock began to fall rapidly. Implied volatility jumped, too, and reached an interim peak in January of 1995 at over 70 percent (point B on chart). The stock was trading in the 33–35 area by that time.

Figure 4.17
TELEFONOS DE MEXICO (TELMEX)

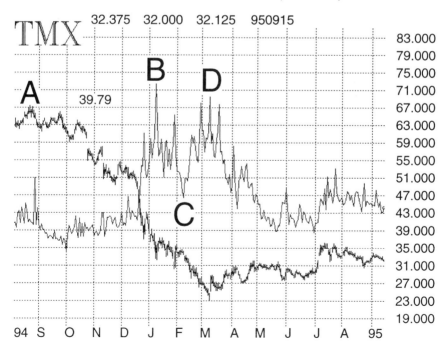

In February it appeared that implied volatility had peaked (point C on chart) and covered writes might have been established at that time. As it turned out, that was premature, as prices dropped to near 25 and implied volatility shot back up again in March (point D on chart). By late March, it again appeared that implied volatility had peaked, so covered writes were again warranted. The stock was at or just below 30 then. So, whether you had established the covered writes in February with the stock near 35 or in March with the stock near 30, you still had a good position. As you can see from the chart, the stock stabilized for months, trading sideways through the whole summer of 1995. Eventually, implied volatilities dropped back down into the 35 percent range and the scenario was finished.

This example again demonstrates the viability of looking for situations where implied volatility is skyrocketing while the stock is falling. Once the volatility peaks, covered writes are a preferred strategy. The example also demonstrates a problem with the strategy in that volatility may appear to have peaked, only to increase once again. This problem can be at least partially countered by taking only a half-position on the first decline in volatility, with plans to add to the position as time passes.

One might think that, given the apparent success of looking for *high* implied volatility, there might be a corresponding strategy associated with *low* implied volatility. If there is, it is much less evident for stock options (we'll see shortly that it's better used with index options). Obviously, if you feel implied volatility is too low, and therefore that the options are too cheap, you can consider option-buying strategies. These would primarily be straddle purchases, but stock options can get cheap and stay cheap for a long time, causing woe for straddle owners. So watching for exceedingly low implied volatility in stock options may sometimes be worthwhile, but it is a strategy that has to be used selectively. It is discussed extensively in Chapter 6.

Implied Volatility of Index Options

Since indices are composed of stocks, some of the same philosophies regarding implied volatility can be applied to index trading. This is especially true of the broad-based indices, such as OEX. When implied volatility gets too high—especially if it increases to that high rapidly—the market is near a bottom. Conversely, if implied volatility gets too low, we can expect a market explosion (not necessarily a drop in the market), for a large move is possible in either direction.

The CBOE publishes an index that is a measure of implied volatility of OEX options. This is the Volatility Index, and its symbol is VIX. Thus, even if you don't have any option calculation software, you can still observe OEX's implied volatility by charting this index.

The index was created in January of 1993, so its history is limited. But even since its inception, there are enough examples to demonstrate how OEX volatility relates to the stock market.

The chart of VIX is shown in Figure 4.18. During most of 1993 (not shown in Figure 4.18), OEX implied volatilities were stuck in

Figure 4.18
VOLATILITY INDEX—VIX

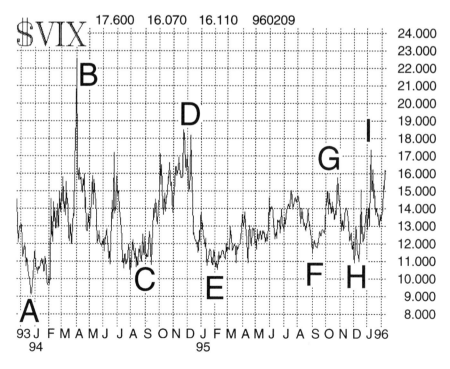

a range of about 11 to 14 percent. The graph shows the last few months of 1993, when volatility began to trend lower. In fact, it broke below the yearly range, falling all the way to 9 percent in December of 1993 (point A on chart), and remained below 11 percent through January of 1994. Anything below 10 percent is considered to be extremely low.

For broad-based index options, extremely low implied volatility normally precedes a market explosion. This explosion is often on the downside, but not always. Sometimes the market takes off to the upside instead. Thus, the preferred strategy is to buy straddles or establish backspreads when VIX makes an extreme low. In this particular case, the market was rallying and making new highs through January and into the beginning of February of 1994. The chart of OEX for the same time period is shown in Figure 4.19. Then the Fed raised rates for the first time in years, and OEX quickly fell nearly 50 points in just a couple of months. So the low volatility on the VIX chart was a good warning sign for what eventually turned out to be a major market decline.

All the while that this decline was taking place, OEX implied volatilities were rising. As the declines accelerated in late March, and especially the first trading day of April, VIX shot up to nearly 22 percent (point B on Figure 4.18). Implied volatility quickly retreated from those extremely high levels, leaving a spike high on the chart. *An extremely high implied volatility reading, especially if it occurs as a spike, is generally a sign that a short-term bottom is at hand for the broad market.* OEX rallied right after that spike in implied volatility, and the rally carried into the middle of June 1994. So the spike in implied volatility at the very beginning of April was a good time to buy the "market," or OEX in particular.

If you look back at the chart of the VIX, you will see that it reacted all the way back down to 11 percent while this market rally, which began in April, was going on. In June, a short, sharp market drop followed. By late June, this decline sent VIX spiking back up to 17 percent. This was a very short-term movement, so many traders may not have caught it. However, with the aid of VIX, you would have at least been aware that a trading high and low were likely.

In the late summer of 1994, the broad market was rallying once again. As is customary during steady rallies, implied volatility

Figure 4.19
OEX

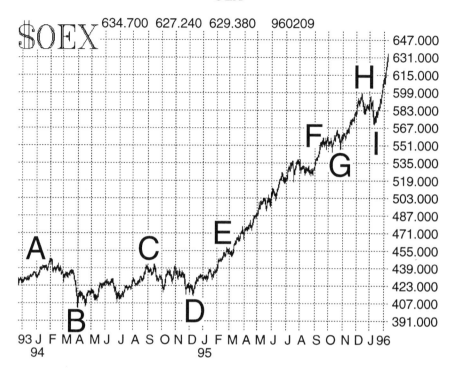

remained low, in the 11 to 12 percent range (point C in Figure 4.18). At about the same time that VIX broke out to higher volatility numbers over 12 percent, another relatively quick and sharp market decline began (in September). Once again low volatility had preceded a falling market. Often, the timing of the market move, whether up or down, can be refined by noting when volatility begins to increase.

Even though the broad market rallied a little in October of 1994, it eventually made its way to a new low in early December. Implied volatility, as measured by VIX, climbed rather steadily during that whole time, once again reaching levels above 18 percent (point D in Figure 4.18). From there it spiked down, a buy signal. In fact, this turned out to be a very large buy signal, as OEX and the broad market embarked on one of the largest rallies in recent memory. So, during

1994, using VIX as a guide to short-term market movements was very profitable.

As the large rally that started in December of 1994 worked its way higher over the next couple of months, VIX fell below 11 percent again (in February, 1995; point E in Figure 4.18). As it turned out this time, the market roared even higher. This, then, is an example of low volatility preceding an *upward* move in the market. After that, implied volatility settled into a trading range between 12 and 15 percent, neither spiking too high nor reacting to a new low.

In order to have profited from each of the low volatilities during 1944–1945, you would have needed to buy straddles each time, for you did not know whether the market was going to move higher or lower. Since the moves were large, profit would have resulted. Backspreads would have worked as well, as we'll see in Chapter 6.

Prior to the CBOE's initiating the VIX Index, there were other notable periods of extremely high or low implied volatility in OEX options preceding important market turns. Some of the low volatility examples include both August of 1983 and August of 1984. Both times, the market exploded higher shortly thereafter. Then, in 1987, OEX implied volatility reached very low levels just after the market peaked, but before the crash. Thus, followers of option premium were long straddles when the crash came.

High implied volatilities have signaled buying opportunities over the years. After the crash of 1987, volatilities rocketed to levels in the 40 percent range—levels never seen before or since for OEX options. That turned out to be a buying opportunity, although the volatility didn't exactly spike; it stayed at inflated levels for quite some time. The minicrash of 1989 (caused by the failure of the UAL leveraged buyout) saw volatility spike to high levels and then fall back, and that was a very good buy indicator.

In September 1987 the market had made some attempts to retest the all-time highs made in August, but those attempts were unsuccessful. At about this time, implied volatilities of OEX options and S&P 500 futures options were trading with an extremely low volatility.

The December S&P 500 straddle could be purchased for 15 points, with the index at about 320. That was a very low level of volatility, considering that the market had been rather volatile while rising all during that year. In fact, no three-month trading range had been contained within a 15-point wide band since the middle of 1985 (i.e., for over two years). Mathematically speaking, statistics indicated that there was a 93 percent chance that the market would move at least 15 points in three months.

As it turned out, the market moved much more than that, of course, falling over 100 S&P points during the crash.

Thus, not only is index option implied volatility useful as a market indicator, it is also useful as a *strategy* indicator. That is, when implied volatility is too low, option buying strategies are better, for a market explosion may be at hand. But when implied volatility is high, selling strategies may be good for strategists, while speculators can consider buying the market. Let's now take a look at another technical indicator based on daily option trading volume.

THE PUT–CALL RATIO

The put–call ratio is simply the number of puts traded in a day, divided by the number of calls traded on that same day. Normally options are grouped into similar categories when calculating the ratio. For example, an *index* option put–call ratio, or maybe a *gold* option put–call ratio, might be calculated. In order to smooth out the fluctuations of the daily numbers, some moving averages of the put–call ratio are usually tracked.

Technicians have been calculating the put–call ratio for a long time, even before the advent of listed options, for it is known to be a valuable *contrary* indicator. When too many people are bullish (when they are buying too many calls), then contrarians short the market because the majority is usually wrong. Similarly, when too many traders are bearish and buying puts, then a contrarian will look to buy the market. The put–call ratio is a measure of how many puts are trading with respect to calls, so that the contrarian can attempt to quantify his measurements.

The general patterns to compare are shown in Figure 4.20. When the put–call ratio is at a high level, a lot of puts are being bought, and that indicates a market buy. Then, the put–call ratio declines while the market is rallying. Eventually, bullish sentiment

Figure 4.20
PUT–CALL RATIO

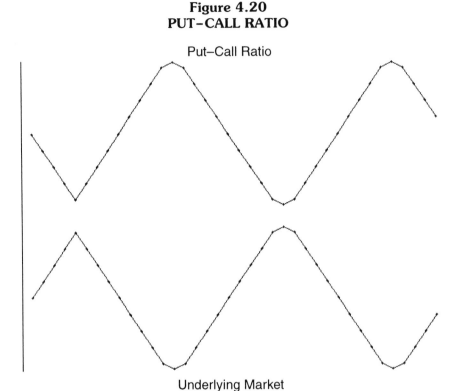

Put–Call Ratio

Underlying Market

becomes too strong, and the put–call ratio bottoms just as the market is making a top. After that, the put–call ratio rises while the market is falling, until the whole cycle begins again.

There are two major put–call ratios that are widely followed. The first is the *index* option put–call ratio, which is generally best computed by using only OEX options, for that is the index with which most people speculate. Therefore the OEX put–call ratio will normally give the best clues regarding what the "average" trader is doing. I have looked at the put–call ratio of all index options, and it is not a useful number. Many of the indices besides OEX are dominated by institutional orders and do not accurately reflect the speculative activity whose observance is necessary in order to develop a contrary opinion.

The second major put–call ratio is the *equity-only* put–call ratio. As the name implies, this ratio is calculated by using the volume of all stock options. You can also combine the index and equity-only ratios to arrive at a *total* put–call ratio.

These are the most reliable ratios because there is a lot of option volume each day in these categories. If we were to calculate the put–call ratio on an individual stock, there would normally be so little volume that the figures would be quite distorted and would not be useful in predicting the direction of the stock's movement. Very active equities such as Intel or IBM might be exceptions, but even with those, there may be little correlation between the put–call ratio and the direction of the trend in the stock.

A sort of middle ground can be reached with futures options. It makes no sense to calculate a futures put–call ratio wherein all futures contracts are included, because, for example, there is no relationship between grain options and oil product options. However, if futures options are relatively active on a particular commodity, then you could use the option trading across all months for those specific futures options. Thus, you might compute a *gold futures* option put–call ratio, or a *soybean futures* option put–call ratio.

The Data

All of the data are available in the newspaper every day, although the equity-only put–call ratio is somewhat difficult to calculate. The easiest broad ratio to determine is the index put–call ratio, for you merely have to divide the total number of OEX puts traded by the total number of OEX calls traded. These two numbers are reported in the *Wall Street Journal* or *Investors Business Daily* every day. On any given day, there are normally more index puts traded than index calls, which is a result of the fact that many investors and money managers buy OEX puts as protection for their long stocks. In recent years, as more and more money managers utilize this protective feature of index options, the index put–call ratio has crept higher and higher. We discuss this fact in more detail when we discuss how to interpret the ratios.

Computing the equity-only put–call ratio is a little more difficult, although you can arrive at a fairly accurate estimate in a short period of time. The same newspapers report the *total* volume, by exchange, and then by grand total; they also report all the index option trading in one place as well. The "total" figures include every stock-related option that trades on the exchange: all the index options are included in this total as well. So, in order to arrive at the equity-only put–call ratio, you need to subtract the index option trading from the total trading.

This example shows what numbers to use from the daily financial pages in order to construct the CBOE equity-only put–call ratio on a daily basis. The figures were taken from *Investor's Business Daily*, but the same information can be found in the *Wall Street Journal* as well, or by calling 1-800-OPTIONS.

The total volume is listed under "Option Totals," for each option exchange. This information is normally found on the same page that lists all the option quotes for various stock options. On the particular day used for this example, we find:

Exchange	*Total Call Volume*	*Total Put Volume*
CBOE	322,941	252,373

Now, turning to the "Index Option" listings, we find these various indices listed:

Index	Total Call Volume	Total Put Volume
S&P 100 (OEX)	73,676	110,942
S&P 500	22,522	46,925
NASDAQ-100	3,437	5,379
Total index	99,635	163,246

These three indices all trade on the CBOE, and they are the most active. You might even want to ignore the NASDAQ-100 because its volume is so small in comparison to the others. In any case, if we subtract the total of these three indices (total index) from the prior total of all options traded on the CBOE, we get:

	Total Call Volume	*Total Put Volume*
Equity-only estimate:	223,306	89,127

Thus, the CBOE equity-only put call ratio would be the quotient of these two: 0.399.

You might think it's not worth the bother to compute the equity-only ratio, since many speculators trade OEX options. It turns out that in recent years the equity-only ratio has given some important signals with far better timing than the index ratio. In fact, some analysts think that the equity-only ratio is the "purer" one because there is so little arbitrage in equity options anymore and most money managers don't buy equity puts for protection—they buy index puts. Therefore, equity options may represent a better picture for contrarians.

The daily numbers can either be expressed as the absolute ratio, or as a percent. For example, if an equal number of puts and calls traded, then the daily number would be 1.00 (absolute) or 100 (percent). I prefer to use percents because, when you're speaking about the ratios, you don't have to keep saying "point" (as in one point fifteen for 1.15, for example). The index put–call ratio tends to have daily numbers in the 100 to 130 range (circa 1995). The equity-only ratio, however, is far different. Since there are normally many more equity calls traded than puts, the equity-only ratio is normally in the 30 to 50 range. That is, only 30 to 50 equity puts trade for every 100 equity calls that trade on a given day. The "total" put–call ratio (all options traded) is typically in the 50 to 70 range. These ranges tend to change over time, so you should understand that these ranges refer to the early-to-mid 1990s time period. We will soon discuss how and why these ranges change.

Different technical analysts keep track of different moving averages of the ratios. I prefer to use a 21-day moving average and a 55-day moving average. However, some prefer to keep shorter or longer moving averages. I find that the 21-day average is useful in catching short-term moves that might last from a few days to a few weeks, while the 55-day identifies more intermediate-term trends.

Interpreting the Ratios

The concept of interpreting the put–call ratios is an easy one in theory, but in practice, things become a little more complicated. It is an easy matter to say that when the ratio gets "too high," you should buy the market. Conversely, if the ratio gets "too low," you should take bearish positions. Quantifying "too high" and "too low" is where things get tricky. Past experience has shown that static interpretations of the put–call ratios are an incorrect approach, for investors and traders change their investing patterns. Rather, a dynamic approach is best. A dynamic approach means looking for peaks and valleys—at whatever absolute levels they may occur—in the put–call ratio to indicate buy and sell points.

Let's begin with some historical examples. Recall that put options didn't start trading until 1977, and index options until 1983. Therefore, it wasn't until after 1983 that traders had the index put–call ratio and the total put–call ratio available to them. Since there was very little use of index puts as protection in those days, the index ratio was considered to be the best source for the speculative pulse of the market. Moreover, there was a lot of arbitrage in equity options, so the equity-only put–call ratios were somewhat distorted by this arbitrage.

In those days, the index put–call ratio ranged between about 60 and 100 at the extremes, much lower than today's average range.

Figure 4.21
55-DAY INDEX PUT–CALL RATIO

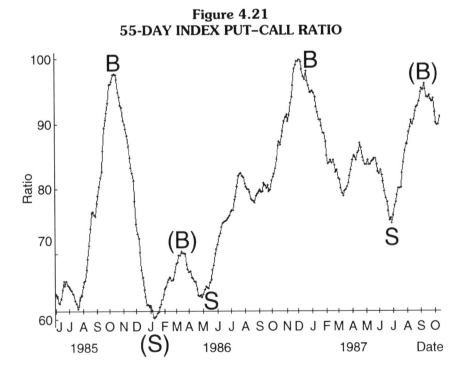

When the ratio rose to near 100, the market could be bought, and when it fell to 60, it could be sold.

In October of 1985, the index put–call ratio reached 100, and the market embarked on a huge 8-month rally. OEX moved from 175 to 239 by July of 1986. Then, in December of 1986, the index put–call ratio reached 100 once again, and the market rallied for another eight months, setting many all-time highs along the way. OEX rose over 100 points in that time. The ratio reached very low levels in March of 1985 and April of 1986, neither of which was a tremendous sell point, but in both cases the market leveled off and went sideways for several months after each occurrence.

These buy and sell signals, using the intermediate-term 55-day moving averages, are shown in Figure 4.21, while the graph of OEX over the same period is in Figure 4.22.

Figure 4.22
OEX DURING 1987

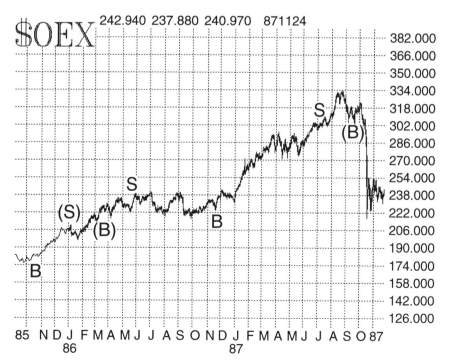

What happened next made many technicians discard the put–call ratio as a useful indicator. The index put–call ratio (coming off the December 1986 buy signal) gave a sell signal in July of 1987. You may not think that's so bad, since the market actually peaked in August, but the index ratio began to climb back toward the 100 level by September of 1987, and actually gave a buy signal at that point (September 1987). Thus, if you were only paying attention to the *index* put–call ratio, you were long going into the crash of 1987.

The saving grace was that the equity-only put–call ratio also gave a sell in July, and remained on that sell signal through the crash and on into early 1988. So even though the equity put–call ratio sell signal was early, it was correct, and it did not reverse before the crash (see Figure 4.23).

Nevertheless, the index signal was a disaster. What had gone wrong? Had the public actually been right? Did they really buy so many puts during the July–September period of 1987, and therefore

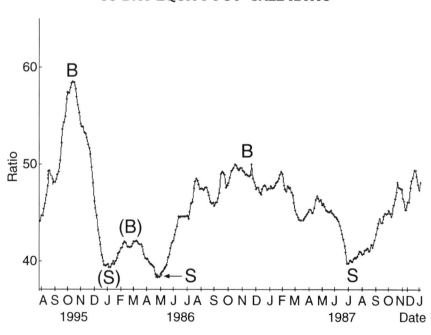

Figure 4.23
55-DAY EQUITY PUT–CALL RATIO

correctly anticipate the crash? I think any one who survived the crash or even read about it knows that the public most certainly did *not* anticipate it. Therefore, the public was not buying puts before the crash (in fact, you may recall our comments in Chapter 2 concerning how many public customers were actually *selling* naked puts just before the crash).

If you think about it logically, a rising market should always culminate with lots of call buying. The public will always chase a trend, not fight it. That's why contrary indicators work. At the exact top of a market, the public will be displaying its most bullish sentiment. In option terms, that means the public will be buying *calls* heavily at the top of a bull market. By logical extension, then, you would not expect to see *put* buying increase heavily while a market is rising; rather, put buying should increase while a market is falling. Thus, if you do see put buying increasing during a rising market, you should suspect that something besides speculation is behind that increase in put volume.

So why did the put–call ratio shoot up that summer? There is only one plausible answer: institutions were buying puts in order to protect their stock holdings.[1] In Chapter 3, we discussed how portfolio insurance played a role in the crash. Those money managers were (theoretically) using futures to hedge their stock positions, but many others were buying index options as protection. So, during the summer of 1987, as the market drove into what was considered by many to be overvalued territory, some institutions took the precaution of buying puts. *This* is what caused the index put–call ratio to accelerate to the upside. Apparently, by late September (see Figure 4.21), the institutional put buying slacked off and the index put–call ratio began to trend down—a buy signal.

The institutions tend to buy index puts more readily than individual equity puts, because with one large buy order in OEX puts, they can acquire a lot of protection. It would be much more work to buy

---

[1]Some analysts may offer another explanation: that the public was selling naked index puts and thus inflating the volume. True, there was some of that going on, and the losses subsequently suffered by those put sellers made front-page news in the financial section. But, in reality, there wasn't enough naked put selling to make a real dent in the overall volume figures. Institutional put buying, however, *was* significant in terms of volume.

puts on each stock that they own, to say nothing of the fact that many of the individual equity puts would be so illiquid that the institutions could not even purchase the quantity of puts they need.

We will never know what happened to all those puts that were bought, of course, but it wouldn't be too shocking to discover that they were puts expiring in October or earlier. Of course, those puts, while useful, expired on October 16, 1987, just before the actual crash on October 19th. A less cynical view, of course, would allow that the institutions bought puts expiring in November or December.

Earlier, we stated that, during the early days of listed index options, the index put–call ratio was considered to be the best measure of speculative activity because there was very little use of puts for protection. Obviously, that situation changed during the summer of 1987. Index puts suddenly became a very popular item among institutions, which tend to have a herd mentality about such things. As the theoreticians were convincing some money managers of the viability of using puts, the word was spreading and many of them rushed in to buy these puts. During the years since then, even more money managers routinely use index puts as a form of protection. This is why the average put–call ratio readings of index options have moved from the 60–100 range in the 1980s up to the 100–130 range in the 1990s.

Interpreting the put–call ratio as strictly a contrary indicator results from the tacit assumption that most option buying is speculative and can therefore be interpreted by the contrary-opinion theory. In reality, there are other factors at work besides speculation. Index options at first *were* mostly pure speculation, but then became speculation mixed with protective put buying. Ironically, *equity* option volume in the early 1980s contained a lot of arbitrage activity. That arbitrage activity was so prevalent that it even distorted the NYSE short-interest figures, so that technicians had to basically give up on short interest as a means of measuring market sentiment. The equity arbitrage that was so prevalent in the early 1980s has disappeared (because of competitive pressures), so that the *equity* put–call figures today may be a purer measure of sentiment than the index ratio.

So, when we see a lot of index puts being bought while the market is rising, are we to interpret this as bullish because the public is looking for a top in a rising market, or should we figure that the put volume is due to institutional put buying? Almost certainly, it's the latter, for reasons already discussed—the public doesn't get bearish at tops, they get bullish. But, even though he knows the put volume is increasing from institutional activity, the contrarian is still in a difficult situation. What is the institutional manager's true bias? Is he bullish because he still owns stocks, or is he bearish because he is buying puts? This is the bane of contrary analysis—attempting to accurately interpret the data being received.

Before getting to more recent examples, one more historical footnote might be helpful. In the 1980s, the put–call ratios were more or less static, ranging between the same highs and lows. However, as noted earlier, with the more prominent use of puts for protection, the ratios have crept higher over the ensuing years. This means that a static interpretation (such as "buy when the index ratio gets to 100 and sell when it falls to 60") is irrelevant. In the late 1980s and early 1990s, however, some technicians were still trying to stick with their old, static measures and were especially hurt by the mini-bear market of 1990. In that year, the ratios were trending higher, so static interpreters bought the market when the ratios reached their old, (un)reliable buy zones. This got them long too early, and created even more bad publicity for the put–call ratio as a technical indicator. Feature articles were written about the fact that the put–call ratios just didn't work anymore.

They still work, but you must interpret them dynamically—looking for local maxima and minima as buy and sell points—and not rely on fixed numbers. You will never again see the 50-day moving average of the index put–call ratio down to 60, even if the market goes straight to the moon. The following charts contain several examples of buys and sells occurring at differing levels; however, each of those buys and sells is a turning point in the trend of the ratio (a peak or a valley). This, then, is the *proper* way to interpret the put–call ratios.

Situations similar to 1987 occurred again in the big bull market of the 1990s, most notably in 1995. The market began to rise strongly in the first part of the year. Initially, both the equity and index put–call ratios had confirmed this with a buy signal in December 1994 (point **a** on Figures 4.24 through 4.26; these charts use the short-term 21-day moving average).

However, the rise began to accelerate and both ratios issued sell signals in February of 1995 (point **b** on the charts). This was an incorrect sell signal, as the market only paused briefly and then blasted ahead. The equity put–call ratio quickly turned back to a buy (point **c** in Figure 4.24), but the index ratio did not. In fact it continued on to much higher highs.

What was happening was the same thing as in 1987: institutions were buying puts en masse to protect their stock holdings. Many money managers already felt that the market was overvalued even *before* the 1995 rally began, and by the spring they were getting very nervous. So they bought index puts. Note that we can't necessarily derive any market prediction from the institutional index put buying; in 1987, a bear market followed, while in 1995, a bull market ensued.

Finally, the index put–call ratio got back on a buy signal (point **c** in Figure 4.25). The ratios were then again in synch. This time, the buy was correct, as the rally continued well into the future.

Figure 4.24
21-DAY EQUITY-ONLY PUT–CALL RATIO

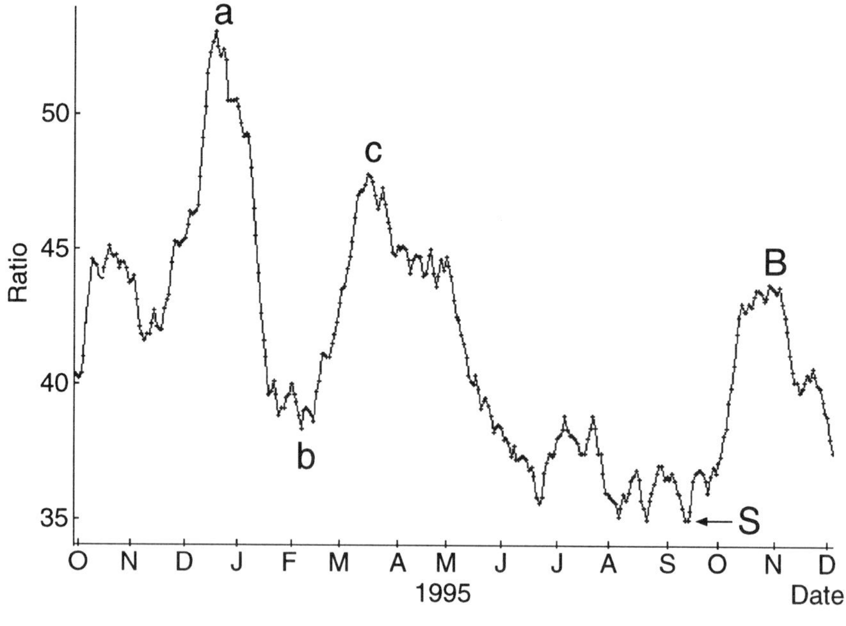

   These 1995 and 1987 experiences seem to dictate that both the index and equity put–call ratios must confirm signals. Also, heavy index put buying during a fast-rising market should be regarded as institutional activity, and not as a true contrary indicator at that time. In fact, many contrary indicators can be distorted by arbitrage or nonspeculative activity. That is why it often pays to think about what's going on, and not just blindly follow *any* indicator, especially a contrary indicator.

   You can see the other points marked as buys (B) and sells (S) on these charts, and how well they correspond to market bottoms and tops on the OEX chart. This confirms the viability of using the put–call ratio as an indicator. Notice that the index buy signals generally occur with the ratio in the 130–140 range, and the sells in the 110–120 neighborhood. These levels will change as the years go by, as the relative definition of how much is "too much" mutates. However, the dynamic interpretation of using local maxima as buy signals and local minima as sell signals will persevere.

Figure 4.25
21-DAY INDEX PUT–CALL RATIO

Figure 4.26
OEX, 1994–1995

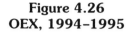
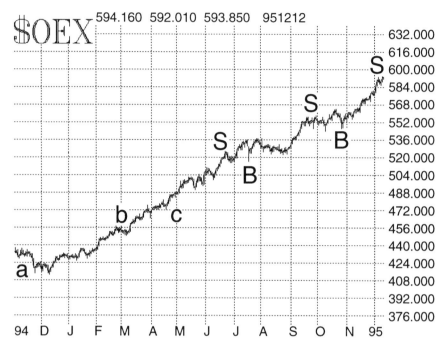

I expect the index ratio to eventually head much higher if and when we ever have a bear market. The bulls who buy because the index put–call ratio is "too high," or those who just use a static level as a buy point, will be buried when that happens. You should *not* be fooled, however, for when that happens, you now know not to turn bullish until the index ratio actually *peaks*, even if that doesn't occur until the ratio reaches now-unheard-of levels.

Sector Index Options Put–Call Ratios

Put–call ratios can be used in a similar manner for the more liquid sector options. Since sector options are quite a bit less liquid than OEX options, you would expect the signals to be less accurate—and they are—but they are still quite useful most of the time. At the time this book was written, the following sectors were responding best to put–call ratio signals. The index symbol is given in parentheses (we use a dollar sign to denote that it's an index):

Banking ($BKX)	NASDAQ-100 ($NDX)
Broker-Dealer ($XBD)	Natural Gas ($XNG)
Computer ($XCI)	Oil and Gas ($XOI)
Consumer ($CMR)	Pharmaceuticals ($DRG)
Cyclical ($CYC)	Semiconductor ($SOX)
Gold and Silver ($XAU)	Tech Stocks ($TXX)
Hong Kong ($HKO)	Telecommunications ($XTC)
Japan ($JPN)	Topix ($TPX)
Major Market ($XMI)	Utilities ($UTY)
Mexico ($MEX)	

For those not too familiar with sector index options, the categories in the preceding list are fairly self-explanatory with the following exceptions: Major Market (an index of 30 stocks that simulates the Dow-Jones Industrials), and Topix (the 100 largest American companies). Specific details of the components of each sector index can be obtained from your broker or from the exchange where the options are listed.

It is interesting to note that three foreign stock markets are among the sectors with active option trading in the United States: Mexico, Japan, and Hong Kong. The put–call ratio has proven to be a good trading vehicle for all three of these sectors. Consider Figures 4.27 and 4.28. These figures are of the Japan Index ($JPN) and its put–call ratio during a period of 1994–1995. Note that the put–call ratio can reach very high extremes in these sector options. Using the same logic as with the OEX put–call ratio earlier, we see that there are buys when the put–call ratio peaked in September 1994 (a poor signal), February 1995 (also a poor signal), and July 1995 (an excellent signal). On this same graph, sells coincide with bottoms on the put–call ratio chart. These occurred in January 1995 (a superb signal), May 1995 (a decent signal), and October 1995 (another good signal). So, on this chart alone, profits were registered in four of six situations, and two of the signals preceded very large moves by the index. If you were to have bought an at-the-money option at the time of each signal, you would have profited handsomely: two would have

Figure 4.27
21-DAY JAPAN INDEX PUT–CALL RATIO

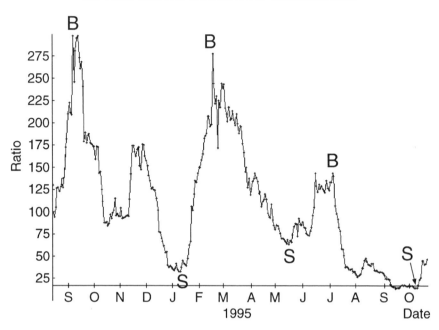

expired worthless, but two would have returned many times their initial value, and two would have generated smaller profits. Figure 4.28 extends back to late 1993, and two good put–call signals—a buy in December 1993 and a sell in June 1994—are noted for that time period as well.

There are several other indices whose options are active enough to use for put–call ratio signals. The best ones at the time of this writing included the NASDAQ-100 (symbol: $NDX), Semiconductor Index ($SOX), Broker-Dealer Index ($XBD), Technology Index ($TXX), Gold and Silver Index ($XAU), Mexico Index ($MEX), and the Utility Index ($UTY). We won't go over all of these, since they may change in the future when technology cools off, and something else becomes hot. However, the NASDAQ-100 is typical, as seen in Figures 4.29 and 4.30. These figures show the put–call ratio for the NASDAQ-100 Index ($NDX) during 1995, and the price of the index itself. In late 1994 and through the middle of 1995, put volume was very heavy and the put–call ratio reached lofty levels several

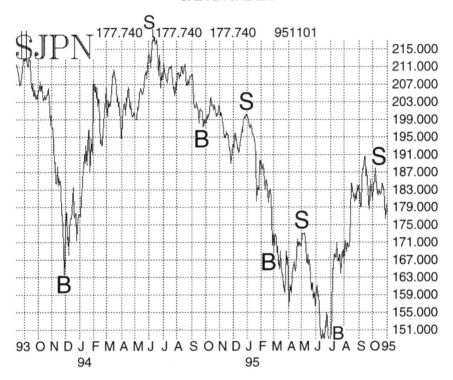

Figure 4.28
JAPAN INDEX

times—over 250 on the put–call ratio. Buy signals in December 1994 and April 1995 were especially rewarding. Also, the index suffered its first serious setback in July 1995, and the put–call ratio raced up to about 260 again that time, resulting in another profitable buy. Sell signals seem to come from local minima in the 80–90 area. There was a modestly profitable one in January 1995, but you would have had to be quick to register much of a profit then. However, the sell in September 1995 was an excellent one.

Futures Options Put–Call Ratios

Put–call ratios can also be calculated for futures options. As stated previously, though, it only makes sense to compute such a ratio for

Figure 4.29
21-DAY $NDX PUT–CALL RATIO

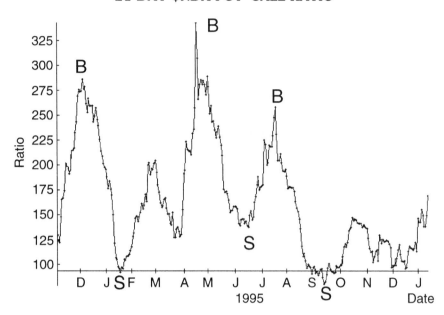

one commodity or set of futures contracts at a time. Thus, to compute the gold futures options put–call ratio, add the put volume for all of the existing gold contracts (February gold futures puts, April, June, August, October, and December, for example). That total would then be divided by the call option volume totaled over the same contracts. The result would be the gold put–call ratio for the day. The number of puts and calls traded is reported, subtotaled by commodity, in the daily newspaper listing of futures option prices.

Since the total volume of gold options traded in a given day is a very small number compared to OEX options or total equity options, you must be a little careful in interpreting the indicator. One or two large orders can distort the gold put–call ratio daily because volume is relatively thin. Thus, rather than interpreting each local maxima and local minima as a sell or buy signal, respectively, you may be better served by looking for *extreme* maxima and minima as signals.

Figure 4.31 is a chart of gold's put–call ratio extending from January 1994 through August 1995. You can see that the ratio had

Figure 4.30
NASDAQ

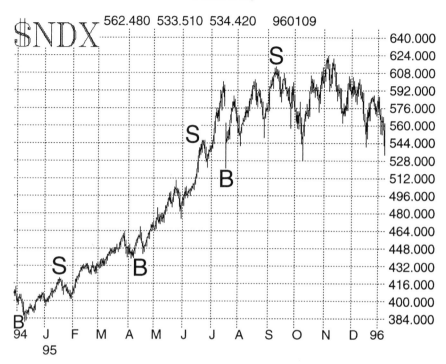

an extreme peak near 100 (point A) in August 1994. That was a good buy signal, as gold rallied from about 385 to 410 over the next two months. See the chart of continuous gold futures, Figure 4.32, to verify this.

The continuous charts shown in the remainder of this chapter are constructed by sequentially linking futures contracts and eliminating the gap that occurs between them. For this gold chart, for example, during April and May, the price is that of the nearest June futures. Then during June and July, the continuous price uses the nearest August futures, and so forth. However, the price of each sequential contract is adjusted to eliminate the gap that exists (between June and August futures, for example). Essentially, this chart represents the actual results a trader would have experienced had he bought gold futures in August of 1993 and continually rolled

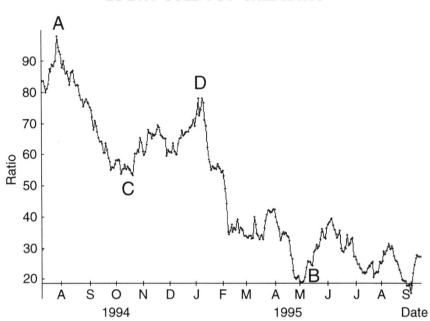

Figure 4.31
21-DAY GOLD PUT–CALL RATIO

to the nearest contract about a month before expiration. The October 1995 prices (on the right side of the chart) are *lower* than the actual December 1995 gold futures prices. This is reflective of the fact that a trader would have *lost* some ground each time he rolled forward, since the longer-term contracts trade at a premium to the current contract. In a situation where the longer-term contracts trade at a discount to current contracts (T-bonds, for example), the continuous price chart would have a *higher* price in October of 1995 than the actual December T-bond futures. We use this continuous price chart to evaluate the signals because it reflects how a trader would have done at any time by trading the most liquid contract over the length of the chart, without artificial gaps in prices.

Back to our example. In May 1995 the put–call ratio reached an extreme low, getting all the way down to 20 (point B). That means that there were five calls traded for every put that traded, on average. That low level is certainly reflective of an extreme bullish opinion on

Figure 4.32
CONTINUOUS GOLD FUTURES

gold. Therefore, by contrary-opinion theory, a sell signal was issued. Gold was much less volatile at that time, but did manage to decline about $20.

So, using the extremes seems to work fairly well. But what about the other two significant turning points in the gold put–call ratio (points C and D on the chart in Figure 4.32)? It turns out that these were good signals also. Point C identifies a sell signal in October 1994; look again at the chart of continuous gold, and you can see that it declined from about 390 to about 355 in January.

Point D on the put–call ratio chart in Figure 4.31 is a local maxima—a buy signal. It worked pretty well also. Gold rallied from that January buy signal to a high in April (355 to 378, approximately). Then, shortly thereafter, the extreme sell signal of May 1995 occurred.

Gold options trade between about 5,000 and 20,000 contracts a day normally, but occasionally volume is above that range. As options go, that's not a lot of contracts. In fact, a large wholesaler or institutional account could probably dominate the volume on any given day. Whether they would be active enough to dominate it for 21 days (the length of the moving average that we are using) is unlikely, but still possible. That's why we usually prefer to stick with only extreme readings as signals. However, you can see from the preceding charts that even the intermediate readings (points C and D) can also present good trading opportunities. However, I would still caution you to be a little more careful with the intermediate readings.

Since each futures option market is more or less a separate entity, we have taken extensive looks at each one over time in order to determine whether or not the put–call ratio is a useful indicator. The low-volume ones are the easiest to eliminate. These include

Figure 4.33
CONTINUOUS LIVE CATTLE FUTURES

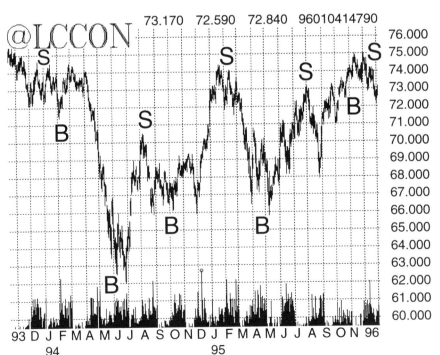

cocoa, the U.S. Dollar Index, copper, orange juice, the CRB Index, and T-bills. *Avoid these contracts, as far as the put–call ratio indicator goes, because the volume is just too low to give meaningful signals.* If volume should increase in any of these contracts in the coming years, then that assessment may change.

There are other contracts where the put–call ratio seems to have no correlation to the price movement of the underlying futures. These should be avoided as well. Avoid corn, soybeans, wheat, crude oil, heating oil, and unleaded gas. For whatever reason, the maxima and minima on the put–call ratio—even at the extremes—do not correspond very well at all with buy and sell points for these futures. Perhaps the option volume is dominated by true hedgers; that's usually what distorts the put–call ratio. In any case, we would *not* recommend trading these contracts with put–call ratio signals.

Now that we've eliminated those, let's discuss more profitable ones. As noted earlier, gold futures can be profitably traded with the put–call ratio. One of the best is live cattle. Figures 4.33 and 4.34

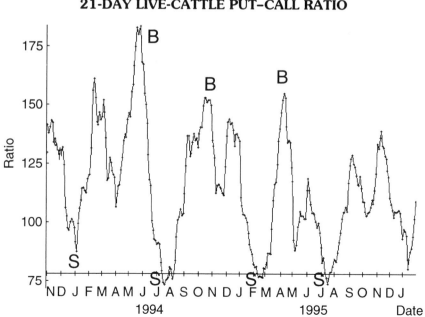

Figure 4.34
21-DAY LIVE-CATTLE PUT–CALL RATIO

show the put–call ratio for live cattle over the past couple of years, and a composite chart of live-cattle futures over that same time.

Note how well the local maxima and minima—marked as buys (B) and sells (S)—correspond with the similar points marked on the price chart. At least over this time period, the put–call ratios seem to remain fairly stable. Buys have originated with the ratio in the 110 to 130 area, and sells in the 75 to 85 neighborhood.

Another very good futures contract to watch for put–call ratio signals is T-bonds. The charts of T-bond (continuous) futures prices and put–call ratio are shown in Figures 4.35 and 4.36. The buys and sells are marked. Note that this is another futures contract where *all* the local maxima and minima can be used as sell and buy signals.

Over the time period shown, the sell signals generally originated with the put–call ratio in the 110 to 130 area, and the buy signals in

Figure 4.35
CONTINUOUS T-BOND FUTURES

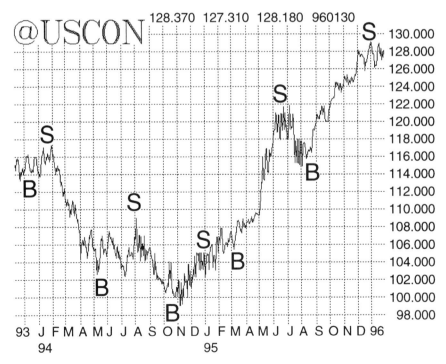
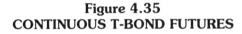

the 70 to 80 area. The buys and sells are marked on both charts, so that you can see how they correspond. Not every signal was a winning trade, but the vast majority of them were winners.

Another contract that can be traded well using the put–call ratios is the S&P 500 futures contract. This is something of a duplication of the index put–call ratio signals given by OEX options, but the two can be used as a confirmation of each other. The put–call ratios for S&P 500 futures options are much higher than for OEX options, indicating that more puts routinely trade in this market. Nevertheless, the signals have been reliable.

The chart of the S&P 500 futures options put–call ratio is shown in Figure 4.37. Compare the buy and sell signals with those of OEX, shown in Figure 4.25. You will see that they confirm each other quite well.

The next group of futures contracts that we look at have less reliable signals than those just presented. These include sugar, coffee,

Figure 4.36
21-DAY T-BOND PUT–CALL RATIO

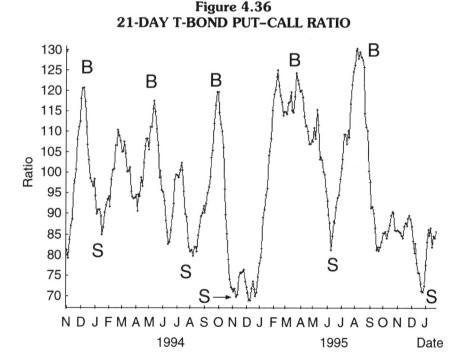

Figure 4.37
21-DAY S&P PUT–CALL RATIO

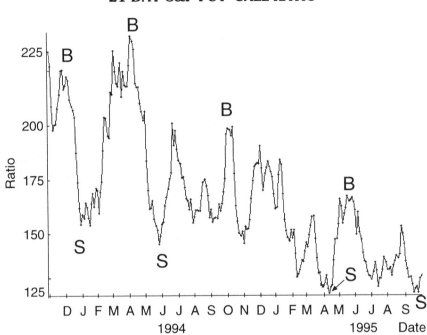

cotton, live hogs, and natural gas. In general, the put–call ratios on these four give pretty reliable signals. But the percent of winning signals is lower than gold, cattle, S&Ps, or T-bonds. The charts are presented in Figures 4.38 and 4.39.

The only signals in sugar that are worth using are the extremes: either buys with the ratio well over 100 or sells with the ratio under 50. Local maxima and minima at intermediate levels have not proved to be reliable in sugar over the length of time shown in Figures 4.38 and 4.39. The best signal was the buy signal in October of 1994, when the put–call ratio had risen to its highest point on the chart—110. Anytime the sugar put–call ratio exceeds 100, you should be looking for it to roll over and give a buy signal. The varying sell signals were much more modest in nature, but each was somewhat profitable.

Figure 4.38
CONTINUOUS SUGAR FUTURES

@SBCON   13.940 13.740 13.930 96011863220

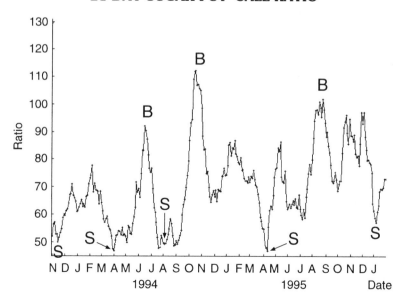

Figure 4.39
21-DAY SUGAR PUT–CALL RATIO

Coffee is another commodity that has had some very profitable moves on the back of put–call ratio signals. The put–call ratios reached a peak in March of 1994. That was an excellent buy point, as coffee exploded over the next few months (Figures 4.40 and 4.41). A sell signal then followed in July 1994, and it was a good one too. The other buy signal—near the first of November 1994—wasn't quite so successful. The only other extreme in the put–call ratio came as a sell signal near the first of September 1995, and that was a very profitable signal as well. Clearly, not all the moves in coffee are captured by the put–call ratio, but some very good ones are—enough to make it worth your while to keep track of the ratio.

Cotton has been very tradeable, using the put–call ratios, as well. The first signal shown in Figures 4.42 and 4.43—a sell occurring in mid-February 1994—wasn't all that good. However, the next one

Figure 4.40
CONTINUOUS COFFEE FUTURES

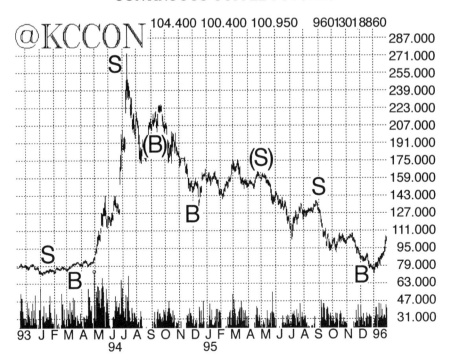

was: the buy of October 1994, which came with the put–call ratio at nearly 200, was a spectacular buy and caught the beginning of the huge bull market. This buy signal is an extremely illustrative one for another reason: it clearly shows the benefit of the dynamic approach. By waiting until the put–call ratio rolled over and headed down, a trader would have avoided getting in too early. The put–call ratio was not anywhere near that extreme level at any other time in the two years of data; and it may not be again for a long time.

A poor sell signal occurred in February of 1995, but the following buy signal in April of 1995 was another excellent signal. Note that this buy signal came at a much lower level—160. Then, just to show that the cotton put–call ratio *can* issue a good sell signal, the sell of late June 1995 was a nice signal as well. Finally, the last buy signal—which came from a lower extreme when compared with the other two buy signals—near September 1, 1995 was a good one as well. Note that the sells generally emanate from the 50 to 60 range

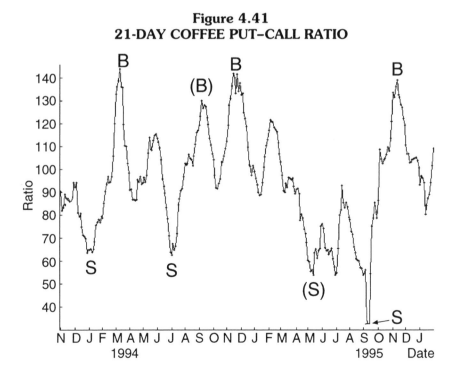

Figure 4.41
21-DAY COFFEE PUT–CALL RATIO

Figure 4.42
CONTINUOUS COTTON FUTURES

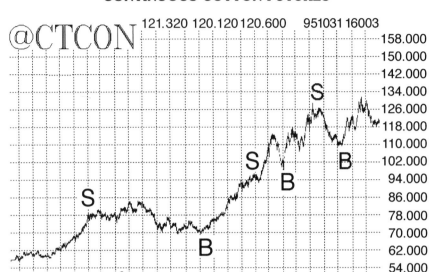

on the put–call chart. However, the buys all came from different levels, so while the static approach might have worked for the sells (which signals, by the way, were not as good as the buys), the dynamic approach is the only one that would have gotten you in at the right time on the buy side.

Sugar, coffee, and cotton are somewhat related. Futures traders who trade one of these markets often trade all three. However, the fourth member of the group of "pretty good" put–call ratio signals is live hogs. Since live-cattle options have a useful put–call ratio, it is not unusual to find that live hogs do as well.

The first signal that we see in Figure 4.44 is in February 1994, when an extremely good sell signal was issued. Eventually, option traders switched sides and the put–call ratio peaked, issuing a short-

Figure 4.43
21-DAY COTTON PUT–CALL RATIO

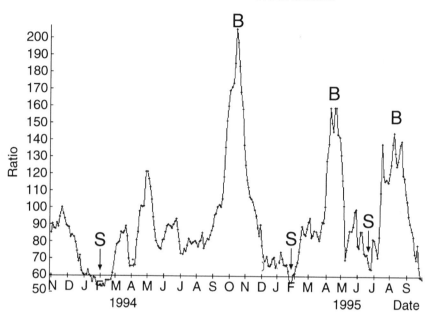

lived buy signal in June of 1994. As you can see from Figure 4.45, the chart of continuous prices, a quick rally ensued, but only lasted a couple of weeks. This signal once again reconfirms an important point: *the strength of a signal is not necessarily related to the level at which the signal occurred.* As you can see, the put–call ratio was almost up to 200 when this buy signal occurred. However, the ensuing rally, while profitable, was only a small bounce in an overall bear market.

After that, the market began falling in earnest once again. In August of 1994, another sell signal was issued and, while it was rather late in the overall downtrend, it did manage to capture about 10 points of the decline, from 39 cents down to 29 cents, which is a very good trade. At that point, the put–call ratio stayed very low for several months, issuing repeated sell signals. These didn't really pan out, although the market didn't rally a great deal during that time, either. It appears that a large number of call speculators were trying

Figure 4.44
CONTINUOUS LIVE HOG FUTURES

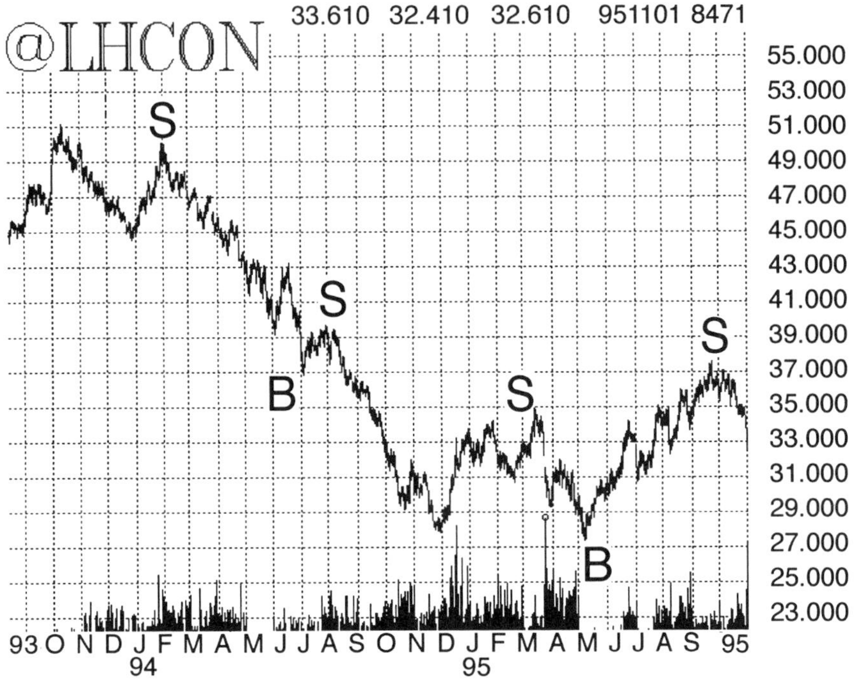

to pick the bottom during the November 1994 to February 1995 time period. And for a period they were right. However, the market collapse to new lows in April of 1995 attracted massive put buying, eventually culminating in a buy signal in June of 1995. The market then rallied into a sell signal in early October, which was a successful signal as well.

Overall, it appears that most of the sell signals for live hogs arrive with the put–call ratio in the 40 to 50 neighborhood, while the buy signals are in the 130 to 150 neighborhood, except for the one big spike in June of 1994.

The fifth member of the group of "pretty good" put–call ratio signals is natural gas. This is normally thought of as a contract that is related to the oil and oil-product contracts. However, natural

Figure 4.45
21-DAY LIVE HOG PUT–CALL RATIO

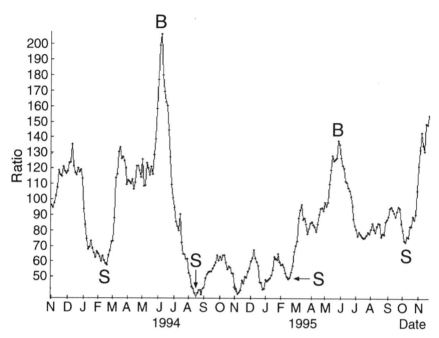

gas options give much better signals than do the oil and oil-product options.

Figures 4.46 and 4.47 are those of natural gas, both the put–call ratio and the continuous futures chart. One thing that immediately stands out from the put–call ratio chart is that the numbers are quite high. Apparently, there is a fair amount of put trading in natural gas options at all times. This is just an observation, for with the dynamic approach, we really don't care at what absolute levels the signals occur. The first signal—a buy in December 1993—was an excellent signal. Then, a local minima (sell signal) occurred with the ratio near 60 in March. It was also a good signal. The next signal was also a sell—the 70 level in August 1994—and it was a tremendous one, as natural gas futures went into a prolonged decline.

Figure 4.46
CONTINUOUS NATURAL GAS FUTURES

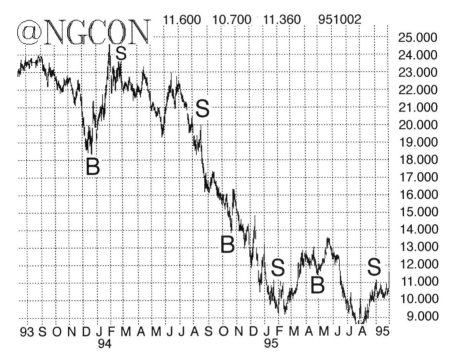

However, the next few signals were not as good, assuming you are just trading the extremes. A sell signal at the 80 level in January 1995, and buy signals in October 1994 (at the 160 level) and in April 1995 (at the 180 level), were either poor or just barely profitable. However, the May 1995 sell signal, also from the 80 level, was another good one.

So, natural gas options' put–call ratio can be traded from the extremes. In the past, this has meant sells occurring in the 60 to 80 range, and buys in the 150 to 180 range. However, don't rely on those static numbers—use a dynamic approach.

The last group of futures that we discuss do not respond as reliably to put–call ratio buy and sell signals as do the preceding ones, although there are some excellent signals in this group. You may have noticed that thus far we have not mentioned currency options. The deutsche mark, British pound, Swiss franc, and Japanese yen

Figure 4.47
21-DAY NATURAL GAS PUT–CALL RATIO

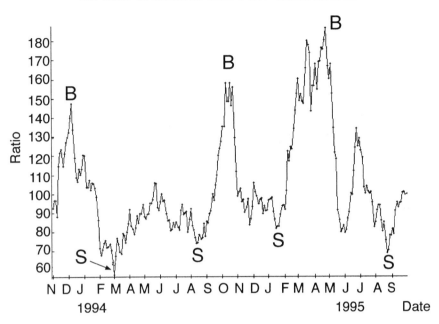

futures all have somewhat spotty track records with regard to put–call signals.

The deutsche mark is a typical example. There are two extreme lows in Figure 4.48—one in January 1994, and the other in April 1995. The first one was *not* a good sell signal, while the second one in April of 1995 was a very good signal (see Figure 4.49).

Since the put–call ratio tends to range between 90 and 130 for almost all of the rest of the time, it's not clear whether the peaks near 130 should be considered buy signals or not. They do seem to work out fairly well, though, as the D-mark generally moved higher after each of those peaks near 130. These came in March–April 1994, June 1994, December 1994–February 1995, and September 1995. You can see from the continuous price chart that these were all reasonably good places to buy the mark futures.

The signals in Japanese yen futures have been spotty as well, although the buy of January 94 (from the 150 level) was a tremendous buy (see Figures 4.50 and 4.51). The peaks on the put–call

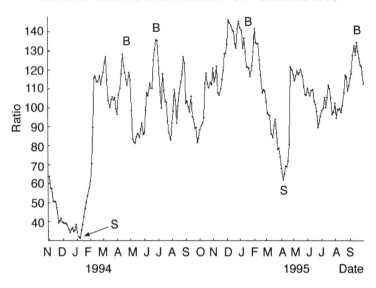

Figure 4.48
21-DAY DEUTSCHE MARK PUT–CALL RATIO

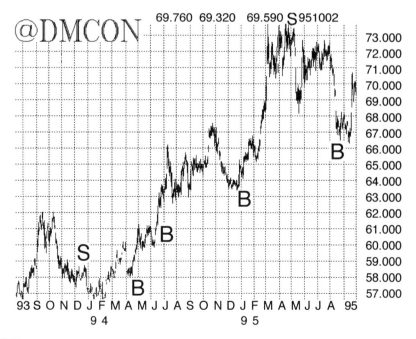

Figure 4.49
CONTINUOUS DEUTSCHE MARK FUTURES

Figure 4.50
CONTINUOUS JAPANESE YEN FUTURES

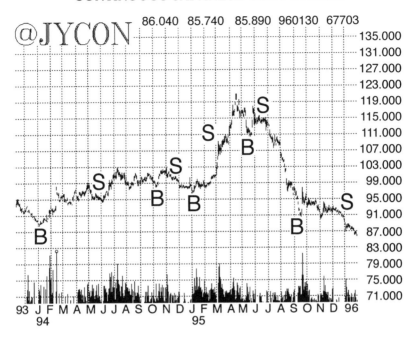

Figure 4.51
21-DAY JAPANESE YEN PUT–CALL RATIO

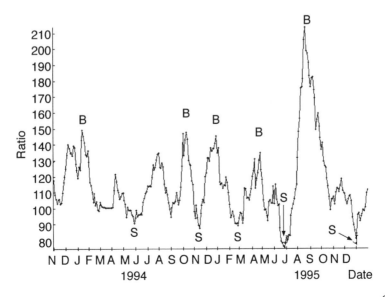

ratio chart are more easily spotted because they are more extreme. Unfortunately, neither the buy of October 1994 nor the one in August 1995, were very good signals.

The sell signal in June of 1995, which came from about the 75 level, was a good signal. The other local minima on the put–call ratio chart, which all occurred near the 90 level, would *not* have made good sell signals. Thus, while not every signal is profitable, you should pay attention to extreme peaks and valleys in the Japanese yen put–call ratio, for some excellent signals are generated.

British pound futures and put–call ratios are shown in Figure 4.52 and 4.53. There was an excellent buy signal when the put–call ratio peaked out at an almost unheard of 430 in July 1994. Another good buy signal came from the 360 level in February 1995, but most of the other signals—both buy and sell—were either incorrect or

Figure 4.52
CONTINUOUS BRITISH POUND FUTURES

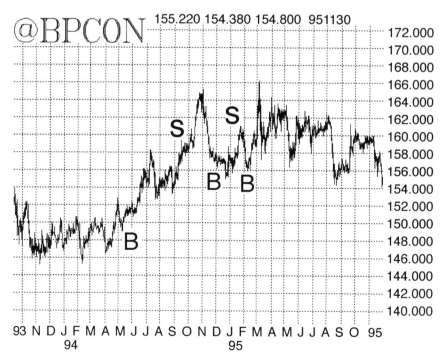

were premature. Thus, as far as this data goes, you can rely on buy signals, but should probably not trade the sell signals. Perhaps sell signals generated from lower extremes than those seen in the data on the chart in Figure 4.53 would have a better chance of success.

Swiss franc futures are similar to the British pound when it comes to the put–call ratio—there are some good buy signals, but sell signals are not good. The data is presented in Figures 4.54 and 4.55. There was a spectacular buy signal in May of 1994, coming from a peak of 135 in the put–call ratio. The buy extreme at 170 in November 1994 was not a good signal. Then, one more buy extreme—at 140 in September 1995—*was* a good signal. Very few of the sell signals were successful, although none of them were from excessively extreme levels.

So, in order to use the put–call ratio for trading Swiss franc futures, you can surmise that buy signals emanating from extreme levels at 130 or higher have a reasonable chance of success. However,

Figure 4.53
21-DAY BRITISH POUND PUT–CALL RATIO

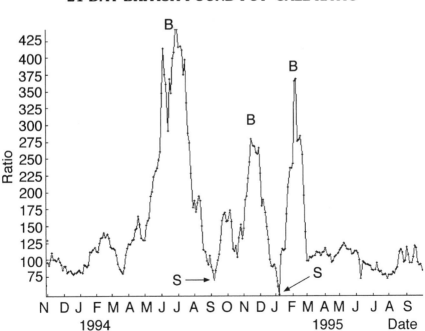

Figure 4.54
CONTINUOUS SWISS FRANC FUTURES

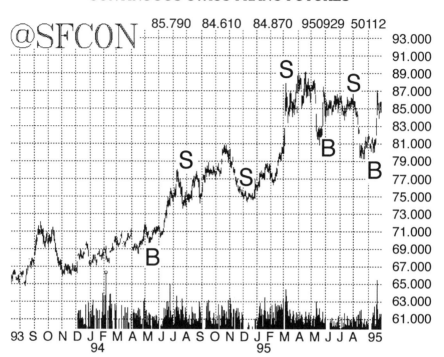

the sell signals in the 60 to 70 area, as shown on the chart in Figure 4.55, are not particularly successful. Perhaps sell signals from lower extremes would be profitable, but we have no data to support that conclusion. Thus, buy signals can be used, but be wary of sell signals.

The track record for trading silver futures with the put–call ratio is spotty. This is somewhat surprising since the system works well for gold futures. Notice from Figure 4.56 and 4.57 that the absolute levels of the silver put–call ratio are quite low, ranging from about 25 to 80 at the extremes. Once again, buy signals seem to be best. The buy signal of December 1993 at the 70 level produced a large profit, and the buy of May 1994 at the 80 level would probably have produced a small profit. The final buy on the chart—in August 1995, at the 65 level—was actually the best one, as silver futures jumped higher shortly thereafter. The sell signals were not good, with the

Figure 4.55
21-DAY SWISS FRANC PUT–CALL RATIO

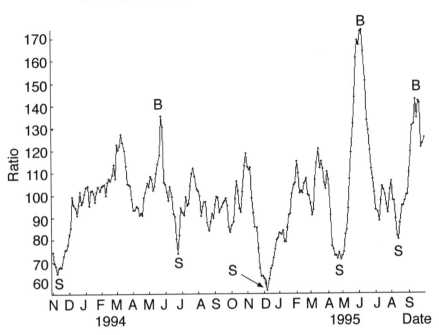

possible exception of the November 1994 sell signal that came in the middle of a downtrend, but just before prices broke sharply lower. The other sell signals were not profitable.

Eurodollar futures options are the most active futures options traded. However, this excess activity is dominated by true hedgers, so that the speculative qualities that we look for in order to use the put–call ratio as a contrary indicator are not primary in Eurodollar futures options. The continuous chart of Eurodollar prices is in Figure 4.58, while in Figure 4.59 you can see that the absolute levels of the put–call ratio are quite high for the Eurodollar, which indicates that hedgers are buying puts.

Nevertheless, there are some good buy and sell signals on the put–call chart, although there are some losers as well. On the left side of Figure 4.59, you can see three buy extremes, each at a successively higher level. The first one, from the 170 level in November

Figure 4.56
CONTINUOUS SILVER FUTURES

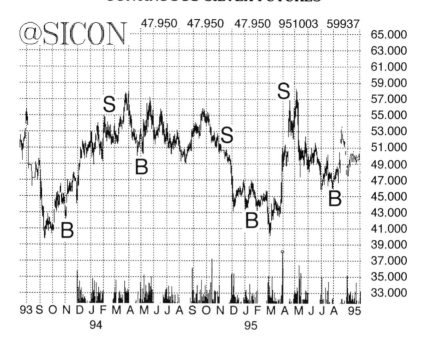

Figure 4.57
21-DAY SILVER PUT–CALL RATIO

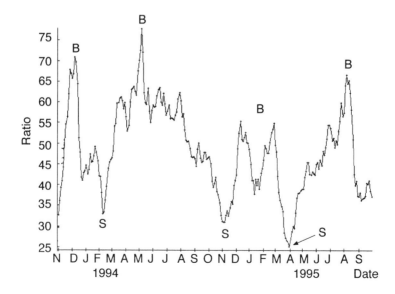

Figure 4.58
CONTINUOUS EURODOLLAR FUTURES

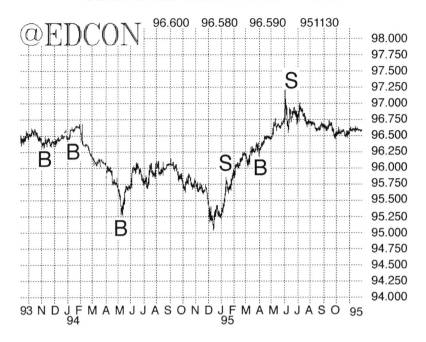

Figure 4.59
21-DAY EURODOLLAR PUT–CALL RATIO

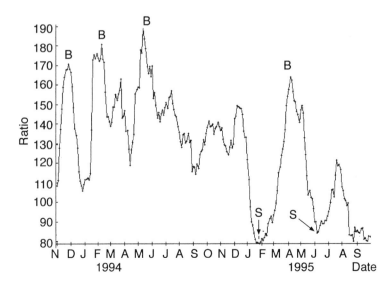

1993, was a modestly profitable signal. The second one, in February 1994 from the 180 level, was a losing trade. But the third one was the best, as Eurodollar futures rose rather nicely after the May 1994 buy signal from the peak at 190. There is one other buy on the chart, in April 1995 at the 160 level. It would have been a good time to buy, as Eurodollar futures were in the midst of a steep uptrend, but it certainly seems like a strange place for extreme pessimism, so perhaps this signal was coincidentally profitable.

There are really only two sell signals from extreme low levels on the chart in Figure 4.59. The first, from the 80 level in January of 1995, was a losing signal. The second, from the 85 level in June of 1995, was a good signal, but only after an initial rally, which was subsequently followed by a decline in prices.

In sum, then, the put–call ratio *can* be useful for trading Eurodollar futures, but once again the best signals seem to be buy signals.

FUTURES OPTIONS VOLUME

Since we are discussing futures options in some detail, this may be an appropriate place to insert a brief item about the liquidity of futures options. This liquidity is not a predictive quality, like the features we have discussed previously in this chapter. Rather, this is more for information purposes. The various futures options are divided into four broad categories.

Very Liquid	Liquid	Somewhat Illiquid	Very Illiquid
Crude oil	Corn	Heating oil	Cocoa
Eurodollar	Cotton	Unleaded gas	Dollar index
S&P 500	Gold	Live cattle	Copper
T-bonds	Coffee	Natural gas	Orange juice
	Soybeans	Sugar	T-bills
	Silver	Swiss franc	CRB index
	British pound		
	Deutsche mark		
	Wheat		
	Japanese yen		

As time goes by, some of the futures options in this list may change positions. In general, I would expect them to become more liquid. It is unlikely that any of the "very liquid" contracts would lose their status—they have been very liquid for a long time and represent a true hedging market as well as a speculative market, so continued volume is likely in Eurodollars, T-bonds, crude oil, and S&P 500 options.

ON MOVING AVERAGES

This section ideally belongs in a chapter on technical analysis, but since I don't have one of those in this book, this seems the best place for it. You have noticed that our use of the put–call ratio necessitates locating the local maxima and local minima of a moving average in order to identify buy and sell signals. There are many other technical indicators in use that require similar identifications. So, just how *do* you go about deciding whether a local maximum or minimum has been reached? It's easy to look at a historical chart, such as those shown throughout the second part of this chapter, and see where the tops and the bottoms were in retrospect. But can they be identified in a timely manner while they are being formed? The answer to that question is a qualified "yes," and we demonstrate why, in this section.

You may have judged by now that I am not a fan of using *absolute* levels to identify trading opportunities with moving averages. The whole discussion of the index put–call ratio pointed out that the market is dynamic, and it is often the *direction* of a moving average, and not its actual value, that is important. This analysis can be applied to many other moving averages. For example, I have found that it applies quite well to the TRIN, or Arms Index, also. Advocates of the Arms Index use a 10-day, 50-day, or other moving averages to judge whether the market is overbought or oversold.

The Arms Index is computed daily as follows:

$$\frac{\text{Number of advancing issues}}{\text{Number of declining issues}} \times \frac{\text{volume of declining issues}}{\text{volume of advancing issues}}$$

In theory, the number would be 1.00 in a balanced market. What really happens is that volume is generally dominant, so small numbers occur on bullish days (the smallest I recall is about 0.25), and large numbers occur on bearish days (large selloffs can generate numbers higher than 3.00). If the numbers are too high for too long, as identified by a moving average of the daily numbers, the market is getting oversold and we look to buy the market. On the other hand, if the moving average gets too low, the market is overbought, and we look for a sell signal.

I have found that absolute levels might work okay for the short-term averages (1.20 is oversold for the 10-day Arms Index, while 0.80 is overbought). However, the longer-term averages don't adhere to such rigid interpretation. Buy and sell signals come at various absolute levels, but when the longer-term Arms Index moving averages peak, a market buy signal is at hand; when they bottom out, a market sell signal is generated. So, the following discussion is applicable to those moving averages as well, and, in fact, it was the observation of the Arms Index signals that led me to explore the following concepts originally, back in 1977.

Any trader who uses moving averages to generate buy and sell signals knows that he can tell what level is needed on the next trading day, in order to generate the given signal. A typical moving average trading system, employed especially by commodity technical traders, is the moving average crossover system. You keep two moving averages, with differing number of days in each moving average, and when they cross each other, you have a buy or sell signal. Typically, the shorter-term average is used as the directional signal.

Thus, if we were keeping a 10-day moving average and a 20-day moving average, we would have a buy signal when the 10-day average crossed the 20-day one from below to above. Conversely, we would have a sell signal when the 10-day average crossed the 20-day one from above to below. This would generally be identified as a trend-following system, and would generate big profits when a long trend emerged, but would do poorly in a trading range market that oscillated back and forth.

Any trader using a crossover system should know at what levels he will get a signal on the following day. Suppose we know the following information:

Closing price 20 days ago: 80
Closing price 10 days ago: 60

Current 10-day moving average: 62.0
Current 20-day moving average: 63.5

At the current time, the 10-day average is lower than the 20-day average, so we must assume that we are in the midst of a sell signal. However, we also want to be alert for a possible buy signal, since the two averages are relatively near each other.

So the pertinent question is, "What closing price today would cause the 10-day average to cross over the 20-day one and generate a buy signal?" This is an easy matter to figure out. We merely need to compute the sum of the intervening closes, and see what close today would cause the desired result.

Sum of 10 closes in current 10-day moving average: 620
Sum of 20 closes in current 20-day moving average: 1,270

The 10-day sum is merely the moving average, 62.0, times 10. The 20-day sum is that moving average, 63.5, times 20.

Now we know for sure that the closing price of 10 days ago will not be part of the 10-day moving average after today's close. So the 10-day sum *after* today's trading will be the current sum, less the close from 10 days ago, plus today's close:

New 10-day sum = 620 − 60 + today's close = 560 + today's close

Similarly, we can compute the new 20-day sum:

New 20-day sum = 1,270 − 80 + today's close = 1190 + today's close

So now we have a simple arithmetic equation to solve to see what level for today's close would make the 10-day moving average be greater than the 20-day moving average. Let t stand for "today's close," so that the formulas are shorter. When will the 10-day average be greater than the 20-day moving average?

$$\frac{\left(560 + t\right)}{10} > \frac{\left(1190 + t\right)}{20}$$

Solving, we get $t > 70$. Thus, if the stock (or commodity, or whatever) closes above 70 today, we will get a buy signal. Futures traders, whose brokers take such stop orders, could enter an order such as "buy at 70¼, stop close only." Then they could go fishing or play golf.

This simple method can be used to decide what level of trading is needed on the next trading day in order to make the moving average be at a specific level—presumably a level that would generate some sort of signal for whatever trading system you are using.

Now, let's look at a put–call ratio signal. Suppose, for example, that we define *local maximum* for a put–call ratio moving average as occurring when "the average forms a top that is not exceeded for 10 trading days." If that happens, we will call the point a local maximum. Using the method from the preceding example, we could always tell, after nine days had passed, what closing price for the 10th day's trading would keep the moving average below that peak level of nine days ago, thus ensuring that 10 days had passed since the peak was seen. Hence, we would have our local maximum, by the 10-day definition.

That is interesting, but hardly useful enough for our purposes. It would only alert us to a buy or signal after nine days had passed. We could miss a lot of market movement in that time period. What we'd like to know, if possible, is if a local maximum or local minimum is forming on the first or second day of the 10-day period. Now *that* would be something truly useful. In the context of the previous example, that would be tantamount to predicting where the sums will be in 10 days. We know what numbers are coming "off" the moving average in that time (the closes for the previous 10 days), but we have no idea what the closing prices will be for the next 10 days, in order to add back onto the sums. Thus, it seems as though we have no chance of predicting where a moving average might be 10 trading days from now.

Unfortunately, unless you're clairvoyant, you can't predict with certainty what tomorrow's trading will bring—much less the next 10 days—but you can often come up with a good guess, based on the probability of what's happened in the past. This is especially true if you're dealing with items that are confined to a range, such as the daily Arms Index readings or the put–call ratio, rather than stock, index, or futures prices themselves.

The first thing that you must do, if you hope to predict where a moving average will be some days hence, is to define the distribution of the closing values that will be added to the moving average during that time. The *equity put–call ratio* is defined as the number of equity puts that trade on a given day, divided by the number of equity calls that traded on that same day. Typically, this number is between 0.30 and 0.50. Occasionally it falls outside of that range, but if we summarized the daily numbers for a long period of time, we would find that almost all of them fall within this range.

For simplicity's sake, let's assume that on any given day the equity put–call ratio can only be equal to 0.30, 0.35, 0.40, 0.45, or 0.50. Furthermore, let's assume that these five results all occur randomly, with equal probability. Now, these assumptions are not completely correct, but they are reasonable and are simple enough to allow us to demonstrate the technique needed to predict a moving average some days hence.

Once this step—defining the distribution—is accomplished, the technician is well on his way to achieving the desired result of being able to predict the moving average forward in time. Let's start real simple, and see how a two-day prediction would be accomplished.

In this example, we continue with the previous equity put–call ratio moving average example. However, in order to eliminate the use of decimal points as much as possible, we use 30, 35, 40, 45, and 50 as the possible daily closing values.

Suppose that we know the following information:

Current 10-day moving average: 40

Daily ratio reading of 10 days ago: 50
Daily ratio reading of 9 days ago: 45

We also know that the sum of the 10-day moving average is 400 (10 times 40).

Given this information, we can now compute with some certainty where the moving average might be in two days. There are five possible daily values for the first day—30, 35, 40, 45, and 50. And likewise there are the same five values for the second day, for *each* of the possible values on the first day. Thus, in all, there are 25 possible outcomes of two days' worth of equity put–call readings (five on day one times five on day two).

We know that the current sum of the last 10 day's worth of data is 400. In addition, we know what numbers are coming "off" the sum (50 and 45, as given earlier). Thus, the sum will be reduced by 95 over the next two days and then will be increased by whatever actual daily numbers are added on. The top line's moving average of 36.5 is computed as follows: $400 - 95 + 30 + 30 = 365$; $365/10 = 36.5$. Hence, we can then calculate all the possible values for the moving average over the next two days (all the while remembering that we have made the assumption that only five values are possible for any trading day).

Day 1 Possible Values	Day 2 Possible Values	10-Day Moving Average
	30	36.5
	35	37.0
30	40	37.5
	45	38.0
	50	38.5
	30	37.0
	35	37.5
35	40	38.0
	45	38.5
	50	39.0
	30	37.5
	35	38.0
40	40	38.5
	45	39.0
	50	39.5
	30	38.0
	35	38.5
45	40	39.0
	45	39.5
	50	40.0
	30	38.5
	35	39.0
50	40	39.5
	45	40.0
	50	40.5

This list of 25 outcomes is the total spectrum of possible 10-day moving averages after the next two trading days, under our assumptions.

Now that we have calculated this list, here's how to use it. Suppose that we want to know if the current 10-day moving average is going to be a local maximum. From the list, we see that only 3 of the 25 outcomes result in a moving average that is equal to or greater than the current value, 40. Conversely stated, 22 of 25 possible outcomes result in a lower moving average after two days. Therefore there is an 88 percent chance (22 divided by 25) that the current value of the moving average is going to be a local maximum for two days. If we were using that as a trading signal, we would probably go ahead and buy the market, based on the knowledge that there is such a high probability of the current value becoming an actual local maximum (a local maximum in the put–call ratio identifies a buy point).

This technique is a very useful one. We can extrapolate it for longer time periods. As stated earlier, I prefer to define a local maximum or minimum as a point, usually on the 21-day moving average, that is not exceeded for 10 trading days. Therefore, we could extend the "trees" in the preceding example out to 10 nodes (using a computer, of course) and calculate all the possible 21-day moving averages after that time. Then, we can see how many of those possible outcomes exceed the current maximum, in order to predict the probability of that maximum actually holding for the entire 10-day period.

The technique can be used for predicting moving averages in any sort of market as long as the daily values are numbers that generally lie within a range. It is therefore applicable to moving averages of the Arms Index (where daily values normally lie between 0.60 and 1.40), or equity put–call ratios (values between 0.30 and 0.55), or index put–call ratios (values between 0.90 and 1.50). There are many others that would fit the pattern as well—you can see from the put–call ratio charts in this chapter that the daily ratios fall within very well-defined ranges. A lot of technical indicators are based on oscillators that generate signals on crossovers or on exceeding a certain level. Any of those could be estimated with this system also.

You must remember, of course, that real market conditions can bring unexpected results. For example, on the day of the crash of 1987, the Arms Index was 14.07! You certainly wouldn't allow for *that* in your distribution of possible values when making predictions, but it did actually occur. Therefore, the result of your calculations can define a highly probable maximum or minimum, or buy or sell, or whatever, but there is always a chance that, over the ensuing days, the actual values for the daily readings may be outliers. If that happens, it's possible that you won't get the signal you were anticipating, and, if you had taken a trade in advance of the signal, you will probably have to take a loss to extricate yourself.

When I first completed the research for this system, I was using local maxima and minima in the 50-day Arms Index to predict intermediate-term buy (maxima) and sell (minima) points in the broad market. At the time (1977), I was working for Thomson McKinnon as the retail option strategist, and the head of the department and his superior—an executive vice president— both scrutinized the system. They thought it looked workable, and we waited for a signal to occur.

At the time, I was using 90 percent probability as evidence of a signal. I have since tightened that to 95 percent. In any case, in August of 1977, the system said that there was a 90 percent chance of a "market" buy signal occurring. There were no index options trading in 1977, so we had to buy stock options—or a set of several different stock options—in order to trade "the market." We put together a package of three recommended options— IBM, Kodak, and General Motors—and called some of the firm's larger option brokers to give them this research.

As it turned out, the signal *did* actually occur (that is, 10 days later, we had a local maximum in the 50-day moving average of the Arms Index). However, the market was very dull, mostly trading sideways, and we eventually had to advise the brokers to sell out their positions at a loss. No one was particularly upset—an honest effort had been made to identify a profitable trade—but the executive vice president jokingly said that I must have made a mistake, accidentally calculating that there was a "90 percent chance of rain" instead of "90 percent chance of a rising market." From that time on, the system became known as the "probability of rain" indicator.

For those readers who are intending to program this type of system on their computer, or are going to hire someone to do it, I should point out that you can reduce the number of calculations greatly when you are constructing the trees. For example, if you are looking for a local maximum over the next 10 days, and you calculate a node of a tree only three days out that exceeds the current moving average value, then you don't need to calculate any more nodes on that branch of the tree. They are irrelevant, since the current value was already exceeded. All you need to do is count all the possible outcomes that *would* have emanated from that node as outcomes that exceed the current value. You don't actually need to evaluate the outcomes, you just need to count how many there would be, and that is a simple matter (for example, if we are three days out, then there are seven days to go, and if there are nine possible values each day, then there would be 63 outcomes that would be considered to have exceeded the current value). However, with today's very fast computers, you may not want to get so esoteric—the computer can blast its way with brute force through the entire array of calculations.

The advantage of knowing the probability—in advance—of a signal occurring is very useful. It allows you to get into a position much closer to the actual local maximum or minimum, if you are using that type of system. Also, it can assign a probability that two moving averages will cross over each other in the next few days (in order to calculate this type of system, you need to apply the technique to both moving averages and then see how many of the possible outcomes result in a crossover).

SUMMARY

This chapter has demonstrated that options can be used in various ways to predict markets. Unusually heavy stock-option trading is often a tipoff that the underlying stock is about to experience a significant move. Also, option premium levels can be an important indicator in several situations. In some cases, it is a warning of a large move by the underlying stock. In others, it may indicate the end of a downtrend when options are expensive. Similar conclusions can be drawn from index-option premiums; when they are extremely expensive, the market may be reaching a bottom, and when they are very cheap, a market explosion may occur (often to the downside). Finally, the put–call ratio is a valuable indicator for the broad market as well as for certain futures contracts.

We also presented you with a method for predicting whether a moving average is making a local maximum or minimum. This is extremely useful in conjunction with the put–call ratios, since that is how we identify buy and sell points.

5 Trading Systems and Strategies

In this chapter, we describe a number of trading strategies that have profitable track records. These include day-trading systems, intermediate-term market timing systems, intermarket spreads, and a number of seasonable strategies. It is not necessary to trade options to employ most of these strategies, although, as with any trading decision, it may behoove the trader to use options in many circumstances.

We have already discussed one very profitable set of strategies—those having to do with trading at the time of option expiration, especially during the week of expiration and the week after. Several strategies for expiration trading were presented in Chapter 3. These included a hedged strategy for expiration Friday itself, a way to determine if there was a possibility of expiration-related buying in the days prior to expiration Friday, and finally a strategy for trading the week after expiration (the postexpiration effect).

INCORPORATING FUTURES FAIR VALUE INTO YOUR TRADING

In Chapter 3, the concept of fair value for S&P futures was presented. This is an important concept—especially for day-trading of S&P futures, OEX options, or other index options—and the reader should review it if he is not familiar with "fair value of futures." When the S&P futures are overvalued, OEX calls will be overly expensive as well. However, OEX puts will be cheap. Therefore, it is not normally an appropriate time to buy either the futures or the calls, for you will almost immediately suffer the after-effect of overpaying when the futures return to fair value. On the other hand, if you happen to be buying puts, it is a most opportune time to do so. Similarly, if the S&P futures are undervalued, then OEX calls will be cheap and puts will be expensive. In that situation, if you are bearish, you would be hurt by selling the futures or buying the puts, but if you are bullish, the calls are a good buy.

Thus, if you have a broad market trading system that has given a signal, it doesn't always pay to rush right in and take a position. You should first look at the relationship of the S&P futures to fair value. If they are expensive, and you are looking to buy the market, you may want to wait until the futures return towards fair value before making your purchase.

This statement makes the tacit assumption that the futures *will* in fact return to fair value rather quickly. Normally, they do, especially in this day of efficient arbitrage. However, they don't always spring back to fair value if there is an extenuating influence on the market, particularly on the downside. Recall the description of how futures traded at huge discounts to fair value during the crash of 1987. While that is an extreme example, more common ones might involve some piece of bad news that affects the entire market—an unexpected government unemployment figure, for example. This might cause the futures to trade at discounts for more than a brief period of time.

A trader should use judgment in deciding when to trade even though futures are not "fairly priced." Typically, if the market is relatively stable and is not reacting to some sort of extreme news, then you can be choosy, refusing to buy when the futures are overpriced or to sell when the futures are underpriced. However, in a fast-moving market where news is a factor, and perhaps T-bond futures are moving fast in the same direction as well, discretion may dictate that you trade without consideration of fair value. For example, when these fast market conditions exist and you are already long, if the market drops down through your mental stop price, you probably should be more willing to sell at the market rather than wait for the futures to return to fair value.

So, in the discussion of trading strategies in this chapter, you should realize that you may sometimes be able to improve your overall profitability by paying attention to premium levels at which the S&P futures are trading before actually entering your order.

DAY-TRADING VEHICLES

In many of the systems to be presented in this chapter, we are going to be trading "the market," often over a fairly short-term time horizon. The question inevitably arises as to what trading vehicle to use, futures or options. In some of these systems, there will be specific comments on when to use options (in intermarket spreads, for example). However, in others, the choice is the trader's.

In general, I prefer to use the S&P 500 futures to day-trade, but I prefer the OEX options for a trade with a longer time horizon (3 to 15 days, for example). There are a couple of reasons behind my choice, and I will attempt to explain them.

The S&P 500 futures are the "truest" trading vehicle that there is, as long as you are aware of the fair value. There is no implied volatility that can collapse your value as it can with an OEX option. It has been my experience over the course of the 14 years that the S&P 500 futures have been trading that they more accurately mirror the movement of the underlying cash index than OEX options do, by a wide margin.

Here is an actual story from a trading day in 1995, December 1st, to be exact. The market gapped open, higher, on a good economic report. This triggered a sell signal from the TICKI System (to be discussed shortly). The S&P 500 futures were trading at 608.50 and the OEX Index was almost exactly at 581. The following prices sum up the position that I, or any trader, was facing at the time:

> S&P 500 Cash Index: 607.60
> S&P 500 Futures: 608.50
> Futures Premium: 0.90
> Fair Value: 1.25
>
> OEX: 580.98
> OEX Dec 580 put: $4^5/_8$
> Implied Volatility of the put: 12.5%
> CBOE Volatility Index: 11.5%

The controlling factor in all of this was the premium on the S&P futures. It was then at 0.90, which was below fair value. This means that

OEX puts were going to be on the expensive side, since OEX market makers are quite diligent about watching the S&P futures premium.

You can often get a quick idea of how expensive an OEX at-the-money option is, by comparing its implied volatility with the CBOE's Volatility Index (symbol: $VIX), which can be quoted on any quote machine. You can see that this particular Dec 570 put was "overpriced" in that its implied volatility of 12.5 percent was a full point over the VIX level of 11.5 percent. In the case of this option, that one point of implied volatility was worth 0.45 to the price of the option. That is, if the implied volatility fell to 11.5 percent and OEX were at 580.98, the option would sell for about 4⅛. That's a huge amount of the price of this option.

As it turned out, I shorted the futures and the market *did* top out, but only lazily, and it slid slightly lower so that by 3:45 P.M. Eastern time, 15 minutes before the close, the following prices existed (the net change of each price from the earlier prices in this example is included in parentheses):

> S&P 500 Cash Index: 606.20 (–1.40)
> S&P 500 Futures: 607.40 (–1.10)
> Futures Premium: 1.20 (+0.30)
> Fair Value: 1.25
>
> OEX: 579.60 (–1.38)
> OEX Dec 580 put: 4¾ (+⅛)
> Implied Volatility of the put: 11.5 percent (–1.0%)
> CBOE Volatility Index: 11.2% (–0.3%)

The futures had dropped 1.10, and I was able to cover and make $550, less commissions. But look at the OEX Dec 580 put—it only advanced an eighth of a point! Moreover, if you went to sell it, you'd probably have to take an eighth less to hit the bid. What happened here?

Well, let's analyze it. The implied volatility of the put dropped back to be much more in line with the Volatility Index (11.5 percent versus 11.2 percent). As was pointed out, that drop in volatility cost the option 45 cents. Moreover, the delta of the put option was only about 0.43 to begin with, meaning that if OEX fell by a point, the option was only going to increase in value by 43 cents. As it turned out, OEX fell by about the same distance as SPX, but the loss of implied volatility in the option essentially wiped out all the profit potential. Thus the futures were the much better buy; they closely mirrored the 1.40-point drop in the SPX, except for the amount lost when they returned to fair value (30 cents).

This is a fairly typical occurrence. The OEX options are over-priced because of the premium on the futures contract. If you get only a small market move, the futures are going to be the better choice as a trading vehicle. Of course, if the market move is larger, then you probably won't notice much difference. Also, this example indicated that implied volatility fell; that doesn't always happen, either, although it often does when the ensuing market move is a small one.

Thus, for day-trading purposes, I prefer the S&P 500 futures because they more closely mirror the performance of the SPX Index itself. However, for longer-term speculative positions that I might be carrying for a couple of days or even a couple of weeks, I will often use the OEX in-the-money options because of their limited risk nature and the smaller capital outlay required. However, if implied volatility were too high, I would be leery of buying OEX options, even in those longer-term situations.

THE TICKI DAY-TRADING SYSTEM

This is a system that I devised a number of years ago for day-trading S&P 500 futures. It is based on the following basic concept: if an artificial buy or sell program (see Chapter 3 for definitions) is executed in a stable market, the market has a tendency to return to its previous price once the artificial buying or selling is over with. Over the years, this has been a correct observation much of the time. Of course, there is the aberrant case where wave after wave of programs hit the market, but those are the exception, not the rule.

So, in order to create a system to take advantage of this concept, we need a way to identify when a program trade is taking place, and we also need a way to identify when it is over. I have found a very simple way to determine both of these things. It is called the TICKI, and it is something that you can quote on any quote machine, including at-home systems such as Signal or Bonneville.

TICKI is the net plus or minus ticks of the stocks in the 30 Dow-Jones Industrials. For example, if at the current time, 20 Dow stocks are trading on plus ticks (or zero-plus tick), and 10 are trading on

minus ticks (or zero-minus ticks), then the value of TICKI would be
10 (20 minus 10).

A small example will define the terms *plus tick*, *zero-plus tick*, *minus tick*,
and *zero-minus tick*. Suppose that XYZ stock trades at the following prices
over a short time period during a trading day. Each trade is identified as the
appropriate type of tick:

Price	Type of Tick
50	
50⅛	Plus tick
50	Minus tick
50	Zero-minus tick (same price as last trade, which was a minus tick)
50⅛	Plus tick
50¼	Plus tick
50¼	Zero plus tick (same price as last trade, which was a plus tick)

TICKI shows where the 30 Dow-Jones Industrials' last ticks are
at any point. Since there are 30 stocks in TICKI, the highest that it
can get is +30, and the lowest it can become is –30. *If TICKI gets to
+22 or higher, buy programs are being executed in the marketplace; if TICKI drops to –22 or lower, sell programs are being executed.* Note that for TICKI to be +22, 26 stocks have to be on plus
ticks and 4 on minus ticks. Thus nearly all of the 30 Dow-Jones
Industrial stocks have to be on plus ticks for TICKI to get to +22. The
downside is similar: 26 of the 30 stocks would have to be trading on
minus ticks in order for TICKI to be –22.

Since nearly all program trades that are large enough to move
the market noticeably involve the 30 Dow-Jones Industrials, TICKI is
a good way to identify program trading. There is a similar measure,
called the TICK—the net of plus and minus ticks on all NYSE-listed
issues. TICK is too broad-based to quickly and accurately detect
when a buy or sell program is hitting the market. Thus, TICKI is our
choice for making that identification.

Having quantified the first half of what we need to know—when
a program is being executed—we now need to address the other

half, which is how to identify when the program is over. No matter how large a buy program is, it has an end. During the program, TICKI may rise to +22 and stay at or above that level for some time. When the program ends, TICKI will begin to fall, reflecting the fact that some of the stocks are beginning to trade on minus ticks. *When TICKI drops back to +12 after having been at +22 or higher, the buy program is over; conversely when TICKI rises to –12 after having been at –22 or lower, the sell program is done.*

Obviously, some buy or sell programs may be executed in a more discrete manner, but a lot of them are executed just by pushing a computer key, and letting a flood of orders race into the marketplace. This type of program trading causes the TICKI behavior just described. Moreover, it is this type of program trading that draws out traders with opposite opinions. A trader who sees a stock that he owns jump up in price may often sell his stock into the program, thereby obtaining a better price than he would have in a stable market.

Having established the criteria for determining when the programs begin and end, we can now lay out a trading system that is geared toward making money when the market reverses direction after a program is finished:

- When TICKI rises to +22, and then falls back to +12, sell the S&P futures. Hold the position until one of the following occurs:

    (a) The end of trading day
    (b) TICKI trades back up to +22
    (c) The S&Ps exceed the highest price reached during the buy program by 0.20

- Similarly, when TICKI falls to –22 and then rises back to –12, buy the S&P futures. Hold the position until one of the following occurs:

    (a) The end of the trading day
    (b) TICKI trades back down to –22
    (c) The S&Ps fall 0.20 below the lowest price reached during the sell program.

- Don't enter into any trades after 3:30 P.M. Eastern time, for programs near the close of trading may not have enough time to reverse direction.

- If you take two consecutive losses on one trading day, cease trading the system for the remainder of that day.

Note that this system often has a built-in advantage: since you are selling right on the heels of a buy program, the futures may be inflated (trading above fair value), which is an additional benefit. Conversely, when you buy immediately after a sell program, you may find that you purchase the futures below fair value.

Some comments on the system are in order, for I don't believe in totally ironclad adherence to rules. It's a day-trading system, so we generally don't hold any positions overnight; positions are closed out at the end of the trading day if they haven't been stopped out by then. However, some well-known traders have modified their stance on day trades: if you are holding a profit at the close, and the market accelerated in your direction, then close out the trade the next morning. Of course, since S&Ps trade all night on Globex, you can literally close out your position at any time.

You should note that *when* you close out your position will affect your margin requirement. Most brokerage firms require less margin for a day trade than they do for a position held overnight. For S&P futures, a "day" begins at 4:45 P.M., when the Globex market opens and continues through 4:15 P.M. the next day, when trading ceases on the Chicago Merc. Thus if you don't close out your position by 4:15, you will be required to margin the position as an overnight position.

Back to the system. Note that if you are stopped out by rule (b), you will be reentering another trade as soon as *that* program ends. Thus, rule (b) is sort of a temporary stop—it momentarily takes you out of the market since there is another program being executed, but you will reenter your trade shortly.

Finally, the stop loss defined as rule (c) may take a little explaining. This is a rule that I have instituted after years of observing the market's behavior in line with program trading. Generally, if prices exceed the highest point reached during a buy program, then there isn't much hope of the program's effect being reversed, so you should close out your position. Similar thinking applies to the downside. Here's an example.

Suppose that the following prices are observed during a buy program:

S&P Price	TICKI	Comments
550.00	+22	Buy program is taking place
550.50	+26	Buy program is accelerating
551.00	+26	Program still going on
550.75	+20	Program winding down
550.50	+12	Sell signal

In this example, the S&Ps reached a peak price of 551.00 during the height of the buy program. Then, typically, they backed off a little bit before the system issued a sell signal. That sell signal came with the S&Ps at 550.50. You would set your stop at 551.20, just above the highest price reached during the program.

Since traders are allowed to *think* when trading, the setting of the stop in rule (c) is one of those places where thinking may come in handy. I typically adjust my stop based on the level of premium in the futures. If the premium is large—in excess of fair value—then I use the tightest stop because I fear that another buy program may be lurking just around the corner. However, if the premium on the futures is at, or especially if it's below fair value, then I may give the position a little more room than just 0.20 over the high price reached during the program.

I generally trade only with *mental* stops, which forces me to think every time I reach a stop. I do this because I want a chance to evaluate the premium on the futures before I buy or sell them. I do *not* try to outguess the market; any system depends on adherence to a stop-loss point. It's just that I've found, through experience, that there is something to be gained from observing the level of the futures' premium before I make a trade.

Once the position is in place, if unrealized profits begin to build up, I recommend using a trailing stop to lock in some of those profits. Generally, you should use a trailing stop of 1.75 or 1.80 S&P points. So, if you sell the futures, and they subsequently drop by 1.80, begin to use a trailing stop of 1.80 from any subsequent low price for the rest of the day. In this manner, if you get a large move in your favor, and it is later reversed, you will take some profits out of the position.

I would call someone a real-time trader if he is trading this system, since he should be able to watch the market and make these real-time decisions. However, if you would rather use a fixed level rather than risk getting too emotional over the choice forced on you by a mental stop, then use the fixed 20 cents as specified in rule (c).

Here is the chronology of some actual trading that took place during a typical week during the summer of 1995. It will help to explain how the system actually works.

Date	Time	Sep S&P Futures	Premium	TICKI	Action
Aug 24	12:20 P.M.	560.10	1.80	+22	On alert for a sell
	12:27 P.M.	559.70	1.20	+12	SELL
	4:15 P.M.	559.10 (never stopped)			Buy @ close (+0.60)

At the time of this example, fair value premium of the September S&P futures was about 1.10 points. Just after noon on this day (a Thursday, although that's not really important), a buy program entered the market. This program ballooned the premium to 1.80—well above the 1.10 fair value—and got TICKI up to +22, which put us on alert for a sell signal. A few minutes later, at 12:27 P.M., the buy program had abated, and TICKI was back down slightly to +12. That gave us our sell signal, and we sold the S&P futures at 559.70. Notice that the premium had shrunk back to 1.20 by that time, only slightly above fair value. As it turned out, this was a rather mediocre signal, as the market drifted quietly lower in the afternoon, and the trade resulted in a 60-cent profit when it was closed out at the end of the day.

That was the only trade of the day. However, over the next few days the system was active, and when it is active, that is generally when the best profits occur. The trading history for the next four days is listed below:

Date	Time	Sep S&P Futures	Premium	TICKI	Action
Aug 25	9:40 A.M.	560.60	2.00	+22	On alert for sell
	9:45 A.M.	560.40	1.20	+12	SELL
	3:18 P.M.	561.60			Stopped (–1.20)

The highest point that the futures had reached during the buy program of the early morning was 561.40, so when the futures eventually exceeded that point in the last hour of trading, the trade was stopped for a loss.

Date	Time	Sep S&P Futures	Premium	TICKI	Action
Aug 28	9:35 A.M.	563.00	1.65	+22	On alert for sell
	9:40 A.M.	563.10	1.20	+12	SELL
	4:15 P.M.	559.40 (never stopped)			Buy @ close (+3.70)

Early buy programs produced a nice sell signal point early in the day, and the market traded down all day, resulting in a very good profit.

Date	Time	Sep S&P Futures	Premium	TICKI	Action
Aug 29	9:40 a.m.	559.50	1.30	+22	On alert for sell
	9:44 A.M.	559.00	0.90	+12	SELL
	12:07 P.M.	556.50	0.40	–22	On alert for buy
	12:13 P.M.	557.20	1.20	–12	BUY *two* (profit +1.80)
	12:24 P.M.	556.40	0.50	–22	Stopped: rule (b) (–0.80)
	12:30 P.M.	557.00	1.15	–12	BUY
	4:15 P.M.	560.55 (never stopped)			Sell @ close (+3.55)

The action was interesting on this day, as the system generated profits in both directions. Initially, another early buy program resulted in a sell signal, which was closed out when sell programs came into the market just after noon. These sell programs resulted in a buy signal, and we bought *two* futures: one to close out the short sale, and one to go long on the buy signal. This buy signal was aborted, however, at 12:24 P.M. when another sell program hit the market; we were stopped out of our long position because TICKI fell back down to –22 at that time. Finally, the second buy signal was generated at 12:30 P.M., and the market spent the rest of the day rallying, resulting in a very profitable trading day.

Date	Time	Sep S&P Futures	Premium	TICKI	Action
Aug 30	9:42 A.M.	561.50	1.75	+22	On alert for sell
	9:51 A.M.	562.00	1.30	+12	SELL
	4:15 P.M.	561.15 (never stopped)			Buy @ close (+0.85)

Again, the market traded higher early and those buy programs generated a sell signal. This was a moderate profit by the day's end.

When the market is in a trading range, the system is particularly effective. I'm sure everyone remembers days when a bit of news that was released before the market opened caused a gap opening, which was then reversed as the market spent most of the day trading in the other direction. This system is excellent at getting you into a profitable trade on days like that. Such news items are often the release of government figures such as unemployment, the consumer price index, or some similar item that affects both the bond and stock markets. The preceding examples occurred during such a period. You can see the number of signals that occured right after the opening of trading on four successive trading days: August 25th through the 30th.

When the market is moving steadily in one direction during a trading day, the system is least effective. That's why we recommend ceasing trading on any particular day in which you are forced to take losses on two consecutive trades. Note that to take two consecutive losses there have to either be three programs in the same direction or two programs followed by prices moving against you. The following examples demonstrate this fact.

Two consecutive losses could be created by three successive sell programs; for example:

1. Sell program #1: you buy the S&Ps when it's done.
2. Sell program #2: you stop yourself (presumably at a loss) when

TICKI goes to -22 during program #2; when program #2 ends, you again buy the S&Ps.

3. Sell program #3: you stop yourself when TICKI goes to -22.

Two consecutive losses could also be created in this way:

1. Sell program #1: you buy the S&Ps when it's done.
1a. The S&Ps trade lower anyway, and you are stopped out.
2. Sell program #2: you buy the S&Ps when it's done, again.
2a. Again, the S&Ps trade to new lows, stopping you out.

There are a couple of other scenarios—combinations of the ones in the preceding example—that could cause two consecutive losses also. In all cases, however, there are two or three programs in the same direction consecutively that caused the losses. It is my experience that, on days like that, there are more programs to come, and it is best to stand aside rather than get run over. Fortunately, such days are rare, and the damage is limited by retreating to the sidelines after two consecutive losses are taken.

The Intraday Market-Reversal Corollary

The market has made some very impressive intraday reversals over the years, both on the upside and the downside. Every day trader would like to be a participant during these times.

While there have been many significant market-reversal days over the years, two of the largest have occurred in the 1990s. On Monday, October 5, 1992, the market was in a tenuous state. The market had dropped 75 points on the previous Thursday and Friday, including down 54 on Friday. To make matters worse, there had been selling overseas on Sunday night, so the market opened on the downside and began to melt down. By noon it was down 115 Dow points, and over 13 OEX points. The premium in the S&P futures can be used to illustrate the level of panic in the market: at the low of the day, the S&P Index (cash) was down 13.67 points, but the futures were down 19.90, and trading at a discount of 6.80! In early afternoon, however, the market began to stabilize and then it rallied heavily.

Eventually, the Dow closed down 21 points on the day, while OEX was down only 2.42, and the S&P futures only lost 1.75 by day's end.

Another violent reversal day occurred on July 19, 1995, when technology stocks sold off heavily. The Dow dropped 134 points at its nadir, and OEX was down almost 16 points. There wasn't the same level of panic in the 1995 selloff as there had been in the 1992 selloff, however, as the S&P futures never even came close to trading at a discount all day. Once again, the market was able to stabilize and rally. On this day, it didn't come all the way back, but the Dow did manage to regain over 70 points from its lows by day's end. OEX, SPX, and the S&P futures all managed to rally between eight and nine points from their intraday lows.

The TICKI system will get you "in" on these reversals if they occur or the first on second TICKI signal. But you might be concerned about missing out on a good trade on days that reverse direction after more than two or three programs in one direction. By the rule for limiting losses on the TICKI system in one day, you would be standing aside and would miss the reversal. On the two major reversal days described just previous, there were repeated sell programs before the market eventually stabilized and rallied. Anyone trading the TICKI system would have taken two small losses during the morning and then would have been idle for the remainder of the day.

In order to be able to trade reversals after a large move, I have defined the following corollary to the TICKI system and used it with good success throughout the years: *after having sustained two consecutive losses with the TICKI system, reenter the market if it reverses by 1.75 off its extreme point.*

Example: The market has been selling off, and you have attempted to buy it twice after sell programs. However, both attempts were unsuccessful. The market then continues to sell off even more, perhaps under the influence of more sell programs.

However, by early afternoon, the market stops going down and begins to rally. Suppose that the low on the S&P futures at that time was 551.00. If the S&Ps then rise to 552.75, you would buy the market under this reversal corollary.

Similarly, to the upside, if you were forced to take two consecutive losses by the TICKI system as buy programs repeatedly entered the market, then you would use the reversal corollary if the S&Ps fell by 1.75 from their ultimate daily high.

- Once a position is taken under the reversal corollary, you should stop yourself out if the futures subsequently move to new highs (if you are short) or new lows (if you are long).

- If you are not stopped out, close the position at the end of the day.

I have also found the 1.75-point reversal to be useful in taking profits on a TICKI trade. For example, if you are short the S&Ps because of a TICKI signal and they then trade down substantially, you have a nice unrealized profit. If the futures then rally 1.75 points from their low, you would cover your short futures and take your profit. I wouldn't use this type of reversal to go long also, just to cover the short as a sort of trailing stop.

Note: A 1.75-point reversal works well when S&P futures are trading somewhere near 500, but it would obviously need adjustment if the "handle" on the S&Ps changes substantially. For example, if S&Ps were to drop back to the 250 range or rise to the 1,000 neighborhood, the size of the reversal move would almost certainly need to be changed. There are two ways you can make this adjustment. One is by trial and error: if you notice that you are trading many more reversals than you used to, or if you are missing out on almost all reversals, your reversal point needs to be changed. The other approach would be to use a reversal of about one-third of one percent of the S&P's value. The second approach is more dynamic and is the preferred approach.

There are a few other pertinent facts about the TICKI system. It will generally give you about one trade a day, on average, although the trades tend to come somewhat in bunches. That is, some weeks may be very dull with only a little program activity; in those weeks, you would only have perhaps two or three trades. However, in a more volatile, trading-oriented market, you may get more trades, perhaps as many as 8 to 10 in a week.

As for profitability, I can only relate my personal experiences since I don't know of any database that contains historic intraday values of the TICKI. The system generates 54 percent winners, the average winning trade is +1.51 S&P points, the average losing trade is –0.86 points, and the maximum drawdown was 3.39 points.

A SHORT-TERM TRADING SYSTEM

This is a trading system with a slightly longer time horizon—usually a matter of at least several days to as much as several weeks, as opposed to the intraday nature of the TICKI System described in the last section. This new system is based on detecting extremely over-bought and oversold levels in the stock market, by using the number of advancing issues and the number of declining issues on a daily basis. When there is too large a preponderance of advancing issues over declines, the market becomes overbought, and this system looks to go short (or buy puts). Similarly, when there are too many declines, the market becomes oversold, and the system looks to go long.

There are many ways to view the advance–decline line, but generally most of them use the *net* of daily advances minus daily declines as the starting point. This system does as well. The crux of the system depends on calculating a momentum oscillator each day. The oscillator itself is rather simple to compute and can be done at home by any reader, as long as he has a starting point.

Here are the specifics:

1. Subtract NYSE declines from advances = *net advances.*
2. Multiply yesterday's exponential moving average by 0.9 and add it to 0.10 times today's *net advances.*

Stated as a formula, the daily oscillator value is

$$M_1 = 0.9 * M_0 + 0.1 * (\text{Advances} - \text{Declines})$$

where M_0 = yesterday's oscillator value
Advances = number of advancing issues on the NYSE today
Declines = number of NYSE declining issues today

For example, if the oscillator closed with a value of 100 yesterday, and today there were 1,200 advances and 900 declines, then the new oscillator value would be 120:

$$M_1 = 0.9 * 100 + 0.1 * (1,200 - 900) = 120$$

because $M_0 = 100$; Advances = 1,200; Declines = 900.

This type of computation is called an *exponential moving average*. In calculating an exponential moving average, we take a certain percentage of "yesterday's number" and add 1.0 minus that percentage of today's values. In the preceding example, we are using 90 percent and 10 percent, which gives a heavier weight to past data and only a 10 percent weight to today's data. We can change the mixture by using 80 percent and 20 percent, or 75 percent and 25 percent, and so forth.

The oscillator, as just defined, generally ranges between about +200 and –200. These are considered to be the "normal" values. Whenever the oscillator exceeds that range, however, you should take notice, for the market has become overbought or oversold.

The actual rules for entering a trade are very simple:

1. If the oscillator is less than –200, the market is oversold.
   • Once it is oversold, buy the market at the close, on the day that the oscillator climbs back above –180.
2. If the oscillator is greater than +200, then the market is overbought.
   • Once it is overbought, sell the market at the close, on the day that the oscillator falls back below +180.

This is a very reliable way of determining overbought and oversold conditions in the stock market. It has worked well for many years. It usually marks an intermediate-term turning point in the market. However, in some cases, it only identifies short-term movements.

In the ferocious rally that consumed the first half of 1995, the oscillator became overbought by exceeding the +200 level in May. At that time, the

Dow had rallied 220 points in under a month. The oscillator remained over-bought for eight consecutive trading days, while the market pushed another 40 points higher. Finally, the oscillator fell back below +180 and the Dow dropped 81 points in one day. However, that was the end of the decline, and the Dow went on to much higher highs over the course of the year.

On the other hand, the oscillator signals can also sometimes identify major turning points that last for months.

In late 1994, the market had been selling off rather steadily between September expiration and late October. At the time that the oscillator fell below −200, the Dow was down about 100 points from its September high. However, a succession of negative days followed, as there were consistently more declines than advances on most days. Over the next 35 trading days, the oscillator remained below −200 on 26 of those days. At its worst, it fell to −454. During those 35 days, the Dow lost another 180 points. Eventually, when the oversold condition subsided, the buy signal was generated in mid-December 1994, and the Dow rallied 1,200 points over the next nine months.

So this oscillator is useful in getting into a market that has short-term trading potential, and may have even intermediate-term prospects. We have given the entry criteria, but have not specified how to exit the trade. Obviously, if we use too close a stop, we will not be able to capitalize on the intermediate-term moves. Conversely, if we use too wide a stop, we will not profit when the market moves only a short distance in our favor and then reverses.

Personally, I usually use a close stop of 3.10 OEX points and use a trailing stop after OEX has moved three points in my favor. This results in a good accuracy rate, but limits profits on larger moves. Therefore, in order to discern the best system for trading the oscillator, we ran a number of scenarios through the computer in order to optimize the results. The general scenario was that we wanted to trade the OEX index with these signals. The system was to have a stop-loss point to begin with, but if OEX went in our favor, we would use a trailing stop to lock in profits. Furthermore, partial profits would be taken at two fixed points—one-third of the position being sold at each partial profit point. With these criteria, the system was further refined by setting the size of the stops and the partial profit points. It turns out that these points were best set in terms of percent of OEX, rather than fixed distances.

This is the system that tested best in the computer simulation, although individual traders may want to modify it to their own tastes:

1. Set the initial stop to be 2 percent of the value of OEX at the time the trade is entered. For example, if OEX was 500 and a buy signal was generated, the initial stop-loss sell point would be at 490 (500 less 2 percent of 500).
2. Sell one-third of your position to take partial profits if OEX moves 2 percent in your favor.
3. Sell another one-third of your position to take partial profits if OEX moves another 2 percent in your favor. Thus, if OEX was at 500 to begin with, you would take partial profits at 510 and again at 520.
4. Whenever you begin to take partial profits, from then on use a trailing stop of 2 percent of the value of OEX at that time. Raise the trailing stop each time OEX closes higher. Thus, if OEX was initially bought at 500, and then rose to 510, partial profits would be taken and the stop would be raised to 499.80 (98 percent of 510).

Using these criteria, the results shown in Table 5.1 were achieved, by year. The maximum gain was 23.65 points, while the maximum loss was 11.05 points. The gain occurred in 1991; the loss in 1995. The median trade was a gain of 2.99 OEX points. The longest time any trade lasted was 95 days, while there were three trades that were stopped out after one day. The median holding time was 15 days.

The reason that we used OEX for the purposes of the simulation was the limited risk of owning options. We could either trade S&P 500 futures or we could trade OEX options. The median gain of about three OEX points is enough to produce profits using either vehicle, assuming that, if we're trading options, we buy at- or slightly in-the-money options.

Table 5.1
RESULTS ACHIEVED BY THE SHORT-TERM
TRADING SYSTEM

Year	Signals Profitable	Net Result in OEX Points
1984	3 of 5	+9.95
1985	5 of 7	+27.38
1986	4 of 7	+9.76
1987	7 of 10	+15.50
1988	7 of 8	+32.93
1989	3 of 4	+12.08
1990	5 of 8	+23.95
1991	5 of 6	+32.96
1992	4 of 4	+18.51
1993	4 of 4	+34.30
1994	7 of 11	+39.23
1995	5 of 9	−1.94
Totals	59 of 83	+294.28

Monitoring the Oscillator Intraday

In certain cases, you can improve the entry point by anticipating the signals. In order to anticipate the signal, you need to observe the relationship between advances and declines in the afternoon of the pertinent trading day. Even if the broad market moves late in the day, it is often unable to effect much change on the relationship of advances and declines. This is true because many smaller and less liquid stocks make their initial moves in morning trading and won't follow a large market reversal much in the afternoon. As an example, assume the Dow is down 30 and declines outnumber advances by 800 issues in late afternoon. Even if the Dow rallies to unchanged, or maybe even slightly positive, levels, declines will still dominate at the end of the day—not by 800 issues certainly, but probably by several hundred anyway. Obviously, the *depth* of some of the declines will not be as great at the close as when the Dow was down 30, but most of the stocks will still wind up losing ground on the day. This fact can be useful in anticipating signals from this oscillator.

Going into any trading day, you know what level of advances and declines will produce a signal. For example, if the oscillator is at +220 the end of a trading day, then you know what level of advances and declines will produce a sell signal on the next trading day. The next day's oscillator will be the *net* advances plus 0.90 * 200 (=198 + net advances). It is obvious that if there are 180 more declines than advances, you will subtract at least 18 (10 percent of −180) from 198, and you will get the desired 180 to trigger the signal. So when the next trading day begins, you can look for that level. For example, if declines are outnumbering advances by 500 issues or more, and it's midafternoon, it is likely that the sell signal will be confirmed. Thus, you might decide to establish your position at that time—a few hours early.

The 81-point one-day decline in the Dow, mentioned in a previous example, is a classic case in favor of anticipating the signal. The oscillator had closed at 201 the previous night. Ninety percent of 201 is 180.90. So, on the next day, if declines outnumbered advances by *any* amount, a sell signal was going to ensue. By 1:00 P.M., the Dow was down about 35 points and declines were swamping advances by about 800 issues. It was fairly apparent that the advancing issues would not be able to recover. I bought puts at that time. The subsequent late-afternoon rout drove the Dow to its 81-point loss, making the put purchase very profitable. As was often the case that year (1995), market declines were fierce but short-lived. The entire down move had taken place in that one day.

Another use of monitoring the signal, intraday, is illustrated by the following example. In this particular situation, which can occur in extremely fast-moving markets, the oscillator becomes overbought or oversold intraday, but doesn't hold those levels for the close of trading. Technically, then, you do not have a trading signal. However, as a practical matter, a short-term trade may be at hand, even though it doesn't conform to the system in the strict sense.

In October 1995 the market was selling off rather swiftly (that selloff, by the way, *had* been correctly signaled by an oscillator signal in mid-September).

On October 9th, the Dow closed down 43 points and the oscillator stood at −147.18. The next day, the market was under tremendous pressure and was down 67 points at midday. Declines outnumbered advances by about 1,300 issues at that time, so the intraday calculation of the oscillator would have shown it to be well into oversold territory with a reading of about −262 $(0.9 \times -147.18 + 0.1 [-1,300] = -262.46)$.

At that point, the market began to rally as tech stocks recovered rapidly from their lows; the tech stocks had been the market leaders for most of 1995, so their movements were important to the market as a whole. As the rally progressed, shorts began to cover, and the Dow nearly recovered all of its lost ground. It only closed down five points on the day. Meanwhile, the differential between advances and declines shrunk also, although, as was pointed out earlier, it is virtually impossible for that many declines to turn into advances in the afternoon of any trading day. In any case, at the close, declines only outnumbered advances by about 500 issues. Therefore, the oscillator value at the close of trading was about −182.46, *not* in oversold territory.

So, even though a buy signal was not generated by our rules (the oscillator never closed below −200, which is the first criterion), it was fairly obvious that the market had been deeply oversold at midday. Moreover, the large reversal rally was obviously impressive, bringing the Dow 62 points up off the lows. So, was a buy signal generated by the intraday action or was more selling due because the oscillator closed just above the oversold −200 level? In this particular case, the Dow rallied another 73 points over the next three days. Thus, the intraday buy signal was correct.

The point that can be drawn from this example is that the oscillator can be used for confirmation of an intraday move. You might have been tempted to buy the market anyway, based on the large reversal move in the Dow (62 points from the low). However, the fact that the oscillator had penetrated so deeply into oversold territory during the day, and had then risen out of oversold territory by the end of the day, was good confirmation that the selling pressure was over and that a short-term upward move was probable.

This is not to say that you have a buy signal every time the oscillator penetrates the oversold level intraday and then closes outside of it. However, when you have a concomitant market reversal, as in the preceding example, then the intraday oscillator acts as a confirming indicator. Obviously, similar scenarios can be constructed for intraday overbought situations when the oscillator is near the +200 level.

Problems with the Advance–Decline Line

Before leaving this subject, we should address the problems with using advances and declines on the NYSE as an indicator. These problems arise from the fact that many of the issues listed on the NYSE these days are not stocks; in particular, many of them are closed-end bond funds. These funds sometimes move in directions different from the market itself, but their performance is counted in the advance–decline statistics issued by the NYSE. Some technicians call these funds "pseudostocks."

The way in which these pseudostocks affect our oscillator is that they may exacerbate the number of advances or declines on days when the bond market and the stock market move in the same direction. Thus, they may be responsible for the indicator reaching +200 or –200 more frequently than it used to in the past.

I certainly don't feel that the pseudostocks may render any advance–decline indicators totally unusable, but you should be aware that they *do* affect the numbers dramatically on days when the bond market has a big move. In fact, if you use the ARMS Index (named after its inventor, Richard Arms), the pseudostocks have a much more distorting effect. The Arms Index uses both advances and declines, as well as advancing and declining volume. These pseudostocks don't trade with much volume, so while they contribute heavily to the number of advances and declines, they don't contribute much at all to the volume of advances and declines. Without getting into the Arms Index calculations, suffice it to say that with the pseudostocks affecting only half of the equation, they can distort the overall results for that index.

There has been a request by technicians for the NYSE to publish advance–decline numbers based only on common stocks. If and when this comes about, then the pseudostocks will no longer influence any technical indicators using advances and declines (and the volume of same) as variables.

INTERMARKET SPREADS

In option terminology, we usually think of a spread as being long one option and short another option, with both options having the same underlying security. However, in a broader sense, whenever we are long one security and short another, related security, we have a spread in place. Such a spread might be established with stock, futures, or options.

Within this broad concept of spreads, we can divide all spreads into two broad categories: *inter*market spreads and *intra*market spreads. Intramarket spreads involve spreading futures or options that have the same underlying stock or commodity. For example, going long December corn and simultaneously shorting September corn would be an intramarket spread using futures. An intramarket spread using options would be any of the normal options spreads, for example, buying the IBM Jan 100 call and selling the IBM Jan 110 call. This is an intramarket spread because both sides of the spread are options on the same underlying security, IBM.

Intermarket spreads, on the other hand, are ones where, as the name implies, one market is spread against another. They may be closely related markets, such as T-bonds and municipal bonds, or they may be more loosely related such as T-bonds and utility stocks. An intermarket spread may even be a spread between two stocks that have a tendency to move somewhat in unison, a strategy called *pairs trading*. In any case, there is normally a well-defined historical relationship between the two markets. Within that relationship, however, swings can occur. When the swings are wide enough, there are opportunities to profit by trading the two markets against one another.

There are general relationships between many markets. The idea behind interindex spreading is often to capitalize on your view of the relationships between the two indices without having to actually predict the direction of the stock market. Note that this is often the philosophy behind many option spreads as well. For example, have you ever heard some analyst say that he expects small-cap stocks to outperform large-cap stocks? This analyst should consider using an interindex spread between the S&P 500 Index and the Value Line Index (which contains many small stocks), or perhaps between the

S&P and an over-the-counter index. If he buys the index that comprises smaller stocks and sells the S&P 500 Index, he will make money if his analysis is right, regardless of whether the stock market goes up or down. All he wants is for the index he is long to outperform the index he is short.

Before getting into specific markets that have proven to be tradeable over time, we describe the two main strategies for implementing the spreads. The simplest way to implement a spread is to use futures, or the equivalent position. For example, if we were spreading T-bonds against muni bonds, we could use futures in both markets. However, if we were spreading T-bonds against the Utility Index, we would have to use the *equivalent* of futures.

When you are trading an index—particularly a sector index—as part of an intermarket spread, you can't actually buy or sell the index itself and you can't normally buy or sell a futures contract on the sector, either. However, by using options and a knowledge of equivalent positions, you can establish a "futures equivalent" or "index equivalent" position. For example, if you are attempting to buy the index as part of an intermarket spread, then you would merely buy a call and sell a put, with the same terms. As you know, this is the equivalent of going long the index. Since the call and put have time value premium, what you actually establish is the equivalent of a futures contract on the index. Conversely, if you want to short the index, you buy a put and sell a call.

So, whether you use futures or the equivalent thereof, you establish the intermarket or intramarket spread in its simplest form. With this type of position, your profit potential is straightforward—if the two futures move in the correct direction, you will profit; if they don't, you will lose money.

There is, however, another way to establish these spread positions: with options. If, instead of buying (equivalent) futures on one side of the spread, you buy an in-the-money call, you have similar profit potential. You can make unlimited profits just as the futures can, but you give up whatever time value premium you spent to buy the call. If the call is far enough in-the-money, that time value expense will be small. Thus, the profit potential between owning the future and owning the in-the-money call is similar. There is one major difference: the call can only lose a fixed amount, while the (equivalent) futures position has virtually unlimited downside risk. Similarly, if you buy an in-the-money put instead of shorting the (equivalent) futures contract, you have similar characteristics. Thus, the option intermarket spread would be constructed by buying an in-the-money call and an in-the-money put.

What this means is that the option intermarket spread has an additional chance to make money that the (equivalent) futures position does not: it can make money if prices are volatile, even if the spread between the two markets does not converge as expected. For example, suppose that prices fall by a great deal (in both markets), but the spread between the two markets does not converge. Then the intermarket spread using (equivalent) futures would not make money. However, the option intermarket spread *would*, because the call would only lose a limited amount to the downside, while the put would keep making profits. Thus, with the option intermarket spread, you can make money if either (1) the markets converge as expected, or (2) prices are volatile and move a good deal in either direction. The option trader must pay time value premium for this privilege, but if he uses in-the-money options, he can keep the time value expense to a minimum.

Later in this chapter, we specifically discuss intermarket spreads using gold futures and gold stocks, but for now we present a true-life example from those markets in order to demonstrate the advantage of using options in these spreads.

In late 1995, gold stocks had rallied quite a bit, while the price of gold had not. Thus, we thought that the two markets would converge, and we recommended that our customers buy puts on gold stocks and buy calls on gold futures. The recommended prices were:

Gold Stock Index ($XAU): 120   XAU Feb 125 put: 8
April gold futures: 389   Gold April 380 call: 10.50

An equal number of calls and puts were purchased, with each put and call combo costing 18½ points ($1,850).

Things didn't work out as forecast, for gold stocks continued to outperform gold futures. However, both markets started to move higher quickly. This was the saving grace. A couple of months later, these prices existed:

$XAU: 138   Feb 125 put: 1
April futures: 407   April 380 call: 27.00

The combo was now worth $2,800. The call's price had increased in value by quite a bit ($1,650), but the put could only lose a limited amount. Thus, the option strategy made a profit, whereas a straight intermarket index hedge would not have.

European Options

Before discussing the intermarket spreads, it is necessary to spend a moment or two talking about some of the more intricate properties of European options. Most index options and sector options are European style. As you probably recall, this means that they can't be exercised until the end of their life. As a result, their price behavior is somewhat different from the American-style option that most people are accustomed to.

The main difference is that *European options can and do trade at discounts to parity prior to expiration.* This is true for both puts and calls, although it is more prevalent with puts. This discount is strictly a function of the mathematics of arbitrage and option pricing, and has nothing to do with how markets are made or any type of supply/demand situation.

To understand why this is true, you need to look at the situation from the viewpoint of an arbitrageur. First, let's understand why American-style options do not trade below parity. Suppose that a trader has been fortunate enough to have bought an American-style put and then sees the underlying stock decline substantially in price, to the point where the put is 20 points in the money. The trader now decides he wants to sell his put, and he can be certain that he will obtain 20 (or maybe a small fraction of a point less) for it. Why? Because an arbitrageur or market maker can:

1. Buy the put from the trader, and
2. Buy the underlying stock, and then
3. Exercise the put to remove the arbitrage position.

In order to provide this "service," the market maker will generally not pay the full 20 points for the put, but will discount it by a fraction of a point so he (the market maker) can make some money on this transaction also. Notice that the market maker never has any risk, for he is hedged at all times (the stock and option trades—steps 1 and 2—will be executed simultaneously).

The following prices illustrate such a trade: assume the trader owns an XYZ Dec 100 put, and that the stock is trading at 80 in November. He wants to sell the put. The market maker sees that he can buy stock at 80, so he tells the trader that he will pay him 19⅞ for his put. The trader agrees, and the trade is done. The market maker paid a total of 99⅞ (80 for the stock and 19⅞ for put) and got back 100 when he exercised the Dec 100 put (to sell stock at 100). Thus, the market maker made an eighth, without risk, and the trader got out of his put at virtually parity.

The following sums up the transaction from the market maker's point of view:

Buy Dec 100 put @ 19⅞	$1,987.50 debit
Buy 100 shares of XYZ at 80	$8,000.00 debit
Exercise the put to sell 100 shares of XYZ at 100	$10,000 credit
Net credit:	$12.50 credit

Since the market maker pays virtually no commissions, he has a profit on this arbitrage.

Thus, any American-style put can be sold for nearly parity at any time during its life, because of the arbitrage that can be constructed by the market maker to whom the put is sold. The same sort of thing is true for an American-style, in-the-money call. The trader who owns an in-the-money call that is American style can be certain that he can sell that call at any time for nearly parity. In the case of the call, the market maker simultaneously (1) buys the call, and (2) sells the stock (short exempt), and then (3) exercises the call to completely close out the position. Again, the market maker may try to make an eighth of a point by buying the call at a slight, fractional discount to parity.

When European style, in-the-money options are owned by traders who want to sell them prior to expiration, the market makers are generally the ones who are going to buy them. However, the arbitrage takes on a slightly different character because the market maker can't exercise the option as he could in step 3 above, to close out the position. Rather the market maker, after he (1) buys the in-the-money option from the trader, and (2) hedges his risk with the underlying stock, then must *hold the position until expiration*. This ties up the market maker's money for what may be a considerable amount of time, so he must make allowances for this fact by adjusting the price that he is willing to pay the trader for that in-the-money option. Again, an example will clarify this concept.

As in the previous example, a trader owns a Dec 100 put on a stock that is trading at 80, and the trader wants to sell the put a month before expiration. Assume, however, that now the option is European style. The market maker of this option now faces the following situation. He would still like to make a riskless eighth of a point for his trouble. However, when he now (1) buys the put from the trader, and (2) buys the underlying stock, he has to wait a month until expiration arrives before he can complete step 3: exercising the put and removing the position. Thus, the market maker will adjust his bid for the put to reflect his "carrying cost" of the position until expiration. He usually does this by figuring how much it would cost him to carry the striking price, $100 in this case, for the required time—a month, in this example. If his annual rate for borrowing short-term money is 12 percent, then that means that the market maker would have a cost of 1 percent to carry the position for one month. That is exactly $1. Therefore the put will trade at a discount to parity of 1 point.

The whole transaction would go like this, from the market maker's viewpoint:

- A month before expiration:
    1. Buy the put from the trader for $18\frac{7}{8}$ (1 point less than he would have paid for an American-style put): $1,887.50 debit.
    2. Buy the stock for 80 ($8,000 debit).

Thus, his cost is 98⅞ ($9,887.50) so far, which we will assume he borrows from his clearing house or his bank.

- At expiration (a month later):
  3. Pay his bank $100 for the interest on the loan ($100 debit).
  4. Exercise the put and receive the strike price: 100 points ($10,000 *credit*).

His net profit is the same eighth of a point: $10,000 less $9,887.50 paid for the position initially, less the $100 in interest, equals $12.50 profit.

Disregarding the eighth of a point that the market maker takes as profit, the European-style put sells for 19, while its American-style counterpart sells for 20 (parity). You may be thinking, "What if the market maker doesn't have to borrow the money from the bank, wouldn't that lower the cost?" Actually, that would change nothing, because if he uses his own money, then he will still "charge" for the lost opportunity cost of not being able to use his money to earn interest until expiration.

The preceding example was overly simplistic in that it ignored two factors that could help *increase* the price of the European put: (1) dividends and (2) the price of the call with the same striking price and expiration date. The reason that dividends are important is that they increase the price of any put, European or American. For example, if the stock in the preceding example were going to pay a 25-cent dividend during the remaining month of the put's life, then the put would be worth about a quarter of a point more than the prices in the example.

The call price figures into the equation as well, for the market maker or arbitrageur can reduce *his* overall expense by selling that call at the same time that he buys the trader's put. This reduces the market maker's overall expense, which he can pass along to the trader in the form of an increased put price.

Continuing with the previous example, suppose that we have the same situation: a trader wants to sell a Dec 100 put when the underlying stock is at 80, about a month before expiration. However, now we are going to incorporate one other piece of information: there is a Dec 100 call selling for a half point. The arbitrageur's actions can now be summarized as follows:

Action	Cost
Buy the Dec 100 put at 19⅜ from the trader	$1,937.50 DB
Buy the stock at 80	$8,000 DB
Sell the Dec 100 call at ½	($50 CR)
Total Debit	$9,875.50 DB

As you can see, this is the same initial debit as in the preceding example. The market maker will then pay the $100 in interest to his banker, and eventually exercise the put *or be assigned on the call*—collecting 100 points, or $10,000 and closing out the position in either case.

The difference here, though, is that the trader got paid 19⅜ for his put, not 18⅞ as in the previous example. Thus, the price of the call is important in determining the amount of discount (if there is any discount at all) of the in-the-money European-style put.

The more time that remains in the life of an in-the-money European option, the deeper will be the discount, because the market maker's borrowing costs will be larger. In the preceding example, we were talking about the discount on a relatively short-term option—it only had one month of life remaining. However, there are LEAPS options on indices that extend out two years or more. The discounts on these longer-term European-style puts can be very significant.

These deep discounts on longer-term European-style put options are something that traders should factor into their projections.

The first rather widespread encounter between the reality of European-style option discounts and put owners occurred in the AMEX-based Japanese Index puts (symbol: $JPN) in the early 1990s. The Japanese stock market, as measured by that country's Nikkei 225 Index, had peaked out at about ¥40,000 and was in the process of falling to nearly ¥15,000 in the course of the next couple of years. The Japan Index is a surrogate for the Japanese stock market, and it has a value that is about one-hundredth of the value of the Nikkei. So, roughly, the JPN Index fell to nearly 150 (the JPN index didn't exist when the Nikkei was at ¥40,000, but it would probably have been near 400 if it had).

There were European-style LEAPS puts listed on the JPN Index and some had strikes as high as 280, which meant they were over 100 points in-the-money with over a year of life remaining when the JPN Index neared the bottom of that bear market. Consider a Jan 280 put with a year of life remaining and the JPN Index at 180. You can safely assume that the Jan 280 call was essentially worthless, so it was of no help in increasing the price of the put. Even at 5 percent interest, the cost of carrying $28,000 (the strike price) for one year is $1,400. In option terms, that's 14 points. So the Jan 280 put was theoretically selling for 86, when parity was 100.

In reality, with index options, the discount bid by the market makers may be even slightly deeper because it is more difficult for them to hedge an entire index—they have to buy all the stocks in the index, rather than just one stock, as in the previous examples. This increases their clearing costs, to say nothing of their having to buy lots of stocks, each one on the offering price. These factors caused the actual bid for that put to be about 84.

There were even some minor lawsuits by investors who felt that the discount on the puts was arbitrary and unfair. Of course, it wasn't—the puts were properly priced—but in those days, many public traders didn't understand the concept of European options well, and so some felt that the market makers simply lowered their bids to extreme levels because they knew that these traders were long and wanted to sell. Trader paranoia? Yes. Incorrect pricing? No.

Of course, if you were bearish when the market was much higher and bought that put for 10 points, say, you are probably not so concerned with whether you sell it for 84 or 86, since you have a phenomenal profit in either case. However, it is important to understand that you are not going to be able to sell it for 100 if expiration is a long way off.

This concept of discounts on European-style puts could also be important if you are buying the puts as protection for a market decline, since the discounted puts will not provide as much protection if the market falls quickly and there is still a great deal of time until expiration.

Do European-style calls suffer the same fate? The answer is no, unless the underlying pays a large dividend. To understand why, it is again necessary to view things from the arbitrageur's viewpoint. When a trader who owns a European-style, in-the-money call wants to sell it, the market maker buys it and immediately hedges himself by *selling* (*short*) the underlying stock. This transaction creates a credit in the arbitrageur's account, upon which he can collect interest. So, he is perfectly willing to hold the position until expiration and earn interest. Thus, he will pay the trader full parity (or maybe even a little more) for the call.

The exception would be if the underlying pays a lot of dividends during the remaining life of the option. Since the arbitrageur is short the underlying stock, he will be paying out those dividends as time passes. Therefore, he will discount the original price that he pays the trader for the call, by the present value of all the remaining dividends. Note that, in the case of an American-style option, a market maker who is both long an in-the-money call and short the underlying stock will merely exercise his call on the day before the stock goes ex-dividend, thereby saving himself the dividend expense. However, with the European-style option, the market maker cannot exercise prior to expiration, so he is forced to pay out those dividends.

A trader buys a July 60 long-term, European-style call option and subsequently has the good fortune to see the stock rise to 90. At this point, assume there is still a year of life remaining in the call, but the trader wants to sell. Furthermore, assume that the stock pays a quarterly dividend of 50 cents, or a total of $2.00 over the next year. The market maker will bid 28 for the call: that is parity (30) less the 2 points for dividends that he will have to pay out from being short the stock over the course of the next year.

In reality, the present worth of the dividend is not the full $2.00, but it's probably more like $1.80 or something, depending on interest rates, so the *exact* price that the market maker pays might be slightly more than 28, but the concept is illustrated correctly in this example. Also, if the July 60 put is worth anything, its value may increase the value of the call as well.

This feature of European-style calls can be significant if you are dealing with a high-yielding stock or index, such as the Utility Index ($UTY), especially if a significant number of stocks that compose the index are about to go ex-dividend. Many stocks go ex-dividend in early February, May, August, and November, so in-the-money

European-style call options expiring in those months may trade at discounts even though expiration is nigh.

One firsthand experience of the dividend affecting a European-style call option occurred in a 1993 trade of the PHLX's Utility Index (symbol: $UTY). I was long the Dec 210 calls, with the index at about 214. The index made a nice move in my favor, rising quickly to 233, by late November. Thus, the calls were 23 points in-the-money. However, when I checked the market, it was only bid at 21¼. The reason was that many of the stocks that made up the Utility Index were about to go ex-dividend; the total of these dividends was about two points, in UTY terms. Moreover, since there was so little time remaining until expiration, the market maker couldn't really earn any substantial interest from being short the stocks in the index for only three weeks until expiration. However, he was going to have to pay out the dividends against the short sales that hedged his position. Thus, his bid for the calls reflected a discount equal to the $2 in dividends, less a small amount for interest that he could earn over the course of the three weeks.

If you find yourself wanting to sell a European-style option, but you're dubious because it's trading at discount because of dividends, my advice would be to sell it anyway. It's not mispriced—it's supposed to be trading at a discount. You may be tempted to wait until the ex-dividend date is past before selling. First of all, that will gain you nothing theoretically, because the underlying stock or index will drop in price by the amount of the dividends. Thus, even if the call is *then* selling at parity, it will theoretically be selling at the price you are currently seeing. Second, it is generally a mistake to delay a sale for the pure reason of something like this. Taxes are another common example; many people want to sell a stock, but decide not to, for tax reasons, only to see it drop substantially in price, thereby costing them much more than they would have had to pay in capital gains taxes.

This concludes the discussion of European-style options. We have included it here because many of the intermarket spreads that we discuss in the remainder of this chapter involve using European-style index or sector options. If you are trading those options,you should have a thorough understanding of the concepts just described, or you will find yourself at a disadvantage.

Now, let's turn our attention once again to the intermarket spread, using options. Recall that the option spread gives the trader a possible advantage over the (equivalent) futures spread when markets are volatile. Let's look at some of my favorite intermarket spreads. Some of these have longer time horizons than others, but most are held for several weeks.

The HUG/HOG Spread

No, this doesn't have anything to do with giving a loveable squeeze to a farm animal, even though the name might seem like it. Rather it's a spread between the February heating oil futures contract (symbol: HOG) and the February unleaded gas futures contract (symbol: HUG).

It is a rather well-established fact that, in the fall of the year, unleaded gasoline futures outperform heating oil futures. Now, this might seem illogical at first, unless you have an understanding of the way that markets work. After Labor Day, families are no longer vacationing or traveling as much, so the demand for gasoline should slack off, right? Right. Also, as the winter approaches, the demand for heating oil should increase, right? Right. So how in the world can unleaded gasoline futures outperform heating oil futures during that time period? Because it is the job of the marketplace to discount future events.

Historic price charts tell us that the futures market tends to have done most of the discounting for these February futures contracts by September of the preceding year. Moreover, a sort of worst-case scenario is often built into the discounting mechanism. So, if things are "bad" as the fall unfolds and winter develops, then the spread between heating oil and unleaded gas futures will remain about steady. However, if things aren't as bad as the discounting allowed for—as is often the case—the unleaded gas futures will outperform heating oil futures. Thus, it is a low risk spread to buy February unleaded gas futures and sell February heating oil futures against them; the spread is usually established in September or early October and held into December.

You may be saying, "Wait a minute. I hear radio ads all during the fall saying that I should buy heating oil options because winter is approaching. What's going on here?" I would respond to that question in two ways. The first is: are you the only trader who knows that winter is approaching? If you are trading based on obvious information, or information that has already been made widely public, then you can be assured that that information is already factored into the price of whatever you are trading, and you have no edge because of that information. Second, if you are buying options because of what you hear in a media ad, then you deserve what you get as a result. Also, check out the commissions those radio guys are charging and you'll see who stands to make money from buying those options.

It should be pointed out that the price of heating oil may go up as the winter approaches (or it may not), but we have no directional bias in this spread other than to want unleaded gas to outperform heating oil. So, the spread can move favorably for us if prices of both products move higher or if prices of both products move lower. We don't care.

Figures 5.1 through 5.5 cover the history of this spread for the

Figure 5.1
HOG/HUG 1996 CONTRACTS

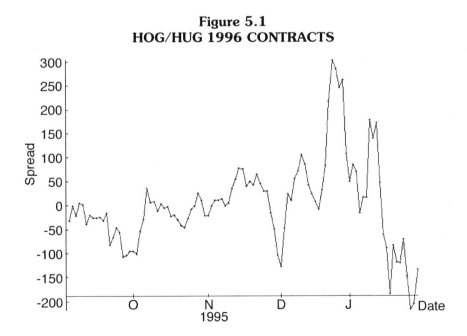

Figure 5.2
HOG/HUG 1995 CONTRACTS

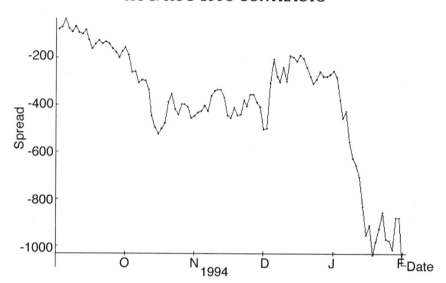

Figure 5.3
HOG/HUG 1994 CONTRACTS

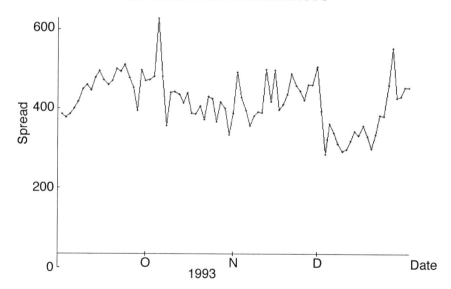

Figure 5.4
HOG/HUG 1993 CONTRACTS

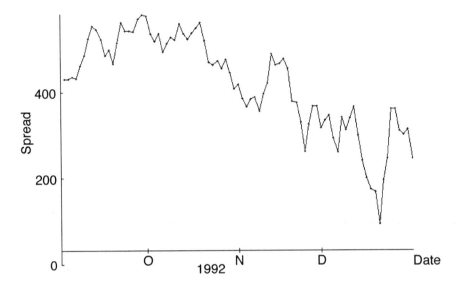

Figure 5.5
HOG/HUG 1992 CONTRACTS

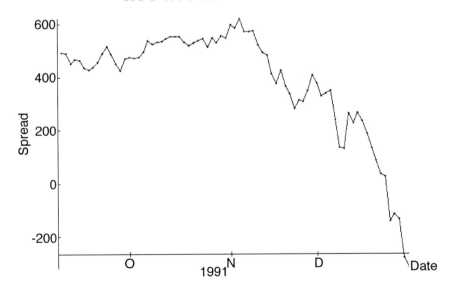

last five years. Note that it doesn't always *start* at the same level in September. In some years (1991, 1992, and 1993) the spread starts out with heating oil trading at a substantial premium to unleaded gas. In the other two years, the spread started out much nearer to zero to begin with (in September). In four of the five years, regardless of the starting level, the spread still moved in the desired direction. These graphs are drawn as *heating oil minus unleaded gas,* so when the price *declines* on the graph, the spread makes money.

The spread's trading history is worth analyzing, for it will give you some feel for how the spread behaves. In 1991, the spread—using 1992 contracts—was trading at about 5.00 in September (heating oil over unleaded), and even crept higher toward 6.00 in late October. But then a serious drop materialized that took the spread all the way to –2.00 by year end. Thus there was a 7.00 point profit from September 1st through the end of the year.

In 1992, similar results occurred, although the spread price was more volatile. The spread was just above 4.00 on September 1st, and managed to climb to nearly 6.00 in early October. It had a small decline through mid-October before beginning to decline in earnest to about 3.00 in December. There was one final downward spike to under 1.00 in late December. Thus, the spread afforded a 3.00 point profit or more that year.

In 1993, the spread did not make money. It started off at 4.00 on September first, had a very short-term spike toward 6.00 in early October, and then traded in a range between 3.50 and 5.00 for the rest of the year.

Better results were posted once again in 1994. The spread started at –1.00 in September (i.e., unleaded was at a premium to heating oil) and quickly fell below –4.00. It then traded between –4.00 and –5.00 for over a month and then rallied to –3.00. At this point, one might have thought that the spread had made its maximum profits for the year. However, in mid-December, the spread began to decline very rapidly and fell to –10.00 by mid-January.

In 1995, the spread exhibited more erratic behavior than in the other years. For a couple of months, it was quite stable and traded in a narrow range. Then, in December, it broke higher—generating unrealized losses—but swifly reversed direction and traded down to spread lows.

In summary, then, the spread usually starts to decline in price by early October, reaching the maximum profit potential by mid-December. In 1991 and 1994, the maximum profit actually came later than mid-December, so a trailing stop would be a good idea.

The margin required for this spread is small, because futures margin requirements realize that the two contracts are related: $1,250. A one-point move in this spread is worth $420. In years when the spread "works," you get moves of three or four points in your favor, or $1,260 to $1,680 on the $1,250 investment. That's a phenomenal return, of course. I view the risk as about two points, and if the spread were to widen more than that distance against me, I would close it out for that year and wait until next year to try again.

You have probably noticed that we haven't mentioned options yet in this analysis. Options can be used in this spread strategy. Simplistically, you would buy a Feb unleaded gas call that was fairly deep in-the-money, so as to minimize time value expense, and would also buy a Feb heating oil put that was deep in-the-money.

These options would be bought *instead* of the futures spread, so the option position would be established in late September or early October of the preceding year. That brings us to our first problem: liquidity. These futures options are not that liquid four or five months prior to expiration. So, you may have trouble finding a striking price that is deep enough in-the-money to allow you to minimize your time value expense. Also, you may not be able to trade enough options to establish the spread in the size that you want.

Remember that the profit potential of the spread is three to four points at best, so if you are spending nearly that much for time value premium when you buy options, then perhaps you should use futures instead. Admittedly, if you are going to remove the spread in December, then there will still be some time value premium left in the options when you sell them—so you might not lose all of the time value premium that you originally bought—but you can't count on that. Moreover, the options expire in January, so they will only have a few weeks of life remaining when you try to sell them in December.

Having stated all the caveats, let's look at the positive side of the option buy combination (we are buying a put and a call) as compared to the futures spread. The advantage of the option position is that it can make money when prices are volatile. The following example, from 1991 prices, shows how this might work.

In mid-September 1991 the following prices existed:

Feb unleaded gas: 62.50   HU Feb 56 call: 6.80

Feb heating oil: 68.00   HO Feb 74 put: 7.50

Futures spread: 5.50   Option combo: 14.30

The futures spread (5.50) is just the difference between the two futures contracts, and the option combo price is the sum of the two option prices. Note that the time value premium in the Feb 56 call is 0.30 and is 1.50 on the HO Feb 70 put. Thus, the option combo requires an expenditure of 1.80 for time value premium. This might represent almost the entire profit of the spread if prices remain unchanged. However, the benefit of owning the option combo was seen when prices became volatile.

As the fall of 1991 unfolded, the futures spread was fairly flat, ranging up to nearly 6.00 in November and down to 4.00 in the first week of December. From the original price of the spread, this would have been a profit of 1.50, basis of the futures contracts.

However, what you can't tell from the spread price is that the absolute level of oil and oil product prices was in a very bearish market in November and December of 1991. Figure 5.6 is a chart of heating oil during this time period. You can deduce that the unleaded gas chart was quite similar, since the spread between the two was remaining relatively stable.

By early December, Feb heating oil fell to 56.00. That means the Feb 74 put had to be worth at least 18.00, which is parity. On the other hand, the Feb unleaded 56 call could only fall to zero (in reality, it was worth 0.20). Thus, the option combo was worth at least 18 points in early December. Since the initial cost of that combo was 14.30, the profit on the option combo was 3.70 points, substantially better than the 1.50 profit available solely from the futures spread.

As it turned out, prices fell even farther during December, which means that the long put generated even more profits.

This example also can be used to illustrate an even more important point in favor of the option combo. Suppose, just suppose, that when Feb heating oil fell to 56.00 in early December, that unleaded gas had fallen even more. Thus, the futures spread would have actually lost money if that had happened. Despite that, the option combo would have had to make money because the option prices would still be the same: 18.00 for the heating oil Feb 74 put and zero for the unleaded gas Feb 56 call. Thus, the option combo can actually make

Figure 5.6
HOG

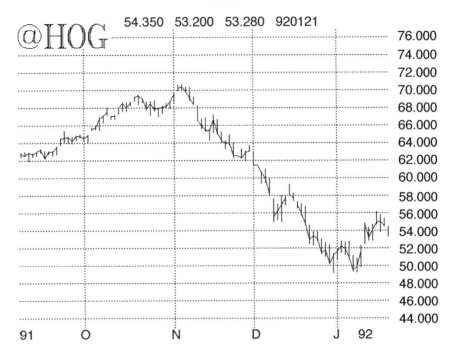

money if prices are volatile (e.g., prices fell dramatically in this example) even though the futures spread might be losing money.

The counterargument, of course, is that if prices remain stable and the futures spread widens by two points or so, you will make all of that two points if you have the futures spread in position, while you would lose time value premium in the same situation if you have the option combo in place. In the preceding example, the time value paid was 1.80, so you wouldn't really make anything from the option combo in that case.

So, which is better, the futures spread or the option combo? I would use the time value premium of the options as the major factor in making that decision. In early September, if the options are trading with an inflated implied volatility or if the time value premium is just plain "too big," then start out by spreading the futures. You can always roll over into an option position if implied volatilities decrease (i.e., if time value premium shrinks). This might happen in October or early November. So, if you have the futures spread in place, I would always keep an eye on the options for an opportune time to switch into the option combo. Thus, *I favor the option combo, but only if time value premium is small enough.*

So get out your calendar right now, and make a note for next September to evaluate the spread between the following February's heating oil and unleaded gas contracts. This is a spread with a good track record.

The January Effect

This is another seasonal spread that can actually be played in *two* directions (not simultaneously, of course). The *January effect* is a term that describes the phenomenon whereby small-cap stocks generally outperform large-cap stocks in the month of January. The reason that this effect takes place is that when the end of the year approaches, people are more apt to sell off their small stocks to take losses. This depresses the small-cap stocks, and then they bounce back in January after the selling abates. However, when January arrives, one would not just want to buy the small-cap stocks (Value Line Index, e.g.) because the overall market might decline. So the preferred spread strategy is to hedge: *buy the Value Line Index and simultaneously sell the S&P Index.* Then if the small-caps outperform the large caps in January, you will have a profit.

That seems simple enough, doesn't it? Unfortunately, when everyone becomes aware of something, the market has a way of making it more difficult to make money. For example, the "conventional" wisdom is that the January effect takes place earlier now since so many people are anticipating it. In fact, there are usually ads on TV by November of the preceding year, urging you to buy Value Line (and possibly to sell S&P as well) to get ready for the January effect.

In order to discern how this spread truly behaves, we decided to do some research on how it has really played itself out in recent years. We didn't want to go back *too* far because spreads such as this tend to implement themselves in different ways as the years go by. We felt that looking at the postcrash (i.e., post-1987) years might be best, since that was sort of a turning point for many investment philosophies. This means that we are looking at data from November 1988 through January 1995, seven examples of the January effect.

The specific prices are listed below, but two broad conclusions can be drawn, and they are very important ones:

1. *Big-cap stocks distinctly outperform small-cap stocks from mid-November to nearly year-end.* Thus one should buy the S&P futures and sell the Value Line futures at this time, holding them until you reverse the spread as stated in conclusion 2.
2. *The optimal time to begin playing the January effect is between December 19th and January 2nd.* At this time you would buy the Value Line futures and sell the S&P futures. The profit potential is large and typically reaches its maximum in mid- to late February.

Conclusion 1 means that mid-November is too early to be entering into the traditional January effect spread: long Value Line–short S&P spread; in fact, you should be taking the *opposite* side of the spread in mid-November. This conclusion makes logical sense, since the original premise is that these small-cap stocks are heavily sold during tax-selling time in November and December. Unfortunately, it seems that many proponents of the January effect are in too much of a rush to establish their positions. Getting in too early can and will hurt you.

The proper time to actually enter the traditional January effect spread is much nearer to the end of the year, when tax selling abates. This usually occurs around December 20th, but in a couple of years recently, it appears that tax selling extended all the way to the end of the year.

You can verify these conclusions by looking at the actual data supporting them as shown in Table 5.2. For example, conclusion 1 says that the spread will actually widen between the November low and the December high. The profits are indicated by the plus numbers in the second column. If you want to take advantage of that fact

Table 5.2

**JANUARY EFFECT DATA, 1988–1995: DIFFERENCE BETWEEN
S&P 500 CASH INDEX AND VALUE LINE CASH INDEX**

November Low Spread Date	High Spread Date and Change from Nov Low	Eventual Low Date and Change from High	Comments
11/11/88	+7.07 (12/19/88)	−8.49 (3/1/89)	Interim low on 1/3/89 with rally to 1/31/89
11/6/89	+15.16 (1/2/90)	−10.33 (2/23/90)	Interim low on 1/22/90 with rally to 1/31/90
11/7/90	+5.12 (12/21/90)	−16.24 (3/8/91)	Interim low on 1/11/91 with rally to 1/18/91
11/20/91	+18.41 (12/30/91)	−34.92 (2/18/91)	The best year recently—both ways
11/16/92	+4.07 (12/21/92)	−22.12 (2/16/93)	The actual low before year-end was on 12/3/92
11/11/93	+3.12 (12/22/93)	−18.85 (2/18/94)	Eventual low reached on 3/25/94
11/4/94	+13.89 (12/14/94)	−10.40 (1/9/95)	Unfortunately, the spread expanded during the rest of January and February 1995

341

in November, you must *sell* the Value Line and *buy* the S&P 500. This "reverse" or "opposite" spread should be established in mid-November. The earliest was November 4th and the latest was November 20th, so the "average" date for establishing this portion of the spread would be November 12th.

Conclusion 2 states that the high point for the traditional spread—the time when you should be taking profits in the opposite spread and simultaneously establishing the traditional spread—takes place near the end of December. Notice that in each of the seven years shown in the table, the peak came at those times (the dates are indicated in the second column). *This, then, is when you should be establishing the traditional spread—long Value Line and short S&P.* The optimum time is between December 14th (the earliest occurrence) and January 2nd (the latest); these dates yield an "average" date of December 23rd for entering the traditional January effect spread. Do not enter into the spread too early (i.e., in November, for example), or you will be looking at unrealized losses before the end of December.

Finally column three shows the large profit potential of the traditional side of the spread. There were some fake-out attempts in January of 1989, 1990, and 1991, as noted in the "comments" column in the table, but the profit potential was large in each year. It has remained very large, even in the mid-1990s when the January effect received so much publicity. In general, there is a very quick profitable move that occurs into early January. In January of 1989–1991, the spread had a reflex rally—back to the highs in some cases—before reaching lows in late February or early March. In 1995, the spread rushed back to new highs and beyond as the S&P stocks dominated their smaller Value Line counterparts after the initial January effect. In the other years, however, the spread has pretty much continued straight down to its low point in mid-February.

Thus, it appears that you should take at least some partial profits on the first move into January. Then, if there is a rally back toward the highs, you can reestablish that portion of the spread, using a stop of 4.00 points or so. This stop is necessary because, in years like 1995, the spread never went lower again. In other years, however, the total position would have been very profitable during the final decline into February.

Implementing the Spread. *The reason that we spread the effect, rather than just buying the Value Line Index, is that there is no guarantee that the market will rise in January; but, whether it rises or falls, the January effect has a good track record going back over 60 years.* To implement the spread, we use Value Line and S&P futures contracts. In both Value Line and S&P 500 futures, a 1.00-point move is worth $500, so there are potentially large profits available, considering the margin for the futures spread is $4500.

There are some pitfalls that should be pointed out, however. First, we are forced to trade futures and cannot trade the indices themselves. Therefore, the futures may have a premium that anticipates some of this January effect, and that premium may reduce the potential profits, as shown by the cash index spread in Table 5.2.

In late December, a trader is thinking of establishing the January effect spread—buying the Value Line futures and selling the S&P 500 futures. He would use the March contract in both cases since that is the "front month" (i.e., most active) contract. The following prices exist:

Value Line Index: 551.13   S&P Index: 582.17
March Value Line Futures: 559.15 March S&P Futures: 585.25

The spread between the cash indices is 31.04, but the spread between the futures is only 26.10. This difference is due to the fact that the Value Line futures are trading with a premium of just over eight points, and those are the ones that are being bought. On the other hand, the S&P futures that are being sold have only a three-point premium. Thus the trader is paying five points of extra premium for the futures spread.

This extra cost is a theoretical disadvantage for the trader, but it reflects the anticipation of the futures market of the coming January effect.

When this large premium appears on the Value Line futures, you might think that you could use the options to establish a more favorable equivalent position. Unfortunately, that's not true. The equivalent option position has just as large a premium, as the calls get very expensive and the puts get quite cheap; thus they are in line with the futures. If the premium is overly large, the only thing that you can do is wait for it to abate somewhat, even though that may mean missing the optimum entry point by a few days.

In summary, the spread can be traded in both directions. In the mid-November to mid-December portion, you are long the S&P and short the Value Line. In fact, this might actually be the most reliable of the two spreads. Its timing is very reliable, but its biggest drawback is that the profit potential is fairly small in three of the seven years shown in the table. Then, in mid-December, you reverse your stance and buy the Value Line while selling the S&P. This also has shown good profit potential in almost every year. Therefore I feel that both portions of the spread should be traded, for the profit potential is obvious.

Spreading the Premium on Value Line and S&P 500 Futures

While we're on the subject of Value Line versus S&P 500 futures, it would be appropriate to discuss another hedged strategy involving those two contracts that has a good track record over the years. We can use this strategy at any time of the year *except* during the December–January time frame, when the January effect spread dominates. In this particular strategy, we are not trying to predict how the one index is going to perform with respect to the other index. That is, we don't care whether the small-cap stocks outperform the big-cap stocks, or vice versa. There is another approach to index spreading, one that does not rely on a fundamental viewpoint of the performance of the stocks in the index: if the futures on two related indices are trading at different levels of premium, then there may be an opportunity for the strategist to set up an index futures spread to take advantage of this discrepancy.

Example: Suppose the following prices exist for the Value Line Index and its futures, and for the S&P 500 Index and its futures:

	Cash Index	Futures	Premium
Value Line	551.00	548.00	–3.00
S&P 500	587.00	587.50	+0.50

Notice that the Value Line futures are trading at a 3-point discount, while the S&P futures have a 50-cent premium! Stated another way, the premium differential between the two futures contracts is a total of 3.50. The *premium differential* is merely the premium on the Value Line futures minus the premium on the S&P futures, which technically is −3.50 points in this case. This is a large discrepancy, because the two indices normally have about the same level of futures premium. Therefore a hedge could be attempted by a simple index spread: *buying a Value Line future and selling an S&P future.*

The object of this spread is to make money when the premium levels of the two futures become more equal. What is the profitability of such a spread? If the two futures premiums converge quickly, a profit will almost always result.

Let's continue with the same example. Suppose we bought the Value Line futures at 548.00 and sold the S&P futures at 587.00. Furthermore, suppose that by the next day, the futures premium on both indices has returned to almost similar levels in a slight bull market:

	Cash Index	Futures	Premium
Value Line	552.00	552.50	+0.50
S&P 500	588.00	589.00	+1.00

At this point, the premium differential in the futures contracts is only 0.50, an insignificant number where these two futures are concerned. At the previous prices, we would have a 4.50-point gain on the long Value Line futures and a 1.50 loss on the short S&P 500 futures, for a nice total gain of 3.00 points, or $1,500.

In this example, the premium differential disappeared quickly—in one day. When the differential disappears quickly, a profit usually results, because there is not enough time for the underlying cash indices to move in an adverse manner. Unfortunately it may sometimes take a while for the differential to disappear. If, during the time that you are waiting, the cash indices diverge, you may not make any money at all even if the futures eventually have equal premium levels.

Even in that case, though, the losses may be small. The following example shows what might occur when the futures premiums don't converge right away.

Recall that the original example had us buying Value Line futures at 548.00 and selling the S&P futures at 587.50. Suppose that a few days pass before there is any improvement in the premium differential between the two futures contracts.

	Cash Index	Futures	Premium
Value Line	549.00	549.50	+0.50
S&P 500	590.00	591.00	+1.00

In this example, even though the premium differential has shrunk to 50 cents, the hedge produces a loss because of the fact that the cash indices have moved in an adverse manner. There is 1.50-point gain on the long Value Line futures (from 548.00 to 549.50), but that is more than offset by the 3.50-point loss on the S&P 500 futures (587.50 to 591.00).

This example demonstrates that the mere fact that the futures premiums converge does not necessarily guarantee a profit if the cash indices diverge. Still, if the original discrepancy is large enough, the loss should be small if it occurs. Moreover, the profits could be sizable if the futures come back into line quickly.

The strategy that we have found profitable over time is this:

1. **Calculate the differential** = (VL future − VL Index) − (S&P future − S&P Index).
2. **Establish the spread** when the differential is greater than +2.00 or less than −2.00.
   (a) If the spread is +2.00 or greater, then buy S&P 500 futures and sell Value Line futures.
   (b) If the spread is −2.00 or less, then buy Value Line futures and sell S&P 500 futures.

   Note: Do not establish the spread in late December, because of conflicts with the January effect.

3. **Remove the spread** as soon as the futures premiums converge, regardless of the profit or loss in the spread at that
time. We define "converge" as the premiums being 0.50 or
less apart, or reversing completely the other direction. This
discipline adds an unemotional exit point to the position.

Figure 5.7 shows the premium differential between the Value
Line futures and the S&P futures on a daily basis over the period of
about a year. Notice that sometimes the differential has gotten as
high as +4 (the Value Line futures have four more points of premium
on them than S&P futures do), and as low as –4 (the Value Lines
have 4 points less premium than the S&Ps). In fact, the differential
has actually gotten as large as +8 and as small as –9 (not shown on
graph). But in nearly every case, the differential quickly returns to
zero. Thus, you are usually not forced to hold this spread for a long
period of time. Rather, the hedger will normally be exiting the spread
within a week or so.

Figure 5.7
VALUE LINE FUTURES PREMIUM MINUS
S&P FUTURES PREMIUM

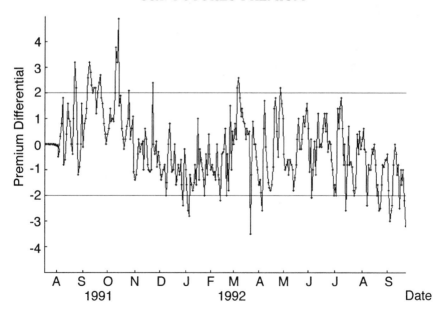

Note that this index spread is *not* an arbitrage; you would have to trade the stocks in the indices as well as the futures in order to construct a true arbitrage, and that would be a formidable task. However, it *is* a hedged position with a built-in advantage. That advantage is the fact that the futures premiums are more than 2.00 points out of line when the spread is established. This advantage does not necessarily guarantee a profit, since the cash indices could move at different speeds and erase the advantage. However, it does mean that the odds are on your side initially, which is all the strategist can ask.

You may be wondering why such a large differential in the futures premiums would occur. In some cases, the futures premium is actually predicting the way in which the "market" thinks the actual cash index will move. An example of that was shown in the previous section, on the January effect, when it was pointed out that the Value Line futures will often get a large premium on them at year-end, in anticipation of the buying of small-cap stocks in January. Thus, I would not use *this* hedged strategy if it conflicts with the January effect spread, for the latter is more dominant. That is, *do not establish this hedge in the latter part of December, even though the Value Line futures may have a huge premium on them*. However, most of the rest of the year, the futures differential can get out of line for no reason other than that there is inordinate trading activity. It is at those times that this hedged strategy works best.

The data in Table 5.3 summarize the results of trading this spread over the three-year period, 1993–1995. There was a surprisingly large number of trades in 1993 and a rather small number in 1994. The total profit is figured on trading one contract, using settlement prices.

The total gain was 19.40 points, or $9,700. Allowing $100 per trade for commission and slippage would reduce that to $7,300, a good profit for a relatively inactive trading system. Since these calculations are based on settlement prices, you might easily be able to achieve better results with intraday trading.

The trades are very short-term in nature, averaging only six days. That average is actually inflated by a couple of trades that were held for 19 calendar days. The median trade was only 4 days, meaning that 11 trades were of 3 days duration or less. This short-term hold-

Table 5.3
SUMMARY OF TRADING RESULTS FOR 1993–1995

Year	Number of Trades	% Winners	Total Yearly Profit from One Contract
1993	12	75	11.10
1994	4	75	6.40
1995	8	50	1.90
Total:	24	71	19.40

Largest Gain: +6.20 points
Largest Loss: −2.70 points

Average holding period: 6.1 calendar days
Median holding period: 4 calendar days
Longest holding period: 19 calendar days (2 times)
Shortest holding period: 1 calendar day (7 times)

ing period is to be expected—just look at the previous graph: the premium discrepancies usually return to relatively "normal" levels quite quickly.

With only 24 trades in 3 years, and with each trade being held for an average of only 6 days, this isn't a system that will occupy a lot of your time or capital. However, since it's got a good track record, it would behoove you to monitor the premium levels of the Value Line and S&P 500 futures for the purposes of trading the spread whenever the conditions warrant. If your quote machine can monitor equations, then plug the equation for this premium differential spread in and set a limit on it at +2.00 and −2.00. Otherwise, calculate the ratio daily from the newspaper—it only takes a few seconds.

Gold Stocks Versus the Price of Gold

There are some stocks whose price is related to a raw material that is extremely important to the company's financial fortunes. Among the raw materials that fall into this category are gold, oil, copper, and fertilizer. In certain cases, an intermarket spread strategy can be devised wherein the stock(s) are traded against futures on the pertinent commodity. The intermarket strategy could be as simple as trading copper futures against Phelps Dodge stock (Phelps Dodge is a major copper producer), or it could be a little more complicated, such as trading an index of stocks—if a sector index, if fact, exists—against the futures contract. This latter strategy is a useful one, and since the index provides some measure of diversification, it is probably a more reliable strategy than merely trading one stock against the futures.

In order to trade the index, you could either buy the appropriate number of shares of each stock in the index, or you could use options on the index, if there are listed options trading. Usually, using options is much simpler because you can get "long" or "short" the index very quickly and easily, as opposed to executing trades in all the stocks that compose the sector index. Moreover, the capital required for the option transaction would be much smaller than that required to buy all of the stocks in the index.

Furthermore, when trading options on the index, there are two approaches that you could take as well. First, you could use the *equivalent strategy* described at the beginning of Chapter 3. For example, if you wanted to be long the sector index, you could buy a call and sell a put—both with the same striking price and expiration date—as a total substitute for owning the index. When using this approach, you have the full upside potential *and* downside risk of the index. The other approach would be to merely buy a call on the index; this means that you would have limited downside risk, but would have risk of time value eroding your option.

Now that we have discussed all those possibilities, it's time to look at one of these intermarket spreads. It is the one between the price of gold (futures) and the price of the PHLX Gold and Silver Index (symbol: $XAU). Figure 5.8 is an approximation of how this spread has looked over a seven-year period from 1989 through 1995. The purpose of this chart is to demonstrate that the relationship between the price of gold stocks and the price of gold itself can change dramatically over time. When you are actually trading the intermarket spread itself, you usually are interested in shorter-term movements than those shown on this broad chart.

Nevertheless, the chart is useful. Note that, as the 1990s began, the price of gold stocks (XAU) was about 30 percent of the price of

Figure 5.8
XAU DIVIDED BY DEC GOLD FUTURES

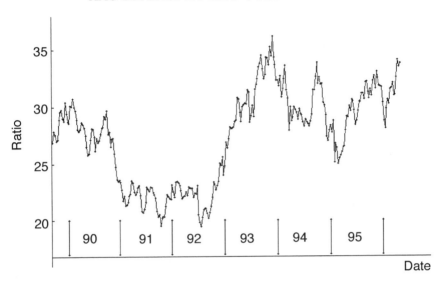

Dec gold futures (30 on the chart). At the time that was historically expensive. Then, both gold and gold stocks went into a prolonged decline in 1990 and the ratio plunged. In fact, gold stocks went down farther than gold itself, as the XAU index dropped over 50 percent from its early 1990 levels, while gold declined about 20 percent. This caused the ratio to eventually drop to levels near 20 on the chart in Figure 5.8.

An opposite move occurred in 1993, as both gold and gold stocks blasted off to the upside, with the XAU doubling in price, but gold only gaining about 25 percent. Thus, the ratio moved higher once again, peaking near 35 at the beginning of 1994. As you can see, when major moves occur, XAU moves farther than gold because it is a more volatile item. So, when both the XAU Index and gold are moving together, we generally would not be looking to establish an inter-market spread. However, when *one* of them is moving and the other is not, we may have an interesting opportunity to establish a position.

The 1993–1995 period is a classic case in point. During that time, gold itself was quite stable, remaining in a very narrow range between about 375 and 410. However, gold stocks, which apparently are more subject to investors' emotions, had some fairly big moves. This caused the action on the chart in Figure 5.8 whereby the ratio peaked in the 33 to 35 area three times, only to decline each time and bottom below 30. These ranges are tradeable via an intermarket spread.

Beginning in February 1995, many institutional investors, money managers, and advisors began to espouse gold stocks as an investment. As a result, the XAU Index rose from just under 100 to over 130. During that same period, gold futures rose about $10, from 380 to 390. This caused the ratio to move from about 24 to 33. Clearly this was a sign that the two were out of line, because there was not a real direction apparent in the price of gold—the gold stocks were moving on their own. When this type of action occurs, the intermarket spread is attractive.

Since it was the XAU that was "ahead" of gold, the proper intermarket spread was to buy gold futures and short the XAU (or buy puts on XAU). The strategy worked quite well, as gold remained quite stable, but gold stocks eventually gave up much of their gains, with the XAU falling back to below 110. The ratio simultaneously fell back toward 28, and the spread produced nice gains.

What made this situation an ideal one for establishing an intermarket spread was that only one of the two components was moving—the XAU, which was rising—while the other was relatively stable. When you see that situation in these related markets, then you have to figure that either (1) the gold stocks will fall back to get more in line with the price of gold (and that's what eventually happened in our example), or (2) the price of gold will rally to catch up with the move in gold stocks.

As a means of describing the details behind setting up one of these types of intermarket spreads, we'll use the same example. Before looking at specific prices, however, we must introduce the formula necessary for equalizing two different trading vehicles on two different markets. This formula gives us the ratio of contracts that we need to trade to have a market neutral spread, one that will capture the true movement of the two indices. It was not necessary to use such a formula for the previously discussed intermarket spread (unleaded gas versus heating oil, and Value Line versus S&P 500) because those markets were very closely related; in fact, they are almost identical. However, when the relationship is looser, then the formula is necessary for determining how many contracts to buy and sell.

$$\text{Intermarket quotient} = \frac{\text{Price}_1}{\text{Price}_2} \times \frac{\text{Unit}_1}{\text{Unit}_2} \times \frac{\text{Volatility}_1}{\text{Volatility}_2} \times \frac{\text{Delta}_1}{\text{Delta}_2}$$

where Price$_i$ = the price of the contract
    Unit$_i$ = the trading unit of the contract (for example, $100 per point, or $500 per point, etc.)
    Volatility$_i$ = the actual (historical) volatility of the contract
    Delta$_i$ = the delta of the options being used in the spread, if options are in fact being used

Once you plug the various variables into this formula, the quotient will tell you quite simply how many of one contract to buy for each one you sell. Thus, it is the basis for every intermarket spread.

Example: Continuing with our example, the following prices existed in mid-September 1995:

XAU Index: 126.62
Dec gold futures: 389.70

In keeping with the overall philosophy of trying to use options in these intermarket spreads, unless the options have too much time value premium in them, the following option contracts looked attractive at the time:

Option	Price	Delta
XAU Dec 135 put:	12	0.71
Gold Dec 380 call:	11.50	0.78

The time value premium of the put is 3.62, while the time value premium of the call is 1.80. Thus the total time value expenditure is 5.42, somewhat hefty, but not unreasonable considering the rapidity with which this ratio can move. Also, remember that using the options gives you the extra chance to make money if prices move a great deal in one direction or the other, even if the intermarket spread itself doesn't converge.

At the time (mid-September 1995) the 20-day historical volatility of the XAU Index was 27 percent and the same volatility for Dec gold futures was 7 percent (that was an extremely low reading for gold, but it had been very quiet for a long time). Finally, the trading units of both options were the same: a one-point move was worth $100. So, we now have everything we need in order to compute the quotient, using the previous formula.

$$\text{Intermarket quotient} = \frac{126.62}{389.70} \times \frac{100}{100} \times \frac{27\%}{7\%} \times \frac{0.71}{0.78} = 1.14$$

This means that you should trade 1.14 Dec gold contracts for each XAU contract that you trade. Ironically this quotient is very nearly equal to one, when small quantities are involved, so most traders would just buy one gold Dec 380 call for each XAU Dec 135 put that they buy. However, if larger quantities are involved, you should adhere to the ratio (for example, buy 114 Dec gold calls and buy 100 XAU puts).

Finally, about five weeks later, the price of gold stocks had retreated substantially, as there was no confirmation from the price of gold itself, and holders of those stocks were getting nervous. The price of gold had fallen slightly, but the price of the XAU had declined rather dramatically. Thus, the spread had performed as expected—the price of XAU had moved back "into line" with the price of gold:

Index	Option
XAU Index: 108.08	Dec 135 put: 27
Dec gold: 383.80	Dec 380 call: 5.00

The option combination was now worth a total of 32 points, as compared to the initial price of 23.50 points—a profit of $850 per combo.

In the preceding example, the prices of the underlying items being spread were *not* volatile during the time the position was held, yet the option strategy made money anyway when the prices converged. This demonstrates that, by using the option strategy, you can profit if the two markets converge, as long as the time value expense of the options is reasonable when the spread is established. As for entry points, I would look for peaks or valleys in the ratio between the XAU and the price of gold futures. The peaks are most significant above 30 percent, and the valleys below 25 percent.

These examples demonstrate that the spread between the XAU Index and the price of gold (futures) is a viable one to trade. The best opportunities arise when one market is relatively stable and the other market makes a substantial move. I would avoid the spread when both markets are trending strongly, for that is when the movements in XAU are more pronounced than those of gold.

Oil Stocks Versus the Price of Oil

Given that you can trade the gold stock index versus gold futures, it should come as no surprise that a similar situation might arise with respect to oil stocks and oil futures. The AMEX trades listed options on the Oil and Gas Sector Index (symbol: $XOI), and, of course, there are futures that trade on crude oil. Once again, the relationship between these two markets is not exact, and the best opportunities arise when one market makes a move that is not matched by the other one.

In 1990, the ratio had dipped due to the price of oil skyrocketing during Iraq's occupation of Kuwait. Oil stocks did not follow suit at that time. Actually, as it turned out, that was a tremendously good time to buy the oil stocks and short crude oil futures. Of course, had Iraq destroyed the Mideast oil fields and thereby sent the price of oil skyrocketing, I'm not sure that oil stocks would have followed.

Figure 5.9 is the chart of the XOI Index divided by the price of crude oil futures over several years. It shows that oil stocks have generally been rising while the price of oil remained fairly constant—especially in 1993. If you had attempted to establish the intermarket spread during this time period, you would probably not have been successful *unless you used options.* In 1994 and 1995, the spread had established a new trading range between the 150 and 175 area on the chart. Thus, at this time it was possible to trade the spread

Figure 5.9
$XOI DIVIDED BY DEC CRUDE OIL FUTURES: 1992–1995

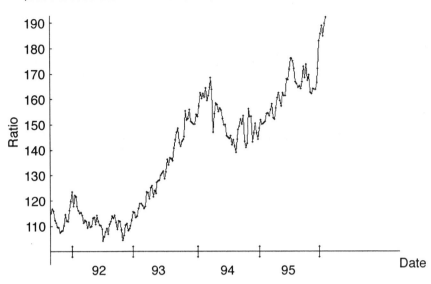

itself and make a profit, without necessarily having to rely on price volatility.

In September of 1993, there was a period when oil stocks advanced and crude oil actually declined. On the chart in Figure 5.9, this is just a part of the overall advance that you see in 1993. However, in Figure 5.10, you can see how there was an upward "bubble" in September, even while the graph was generally trending higher. At the time, it seemed like an illogical market move, so I established the intermarket spread at the following prices:

XOI Index: 260	Nov crude oil futures: 17.38
XOI Oct 265 put: 8	Crude Nov 17 call: 0.84

At the time, the anomaly between the two markets was receiving some attention in the press, and several analysts said that they felt that oil stocks were probably ahead of themselves and should be sold. Option traders might logically translate that kind of statement into an opportunity to buy puts on the XOI. However, knowing that these things have a tendency to

Figure 5.10
$XOI DIVIDED BY DEC CRUDE OIL FUTURES: DETAIL OF 1993

move in ways that you don't read about in the newspaper, I felt the inter-market spread was better, so I not only bought the XOI puts, but I also bought an equal number of the crude calls.

At first, oil stocks *did* decline. And, to make matters even better, crude oil began to rally as well. However, the rally by crude oil eventually caused the oil stocks to rise as well, and they rallied even more than crude oil did. So, whatever factors had made investors buy oil stocks in the first place were only exacerbated by the rally in crude oil.

By early October, the following prices existed:

XOI Index: 273	Nov crude oil futures: 18.90
XOI Oct 265 put: 2	Crude Nov 17 call: 2.13

Fortunately, the rallies in both markets were rather substantial, so that the crude oil Nov 17 calls rose quite a bit and made the whole position profitable, even though the XOI puts lost most of their value. The crude calls made 1.19 ($1,190), while the XOI puts only lost 6 points ($600).

This example is a good illustration of how the use of options in the spread can produce a profit where one would otherwise not have existed. Not only did the intermarket spread not converge (except for the initial move), but the "conventional wisdom" of buying XOI puts was wrong also. Thus, while it is probably safer to trade these spreads in nontrending markets (such as the 1994–1995 time period as shown in Figure 5.9), it is still possible to trade them profitably if you use the option strategy as an integral part of your intermarket spreads.

Utility Stocks and 30-Year T-Bonds

Two other markets that are related are the utility stocks and the long bond futures. Since the utility stocks generally pay rather large dividends, they are interest-rate-sensitive stocks. Obviously, bonds are sensitive to interest rates also. Moreover, since buyers of the utilities are generally investors with a long-term view, these stocks are most sensitive to longer-term interest rates. The bellwether of long-term interest rates is the U.S. 30-year Treasury bond. One of the most active futures contracts is the CBOT's 30-year bond future, typically called the "long bond future."

Figure 5.11 shows the relationship between these two markets for about a six-year period in the early 1990s. You can see that it varies within a range. For the purposes of this graph, we divided the Utility Index (symbol: $UTY) by *twice* the value of the December T-bond futures contract. This division results in a trading range from about 1.05 up to 1.30. Clearly, the intermarket spread can be traded from those extremes. For example, with the ratio near 1.05, you would attempt to buy two T-bond futures and sell one UTY "future" (i.e., buy one UTY put and sell one UTY call).

However, as has been the case with the intermarket spreads discussed earlier, you can also trade the spread whenever one market makes a relatively strong move that is not accurately reflected in the companion market. The 1994–1995 time period contained two such events.

Figure 5.12 depicts the same data as that in Figure 5.11, except that the time period is much shorter, so the chart is "magnified."

Figure 5.11
$UTY DIVIDED BY 2 × DEC T-BOND FUTURES: 1990–1995

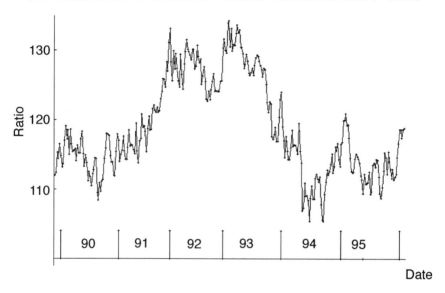

Figure 5.12
$UTY DIVIDED BY 2 × DEC T-BOND FUTURES: 7/94–8/95

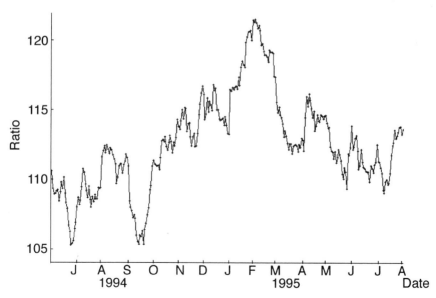

Notice that the ratio, as calculated by dividing the UTY Index by two times the December T-bond futures, had fallen to about 1.05 in mid-September of 1994. What had caused this was a severe drop in utility stocks that was not matched by the bond market: the UTY Index had fallen from about 233 to 209 during August and the first half of September, while the bond futures dropped only modestly—from 103 to 99. So the Utility Index had fallen 10 percent while the bonds only dropped 4 percent.

This discrepancy seemed to be large enough to trade, especially considering that the ratio was near the extreme low end of the chart, at 1.05. In fact, it was rather quickly resolved, as UTY rallied from 209 to 225, while the T-bond futures actually continued to *fall*, dropping down to 96. Over the intermediate term, the UTY Index continued to outperform all the way into early 1995; by that time UTY had risen to 245, while bonds only rallied up to 103. So, you could have profited quickly from the spread, or you could have held on and gotten a large profit from holding the spread even longer. In reality, I would generally recommend taking a partial profit on 50 percent of your position on the initial move, and then holding the balance with a trailing stop. In this case, that strategy would have worked superbly.

That intermediate move can be seen in Figure 5.12, as the ratio rose to over 1.20 by February. While this level wasn't near the all-time highs, it was an extreme move. You can determine an "extreme" move by the quickness with which the ratio rises on the chart. What was actually happening during January was that the UTY Index rose from 227 to 245—an 8 percent up move—while T-bonds were relatively flat, rising 2 percent from 100 to 102. Since the ratio was in the middle of the range as shown on the six-year chart, I would wait until it showed a "peak" before taking a position. By the end of the first week of February, the ratio had declined from about 1.22 to 1.18, so that would be considered a "peak." From that point forward, over the next two months T-bonds rose from 102 to about 105, while the Utility Index actually fell from 241 to 228. Again, this spread produced an excellent profit.

So, this is another ratio that is worth watching. Whenever one of these markets makes a move that is near 10 percent and the other only moves 2 percent to 4 percent, then you have the opportunity to trade the intermarket spread. Moreover, should the ratio reach the extremes of 1.25 to 1.30 on the upside or 1.05 to 1.10 on the downside, the spread can also be established—and, from those extreme levels, you might even want to hold for an intermediate-length trade.

Similar-Sector Index Versus Futures Intermarket Spreads

There are a few other sector indices that have correlation to the futures markets. As such, they may be practical for intermarket spreads. One is the Natural Gas Sector Index (symbol: $NGX) and natural gas futures. This one is a "natural," but since the index was only listed in late 1994, there is not enough of a trading history to conclude what the range of the ratio between the two markets might be. Any strong move by one market that is not matched by the other would be an ideal situation for establishing an intermarket spread between the XNG Index and Natural Gas futures.

Another sector index with only a short history is the Forest and Paper Products Index (symbol: FPP). This might be traded against lumber futures. I would allow a trading history to build up and carefully evaluate this ratio before taking positions, though, since these can be volatile markets. In fact, on the surface, it would seem wise to use options in this intermarket spread because the use of options limits risk.

Since new sector index options are constantly being listed, one should keep an eye out for ones that align rather well with listed futures contracts. Intermarket spreads will probably be viable between such markets.

Utilities Versus the "Broad Market"

It has often been thought that the utility stocks are an early predictor of major market moves. Even Charles Dow noted as much when he first devised the Industrials, Rails (now Transports), and Utilities as separate indices. That is, at the beginning of bear markets, Utilities peak before the overall market does; conversely, at the beginning of a bull market, the Utilities begin to rally first.

The Dow-Jones Utility Average is the most widely quoted utility average and is the one used in most studies that compare utility stocks and the overall market. However, the PHLX Utility Index (symbol: $UTY) very closely mirrors the Dow-Jones Utilities. The NYSE Utility Index (symbol: $NNA) is composed of less volatile stocks and thus moves less, in percentage terms, than the other two utility averages.

Prior to 1994, I could have provided you with all kinds of statistics that show how large moves in the Dow-Jones Utility Average were eventually followed by similar moves in the Dow-Jones Industrials. In fact, virtually *every time* that the Utilities had fallen 20 percent from a peak, or had risen 20 percent from a low, the Industrials followed suit with a similar 20 percent move of their own within 12 months.

However, that analysis went out the window in 1994, when the Utilities declined by over 30 percent, from October of 1993 through September of 1994 (see Figure 5.13). The major broad market averages, however, only fell 8 percent or 9 percent, and their modest decline began *after* the Utilities started to decline and ended *before* the Utilities eventually bottomed. Even using the option form of the intermarket spread would not have helped you in this case.

There was some measure of redemption for the Utilities as a predictor, however, when they began to rally in earnest in September of 1994, setting the stage for one of the biggest advances ever in the Dow-Jones Industrials, which began their monster rally in December of 1994. So, what we can conclude is that turning points by the Utility Averages, after large moves, can *sometimes* be used as predictors of similar large moves by the broad market.

Figure 5.14 illustrates the OEX Index divided by the UTY Index, going back to 1988. You can see that, up until 1994, it was trading in a rather tight range between about 1.30 and 1.60. Then, in 1994, that pattern was broken, and the ratio skyrocketed to 2.00 and above. In late 1994, you can see that the ratio fell from about 2.10 to 1.80; this is when the Utilities began to turn upward ahead of the broad market. However, in 1995, even though both averages were moving higher simultaneously, the ratio kept rising because the OEX average was advancing faster than the UTY average.

Figure 5.13
PHLX UTILITY INDEX

$UTY   214.480 213.040 214.300   940926

Figure 5.14
$OEX DIVIDED BY $UTY: 1988–1995

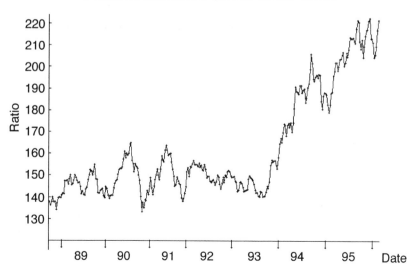

In July of 1994, when the ratio between the two indices had reached 1.90, I recommended this intermarket spread to customers. Relatively deep in-the-money options were used, and *two* UTY calls were bought for each OEX put purchased (as dictated by the "intermarket quotient" calculation—not shown):

OEX: 420.38   UTY: 221.47
OEX Dec 450 put: 35   UTY Dec 210 call: 14

As you can see from the chart in Figure 5.15, things did not go well for the next two months, as the ratio between the two indices continued to climb into September, eventually reaching about 2.10. By that time OEX had risen to 437, while the UTY Index had actually fallen to 218. The option prices, by that time, were:

OEX Dec 450 put: 17½   UTY Dec 210 call: 10½

Thus, for each 2-by-1 combination in place, an unrealized loss of $2,450, plus commissions, was looming. The only mistake that had been made thus far was in taking a position before the ratio actually peaked out. However, we did extract some measure of performance by adding to the position in September, after the ratio peaked and began to turn downward.

Throughout October and the first half of November, there was modest improvement in the position as utility stocks began to rally, but OEX stocks were holding their own as well. Then, in one swift, three-week period, the UTY Index outperformed OEX by 16 points, and the ratio dropped from nearly 2.0 to just under 1.8 (see the sharp drop on Figure 5.15, which is a "blow up" of the 1994 time frame for this same intermarket ratio). By that time, the entire position had turned into a winning trade of over $2,200 per combination.

Recall that when you trade an intermarket spread between two different markets, you first calculate the ratio of one market to the other in order to determine how many contracts to buy and how many to sell. That calculation employs volatility, the prices of the indices, the trading units of the two contracts, and the delta of the options, if options are to be used. These two markets—OEX and UTY—have about the same volatility, and they have the same trading units ($100 per point) so the determining factor of the number of con-

Figure 5.15
$OEX DIVIDED BY $UTY: 5/94–12/94

tracts is the actual price of the indices. Thus, in the preceding spread, that is why we bought two UTY calls for every OEX put purchased.

Again, let me stress that, *when the ratios in these intermarket spreads begin to shoot in a straight line—either up or down—you should probably wait until they have formed a top or bottom before actually taking a position.* The trade in the previous example ignored that advice, and, though the intermarket spread was established at a historical high of 1.90, the ratio didn't peak out until it hit 2.10. Then it began to fall, and the September time period was a better entry point for the spread. In fact, the 2-by-1 spread made over $7,000 from September through early December, when the ratio eventually fell back to 1.80.

So, you can continue to trade Utilities versus the broad market, but as far as saying that extreme turning points for utility stocks are infallible predictors of the overall direction of the broad market, I don't think that holds true anymore. Certainly not after 1993–1994.

The TED Spread

A commonly traded intermarket spread is the TED spread, which consists of Treasury Bill futures on one side and Eurodollar futures on the other. Treasury bills represent the safest investment there is; they are guaranteed. Eurodollars, however, are not insured and therefore represent a less safe investment. Consequently, Eurodollars yield more than Treasury bills. *But how much more* is the key. For as the yield differential expands or shrinks, the spread between the prices of T-bill futures and Eurodollar futures expands or shrinks as well. In essence, the yield differential is small when there is stability and confidence in the financial markets, because uninsured deposits and insured deposits are not that much different in times of financial certainty. However, in times of financial uncertainty and instability, the spread widens because the uninsured depositors require a comparatively higher yield for the higher risk they are taking.

Figure 5.16 shows the TED spread since 1990. Historically, the spread has widened to over 1.50 points (the price difference between T-bill futures and Eurodollar futures). Such things as large bank failures or perceived strains on the credit system affect the spread. For example, just before the Mideast war in January of 1991, the spread jumped to nearly 1.35, and then began a perilous descent. When the war turned out to be less severe than was feared, the spread dropped quickly to 0.75. Since then it has gone into a further descent, to the point where it traded near all-time lows below 0.25. In fact, in the years of the large bull market advance, the TED spread has traded in the 0.25 to 0.50 range, in general.

This narrow range has reduced the profitability of trading the spread. It used to have much wider swings. However, it can be a low-risk, hedged approach to betting on or against financial instability.

This is a popular spread for trading, and when it broke down to what appeared to be relatively low levels in late 1991 and 1992, many traders tried to buy the spread. However, it kept going lower and lower, so buyers of the futures spread—long T-bill futures, short Eurodollar futures—were losing money. During much of that time—from early 1991 through late 1993—the option form of this intermarket spread was able to profit even though the spread itself was shrinking. In the option form of buying the spread, you would buy T-bill calls and Eurodollar puts. The option strategy was able to profit while the futures spread was losing, because the Fed was constantly lowering rates. That action caused prices of both T-bills and Eurodollars to shoot higher. Thus, the T-bill calls were profiting while the Eurodollar puts losses were limited.

Since both T-bills and Eurodollar futures *and* options trade on the Chicago Mercantile Exchange, both the futures spread or the option combination can be entered as a spread order. This fact facilitates execution, allowing the spreader to take advantage of what are normally efficient, tight markets in these futures and options.

There is one other property of the TED spread that is important for traders to understand: *the TED spread has a carrying cost involved with it.* That is, if you buy the TED spread (using futures), there is a time value premium in the spread that will disappear as time passes. An example will illustrate this point.

Figure 5.16
TED SPREAD

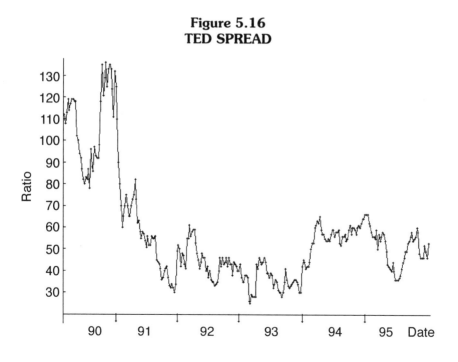

Example: Suppose that the current date is February 1st. Then the following prices might exist for various futures expiration months, for both T-bill and Eurodollar futures:

Month	T-Bill Futures	Eurodollar Futures	TED Spread
March	95.27	94.96	0.31
June	95.15	94.80	0.35
Sep	94.90	94.51	0.39
Dec	94.63	94.21	0.42

Each successive month shows the TED spread to be slightly more expensive than the previous one. This is, in effect, a carrying cost, for if you were to hold the spread for three months, it would lose about 0.03 of value. Of course, this is an advantage to the seller of the spread, for he would make that 0.03 every three months. So, if you are going to trade the TED spread, be aware that there may be a built-in cost involved.

The TED spread, then, is another spread that is tradeable with options. When the spread is small, everything is calm in the financial markets. However, if you expect some unsettling developments in the financial markets, that might be a good time to buy the spread. On the other hand, when there have been some rather troubling developments, the TED spread will widen out, as it did during Iraq's invasion of Kuwait, for example. That may also be a good time to consider entering the spread, but from the short side, if you feel that financial calm will return. In either case, consider using options to establish the spread, rather than futures, if the time value premium of the options is relatively low—and it normally is for both T-bills and Eurodollars, since they are low-volatility contracts.

OTHER SEASONAL TENDENCIES

I'd like to conclude this chapter with a discussion of three strong seasonal tendencies regarding the broad stock market. Ironically, they all occur in the last third of the year, and if you include the Value Line/S&P spread—which sets up in November—you would have four seasonal trades that you can watch for from August through the end of the year. These don't necessarily overlap, although they could at times. We will discuss the three in chronological order, beginning with the one for August, followed by the September-October one, and finally—our favorite—a very short-term seasonal tendency at the end of October and beginning of November.

August: The Dull Month—Or Is It?

There is a common perception that August is a dull month for the stock market, as many traders go on vacation. As a result, implied volatility of options, especially index options, tends to decrease in late July and on into August. However, there have been a surprisingly large number of market explosions that have started in August. In fact, the fall of the year is the most volatile period in general, primarily for the stock and bond markets. Volatile markets make straddle buying—the purchase of both a put and a call with the same terms—attractive. The fact that some of that volatility in the stock market comes as prices fall (sometimes suddenly) only enhances the strategy, because implied volatility increases and inflates the price of the straddle that is owned.

The August–September time period is a pretty volatile one if you consider the data for the 15-year period from 1981 through 1995 as shown in Table 5.4. You can see that August has been the start of serious market movement in most years. In some years, the Dow-Jones Industrials made a sizable move that was self-contained in the month of August. In other years, August was the beginning of a move that lasted through September or October (we'll discuss September and October in the next section). Only in 1990 was the move already underway when August began. That was the year Iraq invaded Kuwait in late July. August was still a volatile month that year, but the move actually began in July. Table 5.4 doesn't even include the fact that a crash occurred in October of 1987, further extending the 8 percent loss shown in the table for that year.

What makes the data in the above table extremely interesting is that the implied volatility of index options—particularly OEX options—traditionally drops in July and August. Since volatility is low

Table 5.4
AUGUST–SEPTEMBER VOLATILITY DURING
1981–1995

Date	General Dow Level	Movement	Percent
Aug 1995	4700	−160	−3.4
Aug 1994	3300	+200	+6.1
Aug 1993	3500	+80	+2.3
Aug 1992	3300	+140	+4.2
Aug–Sep 1991	3000	−90	−3.0
July–Oct 1990	3000	−640	−21.3
Aug–Sep 1989	2700	+130	+4.8
Aug–Sep 1988	2100	+120	+5.7
Aug–Sep 1987	2700	−220	−8.1
Aug 1986	1800	+160	+8.9
Aug–Sep 1985	1600	−60	−3.8
Aug 1984	1100	+150	+13.6
Aug–Oct 1983	1200	+125	+10.4
Aug 1982	800	+160	+20.0
Aug 1981	950	−130	−13.7

entering what has proved to be a rather volatile time period, option buying strategies (such as straddle purchases or backspreads) are favored strategies for this time of the year. Traders often speak about volatility, since it is the most important influence on an option's price. If you own options and volatility increases, it works very heavily in your favor.

Even if implied volatility doesn't increase, the market movements as shown in Table 5.4 are large enough in most years to generate profits on their own. In a rising market, you may not get much of an increase in implied volatility in OEX options, so you are going to be heavily dependent on the market rising far enough to make your straddle purchases profitable. However, in a declining market, implied volatility will normally increase, so you may get a double benefit in that case—increasing implied volatility as well as a falling market—that makes your straddle purchases profitable by falling a distance greater than you paid for your straddle.

In Chapter 1, we related the story of how an OEX call barely lost any money during the crash. The following example is a more every-day one.

You might be wondering just how much of an influence an increase in implied volatility can have on the price of a long straddle. Suppose that a stock is trading at 100 and a three-month straddle is selling for 8, which is a 20 percent implied volatility. If the stock is still at 100 in a month, and implied volatility is still 20 percent, then the straddle will have lost 1¼ points to time decay, and it will then be selling at 6¾. However, if the implied volatility increases to 24 percent at the end of that month, then the straddle will still be selling for 8. Thus, an increase in implied volatility from 20 percent to 24 percent com-pletely offsets the time decay that occurs in that one month.

If the straddle has a shorter life span to begin with, time decay will be more rapid. During the next month, if volatility remains at 20 percent and the stock is still at 100, the straddle will decay to 4½. Thus, it would have lost 3½ points of its original value due to two months of time decay. An increase in implied volatility can offset this loss as well, but it now takes a more dramatic increase to overcome the time decay that occurs during two-thirds of this straddle's life. In fact, implied volatility would have to increase to 36 percent in order for the straddle to again be selling at 8 with one month of life remaining.

Obviously, it's a lot easier for volatility to increase from 20 to 24 per-cent in one month, than it is for implied to increase from 20 to 36 percent in two months. Still, these examples show that implied volatility is indeed a powerful factor on the price of an option.

In the next chapter, we discuss methods of identifying when volatility is "too low" and how to trade it. However, in this seasonal example, you can generally figure that OEX implied volatility is going to be low on the first of August. You can easily tell how expensive or cheap OEX implied volatility is, merely by looking at a chart of the CBOE's Volatility Index (symbol: $VIX). If volatility is indeed low when the beginning of August rolls around, you should buy three-month, at-the-money OEX straddles and hold them for the course of the month.

Other markets often display similar characteristics. That is, implied volatility is low in the late summer, but prices can be volatile in the fall of the year. In particular, these three are also good candidates

Table 5.5
EXTENT AND TIMING OF MOVES IN GOLD, CRB
INDEX, AND T-BONDS FROM 1986 TO 1995

Year	Gold	CRB Index	T-bonds
1986	+40, then −40	Nothing	+9 Sep–Dec
1987	+50	+20 Nov	−8 Sep,+15 Oct
1988	−40 Sep	+20 Nov–Dec	+7 Aug–Nov
1989	+50 Nov	Nothing	+5 Oct
1990	−50 Aug–Oct	−25 Oct–Dec	+11 Sep–Dec
1991	Nothing	+15 Aug–Oct	+5 Dec
1992	Nothing	Nothing	−7 Sep–Nov
1993	−60 Aug +50 Oct–Dec	−10 Aug +10 Sep–Nov	+6 Aug −6 Sep–Nov
1994	+20 Aug–Sep −25 Oct–Nov	Nothing	−7 Aug–Sep
1995	Nothing	+10 August	+10 Aug–Nov

for straddle purchases or other option-buying strategies, beginning near the first of August: gold, the CRB Index, and T-bonds. Table 5.5 shows the extent of moves, and the timing of such moves, over a 10-year period. As you can see from the data, not every one of these three markets has a major move in the fall of every year, but they do occur with frequency. If you are accustomed to trading these markets, you know that a $40 or $50 move in gold is quite substantial—far more than the cost of a straddle, especially if implied volatility is low to begin with. Similarly, a 10-point move in the CRB Index is also a large move, as is a 5-point move in T-bonds. In fact, a $50 move in gold futures, a 10-point move in CRB futures, and a 5-point move in T-bond futures are each worth $5,000 per contract.

Determining the History of Implied Volatility.   Thus, there is plenty of profit potential in looking for low-cost straddles in these markets. The optimum way to analyze the situation would be to evaluate the implied volatility of each market in the beginning of August.

If it is low or at least not above normal, you can buy December futures option straddles. By owning the intermediate-term straddle, you won't be so subject to time decay during the early portion of your holding period. If the underlying market makes a quick move, you will benefit, and you might even get an extra boost if the implied volatility of the options you own increases as well.

In order to determine what is "normal" volatility, you need to know where the implied volatility has been trading over at least the past few months. This information is available from chart books that are published monthly or semimonthly. The Prudential Securities Futures Department publishes one, and so does Opportunities in Options, a futures advisory and brokerage firm. Those with a penchant for computers can find this data as well. Two sources would be Option Vue or Bloomberg.

As we said, these sources allow you to look at where the implied volatility has been trading. This is important, and is different from the historical volatility. As we have noted before, implied volatility in some markets continually trades at higher levels than actual volatility. So what you want to do at the beginning of August is to see if implied volatility is at or below average with respect to where it has been trading over the last few months. Most of these services can give you a moving average of implied volatility for up to a year historically, so that you can easily make this comparison.

September–October: A Very Tradeable Time Period for the Stock Market

We now take a look at another seasonal trading pattern during the period from Labor Day through mid-October. Some of the biggest moves have come during this time, and there are some patterns that stand out. This information does not conflict with what we just discussed regarding the August time period. In fact, it may help to fine-tune your exit points for positions that you already have in place when Labor Day arrives.

As many analysts and media types have observed, September is often a month of decline for the stock market. The period of time surrounding the Labor Day holiday often marks a short-term market top. However, "often" is too vague a term, for there have also been some good rallies in September as well. Thus, you need to analyze the data more carefully in order to be able to construct a trade.

There is normally a rather substantial broad market correction of about 5 percent or more that begins in either September or October. The market *usually* begins a correction on or about Labor Day, but not every September is a down month. What we did find, however, is that even if September is a rising month, a correction will often occur in October.

There are three main scenarios that the market has followed for the last 20-some years: (1) a top is formed near Labor Day, and the ensuing bottom occurs in September (occasionally, the bottom does not come until October); (2) a top is formed in mid-to-late-September, with the ensuing bottom occurring in the first week or two of October; or (3) a top is formed in early-to-mid-October, with the bottom coming in early November. The data are summarized in Table 5.6. Of the 23 years worth of data that we scanned, scenario 1—top near Labor Day—has occurred 15 times; scenario 2—top in late

Table 5.6
SUMMARY OF MARKET DECLINES, SEPTEMBER/OCTOBER 1973–1995

Year	High Date	Maximum Correction (%)	Year	High Date	Maximum Correction (%)
1973	Oct 12[3]	−14.4	1984	Aug 29	−4.2
1974	Aug 30	−12.5	1985	Aug 28	−4.9
1975	Aug 25	−3.5	1986	Aug 27	−8.8
1976	Sep 21[2]	−7.4	1987	Sep 2	−35.3
1977	Sep 7	−7.1	1988	Oct 20[3]	−7.1
1978	Sep 6	−11.4	1989	Sep 1	−7.9
1979	Oct 5[3]	−10.0	1990	Aug 29	−9.1
1980	Sep 22[2]	−5.4	1991	Aug 28	−5.3
1981	Aug 26	−9.6	1992	Sep 4	−5.3
1982	Sep 15[2]	−5.5	1993	Sep 2	−3.3
1983	Oct 16[3]	−6.8	1994	Aug 29	−5.7
			1995	Sep 29[2]	−2.3

[2] Scenario 2.
[3] Scenario 3.

September—has happened 4 times; and the final scenario—a top in October—has occurred 4 times.

So now that it has been established that a correction typically takes place, beginning at one of these three times, we must decide on how the beginning of that correction can be identified. Either that, or utilize a strategy that will make money when the correction finally occurs. Obviously, we don't just want to rush in and buy puts on the trading day before Labor Day. That would be a losing trade in any year that followed scenario 2 or 3.

The put–call ratios that were described in Chapter 4—both the index and the equity-only—and the short-term oscillator that we described early in this chapter are useful in making timing decisions of this sort, especially when you have an inkling of which way you expect the market to go. You only need confirmation from these indicators.

Nineteen ninety-five is a good case in point, because the market rallied quite strongly through the first half of September, eventually topping out for a small correction on September 29th. This fits into scenario 2. When Labor Day arrived, the put–call ratios were all on buy signals, that is, the *trend* of the ratios was down, from a previous peak. In addition, there was no particular reading one way or the other on the oscillator. Thus, no bearish positions were taken at that time.

As the market rose dramatically in the two weeks after Labor Day, the oscillator became overbought and a sell signal was generated on September 22nd. This was a bit premature, and since there was not yet a confirmation from the put–call ratios, I bought bear put spreads. That is, with OEX near 551, the Nov 550 puts were bought and the Oct 540 puts were sold (the reason that Octobers were sold was that they were very expensive in terms of implied volatility and were therefore a better sale than the Nov 540 puts at the time).

The market sputtered a little at that point, but eventually worked higher into September 29th. The put–call ratios finally gave sell signals at that time—on September 28th actually. So we then had the confirmation we wanted. More put spreads were bought, this time using a wider difference in the striking prices and also using higher striking prices: the Nov 560 puts were bought and the Nov 545 puts were sold.

Finally, the market broke—swiftly, but briefly—and OEX traded down to 544 in a matter of a few days. At that time, the oscillator actually became oversold and generated a buy signal. That buy signal was used to take some profits, although the positions weren't completely closed out until the put–call ratios also issued buy signals with OEX near 553 in the final week of October.

There is an additional corollary to this seasonal pattern: there is usually a good trading *bottom* in late September or October. Conventional wisdom holds that the best buying opportunities occur at the October bottoms. That may be true, when the bottom indeed occurs in October. What is, in fact, more correct to observe is that there is often a good bottom at the end of the declines that are part of this seasonal trading pattern. Under scenario 1, when the top is near Labor Day, the eventual bottom is often reached in mid-to-late September—although the decline sometimes stretches into October—whereas under scenarios 2 and 3, the bottom is indeed in October. Some of the most spectacular bottoms have come in October—1974, 1978, 1979, 1985, 1989, 1990, and 1992.

In sum, then, you should be alert for an opportunity to buy puts or short the futures in the time period near Labor Day. If a top does not develop at that time, then a trading top should develop in late September or early October. However, these tops are generally *not* major tops, just good trading opportunities. Eventually, they give way to good buying opportunities in late September or October. This information confirms the observations made in the previous section: that sectors of the market are volatile in the fall of the year. In the next section, a short-term seasonal buying opportunity is described, and it meshes well with these other seasonal patterns also.

Late-October Buy Point

The magazine *Technical Analysis of Stocks and Commodities* printed an article that pointed out a peculiar phenomenon: if you buy the S&P futures on the close of trading on October 27th and sell them on November 2nd, you would have made money every year since 1982, except for one in which you would have lost 0.45 point. The article detailed the years 1982 through 1993, when profits mostly were in the range of 2 to 4 points, although two years had much larger profits. The article pointed out that you may want to use your own judgment in exiting the trade, as a rather large move occurred in only one or two days in some years.

In 1994, the S&Ps closed at 467.20 on October 27th. The next day, they were up 9.00(!) points to 476.20. That turned out to be the high until November 2nd, but it was certainly worth a trade, even if you didn't get the top price when you sold and took your profit.

Using this as a guideline, we decided to go back farther than 1982 (that's the year the S&P 500 futures were first listed, so there is no historical data prior to that time for those futures). In order to go back in time, we used the S&P 500 cash index. What we found was that the S&P 500 cash index has advanced between October 27th and November 2nd in every year since 1978, except one in which it was unchanged. The data in Table 5.7 show this remarkable phenomenon. It should be noted that, if October 27th falls on a weekend, you buy the S&Ps at close of trading on the Friday *before* October 27th. However, if November 2nd falls on a weekend, you don't sell until the close of trading on the Monday *after* that weekend.

Why does it work? There is no good reason, except the ubiquitous one: "seasonality." It reminds me of the best football "system" I ever saw: it was merely to bet on Syracuse the week *after* they played Penn State. The system worked for 19 years in a row (unfor-

Table 5.7
BEHAVIOR OF THE S&P 500 CASH INDEX FOR
OCTOBER 27 TO NOVEMBER 2, 1978–1995

Year	S&P Advance (Oct 27th–Nov 2nd)	Year	S&P Advance (Oct 27th–Nov 2nd)
1978	+1.53	1987	+22.56
1979	+1.95	1988	+1.78
1980	+1.16	1989	+3.43
1981	+4.90	1990	+7.15
1982	+2.22	1991	+7.12
1983	0.00	1992	+4.26
1984	+2.13	1993	+3.83
1985	+4.00	1994	+0.66
1986	+7.03	1995	+10.02

Average profit: 4.76 S&P points.
Average profit, excluding 1987: 3.72 S&P points.

tunately, Penn State terminated their series with Syracuse when they joined the Big Ten). So, even though there wasn't any logical reason *why* it worked, it *did* work. This S&P system also seems to work, so I wanted to point it out to you.

Also, I would use a trailing stop if you get a move in your favor right away—à la 1994—in order to lock in profits, and you might want to take partial profits if the S&P moves three or more points in your favor. As far as a trading vehicle goes, if you don't want to use the futures, I would suggest buying the nearest in-the-money November OEX or SPX call, since you will be exiting the position on November 2nd, at the latest. By using the in-the-money call, time decay shouldn't be too much of a problem for a five-day trade. As always, though, you should check the implied volatility of the OEX options before you buy them since that is what can have the greatest effect on option prices in such a short time. If the options are overly expensive in terms of implied volatility, I would stress using the futures instead as your trading vehicle. I don't think I would use a bullish call spread for this system, since the movements were quite large in several of the years, and you might be unnecessarily limiting your profit potential with the bull spread.

So there you have three good seasonal patterns to trade with during the late summer and early fall of the year. Those, coupled with the January effect, should keep you busy and profitable right on into the new year.

CONCLUSION

In this chapter, we have presented a series of trading strategies that have good track records. Some are very short-term oriented—daytrading—while others are longer-term in nature. You may not follow all of them, but at least choose the ones that are amenable to your philosophy of trading. When the time is right, whether that be daily, or less frequently as with the momentum oscillator, or only once a year as with some of the seasonal trades, analyze the futures and the options before actually trading. Be aware of fair value of the futures and of implied volatility on the options. With careful analysis, you should be able to turn profits with the strategies introduced herein.

6 Trading Volatility and Other Theoretical Approaches

In this chapter, we look at another approach to trading, one based on mathematical evaluations. It is sometimes called *neutral trading* because the price movement of the underlying security doesn't have to be predicted in order to make money. That may be true, but you must understand one thing: *It is certain that you will have to predict* something *in order to profit, for only market makers and arbitrageurs can construct totally risk-free positions that exceed the risk-free rate of return, after commissions.* Moreover, even if a position is neutral initially, it is likely that the passage of time or a significant change in the price of the underlying will introduce some price risk into the position.

In Chapters 3, 4, and 5, we have looked at various trading strategies that rely on pricing projections, many of them based on past history or technical analysis. These methods are successful and rational. What they all have in common is that, in order for these strategies to profit, the underlying security generally needs to move in a favorable direction. There were some exceptions, such as using options in intermarket spreads in order to give yourself an extra chance to make money if prices are merely volatile, but normally the preceding strategies were price-dependent. Each strategy, whether it was based on option volume or on the historical relationship of two markets, had its own particular "edge." That edge will often be good enough to generate superior returns.

However, some traders prefer an approach that relies less on predicting prices, which many mathematicians claim cannot be done, and more on the mathematics of options. This, in essence, *is* the theoretical approach. With the *theoretical* approach, you attempt to construct strategies that will make money based on factors other than price changes. Moreover, since options are a derivative security, there are definite relationships between the option and the underlying security—and between the properties of both of them—that can be exploited without predicting price movements.

This chapter is divided into four broad segments: the introductory material, the basic strategies used for trading volatility within a range, more advanced strategies for trading volatility within a range, and finally, trading a volatility skew, a situation where individual options on the same underlying security have distinctly different implied volatilities.

Before getting into the actual strategies, we define some more terms and properties that are needed for these discussions.

VOLATILITY

In Chapter 1, it was stated that the value of an option is a function of six variables: stock price, strike price, time, interest rates, volatility, and dividends (for equity and index options). All of these are known quantities, except for volatility. As also noted in Chapter 1, there are two types of volatility: *historical volatility*, which tells how fast prices have been changing; and *implied volatility*, which is the option market's perception of future volatility.

In order to calculate implied volatility, all you need to do is to determine what volatility it is necessary to use in your evaluation model, so that the model's theoretical value agrees with the actual market price of the option. The model's general equation can be written as

Option value = f (stock price, strike, time, rate, volatility)

We know the stock price, the strike price, the time remaining to expiration, and the interest rate. We also know at what price the option is actually trading in the marketplace. Therefore, what volatility must we use in the model—along with these other four known values —in order for the model to yield the current option price as the option value? That volatility is the implied volatility.

Most option software will quickly give you the implied volatility of an option or a list of options. The implied volatility is actually determined by an iterative process, which can require a rather large number of calculations, but today's computers are so fast that you don't really notice the amount of calculating that's going on.

When trying to evaluate whether an option is expensive or cheap, we usually state that quality in terms of *implied volatility*. For example, rather than saying "That option is overvalued," it is more commonly said that "That option is trading with a high implied volatility." In this statement, the term "high" would presumably be with reference to the levels of historical volatility or to past measures of implied volatility on this particular underlying security.

Many theoretical traders feel that, not only is volatility the most crucial element of understanding and profiting from option trading, but it is the easiest thing to predict. Therefore, if we could shift our emphasis away from trying to predict the price movement of the underlying security, and toward trying to predict the volatility of the underlying security, we could profit with more regularity and less uncertainty.

In January of 1994, the implied volatility of OEX options dropped to its lowest level ever. A compilation of past readings of OEX volatility showed that it had rarely been measured at a level below 10 percent. In fact it had only dipped to that level two other times. Most of the time OEX implied volatility had traded higher—normally in the 11 percent to 14 percent range in the previous few years—and even at higher levels in the 1980s.

Not only that, but *historical* volatility was low as well, as it stood at about 7 percent. It had occasionally been as low as 6 percent briefly in its 10-year history, and normally ranged in the 9 percent to 12 percent neighborhood, or higher.

Meanwhile, the stock market was making all-time highs after a long round of interest rate cuts by the Fed (although there hadn't been any cuts recently), and bond futures were trading near all-time highs as well. Earnings projections seemed to be quite bullish, and economic activity was positive, although not overheated. There were some troubling items out there—utility stocks had made a peak and turned down about four months earlier, and some fundamental valuations of stocks showed them to be rather high-priced, especially in light of the fact that there had not been substantial stock market correction for three years.

Given these data, which would you feel more comfortable predicting, future volatility levels or the direction of the stock market? If you said volatility, then this chapter is for you. If you said the stock market, then you should read this chapter also—and I'll try to change your mind.

The facts are that volatility was rarely this low, and therefore you would have to suspect that it was going to increase to more normal levels. Sometimes such an increase doesn't occur right away, although with a market as large as the U.S. stock market, you wouldn't expect it to take too long. On the other hand, which way the stock market was headed seemed to be anyone's guess—as it often is—because there were arguments to justify both a bearish and a bullish scenario. Thus, to me, it seems as if a prediction that volatility would increase was much more certain to come true, than a prediction of whether the stock market would rise or fall. A simple strategy to take advantage of this analysis would be the purchase of a straddle, which could make money if prices either rose or fell, and would be benefitted by an increase in implied volatility.

As it turned out, the Fed raised interest rates in early February, touching off a nasty correction in the stock market. Implied volatility exploded to 22 percent by the end of March, and the price of OEX fell over 9 percent. Straddle buyers profited handsomely.

This example may admittedly be an extreme one because OEX implied and historical volatilities were at all-time lows, so it was a pretty safe bet that they were going to rise. But, in more normal situations, you might remain skeptical of anyone's ability to predict future volatility. In the next few sections, we look at two ways of trading volatility, and some simple, as well as complex, ways in which to structure strategies for that purpose.

So now the emphasis of our strategy will be on predicting volatility, and trading its movements if possible, rather than on predicting the price of the underlying security. In fact, we would just as soon be neutral with respect to the price of the underlying, for we don't care if it rises or falls, as long as our prediction of volatility is correct. Thus, we need to discuss how to make a strategy price neutral.

DELTA NEUTRAL TRADING

When most people talk about trading neutral strategies, they mean *delta neutral*. Recall that delta is the measure of how much an option moves when the underlying instrument moves one point. If we calculate the deltas of all the options in a strategic position, and add them together, we can arrive at a *position delta*, which tells us how much money we can expect to make or lose if the underlying instrument moves one point.

Suppose that a trader has a bull spread in place—long the Jan 100 calls and short the Jan 110 calls. He can calculate his position delta by using the deltas of the options in the spread. The pertinent statistics are:

Stock Price: 98

Option	Position	Price	Delta
Jan 100 call	Long 10	5	0.50
Jan 110 call	Short 10	2	0.20

If the stock moves up one point, each of his long calls will increase in value by a half point since the delta is 0.50. Thus, since he owns 10 of them, the long side of his spread will appreciate by 5 points when the underlying stock moves up one point.

Meanwhile, the Jan 110 call that he is short will increase in value by 20 cents if the stock moves up one point. So, the 10 of them that he is short will increase in value by a total of 2 points.

Therefore, his position delta is long 3 points (the longs will increase by a total of 5 points, while the shorts will increase in value by 2 points, hence the net of these is 5 minus 2, or 3). This means that his position will increase in value by $300 if the underlying moves up one point; it also means that his position will lose $300 if the stock falls by one point.

The position delta is also called the *equivalent stock position* (ESP), or if futures and futures options are being evaluated, the position delta can also be referred to as an *equivalent futures position* (EFP). The position delta can be calculated for any complex portfolio merely by calculating each option's equivalent stock position and summing them all together. The simple formula for calculating an equivalent position in an individual option is:

ESP or EFP = quantity × trading unit × delta of option

Again, using the data from the preceding example, we can calculate the equivalent stock position of the two options in the spread. In both cases, the "trading unit" is 100 (for 100 shares per option).

ESP of Jan 100 call = $10 \times 100 \times 0.50$ = 500 shares
ESP of Jan 110 call = $-10 \times 100 \times 0.20$ = −200 shares

Total ESP = position delta = 500 − 200 = +300 shares

Thus, owning this spread is "equivalent" to owning 300 shares of the underlying stock. Of course, as the underlying stock moves up or down, the deltas of the options will change (they will also change as time passes). When the deltas change, the ESP will change as well. But for this moment, the position is equivalent to owning 300 shares of the stock.

So, it is a simple matter to compute the position delta on even a complex option strategy and "reduce" the position to an equivalent number of shares of the underlying stock. If this position delta is very near to zero, then we have a neutral position that won't make or lose money if the underlying stock moves one point. This is extremely useful information because, if you want to hedge the risk of your position, you merely have to use that information to take an equal but opposite position in the underlying stock. In the preceding example, you would sell short 300 shares of the underlying stock in order to neutralize your price risk (at least for the moment).

Such a position is considered to be a *delta neutral position*, because it is neutral with respect to the variable, delta. The neutral position has always held attraction to investors, especially those who are (a) mathematically inclined, or (b) believe prices move in a random manner, or (c) are just tired of trying to predict the market and being incorrect. In theory, if you were able to sell an "expensive" option and hedge its sale with the purchase of a "fairly" priced option, you could capture the differential in price by a neutral position. Mathematics bears out this philosophy, but the reality of trading such a position is more difficult than you might expect. In reality, neutral trading can be very dangerous if you aren't careful.

In a delta neutral position, the other variables that affect the profitability of a position are not necessarily neutral, but at least delta is. When you have a delta neutral position, you have no risk of loss or potential for gain for *small, short-term moves* by the underlying instrument. However, if the stock rises or falls too much, or if time passes, or even if the implied volatility changes, the delta of each option will change. Once these deltas change, the position will generally no longer be delta neutral. In fact, it might acquire quite a bit of risk.

In July 1993, soybeans had rallied quite a bit because of heavy rains and flood conditions in the Midwest. Options had gotten quite expensive, and a strategist might have considered a ratio spread as a way of establishing a delta neutral position. The following statistics describe the position on July 2, 1993:

August Soybeans: 665

Quantity/Option	Price	Delta	Position Delta (EFP)
Long 50 Aug 650 calls	30½	0.63	Long 31.5 contracts
Short 100 Aug 700 calls	12	0.31	Short 31.0 contracts
		Total:	Long 0.5 contracts

This position is very nearly delta neutral, since the EFP of the long options is just about completely offset by the EFP of the short options. Since these options were due to expire on July 24, 1993, they were quite short-term options. This led to the appeal of a neutral position.

A three-day weekend including the Fourth of July followed, so the next trading day was July 6th, and the floods had worsened, so beans opened up the limit and remained there. The following prices existed at that point:

August Soybeans: 695

Quantity/Option	Price	Delta	Position Delta (EFP)
Long 50 Aug 650 calls	59	0.74	Long 37 contracts
Short 100 Aug 700 calls	32½	0.50	Short 50 contracts
		Total:	Short 13 contracts

At this time, the position had become seriously delta short. Not only that, the position was losing significant money. The 50 longs had appreciated by 28½ points, or $71,250. However, the 100 short options had lost 20½ points, or $102,500. The overall unrealized loss was $31,250.

Even though the position was delta neutral initially, it had destabilized significantly in just one trading day, quickly becoming delta short and losing considerable money.

This example demonstrates just how deceiving a delta neutral position can be; such a position is only delta neutral for *small* moves by the underlying security (soybean futures, in this case). Notice that the losses could be significant even for the smaller trader: using the same example, if you were long 5 of the Aug 650 calls and short 10 of the Aug 700 calls, you would still be losing $3,125 on that small position in just one trading day.

The preceding example demonstrates the importance of the relationship between price and delta. However, delta can also be significantly affected by volatility, or, more appropriately, implied volatility. That is, if the options get more expensive or become much cheaper in terms of implied volatility, the deltas of the options can change. Any such change would distort the neutrality of a delta neutral position.

Federal Paperboard (FBO) was trading just under $40 a share in late October 1995, when a vague takeover rumor surfaced. Initially, the rumor was more evident in the price of the options than it was in the price of the stock. That is, the options gained considerable implied volatility, but the stock only rose slightly. The following statistics show how such an event affected a delta neutral position. On October 30, 1995, the following prices existed, and a trader might have established a delta neutral spread, not knowing that there was a takeover rumor:

FBO: 39⅝; Implied Volatility of the Options: 54%

Quantity/Option	Price	Delta	Position Delta (ESP)
Long 10 Jan 40 calls	3	0.52	Long 520 shares
Short 30 Jan 45 calls	½	0.16	Short 480 shares
		Total ESP:	Long 40 shares

This initial position has an ESP very nearly zero, so it is considered to be delta neutral. Within three days, the stock had edged up to 41—not a large move. However, option buyers obviously had some information regarding the takeover rumors and were bidding up the options, which had increased to an 89 percent implied volatility just three days later. This is a significant increase in implied volatility, and the position had thus acquired the following look:

FBO: 41; Implied Volatility of the Options: 89%

Quantity/Option	Price	Delta	Position Delta (ESP)
Long 10 Jan 40 calls	5½	0.60	Long 600 shares
Short 30 Jan 45 calls	2¼	0.32	Short 960 shares
		Total ESP:	Short 360 shares

So this position had now acquired the look of a short position, equivalent to being short 360 shares of FBO. Part of that change in the delta was due to the stock's increase in price from 39⅝ to 41, but the majority of it was due to the explosion in implied volatility. Also notice that this relatively small position was showing an unrealized loss of $2,750 after this change in implied volatility.

The general relationships between delta and time, and delta and volatility, are discussed in more detail later in this chapter.

The previous two examples involved selling naked options. Neutral positions don't always require you to have naked options in them. In fact, you can construct delta neutral positions with long options in them (backspreads, for example). However, that doesn't mitigate the fact that a price change or a change in implied volatility can severely alter the neutrality of the position.

Keeping a Position Neutral

Sometimes, when the neutrality changes, losses result. Even if losses don't accrue, the position acquires market risk as it becomes either delta long or delta short. The position might eventually become profitable, but it is important to understand that merely establishing a delta neutral position doesn't mean that you can just walk away from it and make a profit. Since price changes by the underlying security affect the neutrality of the position, it is necessary to readjust the delta to keep the position neutral.

The easiest way to adjust a position back into a delta neutral status is to use the underlying security. In the most recent example, the position had become delta short 360 shares of FBO after the implied volatility increased. Obviously, that delta could easily be neutralized by buying 360 (or, more likely 400) shares of FBO. Then the position would once again be delta neutral. Of course, it would still be susceptible to further swings in position delta, each of which would require another adjustment.

Another way to adjust the FBO spread back to neutrality would be to buy some more of the Jan 40 calls, which were already long in the position. After the stock rose to 41 and implied volatility ballooned to 89 percent, the position was delta short 360 shares of FBO. Moreover, the delta of the Jan 40 calls was 0.60 (see the preceding example for these details).

Notice that the ESP of *one* Jan 40 call is 60 shares:

$$ESP = 1 \times 100 \times 0.60 = 60 \text{ shares}$$

So, if you were to buy six more of these Jan 40 calls, you would be adding 6 × 60, or 360 delta long into the position. This would completely and exactly neutralize the existing delta short position. Thus the new position would be:

Quantity/Option	Delta	Position Delta (ESP)
Long 16 Jan 40 calls	0.60	Long 960 shares
Short 30 Jan 45 calls	0.32	Short 960 shares
	Total ESP:	0 shares

So, you could either buy stock or buy more of the calls that you are already long in order to adjust. These are the most common tactics used, although you may also buy in some of your short calls. In fact you could buy *any* calls in the proper amount in order to neutralize the position. Usually, small traders will buy one or the other of the calls that are already in the position. However, a market maker or a trader with a large position may be forced to buy whatever is being offered. Thus, he might wind up with a rather complex position. It is no problem to evaluate the neutrality of the larger, more complex positions, though, since the same ESP formula can be applied to each option in the position, no matter how many of them there are, and the result totaled.

Market makers attempt to keep their positions neutral. They prefer to make their money by buying on the bid and selling on the offer. If they have to carry a position, they would just as soon that it not have any price risk. Market makers of listed options can usually extricate themselves from their positions fairly quickly, especially if the options are liquid. However, over-the-counter option market makers (which include several of the largest banks and brokerage houses) and market makers in illiquid options may be forced to carry their positions for quite a while before they can hedge them off completely, or the options expire. These are the market makers who keep their positions neutral and make adjustments as time goes by.

The necessity of these market makers to adjust positions raises the specter of something similar to what caused the crash. Recall from the example in Chapter 3, that practitioners of portfolio insurance had to sell futures in huge quantities in order to protect their stock positions. That practice is no longer being followed. However, what is being done by some of these same institutions for protection, is that they are buying puts as insurance against a large market decline. Many of these puts are of the over-the-counter variety, being transacted directly between buyer and seller and tailored in specific ways as to expiration dates, striking prices, and underlying "security." In fact, the underlying security may be a very specific basket of stocks that resemble the stocks in the institution's portfolio.

Someone, of course, is selling these puts to the institutions that are buying them. That "someone" is the over-the-counter market makers—large firms such as Salomon Brothers, Goldman Sachs, Morgan Stanley, Swissbank, or Banker's Trust. The puts are generally overpriced when the institution buys them—that's why the trading houses are willing and eager to sell them. So all the market maker has to do is hedge his portfolio properly, and he will profit to the tune of the "overpriced" portion of these puts. If he is short puts, that makes him delta long. Since most of these puts are on baskets of stock or on broad-based stock indices, the market maker is thus delta long "the market." He can easily hedge this long by selling S&P 500 futures.

What worries some regulators is that, if the market were to head down in earnest, as it did in 1987, these market makers might have to sell a lot of futures in order to hedge their short put positions. Since these puts were created in over-the-counter transactions, no one really knows how many of them are in existence, in total. Moreover, no one knows the extent of the hedges at any time. So there is some chance that what happened in 1987 to worsen the market decline on the day of the crash could happen again.

These over-the-counter market makers are smart traders. So they understand the ramifications of a portfolio that is too delta long, or has the potential to become too delta long if the market declines. Thus, they have attempted to balance out their portfolios wherever possible, by encouraging institutions or other traders to *sell* puts. This, of course, would transfer the potential of downside liability from the market makers to other traders. Overall, however, it seems to me that most institutions are overall net *buyers* of puts for their insurance value. Thus, whoever sold those puts, be it market makers or other institutions, have potential downside liability. Perhaps the market won't ever decline so severely or so far that it would force those who are delta long to take drastic measures, but you can't be sure.

Other Forms of Neutrality

We have already shown that delta neutral trading is only neutral for a short period of time and within a fairly short price range of the underlying. As long as you understand this fact, you can devise strategies that will compensate and adjust for the changing delta. However, if there is too great a change in price or in implied volatility, there may not be any adjustments that can "save" the position. Throughout history, we have seen such gaps and they have been costly to delta neutral traders. Earlier in this book, we gave several examples of this: the crash of 1987, the large rally in April of 1978, or the Barings Bank problem that began with straddle selling.

When neutral trading first became possible shortly after the introduction of listed options in 1973, there were only a few practitioners. Option premiums were extremely expensive in those times, and the neutral strategies worked fairly well, although even at that time there were problems caused for ratio writers by large rallies in October 1974, January 1975, and January 1976. Then listed puts became available, and straddle selling seemed extremely profitable, so even more "delta neutral" adherents began to surface.

Note that straddle selling is less "neutral" than is the type of call ratio spread that we used in the earlier examples in this chapter. True, you may be able to initialize a position that has no delta to begin with. However, almost *any* movement at all by the underlying will cause a straddle position to lose its neutrality.

Example: XYZ is 50.

Quantity/Option	Delta	ESP
Short 9 XYZ Jan 50 calls	0.55	Short 495 shares of XYZ
Short 11 XYZ Jan 50 puts	−0.45	Long 495 shares of XYZ
		Total ESP: 0 shares

This is a typical, delta neutral short straddle position, established when the underlying is near the striking price of the short straddle. You sell a few more puts than calls in order to make the position delta neutral. Now, if the stock moves a little higher, the delta of the call might increase to −0.65, and that of the put would fall to −0.35. This slight movement exacts a rather large toll on the neutrality of the position; the position delta now becomes *short 200 shares*.

What has happened is that when the stock moves, the deltas of both options in the straddle are changing in the same direction. That is, if the stock moves up, the calls are being *more* delta short, while the puts are simultaneously becoming *less* delta long.

At least with the call ratio spread, this is not the case; there, when the stock moves up, the short calls become more delta short, but that is mitigated somewhat by the fact that the long calls in that spread become more delta long.

The Gamma.   The more serious disciples of neutral trading real-ized that merely being delta neutral was not enough. There was still too much risk to price movements by the underlying security. What was needed was something that helped them reduce their exposure to price risk by the underlying security. If they could have something that would allow them to keep the *delta* constant—presumably, neu-tral—then they could have a more truly neutral position. It turns out that there is indeed just such a measure. It is called the *gamma*, and it is a measure of how fast delta changes. Thus, if you were to con-struct a *gamma neutral* position, then delta wouldn't change at all! And, if delta didn't change, then the position would remain delta neutral. *Voila!* We discuss gamma neutral trading later in this chap-ter, after we have laid some more groundwork.

Mathematicians quickly determined that they could, in fact, quan-tify any position's or portfolio's exposure to any of the variables that go into making up the option price. We already know that exposure to price change is called delta. But, you can also calculate, if you desire, the exposure of a position with respect to time, volatility, and even interest rates (there is no need to calculate the change with respect to the striking price, since the striking price cannot change over the life of the option). The names given to these measures are as follows:

Variable Affecting Option Price	Measure of Exposure
Underlying price	Delta
Striking price	Not applicable
Time to expiration	Theta
Short-term interest rates	Rho
Volatility	Vega

As you can see, the mathematicians gave these "measures of exposure" the names of Greek letters, or names that sound like they're Greek letters (vega is not in the Greek alphabet, but it sounds like it might be).

Moreover, as we saw in the description of gamma, you could get really carried away with this and determine how much exposure each *measure of exposure* has. This information is useful to neutral traders, because they can then establish positions that are indeed quite neutral with respect to many of the things that can go wrong— specifically sudden price changes by the underlying, and sudden swings in implied volatility.

It should be understood that any of these measures of exposure will change as market conditions change. We know that the delta changes when the stock moves, or when implied volatility changes, or when time passes. In a similar manner, these other measures change under those conditions as well. However, the profitability of an option position or portfolio will be much more stable when it is neutral with respect to several of these measures of exposure.

For now, it is sufficient to understand that we *can* use these other measures of neutrality. We return to them, in more specific terms, later in the chapter. For now, we return to the concept of attempting to predict volatility, as opposed to predicting price, the latter being what most of us are accustomed to.

PREDICTING VOLATILITY

If you are able to predict volatility, then you can construct a position that is neutral with respect to price movements, and just concentrate on making money from your volatility prediction. While this is theoretically possible, it's not easy. So, over the bulk of the remainder of this chapter, we address how this can be accomplished. Initially, we use delta neutral examples to illustrate our points. However, you, the reader, know from the preceding sections that delta neutral has its own set of problems. Eventually, we will resolve all of these problems, when we get to the sections on advanced concepts.

Imagine, if you will, that you have found a stock that routinely traded in a fixed range. It would then be a fairly simple matter to buy it when it was near the low end of that range, and to then sell it when it was at the top of the range. In fact, you might even decide to sell it short near the top of the range, figuring you could cover it when it got back to the bottom of the range. Occasionally, you are able to find a stock like this, although they are rather few and far between.

However, in many, many instances, volatility exhibits this exact type of behavior. If you look at the history of volatility in many issues, you will find that it trades in a range. This is true for futures contracts, indices, and stocks. Even something as seemingly volatile as Microsoft, whose stock rose from about 12 to 106 during the 1990s, fits this pattern. Its implied volatility never deviated outside of range between 26 and 50 percent, and most of the time was in a much tighter range: 30 to 45 percent.

Of course, there are times when the volatility of anything can break out to previously unheard-of levels. The stock market in 1987 was a classic example. Also, volatility can go into a slumber as well, trading below historic norms. Gold in 1994–1995 was an example of this, as historic volatility fell to the 6 percent level, when it normally traded above 12 percent.

Despite these occasional anomalies, volatility seems to have more predictability than prices do. Mathematical and statistical measures bear this out as well—the deviation of volatilities is much smaller than the deviation of prices, in general.

You should recall that there are two types of volatility: implied and historical. Historical is a strict statistical measure of how fast prices have been changing. The historical volatility can be looked at over any set of past data that you desire, with 10-day, 20-day, 50-day, and 100-day being very common measures. Implied volatility, on the other hand, is the volatility that the options are displaying. Implied volatility is an attempt by traders and market makers to assess the *future* volatility of the underlying instrument. Thus, implied volatility and historical volatility may differ at times. Which one should you use if you are going to trade volatility?

My answer to that question is this: use a comparison of historical and implied volatility, but only if implied volatility is *not* predicting an usual occurrence for future volatility. Thus, if implied volatility is low with respect to historical volatility, then we would expect implied volatility to increase. In that case, option buying strategies, such as straddle purchases, would be appropriate. However, if implied volatility is high with respect to historical volatility, then we would normally expect implied volatility to decrease and move back in line with historical volatility, so option selling strategies would be appropriate. However, if you have reason to suspect that implied volatility is out of line for a specific reason, then you should avoid trading volatility in that issue. That reason could be impending corporate news.

In Chapter 4, when we discussed the predictive power of options, we noted that it is sometimes the case that expensive options are a harbinger of corporate news. In particular, if the options get very expensive, and particularly if they get active at the same time, then an event may be just around the corner that indicates a large change in price by the underlying security is about to take place—a takeover, lawsuit verdict, ruling by a government agency, or an unexpected earnings report might fall into this category. You would want to avoid selling this type of high implied volatility.

COMPARING HISTORICAL AND IMPLIED VOLATILITY

The situations that are often attractive for trading volatility are when there is a differential between implied and historical volatility. These situations occur with relative frequency. However, it is not enough that there is a big discrepancy between them. In addition, we need to know where both implied and historical volatilities have been over the past months, or maybe even a year; that is, we want to know what range they have been trading in. Even if implied volatility is much higher than historical volatility, we should not automatically sell the volatility unless the trading range of implied volatility confirms that it is high.

If you were to notice that the implied volatility of OEX was 11 percent and the historical volatility was 6 percent, you might think that you should sell options because of the differential between historical and implied volatilities. From this limited bit of information, that *does* seem like a logical conclusion. However, when you investigate more, you will see that it is an incorrect conclusion.

OEX options traditionally trade with a higher implied volatility than the actual (historical) volatility of the OEX Index. There is probably not a logical explanation for this fact, but it is a fact. Thus, it is not sufficient for you to base your analysis on the fact that OEX implied volatility is currently 11 percent and historical volatility is 6 percent. Rather, you should look at past levels of both implied and historical volatility.

In fact, over the past year or even several years, OEX implied volatility has ranged from a low of 10 percent to a high of 22 percent. So you can see that the current reading of 11 percent is actually quite low. In a similar fashion, historical volatility has ranged from a low of 6 percent to a high of about 15 percent over that same period. Hence, the current reading of 6 percent is at the absolute low end of the range. Given this information, it seems that strategies oriented toward *buying* options would be more prudent, because volatility is currently low by both measures, historical and implied.

These were actual readings of OEX volatility, taken from February 1995, just before the market embarked on an upside explosion of historic proportions. Clearly, it was a good time to be buying volatility, not selling it.

This example demonstrates that knowing the previous range of volatility is much more important than merely comparing current values of implied and historical volatility. Using only the latter can lead to incorrect conclusions and losing trades. Moreover, since strategies in which you are selling volatility often involve the use of naked options, you should be extremely careful in your analyses before establishing positions.

An approach to this analysis that works well is to use *deciles* in comparing the volatilities. To break a set of data into declines, merely take all the observations and put the lowest 10 percent in the first decile, the next lowest 10 percent in the next decile, and so forth, until you have 10 deciles worth of data. If the current implied volatility is in the first or second decile, then option buying strategies may be appropriate, for implied volatility is near the low end of its range. Conversely, if implied volatility is currently in the 9th or 10th decile, then option selling strategies should be considered.

In addition, you would want some confirmation from historical volatility, using the same decile method. Historical volatility should be in the same decile or a more favorable one. That is, if implied volatility is in the second decile and you are considering option buying strategies, then you would want historical volatility to be in the second decile or higher. On the other hand, if implied volatility is high (in the 9th or 10th decile), then you would want historical volatility to be in the same or in a lower decile in order for it to confirm the location of the implied volatility. Moreover, you should use several measures of historical volatility in these comparisons.

The following is an OEX example, where volatility was low.

Decile	1	2	3	4	5	6	7	8	9	10	
Implied	10.3>	11.4	11.8	12.3	13.0	13.7	14.5	15.3	16.0	16.7	17.7
10-Day	4.3	5.2	6.2	6.6	7.0	7.7	8.6>	9.4	10.1	10.8	16.5
20-Day	5.4	5.8	6.2	6.6	6.8	7.9>	8.6	9.1	9.8	11.1	12.9
50-Day	6.3	6.6	7.2>	7.5	7.7	8.0	8.6	9.1	9.9	10.3	11.1
100-Day	7.4>	7.7	7.8	8.0	8.5	8.9	8.9	8.9	9.0	9.1	9.1

The implied volatility numbers are the 20-day moving average of implieds. These go back one year, and there are about 250 trading days in a year. So there would be 231 20-day observations in that time period. The ">" character indicates that the current reading is in the first decile.

The other four lines refer to historical volatility. There are four separate measures of historical. You can see that the 10-, 20-, and 50-day historical averages are all in higher deciles than the implied volatility is. The 100-day is in the same first decile as implied volatility.

Overall, this is an attractive picture of volatility for option buying strategies: implied volatility is at its lowest point, and historical volatility is more "normal" with the 10- and 20-day actually being in deciles slightly above average (the sixth and seventh deciles, respectively). Thus, if implied volatility were to return to the middle deciles as well, it would increase, and option buying strategies would benefit.

A similar situation holds for determining when implied volatility is too high. You would compare its percentile with the historical volatility's percentile. There is one exception about high implied volatility that should always be taken into consideration: very expensive options on a moderately volatile stock may signal an impending corporate news event such as a takeover or earnings surprise. A good rule of thumb is to only sell implied volatility if it is at the high end of a previously determined range. But should the volatility break out of that range and rise to new highs, you should probably be very cautious about selling it and should even consider removing existing positions.

We previously mentioned Federal Paperboard (FBO) as an example. It is a classic for demonstrating our point in this case. Traditionally, FBO options traded with implied volatilities ranging from the low 20s to about 40 percent. Not only that, but the price of the stock had behaved in such a manner as to make trading the volatility quite profitable.

Then, in October 1995, the stock ended a small correction at a price of about 35, and began to trade higher. Implied volatility rose above 40 to 41 percent on one day and 44 percent on another—before exploding to readings of 48, 54, 60, 81, and 89 percent over the next five days! This kind of increase in implied volatility above the normal trading range is a warning sign for sellers of volatility to stay away. By this time, the stock had increased in price to 42½—not much of a rise—so volatility sellers could have gotten out or adjusted at a small loss.

As it turned out, FBO was taken over the next week, and it jumped to about 53.

Thus, you should generally not engage in volatility selling strategies when the implied volatility exceeds the previous range, especially if the stock is on the rise. The one exception would be if a stock were dropping rapidly in price, and you felt that that was the reason for the increase in implied volatility. In this situation—as we saw in Chapter 4 with IBM and Telefonos de Mexico—covered writes or naked put sales can often be very effective.

As detailed in Chapter 5, this information on where volatility has been trading is available for all markets from Bloomberg or Option Vue.

TRADING IMPLIED VOLATILITY

So, now that we have outlined the scenarios under which we would buy or sell volatility, let's take a look at what strategies might be appropriate. In this section, use elementary strategies. Later, we see how more advanced strategies can be used. Recall that, as a volatility trader, we don't really want to have to predict where the price of the underlying is going to be. We merely want to predict where the volatility will be. In light of these facts, we normally establish a neutral position to begin with.

With simple strategies, we usually begin with a delta neutral position. We explore those in this section. Remember, though, that a delta neutral position can quickly turn into a position with price risk, so these strategies, while useful, may not be enough to keep us from having to get "involved" with the price movements by the underlying.

Selling Volatility

When the implied volatility is "too high," the strategist wants to sell volatility, intending to capitalize when it returns to more normal levels. *When I want to sell volatility, I favor one of two strategies— the sale of a naked combination, or a ratio spread.* Since both strategies involve the sale of naked options, some traders prefer to purchase deeply out-of-the-money options as disaster protection. That may or may not be a good idea. On the one hand, it allows them to be worry-free about large gap openings, but on the other hand, it costs money and, if these traders have done their analysis correctly, they should be selling inflated volatility, not buying it. I also tend to keep the options relatively short-term in nature when selling volatility.

In a naked combination sale, an out-of-the-money call is sold, as well as an out-of-the-money put. I favor this over a straddle sale because of the wider price range of profitability that is attained.

Figure 6.1 compares the profit potential of a naked straddle sale with the sale of a naked combination, at expiration. Note that the straddle sale can make more money if the underlying is near the striking price at expiration, but that the combination sale makes money over a wider range. Since you are often forced to make adjustments to naked positions when the underlying makes adverse price movements, the use of the combination sale lessens the odds of having to adjust so often.

Before getting into an actual example, there is one other important concept that can be presented visually—the statistical advantage that the position presents. When you are selling high volatility, you expect that volatility will return to more normal levels. In most cases, when this happens, you will make money and you can then exit the position. This return to "normal" volatility may occur quickly, or it may take a while (or may never happen at all). The trader's statistical "edge" is that he is selling inflated volatility, and his profit potential,

Figure 6.1
NAKED STRADDLE SALE VERSUS NAKED COMBINATION

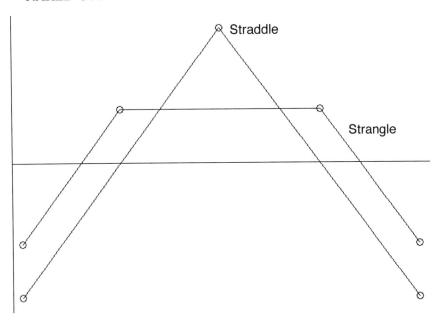

as represented by that edge, is the amount of money that he could make if volatility returned to normal levels.

Figure 6.2 shows the general shape of a combination sale, with two curved lines inside of it. The straight lines are where the profits or losses would lie if the position were carried all the way to expiration. The curved lines are profit projections if the position were held only halfway to expiration. The reason that there are two curved lines is that one represents the results with volatility remaining at high levels (the lower curved line), while the other depicts the results if volatility were to return to normal levels (the higher curved line).

You can see that there are profits under both curved lines if the underlying is near the center of the graph. Likewise, there can be losses as well, as both curved lines penetrate below the zero profit line if the underlying rises or falls too far. What is most important, however, is that there is a definite space between the two curved lines—the shaded area on the graph. This shaded area is a picture of

Figure 6.2
COMBINATION SALE

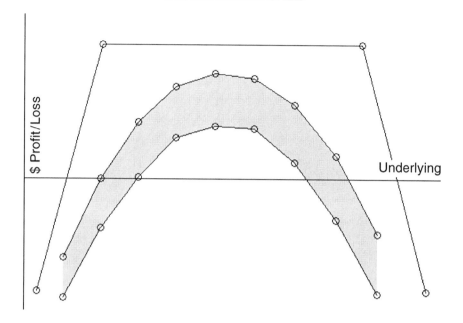

the statistical advantage that the seller of high implied volatility has, for if volatility returns to its normal level, he will profit by the amount of the shaded area.

A similar picture regarding the ratio spread strategy can be observed in Figure 6.3. It is the graph of a call ratio spread. Simplistically, a call ratio spread involves buying one call at a lower strike and selling more calls at a higher strike. Notice that the maximum profit area of all three scenarios—expiration, halfway to expiration with the same volatility, and halfway to expiration with decreased volatility—is at the higher striking price (i.e., the striking price of the short options in the spread). It is at that point where the statistical edge is the largest; the area between the two curved lines is widest at that point.

Now, having established the general theory of trading high implied volatility, some actual examples may prove to be beneficial. Admittedly, this first one is a favorable example, but it is one taken

Figure 6.3
RATIO CALL SPREAD

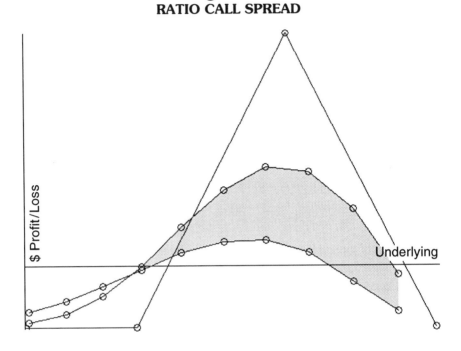

from real-life trading, and the decisions made at the time reflected the philosophies that we have discussed thus far.

The AMEX listed options on the Hong Kong Option Index (symbol: HKO) in 1993. The index was designed to perform similarly to the Hang Seng Index, the main market measure of the Hong Kong Stock Exchange.

The HKO Index is computed just once a day, before the opening of trading in the United States, as the actual Hong Kong market is closed at that time. Closing prices of the stocks used to compute the HKO are taken from actual closing prices in Hong Kong, converted to dollars. Thus, the HKO gaps *every* trading day. Think of it as akin to being able to trade the Dow-Jones only at night, where the only price you had to go from was each day's Dow closing price. This feature raises the implied volatility somewhat.

In late June 1994, the following situation existed with respect to the various implied and historical volatilities of the Hong Kong Option Index:

	Actual (%)	Decile
Implied volatility	34	10th
10-Day historical	16	7th
20-Day historical	18	7th
50-Day historical	19	7th
100-Day historical	21	8th

The previous range of the *implied* volatility of the HKO Index had been from about 21 to 38 percent. Thus, this situation fit both of the stated criteria: (1) implied volatility was significantly higher than historical volatility, and (2) the implied volatility was in the 10th decile, while historical volatilities were high, but not quite as high. What's more, an index is unlikely to acquire a sudden burst of volatility, as a stock might from an impending takeover offer.

The HKO Index itself was trading at about 180 at the time, and the July options, which were due to expire in three weeks were trading at the following prices:

> Date: June 23, 1994
> HKO Index: 180.79
> HKO July 190 call: 1¾
> HKO July 170 put: 2

The fact that short-term (three-week) options were available at reasonably large prices was another added benefit. The combination—an equal amount of July 190 calls and July 170 puts—was sold and, as it turned out, implied volatilities remained high throughout the fairly short life of the options, so there was never a return to "normal" volatility. However, the HKO Index never moved much in price, trading in a range between about 170 and 182 during the next three weeks. The combo expired worthless, and the maximum profit was attained.

Some additional commentary may be beneficial here. First, the naked combo was chosen as the vehicle of choice, because the HKO Index had been trading in a range around 180 for several weeks prior to establishing this position. Therefore, a position with breakeven points centered about the current price (180.79) seemed to be the best choice of a neutral position.

Second, when the HKO dropped to 170, the position had obviously become delta long. Should an adjustment have been made? That is a matter of conjecture, and I always feel it has to do with the size of the position itself. When using an elementary neutral strategy such as a short combo, you are obviously going to have to assume some delta risk eventually (or else you will be making numerous adjustments, and commissions will eat you alive). With these short-term combos, I generally feel that I will leave them room to move and will remove them if (1) volatility drops and I have a profit equal to the statistical edge, as shown in the preceding chart, or (2) they expire, or (3) they violate their breakeven points.

Obviously, no one wants to take large losses—especially in a naked writing situation—so the third criterion is mandatory. Therefore, when the position was established, I was prepared to close out the combination if HKO traded at 167 on the downside, or at 193 on the upside. In either case, only a small loss would have resulted.

The preceding example can be continued because, in a way, no convergence had been reached between historical and implied volatilities. Notice that we said that implied volatility never returned to normal by the time expiration arrived. Therefore, the same situation essentially was available for the next expiration.

At July expiration, the situation had not changed much as far as the Hong Kong Option Index volatilities were concerned:

	Actual (%)	Decile
Implied volatility	33	10th
10-Day historical	24	10th
20-Day historical	22	9th
50-Day historical	20	9th
100-Day historical	21	8th

This was still an attractive situation, although perhaps not quite as attractive as in the previous example. Implied volatility was still at the top end of the range, which was good, but it wasn't that much higher than historical volatility, when measured by the deciles. This could indicate that *all* the volatilities were embarking on a higher move. Still, it seemed attractive enough to repeat the strategy, using the following prices:

Date: July 15, 1994
HKO Index: 176.20
Aug 190 call: 3¼
Aug 165 put: 2

You can see from these prices that the calls were more expensive than the puts, so a neutral position required the sale of five puts and three calls. Such a position took in a credit of $5 \times 2 + 3 \times 3\frac{1}{4} = 19\frac{3}{4}$ points. This makes the breakeven points 196.58 (190 + 19.75/3) on the upside and 161.05 (165 − 19.75/5) on the downside.

During the ensuing four weeks to expiration, the implied volatility once again failed to move below the ninth percentile, and HKO traded in a range from 176 up to about 194, before finishing at 188 at expiration. Since the breakeven points weren't violated, no defensive action was taken, and the combo expired worthless once again.

At this point, I was admittedly feeling fairly fortunate to have had two consecutive combos expire worthless. Even more so, considering the fact that the first one had seen the HKO Index mostly trade lower, even threatening the downside breakeven point; then the second one had the opposite action—the HKO Index traded up and almost went through the upside breakeven point. However, the fact that implied volatility was high when these positions were established made the breakeven points sufficiently far away from the initial index price that it contributed to the eventual inability of the index to exceed those breakeven points.

It surely seemed that this situation couldn't go on forever, but since the implied volatility was still high after even the second combo expired worthless, it seemed worthwhile to attempt a third one.

After the second HKO combo expired worthless, the following situation existed at August 1994 expiration:

	Actual (%)	Decile
Implied volatility	31	10th
10-Day historical	22	9th
20-Day historical	21	9th
50-Day historical	20	9th
100-Day historical	21	8th

The following prices existed at the time:

Date: August 12, 1994
HKO Index: 189.85
Sep 205 call: 1¾
Sep 175 put: 2¼

The deltas of these two options were about the same, so this time the combo consisted of selling an equal amount of Sep 205 calls and Sep 175 puts. Over the next two weeks, HKO traded in a very tight range, between 188 and 193. This had the effect, finally, of causing the implied volatility to contract to 23 percent. At this time, the statistical advantage had finally been realized, and the combos were covered.

Thus ended the profitable saga of the Hong Kong Index inflated volatility. Ironically, the volatility of the index did not return to the 10th decile for over a year and a half after the summer of 1994. Perhaps the market makers and other traders decided that the somewhat disconcerting gap-every-night feature of the HKO did not merit such a large implied volatility on a routine basis.

Selling volatility in this manner is somewhat nerve-racking because naked options are involved. There are always the disasters from naked option writing that you routinely read about and which we have recounted as well—takeovers, crashes, and so on—but with the guidelines that we have set forth, you should be able to avoid those. For example, implied volatility was actually very *low* just before the crash; thus, by our "rule" of requiring it to be in the 9th or 10th decile, you wouldn't have sold it. Also, as was described earlier, implied volatility usually skyrockets before a takeover, so if implied volatility suddenly blasts much higher than the previous 10th decile readings, you shouldn't sell that volatility either. Rather, with these guidelines, losses would generally be more modest, but that doesn't mean that they don't occur. Lest you think that selling naked options when implied volatility reaches the 10th decile is a lock, the following example is provided.

Also in the summer of 1994, UAL Corp's (UAL) options had reached expensive levels, by all measurements.

	Actual (%)	Decile
Implied volatility	36	10th
10-Day historical	28	8th
20-Day historical	26	7th
50-Day historical	28	7th
100-Day historical	25	6th

Thus, implied volatility was not only higher than historical volatility in absolute terms, but it was in a higher decile as well. Note that the *absolute* differential in volatilities is not as large here as it was in the HKO examples, but a 36 percent implied versus historicals in the 25–28 percent range is still a significant difference.

The pertinent prices at the time were:

Date: June 10, 1994
UAL: 116
UAL July 125 call: $1\frac{3}{4}$
UAL July 110 put: $2\frac{1}{2}$

The deltas of these two options were about equal, so an equal number of puts and calls were sold naked. The breakeven points were $129\frac{1}{4}$ on the upside and $105\frac{3}{4}$ on the downside. In line with the philosophy stated earlier, the position was to be given room to "roam" until it hit the breakeven points. With about five weeks until expiration, this seemed like a reasonable amount of room—about 14 points on the upside and 11 points on the downside.

This position didn't have the good fortune of the Hong Kong Index puts. UAL immediately started to move higher and closed at 130 on July 1st. At that time, July 125 calls were offered at $5\frac{3}{4}$ and were covered. The puts were trading at a small fraction and were covered as well.

Moreover, implied volatility had fallen to 23 percent, so it was no longer expensive. Thus, no other position was established in UAL.

The preceding example shows how using the simple neutral position was insufficient to capture the intended volatility decline. In fact, volatility *did* decline—from 34 percent to 23 percent—and that was what we were trying to predict. Unfortunately, with such a simple neutral position, we were left too exposed to price movement by UAL. That price movement overrode the benefits of declining volatility, and the overall position became a loss. It is for reasons such as this that a more sophisticated approach is generally necessary in order to isolate volatility as the important variable. However, for the time being, we want to continue with the simpler strategies, so that we can further lay the groundwork for the more complex material later.

Buying Volatility

The strategist who is attempting to trade volatility will buy it when it is "too low." In such cases, there are three applicable strategies: long straddles, backspreads, or calendar spreads. Note that the first two simple strategies are merely the opposites of the ones used for selling volatility. The introduction of this third strategy, the calendar spread, into the mix gives us a slightly wider range of alternatives.

The simple strategy for selling volatility discussed earlier was somewhat heavily dependent on price movement of the underlying, which was a negative, and time decay, which was a positive. As might be expected, the first two strategies for buying volatility—long straddles and backspreads—are affected in the opposite way: extreme price movement by the underlying is *beneficial* to these strategies, while time decay is an enemy. The ability to use calendar spreads for buying volatility gives the strategist an important alternative: time decay once again becomes a positive factor. The following graphs show these strategies' profitability, both at expiration and at the perhaps more important earlier times.

Figure 6.4 is a graph of owning a straddle. If I am going to use this strategy for buying volatility, I prefer to buy the straddle (both the put and the call have the same strike, which is initially quite near the price of the underlying) rather than buying a combination (out-of-the-money put and out-of-the-call). The curved lines on the graph depict the same sort of things that we saw in the last section: they are the profits or losses halfway to expiration. If volatility remains low, then the profitability will fall on the lower curved line; however, if volatility increases, then profits will be on the higher curved line. The space between the two of them is the amount of profit that can be attributed to volatility returning to "normal" levels.

Trading long straddles can be a somewhat depressing occupation, because of the constant drag of time decay on the position. However, if volatility *does* explode or if the price explodes, profits

Figure 6.4
STRADDLE BUY

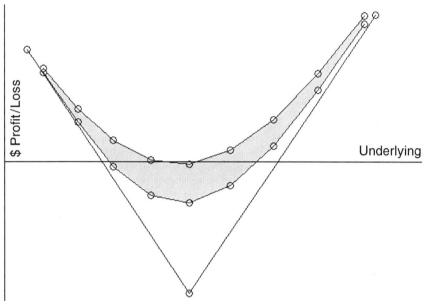

come quickly and can be quite large. The position needs to be handled in a significantly different way from the short combination strategy that was previously discussed. For one thing, when you are *long* the straddle, if the stock reaches your breakeven point, you are most likely only just beginning to make money. Therefore, you must hold onto the position—even though it is in no way delta neutral any longer—if you expect to maximize profits. Another thing that is important is to decide when to take losses. The following examples, again from actual trades, address these points.

In late September of 1995, retail stocks were beginning to come under some pressure. They had had a strong run in the bull market of that year, but had peaked out in late July. There is a sector index that is composed of the retail stocks, and it trades with the symbol $RLX. The index had peaked out at 342 that summer, and had pulled back slightly to 330 by September. At the time, the pertinent volatilities were:

	Actual (%)	Decile
Implied volatility	12	1st
10-Day historical	10	2nd
20-Day historical	9	1st
50-Day historical	10	1st
100-Day historical	13	4th

It is fairly obvious from this data that the Retail Index was at a low ebb, both in implied and in historical volatility. The fact that the 100-day historical volatility was somewhat higher was evidence that the index had been more volatile in the past.

With the index near 330, the December 330 straddle was purchased for 15 points.

There are two ways that a straddle owner can make money: (1) if the implied volatility increases or (2) if the underlying rises or falls far enough in price. The first condition will boost the price of any straddle, whether it be a short-term one or a longer-term one. However, if volatility remains at low levels, the straddle purchase relies on price movement by the underlying in order to make money. You will find that, at low-volatility conditions, the underlying needs to move nearly all the way to the breakeven point in order for the straddle to become profitable.

I usually attempt to buy straddles with about three or four months of time remaining when I am buying volatility. This length of time is selected for two reasons. First, the time decay isn't too rapid for a three-month straddle, although of course time will definitely be working against the straddle owner to a certain extent. Second, the straddle has a good chance to respond if the underlying rises or falls by a reasonable distance. If you go too far out in time, you will be paying too much time value and may find that it is therefore too difficult to make money from price movement by the underlying; you will be overly relying on a volatility increase.

Continuing with the previous example, the retail stocks began to announce poor earnings and earnings forecasts shortly after the straddle was purchased, and the Retail Index fell to 319 in just about two weeks. However, the straddle was still selling for about 15 because implied volatility had only picked up modestly—to 13 percent—and with the put being the in-the-money option, there wasn't much time value premium in the straddle's price.

Options lose time value premium as they become in-the-money options, and in-the-money puts lose their time value faster than in-the-money calls do. This is a fairly typical occurrence, and not a totally unpleasant one: that is, the underlying moves toward the breakeven point, but the straddle price doesn't really respond much because volatility remains at low levels. With the underlying near one of the breakeven points, a long straddle position is by no means delta neutral.

When that occurs, the straddle owner, who, it must be remembered, is really a volatility buyer, must make a decision. He could (1) close out the straddle, (2) readjust it so it becomes delta neutral once more, or (3) go with the flow and try to ride the existing trend. This is not an easy choice, but some guidelines can be given. If volatility has increased, the first choice—to close the straddle—is probably appropriate. The second choice—readjusting—would be more appropriate if the implied and historical volatilities are still in the first or second percentile; that is not normally the case after the underlying has moved far enough to reach a breakeven point. In essence, I only favor the adjustment choice if the position is one that I would initialize if I had no position at all. The third choice—riding the trend—might be appropriate if volatility is still at low levels, and if there is a good technical reason to expect that the trend in prices will continue.

In this same example, after the drop to 319, this Retail Index straddle was quite delta short, as the Dec 330 put had a large negative delta, being 11 points in-the-money, while the Dec 330 call didn't have much of a delta at all, since it was out-of-the-money by an equal amount. Implied volatility had risen only slightly to 13 percent, so the first choice—closing the position—wasn't overwhelmingly the best choice.

In order to assess the second choice—readjusting—it is necessary to compare the implied and historical volatilities once again. The overall volatility picture at this time had become the following:

	Actual (%)	Decile
Implied volatility	13	2nd
10-Day historical	13	4th
20-Day historical	11	3rd
50-Day historical	11	2nd
100-Day historical	12	3rd

This is a picture of low volatilities, but not extremely low ones. I would not normally initiate a position with this volatility picture, so readjusting was therefore not attractive.

The third choice—riding the trend—is sometimes the most risky choice, but it can produce the best profits as well. Figure 6.5 shows the Retail Index at the time it had reached the 319 level in early October. There was previous support there from the bottom that had been made on September 1st. However, should that support give way, it appeared that a much larger drop was possible.

Therefore I decided to ride the trend, figuring that if I was wrong and RLX rallied instead, I could remove the straddle without too much harm since volatilities might still increase. As it turned out, the support *did* give way and the index collapsed to 297. By this time, I was using a trailing stop, and closed the position out on a reflex rally to 304. Thus, the straddle that was purchased for 15 was sold for 27½ (the calls were sold for 1½ on the day the index broke the 319 support level, and the puts were sold via the trailing stop). This entire scenario occurred by November 2nd, so it did not take long to unfold.

Once you have decided on the "go with the flow" choice, you should sell out the unprofitable half of the straddle as soon as the trend is technically confirmed. In the preceding example, that came with the breaking of support at the 319 level, when the calls were sold for 1½. Ironically, the Retail Index rallied all the way back to 328 in late November, so the calls could probably have been sold for more. However, in most cases, when a technical level is broken and you have decided to ride the trend, you should sell out the losing side, for it is probably headed toward zero.

Handling losing straddle positions is actually a much easier proposition. All you have to do is set a mental stop in terms of the straddle price and adhere to it. If the straddle declines in price to your stop, you take your loss. After that, you may want to reestablish a

Figure 6.5
RETAIL INDEX (RLX)

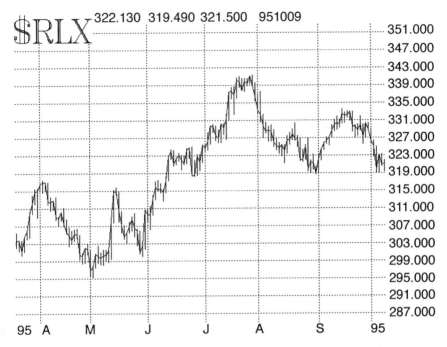

new, longer-term straddle on the same underlying security, although in many cases, it may not be as attractive as the initial straddle was.

We mentioned earlier that the volatility of gold declined to previously unheard of levels in 1994–1995. The decline in volatility began in late 1993, from levels around 20 percent, and had reached low levels by June of 1994. At the time, the following statistics regarding volatility were observed:

	Actual (%)	Decile
Implied volatility	10.7	1st
10-Day historical	6.0	1st
20-Day historical	6.4	1st
50-Day historical	10.0	1st
100-Day historical	11.3	2nd

With deciles like that, the straddles seemed like a very attractive purchase. So the Dec 390 straddles were purchased (Dec gold was trading at
391 at the time) at a price of 18. These straddles had about 4½ months of
life at the time, so that is why they were chosen.

I usually use a stop loss of about 40–50 percent of the value of the straddle, so I set a mental stop at a price of 10 for this long straddle. That is, if the
straddle settled at 10 or less on any trading day, the straddle would be sold.

As it turned out, gold remained in a tight range and volatilities fell even
farther. Gold traded between 380 and 400, never enough price movement
to even approach the breakeven points of 372 on the downside and 408 on
the upside. To make matters worse, implied volatility continued to fall as
well. Finally, by early October, the straddle had fallen to 10, and it was sold
and the loss was taken.

When you take a loss on a long straddle position, you are usually
feeling somewhat frustrated, especially if you did your homework
correctly and bought the straddle when volatility was extremely low.
Your initial reaction is usually to delve into another straddle on the
same underlying security, figuring that *this* time, the volatility will
have to increase. This may be an emotional decision. To remove the
emotion, you should analyze the volatility comparison and demand
the same or better volatility picture before repeating the position.

Shortly after taking the loss on the preceding gold straddle, with April gold
near the 390 level, and volatilities all in the first deciles (albeit at lower actual
levels than shown in the previous example), the April 390 straddle was
bought for a price of 11. This one had just over four months of life remaining. Note the lower absolute price of the straddle, reflecting the diminished
implied volatility.

Without getting overly involved in the details, this time things worked
better, as gold immediately fell below 380, the technical support level that
had been established earlier that summer.

Even if the second straddle purchase had been a loser as well, it
was still well-founded on the basis of low implied volatility. I don't
think you can repeat such purchases repeatedly if losses continue to
occur, and implied volatility continues to decline. For example, the
implied volatility of gold continued to drift lower into 1995, and then
remained at very low levels before finally beginning to climb in early

1996. Our philosophy of trading volatility was based on identifying the *range* of past volatilities; implicit in that philosophy is that volatility is going to *remain* within that range. When it breaks outside of the previous range, you should probably avoid positions in that security until you are confident that a new and relatively stable range has been identified. As a result, no further gold straddles were bought during the subsequent decline in volatility.

The second strategy that we described for buying volatility is the backspread. Figure 6.6 is that of a call backspread—selling one in-the-money call and buying 2 at-the-money calls, for example. You can see by the straight lines on the graph that the call backspread is very similar to the long straddle, except that the profit potential is truncated on the downside. The curved lines show the profit potential halfway to expiration. The higher curved line is the projected profit if implied volatility increases—returning to normal levels. The lower one is the profit if implied volatility remains where it was ini-

Figure 6.6
CALL BACKSPREAD

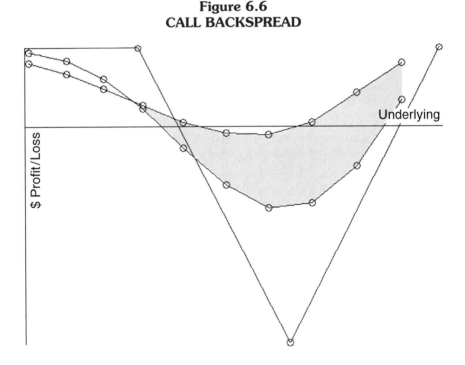

tially. The space between the two lines graphically represents the statistical advantage that can be had by capturing the volatility if it should increase to previously normal levels.

As you can see from the graph, the call backpsread has unlimited profit potential to the upside. A put backspread, however, has unlimited *downside* profit potential. In either case, the maximum loss of the backspread is *less* than that of a corresponding long straddle, because of the profit potential that is forsaken on one side of the backspread.

You might utilize a backspread instead of a long straddle if you think the particular market is more likely to move in one direction or the other. But the neutral strategist is not normally interested in price projection initially. Rather, the strategist would use the backspread when the implied volatilities of the *individual* options in the spread differ. This situation is called *volatility skewing* and is addressed later in this chapter, so examples of backspread positions will be deferred until that time.

The calendar spread is a strategy that benefits from increased implied volatility, but not from volatility of actual prices. A calendar spread involves buying a midterm option and selling a shorter-term option, both with the same striking price. A strategist will normally treat the calendar spread as just that—a spread—and remove it when the near-term option expires. Holding onto the longer-term option after the shorter-term one expires makes you a speculator instead of a spreader.

Figure 6.7 shows the profitability of a calendar spread at expiration of the near-term option. Notice that the maximum profit potential is realized if the underlying's price is right at the striking price. If the underlying moves too far away from the strike in either direction, then losses will occur. However, losses are limited to the initial debit spent for the spread. There are two curves on the graph—the higher one shows what would happen if volatility increased, while the lower one shows profits if volatility remains low. The space between the two is, once again, the statistical edge attributable to an increase in volatility.

Most option traders are familiar with calendar spreads, but they don't often think of them as being so affected by volatility. As a result, novice traders often establish calendar spreads when volatility

Figure 6.7
CALL CALENDAR SPREAD

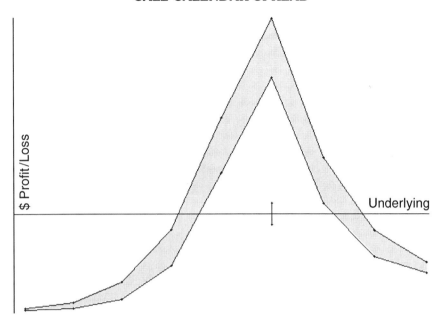

is high because the spread seems attractive when, in fact, it is not. Ordinarily, we use examples to show how to use a strategy, but this is an example of how *not* to use one. The reason that we are including it is because of the propensity of people to use calendar spreads when they shouldn't, that is, when implied volatility is high.

This is a theoretical example using actual prices. In the late summer and fall of 1994, Quaker Oats (OAT) was a rumored takeover for several months. The stock's price had risen from 60 to the 75–80 area, and the implied volatility had risen even more: from 20/30 percent to extremely high levels, ranging up to and even above 60 percent.

When implied volatility increases by this much, it distorts the option prices so that the near-term option seems ridiculously expensive in comparison to the longer-term options. In the first week of October, the following prices existed:

OAT Common: 75

	Price	Implied Volatility (%)
Nov 75 call	6½	60
Dec 75 call	8⅛	57

A calendar spread—buying the Dec 75 call and selling the Nov 75 call—could be established for a seemingly low debit of 1⅝. This calendar spread looks extremely attractive. The near-term November option is selling for a whopping 80 percent of the price of the December option, when both are at-the-money. You don't see that situation too often. Moreover, the November call has a slightly higher implied volatility than does the December call, so a calendar spread would have a slight theoretical edge in terms of the implied volatility options, also.

Furthermore, using a pricing model, you are able to determine that, if the December option holds its 57 percent implied volatility, then the spread will make a profit if OAT is anywhere between 67 and 85 at November expiration (about six weeks away)—a very wide range.

All of those things are true, as far as they go. What has not been investigated is what a contraction in volatility would do to the spread. In fact, it would have a devastating effect. Nothing could prove this more conclusively than what actually happened in real life: on November 9th, Quaker Oats indicated that it would buy Snapple, thereby quashing takeover rumors (most rumored suitors would not be interested in a money-losing venture like Snapple). The stock only dropped about 10 percent—to 67—but the implied volatility collapsed to 37 percent. The prices then looked like this:

OAT Common: 67

	Price	Implied Volatility (%)
Nov 75 call	¹⁄₁₆	n/a
Dec 75 call	⅞	37

By expiration day itself (November 18th), the common had fallen to 65 and the Dec 75 call was trading at a mere half point.

Thus, the calendar spread, which was purchased for 1⅝, was a large percentage loser after volatility collapsed.

This example shows the importance of factoring volatility into your decision when trading calendar spreads. When volatility is already pumped up, as in the Quaker Oats example, it is a potential roadblock to profits for the calendar spread. At the end of this chapter, we present an aggressive strategy for using calendar spreads in inflated volatility situations, but statistically speaking, you should avoid the strategy when implied volatility is too high. It is more advantageous to use the calendar spread strategy when implied volatility is low, thereby reducing the possibility for decreasing volatility to harm the spread and enhancing the probability that increasing volatility will help the spread.

Overall, when trading volatility, the five delta neutral strategies just discussed are generally the preferred ones that you would want to use. To summarize, if you are selling volatility, the two appropriate strategies are the ratio spread (which could be established with either puts or calls) and the naked short combo. If you are buying volatility, backspreads (with either puts or calls), long straddles, or calendar spreads are germane.

THE "GREEKS"

The preceding strategies and examples show the attractiveness of attempting to trade volatility, as opposed to predicting prices. However, since they are such simple strategies, you are often forced to form opinions on prices as the strategies evolve. It is now time to discuss ways in which you can more easily isolate volatility and rely less heavily on price in your strategies.

In order to do that, we must approach things in a more theoretical manner. Thus, this section may seem a little complicated. However, the concepts are not all that difficult. I've often said that statistics on Wall Street is treated like rocket science. That is, math that an undergraduate college math major would routinely understand is imbued with Einstein-like qualities by many traders. Moreover, many traders feel that if the computer says it's so, then it must be the absolute truth. You must not be so awed by what we are about to present. It's not the Holy Grail, nor is it the absolute secret to success. If it were, everybody would be using it. However, it *is* a step above what you normally see in terms of option strategies, and could lead you to more consistent, less risky, investments.

In order to isolate volatility, we need to understand how to isolate *each* of the variables that affect an option's price. Earlier in this chapter, we defined the names of the terms that describe the measure of exposure of an option or a portfolio, for each variable that affects the option price. Since these exposure measures have Greek (or Greek-sounding) names, we refer to them collectively as "the Greeks."

Variable Affecting Option Price	Measure of Exposure
Underlying price	Delta
Time to expiration	Theta
Short-term interest rates	Rho
Volatility	Vega

In addition, we also stated that "gamma," which is the measure of exposure of "delta," is also observed by sophisticated traders who use this approach to neutral trading.

The Model

The basis for calculating all of the preceding measures, as well as for calculating implied volatility and also the theoretical value of an option, is the option model. There are several models that are available to the general public. That is, their formulas have been published and are in the public domain. The earliest and simplest of these was the Black–Scholes model, derived in 1973 by two professors. Since then, many others have attempted to make adjustments and improvements, and many of them purport to give more accurate answers to the question of theoretical value.

One of the more popular alternatives is the Binomial model (the formula for the model, and some examples are given in Appendix C). It involves a lot more calculations than the Black–Scholes model, but in today's world of very fast computers, those calculations can be done rather quickly, although not nearly as quickly as the few calculations required for the Black–Scholes model. What's ironic is that after all these "improvements" over the years, the newer models rarely give "answers"—that is, option values—that differ from the results of the Black–Scholes model by more than a few pennies. In essence, the difference between the results of the Black–Scholes model and the Binomial model is less than the bid–asked spread between the option in the marketplace. Consequently, we see no reason to get more complicated than the Black–Scholes model, especially for a commission-paying, nonmarket maker.

It is necessary to have a model, because "the Greeks" cannot be computed without one. Recall that the model is a function that is based on the five variables that control the price of an option (stock price, striking price, time remaining, volatility, and interest rates). Of these five, only the striking price never changes for an individual option. The others all change as the market trades, day after day. The Greeks measure the effect of one variable, if all the others remain constant. To conceptualize what the Greeks actually are, a simple example may suffice.

Suppose that we are attempting to evaluate an option, where the following data apply:

> Stock price: 50
> Strike price: 55
> Time remaining: 3 months
> Volatility: 25%
> Interest rate: 6%

Under these assumptions, the Black–Scholes model returns a theoretical value of 1.02. Now suppose that we keep all the data the same, except that we recompute the theoretical value with the stock price set to 51. These, then, are the new assumptions:

> Stock price: 51
> Strike price: 55
> Time remaining: 3 months
> Volatility: 25%
> Interest rate: 6%

With this set of variables, the Black–Scholes model yields a theoretical value of 1.33.

What we have just done here is calculate the delta of this option. That is, the theoretical value of this option increased by 31 cents when the stock price increased by one point, with all other variables remaining the same. Thus, the delta is 0.31.

In reality, there is a mathematical equation for computing delta. That equation specifies that the delta of this option is 0.28 when the stock is 50, and is 0.34 when the stock is 51. Thus, the first (less theoretical) method yielded a result that was the average of the two mathematically computed deltas. This example also points out that the delta changes all the time, even as the stock is moving only one point. In any case, you can see that the two ways of computing delta yield very similar results.

You can extrapolate, from the preceding example, that a Greek is computed by changing one of the four variables that are subject to fluctuation during any trading day, while leaving the others unchanged. In this manner, you can measure the isolated effect of the change in any one variable on the price of an option. Almost all option software programs give you all of the Greeks for any option. Mathematically, each of the Greeks is the partial derivative of the model with respect to one of the four variables. Don't worry if you don't know what a partial derivative is; as a strategist you only need to know how to interpret the results of the mathematics, not how to compute the math itself. This is important information, for we can use it to establish positions that are neutral with respect to any or several of the variables. However, before getting into position analysis, let's describe the Greek terms themselves.

Delta

As you should know by now, the delta of an option is a measure of how much the option changes in price, when the underlying changes in price by one point. The delta of a call is a positive number, ranging between 0 and 1; the delta of a put is a negative number, ranging between −1 and 0.

The delta of an option has been discussed somwhat already, both earlier in this chapter and in Chapter 1. In the context of the previous example, suppose that, in addition to allowing the stock price to increase by 1 point, we allowed the other three variables—time remaining, volatility, and interest rate—to change as well. The theoretical value of the option will certainly change, but how much of it is attributable to the change in stock price? It's difficult to say, but it is obvious that these other variables affect the delta, too.

Figure 6.8 shows the relationship of delta and time. Note that the option with a lot of time remaining has a delta that changes rather moderately as the underlying moves from far out-of-the-money (left-hand side of graph) to far in-the-money (right-hand side of graph). However, for a short-term option, the change is much more dramatic, as the call delta rises to nearly 1.00 rather quickly when the option is in-the-money (right-hand side; higher line on graph), and the delta falls to nearly zero rather quickly when the option is out-of-the-money (left-hand side; lower line on graph).

Figure 6.8
COMPARISON OF DELTA AND TIME REMAINING

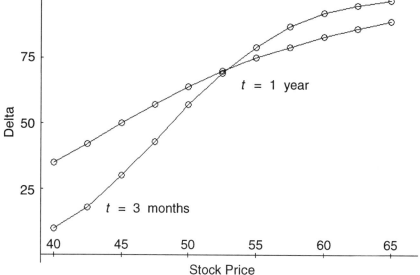

In February 1995, just a few days before February expiration, Motorola announced a slowdown in sales of cellular telephones, their most important product. The stock fell over six points, from 64 to 58, and was down even more intraday. This came one day before expiration of the February options.

Holders of out-of-the-money puts registered varying degrees of success, but nothing shows it more dramatically than the comparison of the Feb 55 puts and the March 55 puts. On the day before the announcement, with the stock trading at 64 (up two points that day, by the way), both of these puts were trading at $\frac{1}{16}$ of a dollar—the minimum value. When the stock dropped (dramatically) the next day, the Feb 55 puts never budged; they *still* traded at $\frac{1}{16}$. However, the March 55 puts jumped to a dollar, rising almost a full point.

Perhaps more vividly displaying the message, the January (1997) 50 LEAPS put, which had almost two years of life remaining at the time, but which was five points farther out of the money, outdid both of these other puts, rising by $1\frac{1}{2}$ points. Thus, the power of time as an effect on the amount an option can move is dramatically shown by this actual example.

The big move by the stock affected the option's deltas as well: the Feb 55 put had a delta of 0.00 before the drop and still had a delta of 0.00 after it, thereby confirming the fact that the delta of a short-term out-of-the-money option doesn't change much when the stock moves (even this far). The March 55 put's delta went from −0.01 before the stock dropped, to −0.16 after, an increase of 0.15. However, the longer-term option, even though it changed more in price, had a smaller change in delta, as its delta went from −0.13 to −0.23, a change of only 0.10. These facts are summarized in the following table:

	Original Delta	Price Change	Resulting Delta
Stock		−6	
Feb 55 put	−0.00	0	−0.00
March 55 put	−0.01	+1	−0.16
Jan (1997) 50 put	−0.13	+1½	−0.23

We mentioned earlier that the delta of an at-the-money option is *not* exactly one-half (0.50). Rather, it is something larger. Even more interesting is the fact that the delta of this at-the-money call changes as time passes. Figure 6.9 is a chart of the call's delta and shows this quite

Figure 6.9
DELTA OF AT-THE-MONEY OPTION AS TIME PASSES

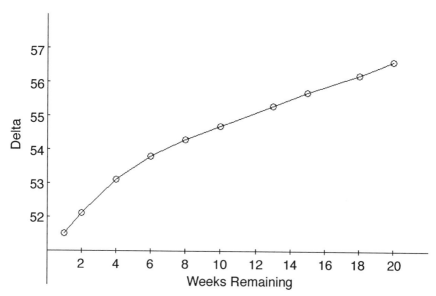

clearly. A put would show a similar change, but the put's delta would be going in the opposite direction, changing from something like –0.43 to nearly –0.50 as time passed (remember that the put's delta is the call's delta minus one). Consequently, the at-the-money put becomes a little *more* responsive to price changes by the underlying as expiration approaches, while the call becomes slightly less responsive. However, the magnitude of difference is small in either case.

We have already seen that the price movement of the underlying security makes the delta change, and it has also been shown that the passage of time changes the delta. The third major influence on a call's delta is *volatility*. Remember that there are two types of volatility, implied and historical. Historical volatility is the measure of how fast the underlying instrument has been changing in price; implied volatility is the volatility that is currently being displayed by the options—a sort of projection of future volatility. Either one can affect the delta of an option, although it is *implied* volatility that usually has the more dramatic, short-term effect.

The options on a low-volatility stock have only a small amount of time premium. Thus, out-of-the-money options are not so responsive to short-term stock movements and in-the-money options are very responsive. This means that the delta of out-of-the-money options on a low-volatility stock are small—perhaps near zero—and that the delta of a corresponding in-the-money option is large. The graph in Figure 6.10 shows this fact. This is somewhat similar to the way options with only a short life remaining behave, as discussed earlier. On the other hand, if the underlying is *very* volatile, then its out-of-the-money options will be more responsive to changes in the price of the underlying security, and its in-the-money options, since they have time value premium, won't be able to move complete point for point with the underlying. This is also shown in Figure 6.10, and is similar in nature to the behavior of a longer-term option.

Implied volatility, on the other hand, can change very quickly. That is, the market's perception of *future* volatility can change overnight. The following example shows how this happens.

Figure 6.10
COMPARISON OF DELTA AND VOLATILITY

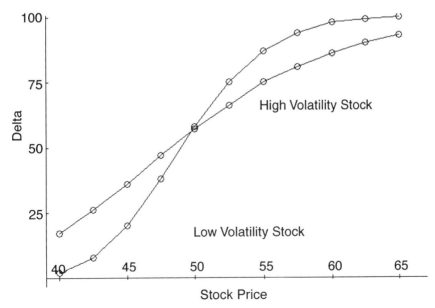

In 1994, Gensia Pharmaceuticals, a fledgling drug company, was a typical high volatility stock. Its normal volatility was about 70 percent annually, which is quite large (the market as a whole is typically between 10 and 15 percent). In July of 1994, the Food and Drug Administration (FDA) announced that it was going to hold hearings on the Gensia's main drug. The stock slipped from a price of about 10 to 8 and then slowly climbed back to 10 over the next month, so the stock was actually *not* volatile, but the options were. The implied volatility of the options immediately jumped dramatically and was up in the 130 to 140 percent area. This was because traders knew that the FDA's ruling would either "make or break" this company. Eventually, in October, the FDA ruled against Gensia, and the stock fell 50 percent in price overnight. However, once that was over, the implied volatility changed overnight from 130 percent back to 70 percent, as traders no longer needed to discount such a volatile event as the FDA ruling in the company's future.

Implied volatility can experience these sudden jumps for a variety of reasons. One is a major corporate announcement, such as the FDA ruling in this example, or as in the lawsuit example that was given earlier. However, another reason for implied volatility to increase dramatically is a *perceived* change in the future price of the underlying. For stocks, this usually means a takeover rumor; for grain futures, it might often mean expectations of bad weather. When these situations occur, there is not such a well-defined reason for the change in volatility (as an FDA ruling, for example). Instead option traders may often find their options changing in price quite dramatically even though there is no apparent news to account for it, and there is no particular price movement by the underlying security either. In essence, the delta of the option is changing dramatically. We can envision this scenario by looking at the previous graph and think of an option's delta lying along one line on the graph and suddenly moving to the other line, without the stock price changing at all.

It is important for the strategist to understand these concepts, so he will therefore also understand that any "neutral" position is not risk-free; it is only neutral with respect to the variable(s) that have been neutralized initially. Subsequent changes in the other variables will adversely affect the neutrality. We saw this in examples regarding delta earlier in this chapter, where an initially delta neutral position became quite nonneutral when the underlying stock price changed.

Vega

This is the nomenclature given to the "Greek" term that describes how a change in volatility affects the price of an option (again assuming that all other variables remain the same). Since the "volatility" that we speaking of here is strictly the volatility that we are plugging into our valuation model, we are really talking about implied volatility. Vega is probably not a familiar term to most option traders, but it should be. For nothing affects the price of an option so dramatically as the volatility. In fact, as has been demonstrated several times in this book, a change in implied volatility can have a large short-term affect on the price of an option.

Since the subject of the chapter is volatility trading, we will be talking about vega a good deal in succeeding sections. For, if we can measure the effect that a change in volatility has on a position, then we will know how much risk we are taking when trading volatility.

Suppose, as we did earlier in this chapter, that we observe that the volatility of a certain security trades in a range between 20 and 34 percent. Furthermore, suppose that volatility is currently 32 percent, and we are considering selling the volatility.

Assume that we establish a position that has a position vega of –5.00. That is, for each one point increase in volatility (i.e., from 32 to 33 percent), we would *lose* $500. This assumes that –5.00 vega is worth $500, which it would be for any option whose unit of trading was $100 per point. If it were a futures option, however, with a larger unit of trading, then the volatility risk would be –5.00 times whatever the unit of trading was.

Vega is stated as a negative number here, indicating that a falling volatility would be profitable for the position, while a rising volatility would be harmful. If we truly believe in our volatility trading range having a top of 34 percent, then our risk due to volatility is two points (from 32 to 34 percent), or $1,000.

If we are looking for volatility to decrease back to 27 percent, for example, which is the center of the volatility's past trading range, then we could make $2,500 ($500 times 5 points of volatility decrease, from 32 to 27 percent) if that happened.

Overall, then, this is a position that has $1,000 of risk and $2,500 of profit potential, as measured by the vega. Of course, as we know, other factors could influence the position, including the fact that implied volatility could trade to higher levels than previously seen. Nevertheless, this example shows that, by using vega, we can measure the volatility risk of a position.

Later in this chapter, we explore ways to isolate volatility from the other variables, in order to produce a position that is neutral to the market with respect to everything except volatility.

Theta

Theta is the measure of time decay on an option. It is stated as a negative number, indicating that as one day passes, the value of an option will decrease in value. Theta is useful in describing just how the passage of time affects a portfolio of options. If you have a lot of short (naked) options in your portfolio, then you will have a very positive theta, because time is your ally. On the other hand, if you own a lot of options, then the theta of your portfolio will be negative, accurately describing the loss that you can expect daily due to time decay.

Rho

Rho measures the effect that a change in interest rates would have on the price of an option. Recall that the interest rate used to value options is the *short-term, risk-free interest rate*, which is normally considered to be the 90-day T-bill rate. Rho is a very small number for short-term options, which is what most traders have in their positions, and is therefore rightfully ignored by most traders. It does have more meaning for longer-term options, such as LEAPS. In fact, the longer the remaining life of the option, the more important interest rates are. Figure 6.11 shows three theoretical value curves for a two-year LEAPS option. The top curve depicts the prices if interest rates are 9 percent, the middle curve if interest rates are 6 percent, and the lower curve if interest rates are 3 percent. You can see from the distance between the curves that there is a significant effect from interest rates.

Figure 6.11
TWO-YEAR LEAPS CALL PRICING CURVE

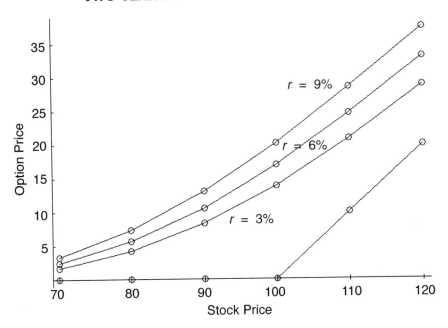

Of course, you wouldn't see short-term interest rates change by 3 percent instantaneously, but you could see such a change over a fairly short period of time if the Fed is aggressively trying to raise or lower rates.

During 1994, the Fed raised the discount rate several times in an attempt to slow down what was perceived to be an overheated economy. During the course of this raising of rates, the risk-free rate rose from 3 to 5.5 percent in about 10 months. Typically, when rates are raised, stock prices falter. Nineteen ninety-four was no exception, as there were three or four fairly steep declines in the broad averages that year, and the averages were off slightly for the year.

What benefitted from this rise in rates was LEAPS options. In fact, the rise in rates over eight months actually negated a large part of the time decay for the longer-term options. Essentially the prices moved from the bottom line on the graph in Figure 6.11 to the middle line, although eight months passed in the interim.

Gamma, Revisited

With the preceding four measures, you can determine how your option positions or your whole option portfolio will react to changes in the marketplace. Still, some theoreticians felt that this was not enough, because two of them—delta and vega—can change so rapidly that it is difficult to neutralize them. So, they thought that if the change in the delta could be measured, for example, it would be useful. This is the *gamma*, which was discussed earlier in this chapter. The gamma measures how much the option's delta changes, when the underlying changes in price by one point. Essentially, it is a measure of how fast the delta changes. Thus, if gamma and delta could be neutralized, then even if the underlying price changed, the option position in question would continue to remain delta neutral. Eventually, if the price of the underlying moved far enough, both gamma and delta would acquire some non-zero value, and the position would lose its neutrality. Still, a delta *and* gamma neutral position has a much better change of remaining delta neutral than does one that was initially only delta neutral.

Gamma is related to the other measures of risk (in fact, as we said earlier, they are *all* interrelated). Figure 6.12 shows how gamma is related to the amount of time left until expiration of the option in question. If there is a lot of time remaining, the gamma is a relatively stable number, whether the option is in- or out-of-the-money. That is shown by the bottom curve on the graph.

This fact can be depicted in tabular form as well. Table 6.1 assumes that the option has one year of life remaining, and that the striking price is 50. It shows the theoretical value of the option and its delta. The gamma is merely the difference in delta for a one-point move in the underlying stock. Thus, in this table, we are showing the observed gamma (the actual difference in deltas), as opposed to the mathematically computed gamma. The two are essentially the same.

You can observe that gamma is fairly stable for this longer-term option. That is, the delta increases rather uniformly as the stock rises

Figure 6.12
GAMMA VERSUS TIME

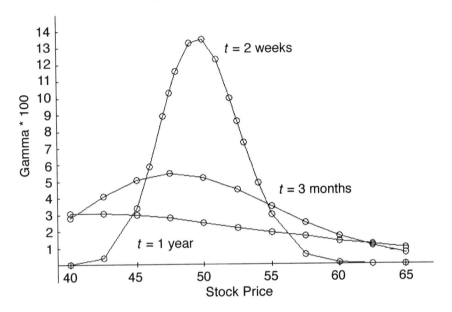

Table 6.1
ONE-YEAR CALL WITH STRIKE PRICE OF 50

Stock Price	Theoretical Value	Delta	Gamma (Observed)
40	1.02	0.24	
41	1.27	0.28	0.04
42	1.57	0.32	0.04
—			
—			
—			
49	4.87	0.62	
50	5.50	0.66	0.04
51	6.18	0.69	0.03
—			
—			
—			
58	11.72	0.87	
59	12.60	0.89	0.02
60	13.50	0.91	0.02

(or decreases uniformly as it falls). However, if we consider a short-term option, then things change substantially. Figure 6.12 shows that the gamma of a one-month option behaves quite violently when the stock is near the striking price. Table 6.2, which is similar to the previous one, shows the situation for a one-month option.

In the case of this short-term option, gamma is stable and nearly zero for options that are only moderately in- or out-of-the-money. This makes logical sense. For example, a moderately out-of-the-money option that has very little life remaining has a delta of nearly zero. Even if the underlying rises by a point, that delta is still going to be very nearly zero. Thus, the one-point rise by the underlying doesn't increase the delta much at all; this is merely another way of saying that gamma is almost zero as well. The same thing holds true for the in-the-money option, because in that case the delta is very nearly 1.00, and a one-point move by the underlying won't change the delta much. Hence, once again, the gamma is nearly zero because the delta doesn't change for a one-point move by the underlying.

Table 6.2
ONE-MONTH CALL WITH STRIKE PRICE OF 50

Stock Price	Theoretical Value	Delta	Gamma (Observed)
41	0.00	0	
42	0.00	0	0
43	0.01	0.01	0.01
—			
—			
—			
48	0.47	0.28	
49	0.81	0.41	0.13
50	1.29	0.55	0.14
51	1.90	0.68	0.13
52	2.64	0.79	0.11
—			
—			
—			
59	9.25	1.00	0
60	10.25	1.00	0

However, near the striking price, things are much more interesting. The delta changes rather quickly, especially for a short-term option or a low-volatility stock. This, too, is logical, for near expiration, the time value of an option disappears quickly. Thus, a small increase in the stock price as it moves higher from the striking price will result in the delta increasing from something just above 0.50 to something very large quite quickly. So, you can see that Gamma is related to time and volatility.

Gamma and Delta Neutral

The next logical step in constructing a price neutral position is to establish one that is neutral both with respect to delta *and* gamma. In this manner, the position will not acquire much risk due to price changes by the underlying instrument. It is a simple matter to construct such a position, although the thought of doing it is somewhat daunting to many traders. There are really only two steps required: (1) create a gamma neutral position, and then (2) neutralize the delta. The second step can always be accomplished with (equivalent) shares or contracts of the underlying security.

Suppose that a stock is trading at 98 at the beginning of the year, and a trader is interested in setting up a gamma and delta neutral position with the following three-month options:

Option	Price	Delta	Gamma
March 100 call	5	0.50	0.030
March 110 call	2	0.25	0.020

Note that gamma is a small number, so you should use at least three decimal places when dealing with it, especially if you are trading large quantities.

Now, in order to create a gamma neutral position, we merely need to divide the two gammas in question to determine the neutral ratio. In this case, a neutral position would be to buy two March 100 calls for every three March 110 calls that we sell, since the gammas are in the same ratio of 2-

to-3 (0.020 to 0.030). This position is going to have a nonzero delta, and in this example we are concerned with neutralizing that delta.

For the purposes of this example, let's assume that our actual trade is to buy 200 March 100 calls and sell 300 March 110 calls. This position has the following ESP, or position delta:

Option	Quantity	Delta	ESP
March 100 call	L 200	0.50	+10,000
March 110 call	S 300	0.25	−7,500
		Position Delta:	+2,500

To neutralize this position, we could sell (short) 2,500 shares of the common stock against the option spread, or we could use our knowledge of equivalent positions and instead sell 25 March 100 calls and buy 25 March 100 puts. If we used the options, our resultant position would be:

> Long 175 March 100 calls
> Short 300 March 110 calls
> Long 25 March 100 puts

Note: The use of the equivalent option position does not change the gamma at all. Neither stock nor the equivalent position has any gamma at all (that is, the gamma of the March 100 call and the March 100 put are equal, and offset each other when we buy and sell an equal quantity).

In the preceding example, it was assumed that we used the gammas to establish a neutral position that was a call ratio write. In fact, we could have done the opposite. Either of these positions would be gamma neutral:

> Buy 2 March 100 calls
> Sell 3 March 110 calls

or

> Sell 2 March 100 calls
> Buy 3 March 110 calls

We would choose one or the other depending on what we were actually trying to accomplish. If we were trying to sell volatility, we would use the first position—the call ratio write. However, if we were attempting to buy volatility, we would use the second position—the backspread. The example did not show that position's exposure to volatility, but from what we have already demonstrated in this chapter, we know that the call ratio write is one of the strategies used when selling volatility, while the backspread is a strategy used for buying volatility. We address the volatility exposure of a gamma–delta neutral position shortly.

First, however, let's examine this position a little more closely so that you can see just what the characteristics are of a position that is gamma and delta neutral. Figure 6.13 is that of the delta of this position for various stock prices. The more horizontal line is where the delta would be after seven days had passed. The other line, which has wider swings, is where the delta would be in 30 days. You can see that, even though the position starts out delta and gamma neu-

Figure 6.13
POSITION DELTA OF RATIO SPREAD

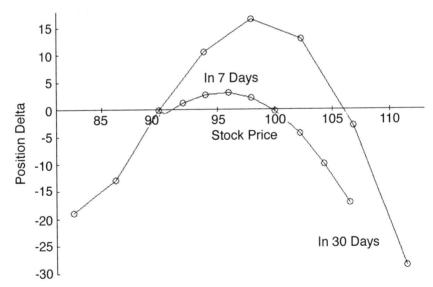

tral, it does acquire a delta after time passes, especially when the underlying stock changes dramatically in price. You must remember, though, that this example position was a rather large position, so the deltas that are acquired are not all *that* large. In fact, the deltas after seven days are rather insignificant—this is the advantage of the gamma–delta neutral position.

Notice that the deltas stay relatively flat over a range—up to a price of about 100 in 7 days, and up to a price of about 107 in 30 days. This means that you would probably not have to adjust your position unless the stock rose above those prices. Above those prices, you begin to get rather delta short. Also, after 30 days, you can see that a large *downside* move will cause the position to acquire a short delta (that's because we are long the 25 March 100 puts). A neutral trader might want to adjust in that case as well.

Suffice it to say that the delta of this example position is much more stable than a typical 1-by-2 call ratio would be (buying 100 March 100 calls and selling 200 March 110 calls, for example, which is only a delta neutral position).

The actual position that we constructed with this gamma–delta neutral position is mostly a call ratio write, but it has a few extra puts added for downside profit potential. Also, the ratio of the long calls to short calls is less than you would have in a strictly delta neutral position (1.75-to-3 instead of 1-to-2), so the position doesn't have as much upside exposure to naked options.

In case you were wondering how this gamma–delta neutral position looked, from a profit and loss standpoint, Figure 6.14 shows the profitability at expiration (straight lines), and in 30 days (curved line). This graph assumes that volatility remains the same, so the profits and losses are accruing strictly from stock price movement and from the passage of time. In reality, we would only take such a position if we were expecting volatility to decrease. We will next see how *that* event would affect the profitability.

This example position initially had an exposure to rising volatility. In other words, the position is short volatility, or in Greek terms, it has a negative *vega*. This is what we would want if we were selling volatility. In order to see how these statements are quantified, let's expand on the previous example by now including volatility in our calculations.

Figure 6.14
PROFIT OF RATIO SPREAD

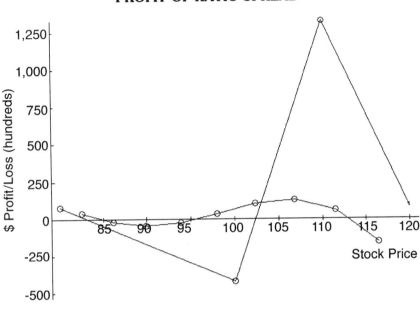

Let's make one more assumption about this position. Let's assume that the trader had observed that volatility typically traded in a range between 20 and 30 percent for this stock. Now, with volatility at 30 percent, he wants to establish a gamma–delta neutral position in order to sell the volatility. Our example position is just the ticket.

The data listed below is exactly the same as from the previous example, except that now we can see the vega of each option as well. Remember, the vega is the amount by which the option price would increase for a (instantaneous) one percent increase in implied volatility. The put has been added to the table as well.

Option	Price	Delta	Gamma	Vega
March 100 call	5	0.50	0.030	0.180
March 110 call	2	0.25	0.020	0.150
March 100 put	5⅞	−0.50	0.030	0.180

Our initial position—long 175 March 100 calls, short 300 March 100 calls, and long 25 March 100 puts—was delta and gamma neutral, but it has a volatility exposure. We can easily compute that exposure by using the vega of the options.

Position	Option Vega	Position Vega
L 175 March 100 calls	0.180	+3,150
S 300 March 100 calls	0.150	−4,500
L 25 March 100 puts	0.180	+450
	Total Position Vega:	−900

Note that vega is always expressed as a positive number; thus long option positions (March 100 calls and March 100 puts in this example) have a positive vega, while short option positions have a negative position vega.

The preceding position vega indicates that if implied volatility falls by one percent—from 30 to 29 percent, for example—then the position will profit by $900. That is an instantaneous measure, of course, and it is affected by stock price changes and the passage of time. Figure 6.15 shows

Figure 6.15
PROFIT AND LOSS OF RATIO SPREAD IF VOLATILITY CHANGES

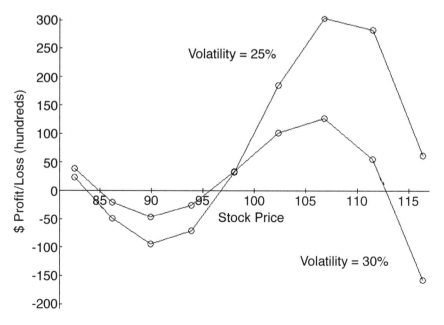

the profit in 30 days, with the lower curve being the same as seen on the previous profit graph—it is the profit if volatility remains unchanged. The higher curve shows what would happen if volatility declined to 25 percent, about back to the middle of the 20–30 percent range that we assumed for this example.

You can see how much extra profit that the decrease in volatility would garner for this position, if the stock is above 98.

This rather detailed example shows how the gamma–delta neutral position can profit nicely from a decrease in implied volatility, while basically maintaining a much more price neutral outlook than a mere call ratio spread would have. We can look at each of our five preferred delta neutral strategies for trading volatility, and see how they would look as gamma–delta neutral positions. The transformation is quite interesting. However, before doing that, we give you one more piece of the general puzzle, and that is how to construct a position that is both gamma and delta neutral and also has the volatility exposure that you feel comfortable with.

This is easily accomplished by solving two equations in two unknowns and then adjusting for any residual delta. As soon as you say, "two equations in two unknowns," many people panic. Relax. There are easy ways to accomplish this. First of all, it's only high school algebra, so if you have a high school or college student in your family, they can probably solve the problem for you. More realistically, there are simple programs that can solve two equations in two unknowns. These are available from shareware, or are possibly even given away. If you still can't find one, call us and we'll send you one if you pay for the postage.

We will continue to use the same example to illustrate this point. We are going to arrive at essentially the same position as we did earlier, but in this case, we are going to approach the whole thing with a specific idea of the risk we want to take. In the earlier example, we merely found the gamma–delta neutral position, and then looked at how large the vega was.

Suppose that you want to establish a call-ratio spread with the March options—as we did earlier—and you want to risk $1,000 for each point that volatility rises. Of course, that means that you will also be making $1,000 for each point that volatility declines, and that is where your profit will come from. In Greek terms, risking $1,000 per point of rising volatility means that the position has a vega of −10.00.

Option	Price	Delta	Gamma	Vega
March 100 call	5	0.50	0.030	0.180
March 110 call	2	0.25	0.020	0.150

Let x stand for the number of March 100 calls to buy, and y stand for the number of March 110 calls to sell. Remember, we want to be gamma neutral and have a vega of −10. The two equations would then be:

$$\text{Gamma neutral:} \quad 0.030x + 0.020y = 0$$
$$\text{Vega risk:} \quad 0.180x + 0.150y = -10$$

Solving, we get $x = 222$, and $y = -333$. That means we should buy 222 of the March 100 calls and sell 333 of the March 110 calls. By doing so, our position will have some delta to it. Since we want to be delta neutral, we need to rid ourselves of this delta.

Position	Delta	ESP or Position Delta
Long 222 March 100 calls	0.50	+11,100
Short 333 March 110 calls	0.25	−8,325
Total Position Delta:		+2,775

So we want to either short 2,800 shares, or use the equivalent option position—sell 28 March 100 calls and buy 28 March 100 puts. The resulting position is:

Long 194 March 100 calls
Short 333 March 110 calls
Long 28 March 110 puts

Hence, this position is very similar to the one from the earlier examples. It is slightly larger because we wanted vega risk to be $1,000 per point, whereas it was $900 per point in the other example.

Now that the theory for determining an appropriate position has been set forth, we can look at the other strategies for trading volatility. The preceding example is a little simplistic in that we have limited our choices of calls to use in the spread to just the two shown—the March 100 and the March 110. In reality, when we are looking at ways to sell volatility, we have many options to choose from. While it is reasonable to expect that we would use the at-the-money call as the long side of the spread, there are still several choices as to which out-of-the-money call to sell. Usually the strategist can narrow the selection process down to very few choices, but as we shall see in the next example, there are times when the selection of the "wrong" options changes the position to something the strategist doesn't really want.

For selling volatility, the one strategy that interests most people is the short naked combo. What happens to this position when you neutralize gamma? The following example illustrates the situation. We start out by showing you a gamma–delta neutral position, with specific vega risk, that is based on a sell combo.

Assume that, as in the previous examples, a trader wants to sell volatility that is currently at the 30 percent level, but normally trades in a range of 20 to 30 percent, and he wants $1,000 of volatility risk per point of volatility increase. However, in this example, he wants to use a sell combo to approach the problem. Recall that we prefer to use a combo (two striking prices) rather than a straddle as the short position in these cases.

With the stock at 98, the trader is considering selling the March 95 put and March 105 call as a sell combo, and then he is looking to hedge that sale by buying out-of-the-money options. In this example, he is going to use the Feb 90 puts and Feb 110 calls as the out-of-the-money combo to purchase as a hedge. When he buys an out-of-the-money combo such as this to protect the short combo, he is said to be buying the "wings."

The following data exists for XYZ: 98, on January 2nd:

Option	Delta	Gamma	Vega
Feb 90 put	−0.18	0.025	0.096
March 95 put	−0.35	0.027	0.167
March 105 call	0.37	0.028	0.170
Feb 110 call	0.18	0.024	0.095

Everything is expressed as a positive number, except for the deltas of the puts. The trader will have two equations as before—one for gamma and one for vega. But it appears as if he has four unknowns, since there are four options listed before. In reality, though, he can consider this as two unknowns, one being the March sell combo, and the other being the Feb combo to be purchased as a hedge. With this simplification, he substitutes the sum of the components in the equation.

So, let x = the number of March combos to sell, and y = the number of Feb combos to buy. The two equations then become:

Gamma neutral: $(0.027 + 0.028)x + (0.025 + 0.024)y = 0$
Vega risk: $(0.167 + 0.170)x + (0.096 + 0.095)y = -10$

Solving this equation, we get $x = -81$ and $y = 91$. That is, if the trader sells 81 of the March combos, he should buy 91 of the Feb combos as a hedge. If he wants, he can calculate the position gamma and position vega to ensure that they satisfy his criteria—gamma neutral and vega risk of -10.

The delta of this position can be computed as:

Position	Delta	ESP (Position Delta)
Long 91 Feb 90 puts	−0.18	−1,638
Short 81 March 95 puts	−0.35	+2,835
Short 81 March 105 calls	0.37	−2,997
Long 91 Feb 110 calls	0.18	1,638
Total Position Delta:		−162

Thus, the position is essentially delta neutral. If the trader wanted to be really picky, he could buy 100 or 200 shares of the underlying to neutralize that delta, but as a practical matter, it is not necessary.

The position that is derived in the example is a little different than you might expect. The "normal" part is that the sale of a combo is hedged by buying a combo that consists of further out-of-the-money options. What is unusual, though, is that the long options expire before the short options do. With this configuration, margin considerations can be considerably different. With futures options, the long options are considered to "cover" the short options until the longs expire, so the margin is merely the spread requirements. However, with equity or index options, which continue to operate with arcane and illogical margin requirements, the short options are considered naked (unless market maker requirements are obtained—that is, the trader is trading for an exchange member).

Having to margin the short options as naked options makes the margin requirement very large—much, much larger than the risk involved. Obviously, no matter how much the underlying moves prior to expiration of the long options—the Februarys in this example— those long options will protect against large losses. That is, the losses are limited. For the collateral requirements *not* to recognize that fact is preposterous.

The margin requirements don't detract from the profit potential of the position itself, although they certainly do lower the *rate* of return. Figure 6.16 shows how the preceding example position would look at February expiration, that is, the expiration of the long

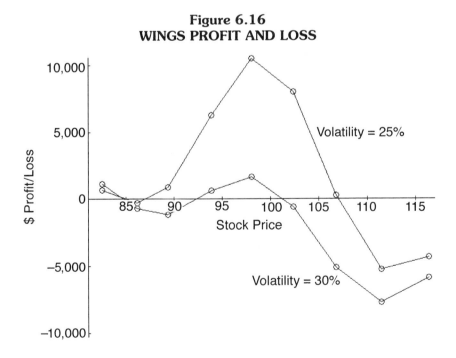

Figure 6.16
WINGS PROFIT AND LOSS

options. The lower curved line depicts the profits if the volatility remained unchanged at 30 percent, whereas the upper curved line shows the larger profits available if volatility declines to 25 percent—in the middle of the supposed range of implied volatility. Once again, it is apparent that, even though the position is initially gamma–delta neutral, it acquires risk due to the passage of enough time and the movement of the underlying stock. Nevertheless, this position has considerably less risk than the mere sale of a naked combo, which of course has unlimited risk if the underlying should move too far in either direction.

You might be wondering why we used the February options instead of longer-term ones as the hedge for the short combo. The reason is this: *in order to begin with the sale of a naked combo and turn it into a delta neutral* and *gamma neutral position by buying the "wings," it is necessary to have the wings expire before the short combo does.* The following example shows how a gamma–delta neutral position would look if you were to use a longer-term combo on the buy side.

Using the same assumptions as in the previous example as far as volatility and wanting to create a gamma neutral position with vega risk of $1,000 per point are concerned, here are the relevant statistics for XYZ: 98, on January 2nd:

Option	Delta	Gamma	Vega
April 90 put	−0.24	0.019	0.170
March 95 put	−0.35	0.027	0.167
March 105 call	0.37	0.028	0.170
April 110 call	0.31	0.022	0.192

Once again, we set up two equations in two unknowns, adding the numbers from each combo. Let x = the number of March combos to sell, and y = the number of April combos to buy. The two equations then become:

Gamma neutral: $(0.027 + 0.028)x + (0.019 + 0.022)y = 0$
Vega risk: $(0.167 + 0.170)x + (0.170 + 0.192)y = -10$

Solving this equation, we get $x = 67$ and $y = -90$. With these data, when we set up and solve the simple set of two equations in two unknowns, we have a solution that gives us a completely different position. Now, x is a positive number, which means that we are supposed to *buy* the March combo and *sell* the April combo. In effect, we are setting up two ratio writes, one with calls and one with puts:

Long 67 March 95 puts
Short 90 April 90 puts

and

Long 67 March 105 calls
Short 90 April 110 calls

This is a totally different position than we had planned on originally, but it is the only way to create a gamma neutral position with the required vega from the four options that we have chosen. Figure 6.17 shows how the position looks in 30 days. Once again, the lower curved line represents the profits and losses if implied volatility remains unchanged, while the higher curved line shows the results if implied volatility decreases to 25 percent.

Note that we haven't really solved the dilemma of margin. Just as in the prior example, we are still short the longer-term options (April options in this case), so the position is going to require a fairly large amount of collateral.

The reason that this position takes on a shape that is somewhat unexpected is that the vega of the April options is so large. In order to create a position that has *negative* vega, which was the original intent here, it is virtually impossible to be able to buy those April options because their vega is so large. The combined vega of the March options is 0.337, but the combined vega of the April options is higher, 0.362. This means that, whenever volatility declines by a point, the March combo will lose about 34 cents, but the April combo will lose even more—36 cents. Thus, it makes no sense to sell the March combo and buy the April combo if we want to make money from declining volatility.

Figure 6.17
PROFIT AND LOSS OF DOUBLE RATIO SPREAD

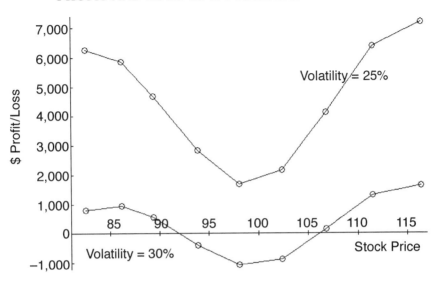

This example points out something very interesting: it is often difficult to "intuit" a gamma neutral position that has the volatility risk that you want. But by using the Greeks, you can see exactly the construct needed to accomplish your goals. In this chapter, we have spent considerable time outlining the groundwork for our strategy: we want to trade volatility and remove as much of the risk as possible due to price changes by the underlying. By using the Greeks, we guarantee that an appropriate position is taken.

I have often seen traders, who want to accomplish the same things as we have outlined in this chapter, take a position that does not work but seems like it should. Typically, if we decide to sell a combo in order to capitalize on an outlook for declining volatility, we will then think that buying the wings that expire at the same time or in a later month will protect us. The previous example shows the fallacy of that thinking. In reality, by buying those wings, we effectively more than cancel out our profit potential from declining volatility.

So far we have seen how two of the more common strategies for selling volatility—the ratio spread and the naked short combo—look when they are transformed into gamma–delta neutral positions. Now we examine how the basic strategies for buying volatility—the long straddle, the backspread, and the calendar spread—can be treated as far as gamma–delta neutral positions are concerned.

The Calendar Spread.   Without going into as much detail as in the previous examples, here is how a calendar spread position that is gamma–delta neutral, with appropriate volatility exposure (vega of +10—note the *plus*, now), would look for XYZ: 100, on January 2nd, with volatility = 20%:

> Long 52 June 100 calls
> Short 44 March 100 calls
> Long 15 June 100 puts

So this looks something like a normal calendar spread, except we are long a few extra calls on the long side, plus long a few puts as well. This is a very attractive position, because it can make money if the underlying moves far enough in either direction, while also profiting if volatility increases (which is our basic assumption). Moreover, the short calls hedge the position if the underlying remains stagnant.

The profitability of this calendar spread is shown in Figure 6.18. The curved lines show the profit at March expiration, the near-term expiration. The lower line on the graph shows the results if volatility remains unchanged at 20 percent, while the higher line on the graph shows the better results that could be expected if implied volatility increased to 25 percent.

The Backspread and the Long Straddle.   These are the other two basic strategies that we use when we want to buy volatility (i.e., when we want to have a *positive* vega). I do not believe that, if we are using these strategies, we should be so concerned with gamma neutrality. When these two strategies acquire a delta, it means we are

Figure 6.18
CALENDAR

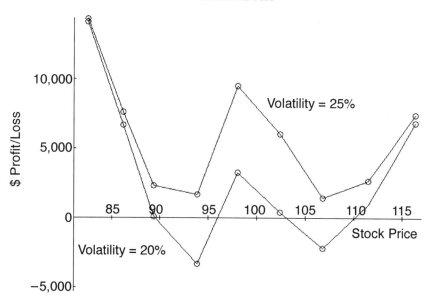

making money, for the underlying instrument is moving. The neutralizing of price movement was much more important for the volatility selling strategies, because a large stock movement could be
devastating in that case. But here, a large movement will be helpful,
so I generally feel that delta neutral, with the appropriate volatility
risk, is sufficient.

Suppose we want to establish a backspread because we think that volatility,
which is currently at 20 percent and at the low end of its historical range,
can go higher. The following data describe the situation for XYZ: 100, on
January 2nd; volatility = 20%:

Option	Delta	Gamma	Vega
March 90 call	0.91	0.018	0.079
March 100 call	0.57	0.043	0.180

Solving these two equations gives us a *delta* neutral position, with a vega of +10. That is, if volatility increases, we will make $1,000 per point of volatility increase.

$$\text{Delta neutral:}\quad 0.91x + 0.57y = 0$$
$$\text{Vega exposure:}\ 0.079x + 0.18y = 10$$

Solving, we get $x = -48$ and $y = 76$. That is, the desired position is:

Long 76 March 100 calls
Short 48 March 90 calls

This is a typical backspread position. Incidentally, this has a fairly small gamma anyway, even though we didn't neutralize it. We can compute that the position gamma of this position is +2.40. That is, if the underlying rises on point, the position delta, which is neutral to begin with, will increase to 2.40, which means that the position will be delta long 240 shares. On the other hand, if the underlying declines by one point, the delta will become −2.40, or the position will then be delta short 240 shares.

The farther that the underlying rises, the more the delta will increase; the farther it declines, the more the delta will decrease. Eventually, you will have a position that has quite a large delta—either positive in a rising market, or negative in a falling market. However, that is a "good" problem, because you will have profits after large moves by the underlying. I feel the same way about the long straddle position as well; it's not necessary to zero out the gamma.

If you prefer a gamma–delta neutral strategy for trading volatility from the long side, then I encourage you to use the calendar spread, as shown in a recent example.

Even More Advanced Constructions

The neutral positions that were described earlier were both gamma and delta neutral. In theory, you could construct positions that had neutrality with respect to as many variables as you might want to consider. Eventually, though, you have to assume some risk some-where—if you're a commission-paying trader—if you intend to make money; only market makers can be neutral with respect to *all* variables, for their intention is to buy on the bid and sell on the offer and take no further risk.

In order to create a position that is neutral with respect to three variables, for example, you would merely have to set up three equations in three unknowns and solve that set of simultaneous equations. For example, you might want to be neutral with respect to gamma and time (theta), but still have volatility risk.

Another risk measure that traders have come to use is the "gamma of the gamma." This measures how fast the gamma changes when the underlying security moves by one point. Thus, many of the more theoretical traders feel they need even *another* measure to help them keep a position neutral with respect to price changes by the underlying security. This shows just how important they consider price neutrality to be.

So the three measures that you might want to use in your equation would be gamma, gamma of the gamma, and vega. You would still neutralize delta at the end, as was done in the previous examples. In this manner you arrive at a position that is *very* neutral with respect to price movement, but still has volatility risk, a risk we want, in the context of this chapter.

The concept can be carried even further—four equations in four unknowns, for example (gamma, time or theta, volatility or vega, and gamma of the gamma), with delta being neutralized at the end. Such a position would be totally impossible to reason out, without using the arithmetic equations.

Without going into too much detail, one of the previous examples can be used to construct a position that is neutral with respect to four variables, and has volatility risk. We will once again begin with the thought of selling the March 95–March 105 combo and using the February 90–February 100 combo as protection. As it turns out, this is the way the position looks after neutralizing the necessary components for XYZ: 98, on January 2nd:

> Long 28 Feb 90 puts
> Short 145 March 95 puts
> Short 45 March 105 calls
> Long 82 Feb 110 calls
> Short 5,400 shares of XYZ

This position has these qualities:

Delta neutral
Gamma neutral
Theta neutral
Gamma of gamma neutral
Volatility risk: $1,000 per point

There is risk to the upside in this position, but the 82 long calls mostly offset the risk of the 45 short calls and the 5,400 short stock. To the downside, there is more obvious risk, as the 5,400 short stock and the 28 long puts are less of an absolute hedge against all those short March 95 puts.

It is not normally necessary for the small- or medium-sized investor to attempt to get this neutral, but the example shows that it can be done.

Summary

This concludes the section on using the Greeks to neutralize positions, so that the volatility risk can more accurately be assessed and assumed. It is really not too complicated, as the examples show. Even with all of this preparation, though, you should realize that you can still lose money in these positions, especially if naked options are involved.

The examples that we used were theoretical, whereas most of the examples in this book have been real ones, attempting to demonstrate the viability of the various approaches in the context of actual market action. However, in this section, since the concept is so new to many traders, we felt that the theoretical examples quite accurately depict the ways in which these positions are analyzed and established. The fact that no actual examples were given does not mean that this approach is strictly a theoretical one. Quite the contrary. In fact, the next time that you see OEX options getting overly cheap or expensive, you may want to try this approach, for it works especially well with broad-based index options. It is also quite appropriate in the futures markets, where volatility sometimes jumps quite high on expectations of drought, flood, or other such conditions.

TRADING THE VOLATILITY SKEW

Up to this point, we have examined the feasibility of trading volatility based upon a two-pronged approach: (1) implied volatility is at the end of its range, and (2) it is at a more extreme level than historical volatility. The idea is that implied volatility will move at some point to the middle of its range, and the volatility trader will profit.

Despite all the careful work laid out in this chapter up to this point, it is possible to lose money by trading volatility in the manner described. For example, if you're selling volatility, you may find that it breaks out of the previous range and trades much higher. This would cause losses, even though the position was essentially delta and gamma neutral. This type of volatility increase has occurred many times in the past. Sometimes, volatility increases occur from an already high volatility.

In the summer of 1991, soybeans had broken *down* from a price of about 575 to 525. Volatilities fell toward the lower end of their range, as is the custom for grain options, declining grain prices are usually accompanied by declining implied volatilities. Then, in July a drought scare developed and beans rallied back up toward 600. This rally brought implied volatilities to the top of their previous range, well above the historical volatilities at that time.

At this point, I established gamma–delta neutral call ratio spreads that had excellent profit potential if volatility declined. What happened was that the drought scare was exacerbated for about another week, during which time beans rallied to nearly 650 and implied volatility skyrocketed to levels way beyond the previous range.

This move was too large even for the gamma–delta neutral position, and I was forced to make adjustments to protect the position. Within a few days it rained, and beans traded down the limit for two days before stabilizing in the 550 to 575 area. Volatilities declined at that point, but it was too late—the adjustments had been so unprofitable that they made the whole position a loss.

One must be mindful of the fundamentals when trading volatility, and when the soybean position was established, I felt that the drought was not serious—I felt it was probably just the typical mid-summer hype that the grain markets often experience. Moreover, I also thought that the implied volatility being at the high end of the range was sufficiently accounting for the stories that were circulating. Obviously this was wrong, as losses, albeit limited ones, were taken.

In a like manner, losses can be taken when volatility is traded from the long side as well. We have already given an example of when gold's volatility dropped to then-unheard-of levels during 1994 and 1995, causing losses for buyers of volatility.

The major problem in these situations was that the historical and implied volatilities never converged, at least not for a while. In fact, that is one of the major problems with trading volatility: *there is no guarantee that implied and historical volatilities will converge, or that they will converge during the lifetime of your position.* As a result, some volatility traders prefer to use another approach. They prefer to look for situations where there is volatility skewing, and trade those.

When different options on the same underlying instrument have substantially different implied volatilities, then a *volatility skew* is said to exist. Certain markets have a volatility skew almost continuously—metals and grain options, for example, and OEX and S&P 500 options since the crash of 1987. Others have a skew that appears occasionally. When we talk about a volatility skew, we are describing a group of options that has a pattern of differing volatilities, not just a few scattered different volatilities. In fact, for options on *any* stock, future, or index, there will be slight discrepancies between the various options of different striking prices and expiration dates. However, in a volatility skew situation, we expect to see rather large discrepancies between the implied volatilities of individual options, especially those with the same expiration date, and there is usually a pattern to those discrepancies. The following examples demonstrate the patterns that we expect to see.

The following example shows the type of volatility skew that has existed in OEX and S&P 500 options—and many other broad-based index options—since the crash of 1987. This data is very typical of the skew that has lasted for over eight years. For OEX: 586 in December 1995:

Option	Implied Volatility (%)
Jan 560	15.8
Jan 565	14.9
Jan 570	14.0
Jan 575	13.2
Jan 580	12.5
Jan 585	11.8
Jan 590	11.2
Jan 595	10.7
Jan 600	10.5

Note that we have not labeled the options in this table as puts or calls. That's because a put and a call with the same striking price and expiration date must have the same implied volatility, or else there will be a riskless arbitrage available.

In the preceding volatility skew, note that the lower strikes have the highest implied volatility. This is called a *reverse* volatility skew. It is sometimes caused by bearish expectations for the underlying, but that is usually a short-term event. For example, when a commodity undergoes a sharp decline, the reverse volatility skew will appear and last until the market stabilizes.

However, the fact that the reverse skew has existed for so long in broad-based options is reflective of more fundamental factors. After the crash of 1987 and the losses that traders and brokerage firms suffered, the margin requirements for selling naked options were raised. Some firms even refused to let customers sell naked options at all. This lessened the supply of sellers. In addition, as we pointed out in Chapter 3, money managers have turned to the purchase of index puts as a means of insuring their stock portfolios against losses. This is an increase in demand for puts, especially out-of-the-money puts. Thus, we have a simultaneous increase in demand and reduction in supply. This is what has caused the options with lower strikes to have increased implied volatilities.

In addition, money managers also sometimes sell out-of-the-money calls as a means of financing the purchase of their put insurance. We have described this strategy in previous chapters as the "collar." This action exerts extra selling pressure on out-of-the-money calls, and that accounts for some of the skew in the upper strikes, where there is low implied volatility.

A *forward* volatility skew has the opposite look from the reverse skew, as you might expect. It typically appears in various futures option markets, especially in the grain option markets, although it is often prevalent in the metals option markets, too. It is less frequent in coffee, cocoa, orange juice, and sugar, but does appear in those markets with some frequency.

The following data shows how a forward volatility skew looks for March corn: 745:

Option	Implied Volatility (%)
March 675	15.8
March 700	16.2
March 725	17.7
March 750	19.8
March 775	21.9
March 800	23.8
March 825	24.8
March 850	26.9
March 875	28.8
March 900	30.7

Notice that in a *forward* skew, the volatilities increase at higher striking prices.

The forward skew tends to appear in markets where expectations of upward price movements are overly optimistic. This does not mean that everyone is necessarily bullish, but that they are afraid that a very large upward move—perhaps several limit up days—could occur and seriously damage the naked option seller of out-of-the-money calls.

Occasionally, you will see *both* types of skews at the same time, emanating from the striking price in both directions. This is rather rare, but it has been seen in the metals markets at times.

The following skew was taken from actual gold option prices for April gold: 390:

Option	Implied Volatility (%)
April 350	10.7
April 360	10.0
April 370	8.8
April 380	8.2
April 390	8.0
April 400	9.6
April 410	11.2
April 420	13.1
April 430	14.9
April 440	16.6
April 450	18.3

Notice that the at-the-money options are the least expensive, while the out-of-the-money options are more expensive, both at lower strikes *and* at higher strikes. This is a dual volatility skew.

The interesting thing about volatility skew situations is that you can ideally establish positions where you sell expensive options and buy cheap options on the *same* underlying instrument simultaneously. Then, if the actual price movement of the underlying adheres to normal patterns, the position should profit. In effect, you are being offered an excellent opportunity to trade two differing volatilities on the same underlying—it's as close to a sure thing as you'll find anywhere.

Price Distributions

Before getting into the specifics of trading the volatility skew, let's discuss stock price distributions for a minute. Stock and commodity price movements are often described by mathematicians as adhering to standard *statistical* distributions. The most common type of statistical distribution is the normal distribution. This is familiar even to many people who have never taken a statistics course.

Figure 6.19 shows the "bell curve," which is a graph of the normal distribution. The center of the graph is where the average member of the population resides. That is, most of the people are near

Figure 6.19
BELL CURVE OR NORMAL DISTRIBUTION

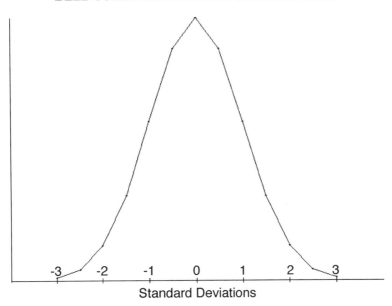

Standard Deviations

the average, and very few are way above or way below the average. The normal distribution is used in many ways to describe the total population: results of IQ tests or average adult height, for example. In the normal distribution, results can be infinitely above or below the average, also called the median. Thus, this is not useful for describing stock price movements, since stock prices can rise to infinity, but can only fall to zero.

Thus, another statistical distribution is generally used to describe stock price movements. It is called the *lognormal distribution*, and it is pictured in Figure 6.20. The height of the curve at various points essentially represents the probability of stock prices being at those levels. The highest point on the curve is right at the average, reflecting the fact that most results are near that price, as they are with the normal distribution shown earlier. Or, in terms of stock prices, if the average is defined as today's price, then most of the time a stock will be relatively near the average after some period of time. The lognormal

Figure 6.20
LOGNORMAL DISTRIBUTION

Current

Underlying Price

distribution allows that stock prices could rise infinitely, although with great rarity, but cannot fall below zero. In fact, they rarely fall to zero.

Mathematicians have spent a great deal of time trying to accurately define the actual distribution of stock price movements, and there is some disagreement over what that distribution really is. However, the lognormal distribution is generally accepted as a reasonable approximation of the way that prices move. Those prices don't have to be just stock prices, either. They could be futures prices, index prices, or interest rates.

Normally, option prices reflect the distribution of the prices that the underlying is expected to follow. For example, the Black-Scholes model is based on a lognormal distribution of prices. However, when a skew is present, the skew is projecting a *different* sort of distribution for prices. Figure 6.21 is a graph of the forward skew, such as you see in the grains and metals. Compare it to the graph of the lognormal distribution in Figure 6.20. You can see that this one has a distinctly

Figure 6.21
FORWARD SKEW

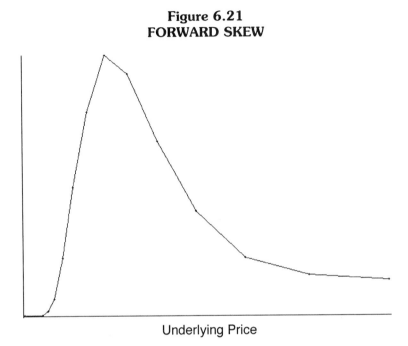

Underlying Price

different shape: the right-hand side of the graph is up in the air, indicating that this skewed distribution implies that there is a far greater chance of the underlying rising by a huge amount. Also, on the left side of the graph, the skewed distribution is squashed down, indicating that there is far less probability of the underlying falling in price than the lognormal distribution would indicate.

The reverse volatility skew is shown is Figure 6.22. Note that it is also different from the regular lognormal distribution. In this case, however, the left-hand side of the graph is lifted higher, indicating that the probability of prices dropping is greater than the lognormal distribution implies that it is. Similarly, the graph on the right flattens out on the right-hand side, which means that it is insinuating that prices won't rise as much as the lognormal distribution says they will.

It is my opinion that skewed volatilities are *not* the correct picture of the way markets move, and that the lognormal distribution is a much truer picture. Therefore, when we find significant volatility

Figure 6.22
REVERSE SKEW

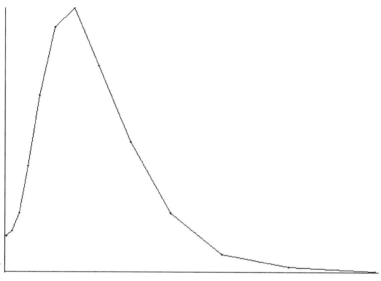

Underlying Price

skewing in a particular group of options, we have a good trading opportunity. A neutral option spread position can be established that has a statistical advantage because the two options have differing implied volatilities.

The best place to look for this volatility skewing is in the options with the same expiration date, as shown in the previous tables of OEX and corn options. The reason that I prefer using options with the same expiration date as the basis of volatility skew trading is that, even if the skew doesn't disappear by expiration, the very fact that the options must go to parity at expiration means that they will then have behaved in a manner similar to the underlying instrument—that is, they will have adhered to the lognormal distribution, not to the skewed distribution.

What we want to accomplish by trading the volatility skew is to capture the implied volatility differential between the two options in question, without being overly exposed to price movements by the underlying instrument. We could use the simple bull or bear spreads, but they are too price dependent. Accordingly, the best strategies are the vertical spread strategies: ratio writes or backspreads.

Trading the Positive Skew

When the volatility skew is *positive*, as it is with grain options, then it is the *call* ratio spread (Figure 6.23) or the *put* backspread (Figure 6.24) that are the preferred strategies. The reason that these are the two chosen strategies is because, in each one, we are buying options with a lower striking price and selling options with a higher striking price. Since the higher strikes have the inflated volatility in a positive volatility skew, these strategies offer a statistical advantage. This advantage arises from the fact that we are buying the "cheap" option(s) and selling the relatively "expensive" option(s) simultaneously, on the same underlying.

Figure 6.23
CALL RATIO SPREAD

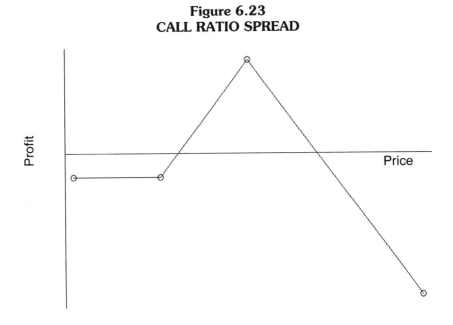

Figure 6.24
PUT BACKSPREAD

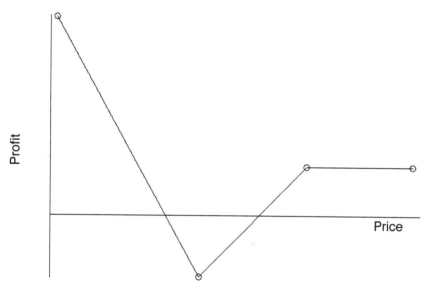

The following data is excerpted from the previous example of the forward volatility skew, using March corn options: 745:

Option	Implied Volatility (%)
March 750	19.8
March 775	21.9

Either one of the two following strategies is delta neutral and takes advantage of the forward skew. The following call ratio spread would be an attractive strategy for trading this volatility skew:

Buy 10 Corn March 750 call
and sell 20 Corn March 775 calls

On the other hand, if you felt that volatility could explode and therefore harm the position, you might want to use a put backspread:

Buy 20 Corn March 750 puts
Sell 10 Corn March 775 puts

Once again, you would be buying options at the lower strike and selling the relatively more expensive options at the higher strike.

You could use the past history of implied volatility to help you decide which strategy to use. If you see that the current implieds are in the lower percentiles, then you might favor the backspread, because there is a better chance that implieds might increase while you have the position in place. On the other hand, if implieds are already near the high end of their historic trading range, then you might favor the call ratio spread, since it will profit if implied volatility declines.

When you trade the volatility skew in this manner, there are several ways in which you can profit. First, you would profit almost immediately if the volatility skew disappeared, because your options would then have the same implied volatility. That is a rather rare occurrence, but it sometimes does happen. Second, you would profit if the underlying were within your profit range at expiration, and, third, you could profit if implied volatilities move in your favor (i.e., higher if you own the backspread or lower if you have the call ratio spread in place). You may want to refer back to Figure 6.3 for another picture of the profitability of this strategy.

The summer of 1995 was a particularly good time for trading the volatility skew in grain options, even though grain prices rose during that time period. The skew was so steep that it presented traders with a good statistical edge. For Sep corn: 278 in early June 1995:

Option	Price	Implied Volatility (%)
Sep 280 call	13½	26.5
Sep 300 call	8	31.5

This is an unusually large difference in implied volatility for two options that are only two striking prices apart. Moreover, implied volatility was in the eighth percentile at the time, thus favoring the ratio spread strategy. Based upon the deltas of the options (not shown), we recommended that customers establish the following basic position:

Long 10 Sep 280 calls
Short 16 Sep 300 calls

This position was established for a small debit of seven points ($350, since one point in grain options is worth $50). Thus, there was very little downside risk. The *upside* risk was theoretically unlimited if corn were to rise too far. The upside breakeven point was approximately 332, so we placed GTC buy stop orders to buy six Sep corn futures at 332 as a means of limiting upside risk. However, since the profit potential was greatest if corn were at 300 at expiration, we were hopeful that the position could be removed for a profit if corn were to rally to 300.

Corn eventually rallied into the 295 area in mid-to-late July, and the position acquired a nice unrealized profit at the time, and the volatility skew had dampened somewhat—27.5 percent for the Sep 280 call as compared to 30.7 percent for the Sep 300 call. Thus, the profit resulted from a flattening of the volatility skew *and* a favorable movement by the underlying. Also, implied volatilities were about at the same *absolute* level—in the high 20s—so that was not much of a contributor to the profit.

When trading the volatility skew with ratio spreads, I generally prefer to use an at-the-money option for the long side of the spread and out-of-the-moneys for the short side of the spread. That is exactly the way the previous example is constructed. In this manner, we will normally have a profit if the underlying moves to the striking price of the spread. In fact, if the volatility skew has disappeared, or at least flattened somewhat, by the time that happens, we should have a very good profit.

It is always something of an art to decide when to take the profit, should it occur. If you are fortunate enough to have the underlying move to the striking price—as Sep corn did in the previous example—then you are tempted to leave the position as is, in order to capture even more profits should the underlying remain near that higher strike. What I recommend is to take one of these two actions: (1) take a profit on half of your position, or (2) set some mental stops that are close enough to the current price so that you will still lock in a good profit if they are hit.

Continuing with the same Sep corn example, we can demonstrate the usefulness of tightening mental stops when a decent unrealized profit has built up. By August 1st, Sep corn had fallen all the way back to 280, and the options, which expired in mid-August, eventually all expired worthless, as corn was at 275 by that time. If there had not been an attempt to lock in some profits with mental stops, the entire unrealized profit would have been lost and a loss equal to the initial debit would have resulted.

So, when corn was in the high 290s, we set mental stops at 290 and 310, intending to remove the position if either of those prices was hit. On the other hand, if corn were to remain between those two prices, greater profits would result. As we have already explained, corn fell in price, so we removed the position when it reached 290 and took a profit. It wasn't as large a profit as had been available when corn was near 300, but it was still a profit.

Of course, one example doesn't demonstrate an entire strategy, but to show that the volatility skew trading does give you a good advantage, I summarized our ratio writes from *The Option Strategist* newsletter over the past four years. All of these were based on volatility skews. There were 39 of them, 24 of which were profitable, 10 of which lost the small initial debit, and 5 of which suffered larger losses. Larger losses can arise from (1) increasing implied volatility, (2) a gap much higher by the futures, (3) or a reversal in trend after an adjustment has been made (a "whipsaw"). None of the five losses was caused by a gap; rather, the cause was either a quick move resulting in exploding volatility, or a whipsaw. The average position was held for 53 days and the average profit on the 39 positions in this strategy was over 50 percent on an annualized basis, assuming that exchange minimum margin requirements were used. Thus, the ratio spread strategy can be quite profitable when employed in our stated manner: there is a forward volatility skew, and implied volatility is relatively high to begin with.

The companion strategy for the forward volatility skew, used when implied volatility is relatively low, is the put backspread. This strategy is used less frequently than the call ratio spread, partially because of the mechanics of the forward volatility skew itself. The only time that implied volatility drops in the grains is when prices have dropped. Since the put ratio backpsread makes its best profits when profits drop even further, it is not often a viable strategy to establish at already-low price levels. However, it is a statistically viable strategy to adopt when the two predominant conditions exist simultaneously: (1) a forward volatility skew, and (2) implied volatility is low.

Trading the Negative Skew

When implied volatilities are skewed in the negative direction, two strategies that are the exact opposite of the previous ones are appropriate: either the *put* ratio spread (Figure 6.25), or the *call* backspread (Figure 6.26). In these two strategies, we are buying the option at the higher strike—the one with the lower implied volatility—and selling the option with the lower strike, which has the higher implied volatility. Once again, there is a statistical advantage, since we are selling an option that is "expensive" on the same security on which we are buying an option. If implied volatility is low, the call backspread is the preferred strategy, but if implied volatility is near the high end of its range, then the put ratio spread would be the better choice of a strategy to trade the reverse skew.

The reverse volatility skew is very prevalent in broad-based index options, although it wasn't always so (prior to 1987, there was a slightly forward skew), and it may therefore disappear once again

Figure 6.25
PUT RATIO SPREAD

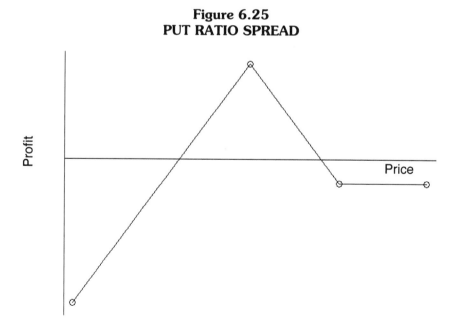

Figure 6.26
CALL BACKSPREAD

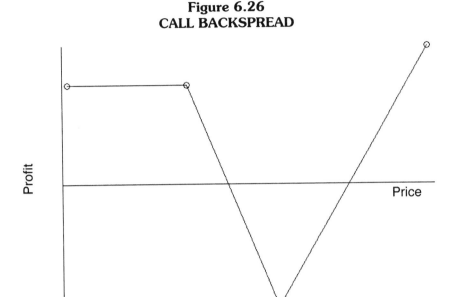

someday. Nevertheless, it appears with some frequency in futures options markets that experience a sudden decline in price. In recent years, it has appeared in cattle, T-bond, and crude oil options. In these cases, the reverse skew disappears as soon as the underlying commodity stabilizes in price. However, with the broad-based options, the skew has persisted for years, mostly due to the margin and supply/demand factors that were discussed earlier.

In Chapter 4, we pointed out that when OEX implied volatility is low, straddle buying is a good strategy. However, we can now refine that statement because of the volatility skew: backspreads are the preferred strategy in OEX options when implied volatility is low and the reverse volatility skew is present. Since 1987, the call backspread in OEX options has served very well as a strategy with which to take advantage of the reverse volatility skew. This is partly due to the fact that OEX options have, for the most part, traded near the lower end of their volatility range. If you wait for those opportunities to establish the backspread, the rewards are worthwhile.

The subsequent story follows a backspread through several months, pointing out how to make adjustments, how to take profits, and when to close the spread.

In February of 1995, the implied volatility of OEX options was relatively low. This can sometimes be considered a market sell signal, but is better interpreted as a precursor of a market explosion in one direction or the other. At that time, the following data was pertinent and backspreads were established for ourselves and our customers:

OEX: 455 on February 23, 1995

With OEX at 455, we would buy calls with a strike of 455 or 460 and sell calls with strikes of 445 or below. These options should generally have about three months or more of life remaining, so time decay won't be a major factor right away. In addition, I sometimes like to purchase some out-of-the-money puts, in order to add some more downside potential to the position, particularly if the striking price of the calls that are being sold is relatively near to the current price.

Option	Price	Implied Volatility (%)
May 460 call	7	9.9
May 445 call	16½	11.7
April 445 put	3½	10.8

The basic backspread position that was established was:

Buy 20 OEX May 460 calls
Sell 10 OEX May 445 calls
Buy 10 OEX April 445 puts
Net debit: 10 points

The May 445 calls being sold were trading with a higher implied volatility than that of the May 460s being bought, the natural by-product of establishing a call backspread when there is a reverse volatility skew. In this case, I used the *April* puts for the extra downside potential because they were a cheaper price. In order to keep the calculations of credits and debits simple, we address commissions at the end of these examples.

Figure 6.27 shows how the position would look at April expiration with volatility still at the low end of the range (middle curved line), at April expiration with increased volatility (higher curved line), and if it dropped to 6 percent (lowest line).

The collateral required for a backspread is essentially the amount of risk. That is, if the underlying expired exactly at the higher strike at expiration, we would realize the maximum loss. That is the margin requirement. Stated in another manner, we must have collateral equal to the difference in the strikes for each of the short calls, plus we must pay for any debit involved. If the position is established for a credit, as is often the case, then the credit may be used to reduce the spread requirement. In this case, the difference in the strikes is 15 points ($1,500), and since we have 10 bear spreads, the collateral required is $15,000, plus the $1,000 debit of the position.

Now, a position such as the one established in this example, is delta neutral to begin with, but has volatility risk *and* it has gamma risk. That is, it is not gamma neutral. This means that as soon as

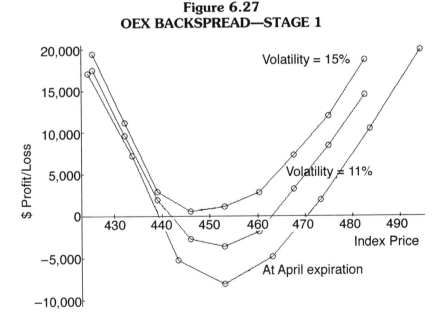

Figure 6.27
OEX BACKSPREAD—STAGE 1

OEX begins to rise, the position will become delta long, or if OEX should fall, the position will become delta short.

When OEX moves, we must decide how to adjust. This problem was addressed earlier when we discussed the handling of long straddle positions. When a volatility skew is involved, we must look at both the volatility skew and the level of implied volatility, in order to determine what to do with the position.

If OEX moves up, for example, and the position becomes quite delta long, we will probably have a profit. If we don't do something, and OEX subsequently falls in price, we will lose his profit. So, we would probably opt to take at least a partial profit if volatility has increased. However, if the volatility situation is about the same as it was originally, we might decide to reneutralize the position. This is quite easily accomplished with backspreads: we merely have to roll the long calls up to a higher strike. This action takes a realized profit on the calls we originally owned, while bringing a credit into our account. Furthermore, we are then positioned to make money if OEX subsequently falls or rises farther.

By the end of March, OEX had moved up to nearly 475, and the position was very delta long. Implied volatility had not really increased, nor had the volatility skew disappeared. In fact, this was the situation:

Option	Price	Implied Volatility (%)
May 475 call	7½	10.9
May 460 call	18	13.0
May 445 call	32	16.0

At first glance, it looks like implied volatility has increased substantially for the options that we own—and it has. But that increase is due to the volatility skew, not to any general increase in implied volatility. Notice that the now-at-the-money May 475 call has a volatility only slightly higher than the May 460s implied was when the position was established (10.9 percent as compared 9.9 percent). The volatility skew is what is causing the in-the-money calls (i.e., options with lower strikes) to have inflated implied volatility. We discuss this phenomenon in more detail later.

The fact that the at-the-money call was still cheap was the overriding factor in my decision to roll the calls up, rather than close the position, which at the time had an unrealized profit of about $3,500 (the April 445 put was still selling for about one point). When rolling up, we should normally buy more than we sell in order to keep the position delta neutral. However, sometimes we're swayed by technical factors, and the market seemed overbought to us, so we only rolled an equal number:

> Bought 20 May 475 calls at 7½ opening
> Sold 20 May 460 calls at 18 closing
> Net credit of roll: 210 points ($21,000)

After this adjustment, the position is:

> Long 20 May 475 calls
> Short 10 May 445 calls
> Long 10 April 445 puts
> Net credit to date: 200 points

Figure 6.28 shows the adjusted position at April expiration. The lower curve on the graph shows the profits if implied volatility remains at the cur-

Figure 6.28
OEX BACKSPREAD—STAGE 2

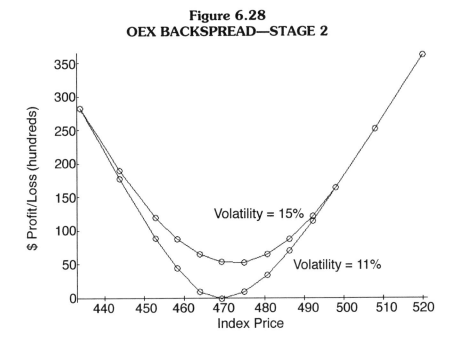

rent low levels, while the higher curve depicts the situation if implied volatility increases.

It should be pointed out that, when we roll up, we increase our margin requirement. In this particular case, the difference in the strikes between the short calls and the long calls is now 30 points ($3,000). We still have 10 of the call bear spreads in the position, so the collateral requirement is now $30,000. Of course, the $21,000 credit that was obtained when we rolled up can be applied against this increased collateral requirement.

In a totally theoretical situation, I would always encourage returning the position to a delta neutral status when an adjustment is made. However, in these examples, we're describing actual trading activity, and sometimes one modifies the theoretical approach in the heat of battle. A slight modification of this sort is a minor condescension to my market opinion—it's not like abandoning the backspread strategy for a totally one-sided position.

In the larger context, I was wrong, of course, about OEX being overbought at that point in 1995—it rallied for the rest of the year, with only a couple of pauses for breath. However, over the next month, it *did* have some trouble advancing as it consolidated to work off its overbought state. This meant that expiration was about a month away. I don't like to hold long, or at- or out-of-the-money options with that little time remaining, so it was time to make another decision.

OEX had crept up to about 479 by the third week of April, leaving only a month of time remaining on the long May 475 calls. Once again, implied volatility was fairly low, so the decision was made to roll out to June options and stick with the position for another month in search of the elusive increase in implied volatility. The following trade was made:

> Bought 20 June 480 calls at 9 opening
> Sold 20 May 475 calls at 9½ closing
> Net credit of this roll: 10 points ($1,000)

In addition, the April 445 puts had been sold for one point a couple of weeks earlier. Since the short calls were now so deeply in-the-money, there was no reason to buy another out-of-the-money put to add downside potential; the short calls were providing plenty of downside capability. These trades brought in a total credit of 20 points, leaving the position in the following state:

> Long 20 June 480 calls
> Short 10 May 445 calls
> Net credit to date: 220 points

Even though the long options were rolled up to a higher strike, a credit was available because of the fact that OEX was just below the 480 strike and implied volatility was low. With three weeks to go, there wasn't much chance of an early assignment on the May 445 calls, but the possibility increased as expiration approached. However, in any OEX spread, should one receive an early assignment notice, he should either quickly sell another, longer-term contract in its place, or he should remove the other side of the spread. He should *not* decide to become a market predictor; that tack is usually not a wise one.

It has been my general experience over the 13 years that OEX options have been trading, that an early assignment is not necessarily an unprofitable thing. True, it is an *inconvenient* occurrence, and it makes a spread position assume a great deal of risk. That is why one should attempt to avoid early assignment. What I am saying, though, is that when I have received an early assignment notice, I have, on average, made money because the market moved favorably after the assignment. Perhaps those traders doing the exercising are doing so because of a short-term market opinion, and that opinion is wrong.

In any case, it is not wise to tempt fate, so with about two weeks to go until May expiration, OEX took off to the upside, and the following adjustments were made.

By the first week of May, OEX was in a fast-rising phase once again. It had rallied to above 490. This was a major move that again made the entire position delta long. Moreover, time was now getting quite short for the May options; the chances for early assignment were increasing with each passing day. In addition, implied volatilities had increased somewhat, although they were by no means expensive:

Option	Implied Volatility (%)
June 480 call	12.9
June 495 call	11.1

Finally, it should be noted that the unrealized profit of the position had now reached about $7,500, less commissions.

Given the fact that the implied volatility of the at-the-money option was still as low as 11 percent, the decision was made to roll the position:

> Bought 20 June 495 calls at 9 opening
> Sold 20 June 480 calls at 20 closing
> Net credit of this roll: 220 points ($22,000)

Also, since expiration was approaching, the May calls were rolled to June calls. When the long calls are so far in-the-money, it is sometimes necessary to roll to a higher strike. The decision as to which short strike to use is usually based on two factors: (1) the time value of the short option that you are considering rolling into, and (2) the collateral requirement; rolling to a higher strike reduces the collateral requirement.

Since there was a reasonable amount of time value premium in the June 445 calls (almost two points), I decided to keep the short strike the same:

> Bought 10 May 445 calls at 53½ closing
> Sold 10 June 445 calls at 54½ opening
> Net credit of this roll: 10 points ($1,000)

These adjustments brought more credit into the position:

> Previous total position credit: 220 points
> Roll of long calls: 220 points credit
> Roll of short calls: 10 points credit
> Net position credit to date: 450 points credit

This is a credit of $45,000 dollars. But it is needed to reduce the collateral requirement, which grew again by rolling to the 495 strike. After this, the profit graph for the position at June expiration had improved, as shown in Figure 6.29 (straight lines). You can see that there is almost no area in which a loss can occur, although we would not want to give back the $7,500 that the position is currently ahead.

Figure 6.29
OEX BACKSPREAD—STAGE 3

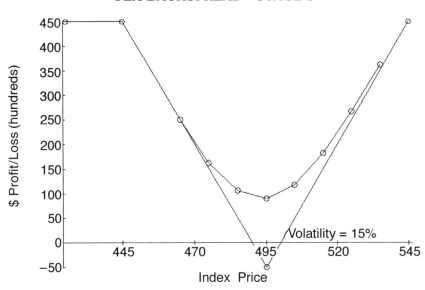

The curved line shows the profit if implied volatility increases by the first of June. It again demonstrates the powerful influence that implied volatility could have, were it to increase to 15 percent or so.

When expiration approaches, the long side of a backspread becomes a concern in terms of time value decay (assuming that the underlying is near the striking price of that long call). In addition, the short side of the spread becomes a concern because of early assignment possibilities. You must remember that the intent of the position continues to be to trade volatility. It is still low, so the decision is made to remain in a backspread position, rather than just close it out.

In the preceding case, the May options were rolled to June options. That one-month roll doesn't add much time value premium to the position. I have always felt that you need to investigate your objectives when rolling the long options. If you roll to the nearest available month, then you are playing it very tight to the vest. You are exposed to time value decay, but your cost for rolling is smallest (i.e., June options cost less than July options). Since I was still having trouble believing that OEX could continue to advance at its then-current pace, I was keeping the rolls short-term, rolling merely from month to month.

OEX wasted no time proving quite clearly that I was misjudging its power. It rose to 505 by the first week of June. Grudgingly, implied volatility of the at-the-money options had increased as well—12.3 percent for the July calls. So, at this time, the position was 3½ months old and the implied volatility of the at-the-money calls had risen from 9.9 to 12.3 percent. This placed the current implied volatility in the fourth percentile, no longer cheap, but not expensive either.

The prices and volatilities of the options being considered were:

Option	Price	Implied Volatility (%)
June 495 call	13	13.4
June 445 call	61	n/a
July 505 call	10½	12.3

At this point, the entire position from inception had an unrealized gain of about $9,000, less commissions.

Since the position had been working so well up until this time, I decided on a halfway measure: I would remove some of the position in order to nail down some profits, but would continue to hold the remainder of the position to see if it could make even more money. The actual decision that I made was to take off a quarter of the position, and to roll the balance to the July 505 calls.

This was the removal of one quarter of the position:

> Sold 5 June 495 calls at 13 closing
> Bought 3 June 445 calls at 61 closing
> Debit on this trade: 118 points ($11,800)

And this was the roll of the remaining longs calls out to July:

> Sold 15 June 495 calls at 13 closing
> Bought 15 July 505 calls at 10 opening
> Credit on this trade: 45 points ($4,500)

The remaining position was now:

> Long 15 July 505 calls
> Short 7 June 445 calls
> Net Credit to date: 377 points

This position had a collateral requirement of $42,000 (seven bear spreads with a 60-point, or $6,000, requirement for each one). The net credit to date of the position was now 377 points less commissions (it had been 450 points credit and was now reduced by the two trades just cited), so that amount could be applied against the collateral requirement.

After these trades, the position once again was approximately delta neutral, but was somewhat smaller. Figure 6.30 shows the potential at June expiration. It assumes that implied volatility remains unchanged at 12.3 percent. Note that the position can no longer lose any money at all, although it could give back some of the nearly $9,000 in profits built up to date, if OEX were to stabilize near 505.

Figure 6.30
OEX BACKSPREAD—STAGE 4

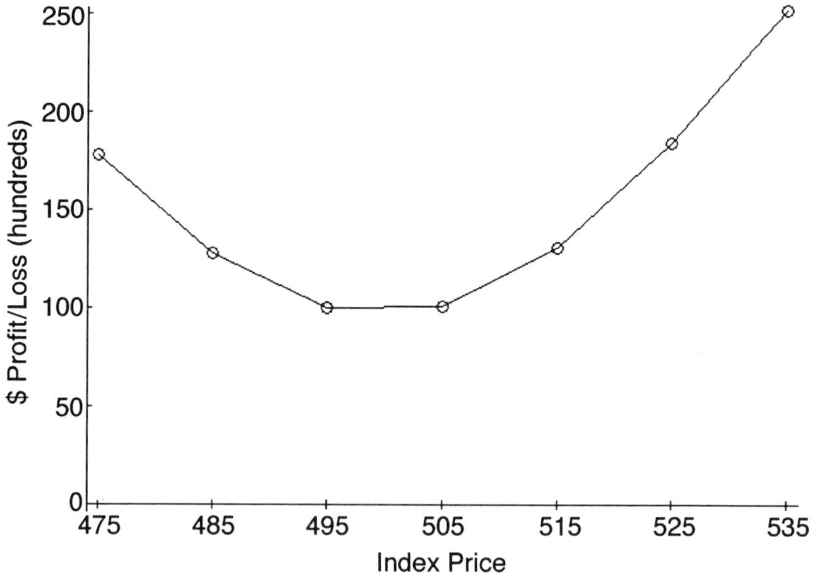

Perhaps in a more theoretical world, the entire position would have been removed before this last roll was made, since implied volatility had risen to 12.3 percent for the at-the-money options. Perhaps it should have been. However, in the real world, we are constantly fighting the battle between theory and reality. Any good trader wants to cut losses and let profits run, even in a hedged position such as this backspread. Since the position had been working so well, I only removed a small part of it, electing to "let the profits run" if they could.

I don't think there's always a "right" and a "wrong" thing to do, when managing a hedged position. In a long volatility position like this backspread, it's important to let the position have some room to move, but when the delta builds up too far, the position should be reneutralized. That had been done for this backspread position several times. As long as you are doing that, and you are mindful of a mental stop, then you are proceeding correctly. The mental stop keeps you from becoming too complacent about time decay. With the current profit at about $9,000, a mental stop at about $6,000 seems reasonable.

OEX moved higher over the next month, but then began to run into some trouble. Moreover, there were some early assignments. The combination of these events "led" me out of the position. The following discussion concerns the handling of an early assignment.

As June expiration approached, the short calls were rolled forward to avoid assignment:

> Bought 7 June 445 calls at 58 closing
> Sold 7 July 445 calls at 60 opening
> Credit for this trade: 14 points ($1,400)

However, within a week, and with nearly a month remaining until July expiration, an early assignment notice was received on two of the July 445 calls. This was highly unusual, coming so far in advance of expiration. Even though the option was very far in-the-money, I still considered it atypical to be assigned a month before expiration. This assignment was received the morning after OEX had closed at 511.31. Thus, the price on the assignment was 511.31 − 445.00, or 66.31.

There were actually quite a few OEX calls exercised that night. As has often been the case after early assignments, the market opened lower the next morning, but then began to recover. In fact, by noon it was well into positive territory. As I said earlier, it has been my experience that this is a common event—early selloff, followed by rally, after an OEX call exercise.

I had been feeling somewhat uneasy about not having taken a larger portion of the position off at the time of the last roll (to the July 505s). Therefore, I used this assignment as an opportunity to remove another piece of the position. I sold out five of the long July 505 calls. This trade occurred around noon of the day of the assignment.

Thus, the complete trade was:

> Bought 2 July 445 calls at 66.31 closing
> Sold 5 July 505 calls at 15 closing
> Net debit for this trade: 57.62 points ($5,762)

The remaining position, after the roll and assignment, was:

> Long 10 July 505 calls
> Short 5 July 445 calls
> Net credit to date: 333.38 points

Handling an early assignment in the manner just described is somewhat risky. As I said, it has been my experience that the initial market selloff caused by a fairly large OEX call exercise is quickly reversed. But sometimes it isn't. In those cases, you would fare worse by waiting to execute an offsetting trade against your early assignment notice. Therefore, if you decide to approach it in the manner that I did, by not selling something immediately on the opening (when everyone else is), but by waiting to see if there is a reflex rally, then you need to have an absolute mental stop in your head. The mental stop will keep you from "freezing" and holding on way too long.

A good rule of thumb is to see where the S&P futures are trading when the initial selling flurry, caused by the OEX call exercise, subsides. The S&Ps would normally be somewhat off their daily lows at that point. I often use this as a mental stop: if the S&Ps *then* make another daily low, I will sell what I need to, in order to balance my position. On the other hand, if a market rally develops, as was the case in the previous example, then I would look for a place to sell into the rally.

I would *not* change my overall strategy, though. For example, if the market was going my way, I would not attempt to remain overly "long" the market over a longer period of time. After an early assignment, you should return to a balanced position at some point during the trading day on which you received the assignment. If you are able to ride a rally, and get a better price for your "resale," so much the better, but don't wait overnight to readjust the position.

OEX continued to rally—confounding me, who was keeping my position delta neutral. When it reached 520 in late June, the implied volatility of the August 520 call was only 11.6 percent. So volatility had actually decreased from the last time that a roll was made—into the 505s.

Therefore, I decided to stay with the position, and executed the following trade:

> Sold 10 July 505 calls at 18 closing
> Bought 10 Aug 520 calls at 10½ opening
> Credit on this trade: 75 points ($7,500)

The total position was then:

> Long 10 Aug 520 calls
> Short 5 July 445 calls
> Net credit to date: 408.38 points

The unrealized profit had grown to over $12,000. *I moved my mental stop up to $9,000. That is, if the position marked at $9,000 on any day's close, I would exit the next day.*

This lengthy position was eventually terminated in August, but not before a couple more early assignments.

I received early assignment notices on back-to-back days in July. On the first one, I was assigned on all five of my short July 445 calls. I sold the Aug 445 calls that day, taking in a net credit on the roll. On the very next day, I was assigned on the *Augusts!* At that point, I decided that the only way to avoid these early assignments was to roll to a higher strike, so I sold the August 475 calls. I chose the 475 strike because the open interest was fairly large in that series. This last trade necessitated a debit, because the strike was moved higher.

The net debit from these two early assignments was 127.45 points ($12,745). This left the position as:

> Long 10 Aug 520 calls
> Short 5 Aug 475 calls
> Net credit to date: 280.93

Eventually OEX rose to over 530 in late July, but then began to slip in early August. Time decay was beginning to become a major factor, and a decision needed to be made as to whether to terminate the position or to roll it once again, this time into September or October options.

With OEX at 525, the implied volatility of the at-the-money September calls was 12.7 percent and the Octobers were 13.0 percent. Since the range of implied volatility had been shrinking all year, these numbers were in the fifth and sixth percentiles. Given that fact, plus the fact that time decay had eroded the value of the long calls as OEX stabilized, I therefore decided to close the position:

> Sold 10 Aug 520 calls at 8 closing
> Bought 5 Aug 475 calls at 51 closing
> Net debit of this trade: 175 points ($17,500)

The net realized credit of position to date was 105.93 points, or $10,593.

A total of 304 contracts had been traded. At a commission rate of $4 per contract, that is $1,216 in commissions. Thus, the net gain on the entire position was $9,377.

The first criticism that a hedged trader usually receives is along these lines: he had to manage a relatively complicated position for six months, making numerous trades, and his net profit was $9,377. Meanwhile, OEX had risen 70 points. Wouldn't you have been a lot better off just to hold the initial position, or to have bought calls in the first place?

Of course you would have, but that's hindsight, and it is not what our goals were when the position was established. In reality, this position had an excellent rate of return and was hedged all the way along. Recall that the $9,377 profit was on an initial invest-ment of $16,000, which represents about a 60 percent gain in six months. This is very attractive for a hedged position. Even more importantly, we were hedged at all times; if there had been a severe market correction, our short calls would have provided very good profit potential (just look at any of the profit graphs in this example).

So, don't confuse hedging with speculation. Yes, speculation has much larger rewards, but hedging is supposed to provide steadier returns. Moreover, when trading volatility with a hedged position, we have the added advantage of having a statistical edge built in.

This example was rather long, but it illustrated most of the deci-sions that the strategist needs to contemplate while such a position is in place: when and whether to roll the long calls up, when to roll the short calls, how to handle early assignment, and collateral and profit/loss considerations. As I said in the preface, I am often asked what I use to make decisions regarding establishing a position and in follow-up action—how I decide which options to use, when to roll, how to handle early assignment, and so forth. Hopefully, the preced-ing example will answer some of those questions.

This concludes the section on using backspreads to trade the volatility skew. Obviously, not all backspreads work so well. How-ever, the strategy is a very attractive one as long as you have a mar-ket where there is a volatility skew. I especially like the fact that you can use simple spreads (rolling up the long calls, in the preceding examples) in order to adjust the spread. This is a distinct advantage of a backspread as compared to a long straddle. With a straddle, when the underlying moves higher, your downside protection gets farther and farther away. The only way to reneutralize a straddle is to sell the entire straddle and buy a new one at the higher strike. I have found that, on average, I personally make better, more profitable, decisions with the backspread than with the straddle.

Put Ratio Spread

The put ratio spread is also a viable strategy for trading the reverse volatility skew. You buy puts at one strike and sell puts at a lower strike. Since the puts purchased have a lower implied volatility than the puts sold (because of the reverse volatility skew), this position has a nice statistical advantage, too. Many OEX traders use this strategy in one form or another because of the attractiveness of selling expensive out-of-the-money puts.

If you buy and sell an equal number of puts, you have a bear spread with a theoretical advantage. That's great, but if the market continues to rise, as it has for over five years, you don't make much money from the bear spreads. Money managers sometimes take advantage of this volatility skew to buy bear spreads to act as insurance for their long stock positions. Admittedly, the bear spread wouldn't provide complete insurance—it's only insurance down to the lower strike—but these money managers figure it's better than nothing, and it isn't so costly where there's a reverse volatility skew present.

The delta neutral version of the put spread is, of course, the put ratio spread—buying perhaps one at-the-money put and selling two out-of-the-money puts. Sometimes these put ratio spreads can even be established for credits, when the volatility skew is steep enough. This means that you would profit unless the market dropped through the lower breakeven point of the ratio spread before expiration. In fact, a modest decline by the market, to the striking price of the written puts, could produce very good profits.

Since the crash of 1987, it has not been at all uncommon to see prices such as these in OEX options. This particular set of prices was recorded at the end of a very volatile day in the market, which saw the Dow up 35 in the morning, then falling 90 points in the afternoon, before rallying 35 points late in the day to finish –20 for the day. The skew is usually quite pronounced after a day like that—which contains a big downdraft—and it is invariably a good time to establish these put spreads.

OEX: 587 on January 4th

Option	Price	Implied Volatility (%)
Feb 550 put	1.81	16.6
Feb 555 put	2.19	16.0
Feb 560 put	2.69	15.4
Feb 565 put	3.19	14.6
Feb 570 put	4.13	14.3
Feb 575 put	5.00	13.7
Feb 580 put	6.38	13.2
Feb 585 put	7.88	12.6

You can see the nice, uniform pattern of implied volatilities increasing as the strikes get lower. This is a classic reverse skew.

What is very interesting is that you can buy almost any one of these puts and sell two of the puts with a striking price 15 points lower, and still take in a credit. This makes a very attractive put ratio spread. For example, if you bought one Feb 585 put at 7⅞ and sold two Feb 570 puts at 4⅛, you would take in a credit of ⅜ of a point. This might only be enough to cover commissions, but it is a very attractive spread, theoretically, since the option you are buying has an implied volatility of 12.6 percent, while the ones you are selling are trading with a 14.3 percent implied. That is a large discrepancy.

The downside breakeven point on this 1-by-2 ratio spread is about 565, which is 22 points below the current OEX price. That's plenty of downside cushion.

A put ratio spread strategy can be operated much like the call ratio spread strategy that was described earlier with an example using corn options. In the put spread, usually no action is necessary if the index rises. However, if the index declines, you would normally have a profit if the underlying gets down to the striking price of the puts that were sold (the exception would be a quick decline, and we'll get to that in a minute). At that point, you can decide if it is best to take some profits or to narrow your action points to protect the profits you have.

The put ratio spread strategy consumes a lot in the way of collateral requirements, so it is best used by traders who have excess collateral in their accounts. Each naked index put requires collateral in the amount of 15 percent of the index value, plus the put premium, less any out-of-the-money amount (if it's out-of-the-money). This can be expensive, although collateral can be equity in your account—it does not have to be cash. Thus, the excess value of your stocks and bonds can be used to finance this strategy.

The problem with the put ratio spread strategy is that everyone remembers the days on which this strategy was particularly poor, the crash of 1987, and the 1989 crash caused by the UAL leveraged buyout falling apart; then there was the 1990 Iraq-inspired bear market. Admittedly, those were nasty times, but you could have hedged yourself so as to prevent disaster.

In the UAL-induced crash of 1989, I had OEX put ratio spreads in place. However, I was able to hedge them with futures even as the market was plunging. As long as the market is open and doesn't gap through your downside, you can protect yourself.

The downside breakeven was about 316 with the OEX index trading at levels above 330. Then, on a quiet Friday afternoon—some self-employed traders had already gotten bored with the market and had gone home—news came out that the UAL deal was going to collapse. UAL itself had been trading at 249, and was halted at 243 due to an order imbalance.

The stock market, though, knew what was coming and headed south—fast! OEX fell over 20 points that afternoon, to close just below 310 (the Dow was off 190 points). OEX put premiums ballooned and there were several trading halts and rotations. No one can adjust a position in the midst of a trading halt, and to attempt to trade in a rotation is an exercise in masochism.

The S&P 500 futures were open for trading, though, and they were available as a convenient hedge. When the market approached the downside breakeven point of the spread (316), enough S&P futures were sold to eliminate the downside risk—one future was sold for every five net naked puts in the ratio spread position. This turns the naked puts into covered puts, in effect, even though the S&P 500 and OEX aren't exactly the same thing. Usually, though, the two indices perform in concert, and when you need a hedge of last resort, you can't be picky about something like tracking error.

Thus, you can use the S&P futures as a hedge for OEX positions. If OEX is free trading, that wouldn't be necessary. But if the CBOE declares fast market conditions in OEX, I would look to the futures as a hedge. You pretty much always know where the futures are trading, and, while they *do* have limits, they are more flexible in fast markets than trying to get an option order executed. It should be noted that, once you have sold the futures as a hedge, if the market changes direction and heads back up again, you could have risk if it rallies above the striking price of your short puts. Of course, this is a problem with any adjustment against short options in any strategy— you can be whipsawed. There is no easy remedy when it occurs. You just have to try to reduce your risk by executing closing trades to remove the short put/short futures position.

A Volatility Skew Biases a Position

It is quite true, but not necessarily intuitively apparent, that when the options in a position have a volatility skew, that position is biased. If the skew is a reverse one—à la OEX options—then the position has a bullish bias. That is, it will do better when OEX rises in price than would be normally expected, and it will do worse on the downside. On the other hand, if there is a positive skew, like grain options have, then the position has a bearish bias; it will do better on the downside than you would think.

These biases will persist as long as the skew exists. If the skew disappears, then the position will behave "normally." The profit graphs in the previous examples, designed to show how to trade the volatility skew, had the volatility skew built into them. Any trader relying on profit projections generated by a computer must be sure that the computer program doing the projections knows if there is volatility skew or not and, if there is one, accounts for it in the profit forecasts.

To verify that a reverse skew puts a bullish bias in a position, consider the OEX backspread example that we have just examined. When the position was established, we had the following situation:

OEX: 455 in February

Position	Implied Volatility (%)
Long 20 May 460 call	9.9
Short 10 May 445 call	11.7

Later, in March, OEX had rallied, and we saw that the following implied volatilities were then evident:

OEX: 475 in February

Position	Implied Volatility (%)
Long 20 May 460 call	13.0
Short 10 May 445 call	16.0

Both options' implied volatility had increased because they were now both in-the-money options. Remember that the deeper an option is in-the-money, when you have a reverse volatility skew, the higher is the implied volatility of that option.

The increase of implied volatility from 9.9 to 13.0 percent on the 20 calls that were long aids the position. Conversely, the increase in implied volatility from 11.7 to 16.0 percent on the 10 short calls hurts the position. Overall, though, the increase in implied volatility on 20 long calls is more dominant than the increase in volatility on the 10 short calls. Thus, the position has been aided by the fact that OEX rose in price while the volatility skew was still in place.

If you would prefer to see actual prices to verify this bias, look at the following table:

Position	Price	Implied (%)	Profit/Loss ($)
Original			
Long 20 May 460 calls	7	9.9	
Short 10 May 445 calls	16½	11.7	
One month later			
Long 20 May 460 calls	18	13.0	+22,000
Short 10 May 445 calls	32	16.0	−15,500
Total Profit			+6,500

However, suppose for a moment that there was no skew in evidence and that the options retained their original volatility as OEX moved higher.

Then the following situation would have existed one month later (according to our option model):

	Price	Implied (%)	Profit/Loss ($)
Long 20 May 460 calls	17	9.9	+20,000
Short 10 May 445 calls	31	11.7	−14,500
Total Profit			+5,500

No increase implied; one month later position.

The presence of the volatility skew, which caused the implied volatility of the in-the-money options to increase, resulted in the position making $6,500 instead of the $5,500 it would have made if implied volatilities had remained as they were when the position was established. This $1,000 increase in profit is the bias attributable to the volatility skew.

In a similar manner, we could show, but won't bother going through the details, that a forward skew biases a position in a bearish manner. Thus, a seemingly neutral position in soybean options, for example, will do *worse* than expected if soybeans rise in price.

We point this out so that you will not be surprised when these results occur in your positions. As stated earlier, a computer program that correctly incorporates the skewing into profit projections will give you these accurate results. You may also want to anticipate this effect when you construct your initial position. For example, if you determine that an OEX backspread is neutral with 20 long calls and 10 short calls, you know that the position will outperform on the upside and underperform on the downside. Thus, you might want to buy only 18 calls while selling 10. This would compensate for the volatility skew's effect.

Finding Where Volatility Skewing Exists

Having discussed *how* to trade the volatility skew, it is also important to know *where* to find one. The easiest method seems to be to compute the statistical standard deviation of the individual striking prices with the same expiration date. That is a simple computation, which we show by example momentarily.

First, though, let's define "standard deviation" for those who are not familiar with the term. In order to determine the standard deviation of a group of numbers—implied volatilities of individual options, in this case—you first find the average of the group of numbers. Then, for each number, you (1) subtract that average from the individual number, and (2) square the result of step 1. You add up all these squares, and, at the end, divide by how many were in the group, less one. Then you take the square root of that final result. What is left is called the *standard deviation*. For the purposes of volatility skewing, we compare that final result with the average implied volatility to see if it is significant.

Mathematically, the formula, for the standard deviation of a group of n numbers, is as follows. The symbol for percent standard deviation is σ:

$$\sigma = \frac{\sqrt{\dfrac{\Sigma\left(V_i - \mu\right)}{n-1}}}{\mu}$$

where V_i = implied volatility of an individual option
  μ = average of all the V_i
  n = number of items in the group

The following example shows the actual calculations used to determine the standard deviation of March soybean options on a particular day. You will be able to see, with your naked eye, that there is a volatility skew here, but our intention is to prove, mathematically, that there is one. In this way, you can have a computer program look for these skews.

The following example is concerned only with March soybean options. The prices are closing prices.

March Soybeans: 758¾

Strike	Call	Put	Implied
700	59¾	1⅜	15.39
725	38½	5¼	16.33
750	24	15¼	18.93
775	14⅜	31	20.74
800	8¾	50	22.70
825	5½	n/a	24.65
850	3¾	n/a	26.91
875	2½	n/a	28.67
900	1⅝	n/a	30.00

Note that there are nine items in this group (i.e., nine different striking prices in the same expiration month, for which we have computed the implied volatility).

First, we compute the average of these nine implied volatilities, which comes to 22.70. Now, we subtract that average from each of these implieds, and we square that result:

Strike	Implied	Difference from Average	Square of Difference from Average
700	15.39	−7.31	53.45
725	16.33	−6.37	40.62
750	18.93	−3.78	14.26
775	20.74	−1.96	3.84
800	22.70	0.00	0.00
825	24.65	1.95	3.79
850	26.91	4.21	17.74
875	28.67	5.97	35.64
900	30.00	7.30	53.26

Now, we add up the "squares of difference," the right-hand column in this table, and get 222.61. The standard deviation is

$$\sigma = \text{SQRT}(\text{"Sum of squares of difference"} / (n - 1))$$
$$= \text{SQRT}(222.61/8)$$
$$= 5.275$$

Finally, we express the standard deviation as a percentage of the average implied volatility:

$$5.275/22.70 = 23.2\%$$

The idea behind using the standard deviation is to see if there is a large distance between most of the implied volatilities of the individual options and the average volatility. A "large difference" is usually defined by the final percentage being over 15 percent. In this example, the final percentage is 23 percent, so we can definitely say, mathematically, that there is a volatility skew in these March soybean options.

You will normally find volatility skews only in index and futures options. It is rather rare to find them in equity options, although occasionally you will see one in a takeover stock situation.

THE AGGRESSIVE CALENDAR SPREAD

Before concluding this chapter, we present one more strategy. It is related to volatility, but isn't technically a volatility trading strategy. In fact, in this strategy, which is a calendar spread strategy, we want volatility to remain the same (or go higher), as we would with any calendar spread. The difference here is that this position is established when implied volatility is already high—a dangerous move for a calendar spreader. However, offsetting that risk is the fact that this is a very short-term strategy, so a position is not in place for more than a few trading days. This often helps to mitigate the risk that implied volatility might collapse while the position is in place.

When takeover rumors surface, implied volatilities tend to skyrocket. Strategists often look for ways to sell the extremely expensive short-term options while hedging themselves with either stock or a longer-term option. The following true-life example demonstrates the situations that we often find in these cases.

In the late spring of 1994, there were takeover rumors surrounding the stock of American Medical Holdings (symbol: AMI). The stock was trading at 25, and the following prices prevailed, with about two weeks remaining until June expiration:

AMI: 25

Option	Price	Implied Volatility (%)
June 25 call	1½	105
July 25 call	2⅞	95

The near-term option is often much more expensive than any longer-term option, when takeover rumors are "hot." AMI was a typical situation in that regard.

On the surface, the calendar spread is an attractive strategy, because it has limited risk no matter what happens. It is often a strategy that we are tempted to establish in high-volatility options because it seems that the risk is small compared to the possible expansion that the spread would undergo if "nothing" happened.

However, the calendar spread strategy in this situation is extremely dependent on implied volatility remaining inflated. If the implied volatility collapses for one reason or another, the strategy will almost surely lose. One way to increase your odds is to establish the calendar spread when there is a *very* short time remaining until expiration, perhaps as little as a week or 10 days. In that case, there is less of a chance that the rumors will dissipate in so short a time, and therefore there is more of a chance that the strategist will be able to capture the decline in premium of the expensive short-term option, while the longer-term option retains its high implied volatility. If that were to happen, the spread would widen and produce a nice profit very quickly.

Any short-term option strategy is a risky one. When you are operating any strategy with so short a time horizon as one week or less, you would have to consider that a speculative strategy. Speculation is not necessarily bad, but you must understand that even though you are hedged, a big swing in returns can occur in the course of one week in this situation.

If a takeover bid is made during the week in which you are holding the calendar spread, there is a significant chance that both options will trade at or close to parity and that the maximum loss—equal to the initial debit paid for the spread—will be realized. A similarly poor result could occur if the stock collapsed during the ensuing week, perhaps on an evaporation of the rumors.

Figure 6.31 is a graph of a 10-lot calendar spread in the aforementioned AMI options. The spread was established with exactly a week to go until expiration. It shows two scenarios. The first is if implied volatilities remain high: rumors still abound, but no actual news is forthcoming. This ideal situation is represented by the higher, profitable, curve on the graph. The second situation is if implied volatilities collapse to the 30 percent level, as represented by the lower curve on the graph. The two curves are so far apart that it appears they are depicting two totally unrelated strategies; *but they*

Figure 6.31
AMI SHORT-TERM CALENDAR SPREAD

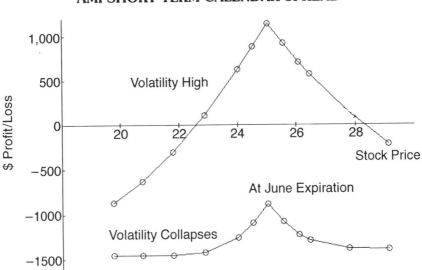

are not! Notice that, even at its best result, the spread would lose nearly $1,000 if volatilities collapse, whereas it could make as much as $1,000 if volatility remains high, and AMI is near 25. This picture graphically depicts the risk/reward aspects of this strategy. Of course, the hope is that the shortness of time that the spread must be held will mitigate the chances of the profits falling on that lower curve.

This type of calendar spread should be removed on the Friday of expiration of the near-term option. It could conceivably be removed slightly earlier if the stock were very close to the strike and the spread had widened. You will probably find, however, that the near-term options will continue to have a large premium (implied volatility) right up to the end, as speculators hope that a takeover bid will come before expiration Friday. This means that you will probably not have much of a chance to remove the spread early.

This strategy could be employed in any case where stock options are trading with an extremely inflated volatility. The only two ingredients would be that the stock is trading fairly close to the striking price when you establish the spread, and that there is a reasonable chance that no news will occur before expiration. This latter criterion would rule out situations where an earnings report, court verdict or FDA decision, for example, was scheduled to be handed down right before expiration.

SUMMARY

There are two basic approaches to dealing with trading volatility, although they are related in that they both rely on using the current percentile level of the implied volatility. In one approach we look for the implied to be near the end of its trading range, either in a very high percentile or in a low one, and for the historical volatility to be more in the middle of the range. If that is the case, we will sell volatility when it is high, and buy it when it is low. Strategies used for selling this type of volatility are the naked sell combo and the ratio spread. If implied volatility is low, we will buy it, using long straddles, backspreads, or calendar spreads as the favorite strategies. These strategies can all be enhanced to remove price risk—especially the sell combo, ratio spread, and calendar spread that are hurt by volatile price movement—by using gamma and delta neutral strategies.

The second method for trading volatility concentrates more on locating situations in which the individual options on the same underlying security have differing implied volatilities. When this condition exists, it is called a *volatility skew*. If the skew is positive—that is, implied volatilities increase at successively higher striking prices—then the applicable strategies are put backspreads or call ratio spreads. However, if the opposite situation exists, which is called a *reverse volatility skew*, then call backspreads and put ratio spreads are the two strategies that are the ones to use. Finally, a method for mathematically computing the extent of a volatility skew was presented.

Experienced option traders tend to view volatility as the most important variable when discussing option pricing and option trading strategies. Moreover, it is somewhat more predictable than prices, so if the volatility can be isolated and identified, then you might be able to construct positions with less risk and more profitability by predicting volatility movements rather than by predicting price movements.

7 Other Important Considerations

In this chapter, we discuss some other important aspects of option trading. One is support activities, which include brokers, order entry, data sources, and software. Also included are some discussions on trading in general, including procedures and money management. Finally, we look at the psychological aspect of trading options—perhaps the most important facet of trading, no matter *what* market you are trading.

SUPPORT ACTIVITIES

Many of today's traders are doing their own research and developing their own trading systems. I assume that is why you are reading this book. Even if you are relying on someone else for advice, such as a daily or monthly newsletter of the type that we publish, you are gathering your own information, apart from your broker. Thus, it is appropriate to discuss brokerage, order entry, data vendors, and software.

Order Entry

When you place an order, it can be done in one of two ways. You can call your broker, or you can use one of the computer order entry systems where you enter the order directly from your computer (or possibly from the touch pad of your telephone). Regardless of which method you choose, the order has to be sent to the floor of the appropriate exchange for execution. This is true for exchange-traded securities; in the over-the-counter (NASDAQ) market, there are some differences.

For most individual customers, the order-entry process begins with a phone call to your *broker*. Then, depending on the size and complexity of your order, your broker will either put the order over the *electronic entry system* (this is often called the *wire system*), or he will phone it to a *special-handling desk* or order desk at the home office of the brokerage firm. If you enter the order electronically yourself, it still goes to a brokerage firm, where it is rerouted into their own wire system. A flow chart of the order entry process is pictured in Figure 7.1.

There are benefits to either method of placing an order. If the order is small and speed of execution is desired, then the electronic method is best, although many customers at home don't have access to computers to do their own electronic order entry. However, even if you call your broker directly with a small order, or if it is a simple market or limit order, it is most likely then entered electronically by a clerk at the brokerage office. Thus it eventually becomes an electronic order as well. One of two things can happen to your order at this point: it will either go to your firm's *booth on the appropriate trading floor*, or it will go onto the *automatic execution* system.

Figure 7.1
ORDER FLOW

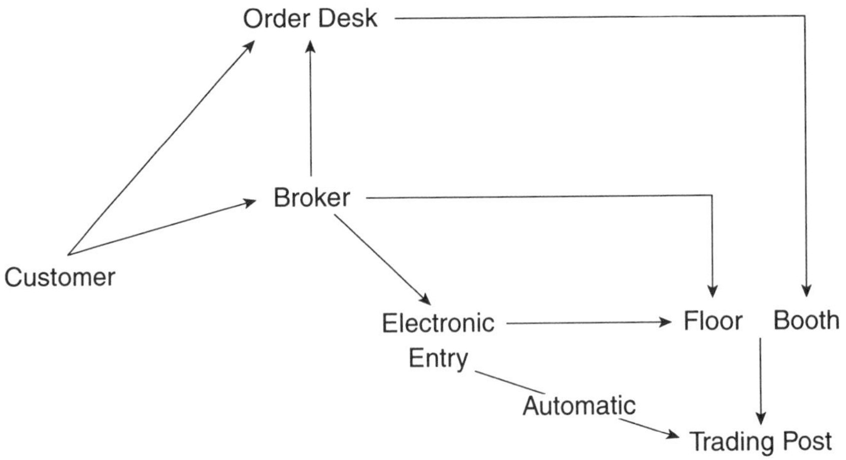

If an electronic order goes into the automatic execution system, it goes into a computer that directs it to the appropriate trading post (the place where the trading in a particular stock or option actually takes place) and gives an immediate, automatic execution. This system is not available for all orders; however, if the order is a small one of 10 contracts or less *and* it is a market order or it is a limit order to buy at the current offer or to sell at the current bid, then the order will go onto the automatic system. Each option exchange has its own particular maxima regarding the number of contracts that are available for automatic execution (for example, they may be larger for index options), and each exchange calls their automatic system by a different name; you should check with your broker for specific details on automatic order entry. When this system is used, another stage in the process—your brokerage firm's floor trading booth—is bypassed.

The other thing that can happen to an electronic order is that it goes to the firm's booth on the trading floor. At this point, the order is given to a *floor broker*, and he physically goes into the trading pit and executes the order.

Remember, though, that there was another way to get your order to the floor. If you are a larger trader, for example, you might demand and require the personal attention that a large order sometimes needs. Your order might be called into a special-handling desk—or *order desk*—which will in turn call the order down to the trading floor. This type of order is then monitored by the order desk in order to stay on top of partial fills, or any other type of personal attention that the order might require. Some clients even give the order desk or the broker some discretion (i.e., leeway in what price to pay), figuring that the professionals on the trading desk and on the trading floor are more in tune with the market.

The order desk is staffed by professional traders who are familiar with the sometimes arcane terminology of options and who generally handle larger orders and/or orders involving spreads and more complex situations. In any case, though, there is usually a minimum number of contracts that you must trade in order to receive the benefits of having the order desk take care of your order. Larger customers, money managers, and institutional option traders talk directly to the order desk to get this special handling. *If you are trading in fairly large size, then you should request that your brokerage firm allow you to talk directly to the order desk.* Your broker will still receive his commissions, but you will be getting faster executions because you have bypassed one phone call in the order-entry chain: the phone call from your broker to the order desk now becomes unnecessary. For some large customers, their broker actually sits next to the order desk so that they effectively gain direct access to the desk by calling their broker; these brokers are generally called *institutional brokers* and are only available to large trading accounts.

Thus, orders that arrive at your brokerage firm's floor booth—whether sent there by the firm's wire system, or called in by the firm's order desk—end up in the hands of a floor broker. Floor brokers are of two general types: those who work for the same firm as your broker, and independents who work for themselves (sometimes called *two-dollar brokers*). The independent broker charges an additional fee for his services, but may be better at obtaining favorable price executions and in handling special orders. Unless you are calling the independent broker yourself (which is possible if your brokerage firm will allow it), then you have no control over which type of broker winds up with your order.

These steps are all summarized in Figure 7.1. Note that the quickest path for large traders is for the customer to call the order desk, from where the floor booth is called, which is where the order is executed. As mentioned in the previous paragraph, it is even quicker to call a floor booth yourself. In order to take advantage of this, however, your brokerage firm would have to agree to process trades executed by the independent broker. As there is a certain amount of "handshaking" that needs to go on, it may not be easy to establish such a relationship.

Brokers and Brokerage

Today, if a trader uses a full-service broker, he uses him more for the services provided than for recommendations. That is, he is interested in technical or fundamental reports, summaries of his account, charts, and other products that the full-service firm can provide. Most important, the full-service broker offers the ability to watch a client's account and to alert him when a previously agreed-upon event occurs. For example, if you are trying to use mental stops—where you want to make a decision in real time when the underlying hits a certain price—you can have your full-service broker call you when the stock, future, or index hits that price. Thus, you, the client, do not necessarily need real-time quotation capabilities if your broker can watch your positions for you.

A discount broker will not be able to give that level of service, but his commission rates will often be lower than those of a full-service firm. If you are using a discount broker, you will need to have some way of knowing prices, so that you can make trading decisions. If your investment horizon is intermediate to long term, you probably are not so interested in knowing real-time prices. However, if you are a short-term trader/investor, then you will most likely need access to prices on a timely basis. A discount broker will not be able to offer those, but we discuss price quotation services shortly.

However, perhaps the most important aspect of any brokerage *firm*—not of your *broker* himself—is what kind of orders they will take, and how they handle those orders. I have had attendees at seminars tell me that their brokerage firm will only take market or limit orders—no spreads, stops, or contingent orders. My advice is always for them to find a firm that will take those orders. Similarly, if your orders are repeatedly slow in getting to the floor and are then sloppily executed, or you have to argue about executions and partial fills, perhaps you should look for another brokerage firm with which to do business. It does little good to save on commissions by using a deep-discount broker, but then to give those savings back in the form of restricted order entry or poor order execution.

One thing you should be aware of in selecting a broker and a brokerage firm is commissions, including those for treatment for exercise and assignment. Commissions are important, but should not be your only concern. I am always hesitant to recommend a specific commission rate that you should seek, because there are other considerations. However, the following are reasonable rates that are attainable from many reputable brokerage firms: stock or index options: $4 per option; stock: 8 cents per share; futures options: $10 per side; futures: $15 per round turn. If your broker charges a little more than that, but you feel you are getting service to justify it, then I would heartily recommend that you stay with him. Exercise and assignment commissions are an important aspect of option trading, particularly for stock and index options. If you are assigned, or if you exercise, you should ask your broker for rates comparable to the option trade that would have occurred.

This situation often arises near expiration: the call option that you own, and want to sell, is trading at a discount. It is more efficient for you to sell the stock (short exempt) and exercise your call. In this manner you achieve parity as the net price for your call. Suppose the following prices exist on expiration Friday of January expiration:

XYZ: 23½ bid, 23¾ offered

XYZ Jan 20 call: 3⅜ bid, 3⅞ offered

At these prices, the market makers are setting the bid an eighth below parity and are setting the offer an eighth above parity. This is fairly typical for an in-the-money option at expiration.

You own the Jan 20 calls, and you attempt to sell them at 3½. However, the market makers don't budge and time is running short. You can sell the stock at 23½ (where it is bid) and exercise your calls, thereby buying the stock at 20. In effect, you have sold your calls for 3½.

How much you have to pay out in commissions has a major effect on the overall net money received from these trades. Suppose you are normally paying $4 per option and 8 cents per share of stock as commission rates.

Let's compare the two choices that this trader has: (1) selling his call at 3⅜, where it is bid, or (2) selling the stock and exercising the call, as just detailed.

(1) Net money from selling call at 3⅜:

Sell call at 3⅜:	$337.50 credit
Commission:	4.00
Net credit:	$333.50 credit

(2) Net money from selling stock and exercising:

Sell stock at 23½:	$2,350 credit
Commission on stock sale:	8 debit
Exercise (buy stock at 20):	2,000 debit
Commission on stock purchase:	8 debit
Net credit:	$ 334 credit

The two methods produce virtually the same result, so you seem to be just spinning your wheels to go through with the stock trades. The better price achieved is eaten up by the extra commissions.

However, many brokers will discount stock commissions on trades involving exercise or assignment. Suppose that you receive a 50 percent discount on exercises and assignment. Then your net credit from method 2 would be $342 ($350 credit from the stock trades, less $8 in commissions). If that were the case, it *would* make sense to use method 2.

Another important feature to consider when selecting a brokerage firm is margin rates, especially for the treatment of naked options. If you are a strategist, you almost certainly will be trading naked options at some time or another. It might arise from selling naked puts to simulate the covered writing strategy, or it might come from ratio writes to take advantage of expensive volatility, or it might even evolve out of something simpler, such as selling out the long side of a bull spread that is out of the money and letting the short side expire worthless.

Some option firms don't allow naked option trading at all. Avoid those firms, unless you never plan to do anything besides buy options. Other firms heartily discourage naked option trading by imposing onerous margin or equity requirements. It has been explained that the exchange sets minimum margin requirements for naked option selling. *Select a broker who uses the same standards—exchange minimum margin requirements.* This goes for futures and futures option traders as well. Use a brokerage firm that adheres to exchange minimum margin requirements. In fact, futures option traders should request SPAN margin, which is even more favorable than exchange minimum. SPAN applies logical price projections, which include the use of volatility, to naked options to arrive at margin requirements. While I wouldn't consider it absolutely mandatory for your broker to allow you to use SPAN requirements for your futures option positions, it would certainly be worth requesting.

The final point I would like to make about selecting a broker is to find one who trades all markets; specifically, this means index, equity, and futures. Later, we encourage *you* to trade all markets, but in order to do that, you have to have a broker who can execute those trades. Even if you don't plan to trade futures options, for example, you will almost certainly have to if you are trading OEX options. You may recall the story of the 1989 crash, where OEX options ceased to trade and the only thing that prevented disaster for those traders who were naked OEX puts was to be able to sell S&P 500 futures. We have also pointed out that it is sometimes more efficient to trade S&P futures than OEX options if implied volatility is too high.

Data Vendors

Many traders and investors are using their home computers to act as quote machines. There is a wide variety of products and services on the market, and more are being introduced all the time. Thus, while we attempt to survey the landscape accurately at the present time, you must understand that technological advances might present other opportunities in the future.

When deciding to select a data vendor, you need to consider several things, including whether you need real-time or delayed prices, how you will physically receive the prices, and what type of software is able to work with the prices you're receiving.

Costs.   When buying stock or futures market data from a vendor, you have two costs to consider: (1) the service charge imposed by the vendor, and (2) the exchange fee imposed by the exchange that originally disseminated the prices. In essence, the vendor buys the prices from the exchange and then resells them to its subscribers. If the end user (you) is only interested in delayed quotes, or end-of-day closing prices, then there is no exchange fee—only the vendor fee need be paid.

However, in a rather archaic setup, the exchange is entitled to collect exchange fees from every end user of its real-time prices. Therefore if a trader needs real-time prices, he must pay the exchange fees, too. In the modern world of competitive (and decreasing) costs for data of all sorts, it seems unreasonable that the exchanges can impose these fees. However, at the present they can, and they do. These exchange fees can be quite modest for individual investors (for example, the NYSE only charges $4 per month for their quotes, if they are disseminated to an individual investor). However, professional investors—and that is defined rather broadly by the exchanges to include everyone who is trading for an account other than their own—must pay considerably more. Moreover, the futures exchanges' fees are quite a bit higher than most stock exchanges.

If you are only interested in stock and option quotes, you can probably get them real-time for less than $100 per month. Delayed or closing quotes can be obtained for $20 a month or less. However, if you want real-time quotes on all the stock, option, and futures exchanges, you are probably going to have to pay costs of $500 a month or more—and that doesn't include much in the way of analysis programs.

Data Connection.   The next feature that must be considered is how you are going to get the prices, physically. Most investors who are interested in doing their own analysis pull the prices into their own computer and then run various software programs (charting analysis programs, for example) on that data. However, it is not absolutely necessary to have a computer and software in order to be able to receive pricing data.

If you only want to see quotes, you can get them on a variety of hand-held devices. One of the more popular is Quotrek (sold by the same people that sell SIGNAL). A Quotrek acts just like a quote machine and receives data over FM airwaves. Thus, it can only be used if you are near an FM radio broadcast signal. You can also get pagers from most of the large paging companies (Mobilemedia, Pagenet, etc.) that have the capability of displaying stock quotes and alerting you when a certain price is hit. These hand-held devices also let you see news headlines.

However, if you are going to perform any analysis, then you will need to have a more sophisticated way of getting and handling data—using a computer. There are essentially three methods by which you can observe and analyze prices by computer: (1) using your own computer for access, you can dial up another computer and observe analyses on that computer; (2) you can use a terminal supplied by the data vendor that performs specific tasks and connects to the data vendor's main computer; or (3) again using your own computer, you can download data and analyze it with your own software.

In method one, the trader doesn't have to actually subscribe to a data service, per se. The vendor whose computer he is dialing pays the exchange fees and charges the end user a unit charge for access to the main computer. This unit charge might be a flat monthly fee, or it might be a fee based upon the amount of time that the user is logged onto the main system. Examples of this type of data connection might include any number of internet providers, where the trader can log into their web site and look at prices or analyses. These providers are generally somewhat limited. A broader array of analyses and pricing services are available from a direct link into a main computer, such as is available with Telescan, a data provider in Houston, Texas. They have a whole catalog of services and analyses that are available to customers who dial into their system. The prices charged are based upon the amount of time spent logged into the system; also, they offer specific services, such as newsletters and more in-depth analyses that can be viewed for an additional fee.

The second method of getting data is to install the vendor's terminal at your home or business site. This can be a rather expensive method, but it has some advantages, especially for sophisticated users. Perhaps the best known of this type of data vendor is Bloomberg. Bloomberg terminals can be found all over the world, mostly in professional trading rooms. A Bloomberg terminal is installed at your office and is connected to the main Bloomberg computers by a direct phone line. A direct phone line is one that is dedicated to a specific purpose, in this case, to linking the terminal with the main computer. A direct phone line can cost upwards of $500 per month. In addition, the rental cost of a Bloomberg terminal is $1,500 per month.

For this rather large cost, you receive a vast, startling array of data. There are voluminous quotes, not only on listed securities, but on bonds and foreign stocks as well, and sophisticated analyses are available at the press of a key on the terminal. Option implied volatilities, and historic volatilities on the underlying—graphed right on the price graph of the underlying security—are readily available, for example. Moreover, some of the most sophisticated research on Wall Street can be read by Bloomberg users, although much of it requires an additional fee for access. In addition, shopping can even be done on the Bloomberg terminal, although that is hardly a reason to go this route—it's just an added feature.

Another vendor is Track Online, in New York. This one is something of a blend of the first two methods; you can either dial in to their computer, or you can hook your computer up to theirs via a dedicated phone line. They specialize in option analyses, including many in which you can tailor your requirements to see certain outputs. For example, if you wanted to see all available covered writes (or the best ones) on options that were at least 10 percent in-the-money, with premium at certain levels, you could do so.

The third method of receiving data is to have the data come directly into your own computer. This is what SIGNAL, Bonneville, PC Quote, DTN Wallstreet, S&P Comstock, and others supply. With SIGNAL or Bonneville, you can subscribe to real-time prices, or 15-minute delayed prices, or just closing prices. Each one has different costs, with the real-time data being the most expensive. The physical setup differs somewhat for each one, but you will definitely need a computer in order to receive the prices from these vendors. SIGNAL attaches a data box, which they manufacture and sell you, to your computer. The prices come into the data box, and their software accesses the box in order to display the prices on your computer screen. The SIGNAL box can hold over 70,000 quotes at any one time. The other vendors put the data right into your computer, but you will probably have to expand memory in order to handle it. In all cases, your computer can act just like a broker's quote machine. Of course, this ties up your computer while the software is running, so many investors actually buy a second computer to act as a quote machine.

There are four ways that data can physically be delivered to your home or office. One is the direct phone line that we mentioned in connection with Bloomberg or Track Online. That is the most expensive method. SIGNAL subscribers use one of the other three methods: satellite dish, FM radio, or cable television; Bonneville data is available via similar format. If you have cable television available in your area, it is the cheapest and most reliable way of getting the data. You merely plug the TV cable right into the SIGNAL data box and instruct the box to tune to one of these channels: American Movie Classics, CNBC, WGN, or C-Span I. There is no additional cost—

you pay your cable TV bill as you normally would. The data is broadcast on a normally unused portion of the cable TV channel. If you don't have cable TV or don't want to pay for it, SIGNAL information is also available via FM radio in certain metropolitan areas. The SIGNAL box can be tuned to a local FM ratio station and can receive the data via that method. This method is less reliable in terms of data accuracy. FM radio signals can be distorted, and your computer will probably interfere with the signal somewhat. Finally, if neither cable TV nor FM radio works for you, then you can buy a satellite dish from the data vendor and put it on your roof. You then run a wire from the satellite down to your computer or to the SIGNAL box and receive the data that way. This is the most expensive method, because you have to buy the satellite dish and have it installed, but it is the most reliable. The data will always be received; with cable, you would have no data if your local cable TV signal goes out, and with FM radio, you would have no data if the radio station goes off the air, or if there is interference with the broadcast signal.

Software

When you connect directly to the host computer, as you do with Bloomberg or Track Online, then you see the results of the output from software that runs on their large host computer. However, if you buy the data yourself—from SIGNAL or Bonneville, for example—then you are going to need to buy or create some software in order to analyze the data.

Along with the data from SIGNAL, you commonly get a basic software package that lets you get quotes, arrange them in any order that you would like to see, and perhaps even do rudimentary profit and loss statements on your portfolio. *Be sure that the vendor's software can display option* pages. That is, you want the ability to type in the stock, index, or futures symbol and hit one key to get a page of options on that underlying. This is an absolute must, whether you intend to trade spreads or not. Even if you are just an option buyer, you will want to be able to look at several options at once and compare them.

If you want more sophisticated analyses, you need to buy software. Most of the major software packages (for example, technical analysis charting programs, option analysis programs) work with data supplied by the major data providers, such as SIGNAL, Bonneville, or PC Quote.

Buying your own data gives you a lot of flexibility and, if you are an accomplished programmer or want to hire one, this method gives you access to the raw data, from which you can construct your own analyses. Even if you're not a programmer, this may be the best method because (1) you can keep your costs down by only subscribing to markets that you have an interest in, and (2) you only need to buy software that performs the analyses that you will use.

As an option trader, you will probably need to buy some option analysis software if you are bringing data into your own computer. There are several major option software packages available; you can normally find them through advertisements in financial newspapers or magazines. Some of them include Option Vue (Libertyville, Illinois), Option Pro (Wheaton, Illinois), and Option Simulator by Bay Options. In addition, some of the more advanced, broader-based analytical tools, such as First Alert or AIQ, do option analysis as well. A more complete list of available software vendors is normally available from the data vendor. For example, if you buy SIGNAL's data, they will send you a rather large book of approved software vendors. From this, you can see who provides charting services, option analysis, and so forth.

If you are going to buy option software, there are several qualities that I would consider mandatory. First is that the software be able to display option prices in *pages*, along with theoretical values, delta, implied volatility, and so on. I mentioned earlier that I would want the data vendor's software to display option pages. However, if the software vendor's program can display option pages, then you might relax the criterion for the data vendor. The option software should also have a portfolio-management system built into it. This portfolio-management system should be able to do more than calculate profits and losses. It should be able to calculate, for example, the position delta of any position, or of your whole portfolio. Ideally, you would also be able to calculate position vega, gamma, and so forth. In this way, you can determine the exposure of your option portfolio to various market conditions.

The specific model that the software uses is not important. As was explained in Chapter 6, there are several option models available, and they give very similar answers to theoretical value questions. Also, if the model does not specifically calculate futures option theoretical prices, that is not a problem as long as the software allows you to change the short-term interest rate (which almost all software packages do). If you set the short-term interest rate in your model to 0 percent, then you will get the correct theoretical value for nearly all futures options. The exception would be deeply in-the-money futures options, which would appear to be somewhat underpriced by our simplistic method. *Be sure that the software allows you to change the interest rate, if you are going to trade futures options.*

The software should also be able to perform what-if analyses. That is, you construct a position that you are considering and the software can describe how that position will perform in the future, under certain assumptions such as time passing and volatility changing. Preferably, it will graph this information. Option Vue is particularly good at this kind of analysis.

Ideally, your software should be able to keep historical records of volatility and underlying prices. Historical records of option prices are not mandatory, for they take up a lot of disk space and aren't really necessary for further analysis. However, being able to track historical volatility (which can be done via the historical prices of the underlying security) and to track the past ranges of implied volatility are necessary for many option trading strategies, particularly those discussed in Chapters 4, 5, and 6.

Before leaving this section on software, it should be pointed out that there *are* some low-level software programs that are "stand-alone." They do not get their data from a real-time data feed. Rather you, the user, type data into a file, and the software analyzes those data. For many traders, this type of software is often sufficient, and it is always quite inexpensive (less than $100) because it doesn't have to link into a real-time data source, such as SIGNAL or Bonneville. For example, to see the implied volatilities of a group of options, all you would have to do would be to type in the stock price, the expiration date, the strike prices, and the current option prices (for this last item, you would need to have some way of quoting prices). The simple computer software program can then display delta, gamma, implied volatility, and so on. Of course, with no historical record of volatility, you would have a hard time deciding whether or not the options were expensive with respect to their history, but you can see how they compare with each other at the current time. Programs of this type are often called *option calculators*. McMillan Analysis Corp. sells one, as does Ken Trester (Institute for Options Research, Lake Tahoe, Nevada).

In sum, there is no "best" data service and accompanying software. Best depends on what you perceive as your needs. If you are a small investor who only wants to see end-of-day quotes, then something very simple will suffice. However, if you are a real-time trader, then you want a more sophisticated data service, although your software needs may not be complex. Finally, if you are planning on trading volatility in the option markets, then you are going to need more sophisticated software and probably real-time pricing as well.

TRADING METHODOLOGY AND PHILOSOPHY

The preceding chapters have concentrated mostly on trading strategies and systems. Thus far in this chapter, we have looked at how to get yourself physically set up to trade. Those are both very important parts of trading, but there is more to trading, much of which has to do with mental preparation and execution.

Managing Your Money

One of the most important aspects of trading is money management. We have presented several systems and strategies in this book, but it is up to the individual investor or money manager to decide how much of his capital he is going to allocate to each position. However, money management encompasses much more than just deciding how much to invest. It also has to do with taking losses, so that the investor can be "alive" to invest another day.

Most people are familiar with a simple form of money management: dollar cost averaging. This simple strategy—buying the same dollar amount of stock at equally spaced intervals—is designed to help an investor avoid putting all of his money into a market at once, lest he should be buying at the top. It's not a bad strategy, but it has little relevance to short- or intermediate-term trading—it is more of a long-term, buy-and-hold strategy.

Rather, most traders approach short-term trading with a fixed amount of money that they feel comfortable risking. Thus, they have a pool of funds and that pool will either make it or break it; further moneys will not be added if the trading is not working out. A professional trading firm approaches the matter differently. The professional trading firm will put a limit on the losses that it will allow from a strategy—if that limit is hit, trading will cease. This is a proper approach, and one that often distinguishes large professional trading firms from individual investors.

Firms that are in the business of trading will often accept new ideas from outside traders or analysts. Traditionally, such firms have been the large brokerage firms, but in recent years they have cut back on their risk-taking, so hedge funds have taken up the slack. It is sometimes possible for a trader, who has an original idea that is well documented to be profitable, to approach one of these firms and receive trading capital. Profits might be split 50-50, perhaps, but the supplier of the capital has the right to terminate the trading if losses get too large. The firm might terminate trading if losses reach 15 to 20 percent of original capital.

In the late 1980s, one new strategy that was quite profitable was Japanese warrant trading. The Japanese stock market was soaring at that time toward its all-time high of over ¥40,000. Many Japanese companies had issued warrants. Warrants are much like options, except that warrants are issued by a company, and that company retains the proceeds from the initial warrant sale. Market professionals have always felt that hedged warrant trading was a viable strategy. The book, *Beat the Market*, written by Edward Thorp and Sheen Kassouf in 1967, dealt solely with this strategy. In hedged warrant trading, you buy undervalued warrants and short the underlying common in a proper ratio, in order to create a delta neutral hedge.

This is much like owning a cheap straddle in the option market. Profits can accrue if the underlying stock moves way up or down in price, or if the warrant returns to "fair value."

Thorp and Kassouf were only discussing trading in U.S. markets, and their warrant model in the book was a rather simplistic one, but the strategy was sound. Over the years, U.S. companies stopped issuing warrants, and the strategy dried up. However, the same strategy appealed to many traders when the Japanese companies began issuing warrants.

One fairly large and aggressive trading firm agreed to open a department to trade these warrants in a hedged manner, having been approached by a trader who had outlined the benefits of the strategy and had documented its theoretical success. The way in which the trading evolved and the trading firm managed its risk are the point of this story.

The mechanics of operating the strategy with Japanese stocks introduced some different variables into the real-world equation: one was the difficulty and high cost of borrowing the actual shares of Japanese companies (they needed to be borrowed so that they could be sold short as a hedge against the warrants); another was the currency risk for U.S. traders—the underlying market was trading in yen, while the warrants were traded in dollars (the warrants were traded out of Hong Kong and London, so they were denominated in dollars).

But an even more insidious problem was built into the pricing structure, and it was a difficult one to foresee. We have discussed the necessity of measuring implied volatility in percentiles, by looking at where it *has* been trading. Most of Chapter 6 was devoted to trading volatility based on this concept. We saw, however, that sometimes volatility will break out of its previous range and cause losses for a volatility trading strategy.

In effect, warrant hedging is a volatility trading strategy: you attempt to buy the warrants when implied volatility is low and hedge them with stock. When the Japanese market was moving up strongly through the late 1980s and into the beginning of 1990, the range of implied volatilities was quite uniform. However, when that market topped out and began to trade down, implied volatilities fell to as-then unheard of levels. In some cases, out-of-the-money warrants were dropping nearly as fast as the stock (in effect, the delta of an out-of-the-money option was nearly 1.0!). Of course, this atypical action was caused by the decrease in volatility.

In any event, the hedges that were established for the firm's account were losing a great deal of money when this happened. When the losses reached the previously agreed-upon amount, the traders were ordered to liquidate their positions in an orderly manner and close the accounts. No excuses or rationalizations, just no more trading.

This is a discipline that individual traders rarely impose upon themselves. It is easy to make excuses, to reason that next time you'll be more careful with volatility estimates, that you'll be in more liquid issues, and so forth. However, the need to cut losses and terminate a strategy can be great, especially if it is a proven winner and you are losing money trading it. You are probably doing something wrong— perhaps emotions are leading you to overrule your "system—and sometimes the only way to stop that wrongdoing is to stop trading that strategy.

This is distinctly different from operating a strategy properly, but running into a series of poor luck that causes losses. For the firm traders in the previous example, it wouldn't be of much help—hitting the stop-loss point would cause them to lose their jobs in any case. However, individual traders, no matter how wealthy, often work with a fixed pool of capital for a strategy, capital that they are willing to risk in order to determine if the strategy can be a successful one. If they are willing to risk the entire pool of capital (which, we assume, is only a portion of their overall assets), then they would not want to use the fixed-loss form of termination, as in the previous example. Rather, they would use a form of investment that allows them to invest more heavily when they are winning, and to reduce the size of their trades when they are losing.

This is an important concept that was first illustrated to me many years ago in a book I read that detailed the life of the famous gambler, Nick the Greek (not *Jimmy* the Greek). Nick was a well-known gambler who had many interesting stories and who mainly played casino games and bet sports. Nick believed in progressive betting, and so should you. In progressive betting, you increase your bets each time you win, but if you lose, you return to your original bet size.

One night when not much was happening in a particular Las Vegas casino, Nick was standing at a craps table, when a Nebraska farm boy entered and bet $1 on the pass line. He won. He then bet $1 again and won again. The farm boy ran off one of the most amazing streaks Nick had ever seen—he rolled 28 straight passes (even if you're not a casino gambler, you should understand that winning 28 straight wagers on any casino game is a pretty remarkable feat). Then he lost. The farm boy had netted out $27 and he left.

Nick, on the other hand, had started with a $10 bet, and had won $40,000 by the time the farm boy was done with his remarkable streak. Nick did this with progressive betting. He increased his bet each time that he won, eventually betting massive amounts—all of which was the house's money—near the end of the streak. If there hadn't been a table limit, Nick might have broken the house itself on a streak of that length.

The book never explained what progressive system Nick was using, but the common one is to increase your bet by 60 percent every time, pocketing 40 percent of the winnings for yourself. If you are lucky enough to be involved in a streak of even eight or nine straight wins, you'll be very happy. At the end of eight wins, for example, your next bet would be 1.6^8 times your initial bet, which is about 43 times your initial bet. If you think it would be hard to remember how much to bet after each win, especially if the streak gets long, just bet the Fibonacci numbers: 5, 8, 13, 21, and so on. Each one is about 1.61 the previous one, but even easier, each one is the sum of the previous two. So all you have to do, in order to calculate the next one, is remember the last two. That's pretty easy to do, even in the heat of battle.

The power of progressive betting is very strong. Of course, in a casino game, you are destined to be a loser if you play long enough, because the house has an advantage. However, if you just gamble occasionally, it's a lot more fun to use progressive betting, because you might hit a streak that is long enough to make you a winner for life, considering that you are only visiting the casinos occasionally.

Mathematicians have attempted to apply this same thinking to the stock market, and specifically to how much to invest in a trade. The main difference between the casino bets and the stock market investments is that you normally have more than one stock market investment going at a time. So instead of getting a series of sequential results, your results are mixed together. Also, it's easy to know when a casino game ends—the shooter passes or craps out, or the card player wins or loses—but in the stock market, only you are in control of how each investment ends. If you are trading with a system, then that system might have specific entry and exit points, and that would make things easier to evaluate in the context of the money management system that we are going to discuss.

Back in the early 1950s, a scientist at Bell Telephone Laboratories was working on a problem. He needed a formula to determine the optimum usage of lines in a telephone cable. His name was J. L. Kelly, Jr., and in 1956 he published his findings in a technical journal on information theory. How his findings found their way into the gambling community is unknown, although most of the big casinos do employ mathematicians to calculate odds, so perhaps one of them saw the article in an obscure technical journal. When the results of Kelly's analysis were applied to gambling, this money management system became known as the Kelly System. It has since been adapted to the stock market as a money management system as well.

In reality, the Kelly System was designed only for use on items that have only two results (win or lose, true or false, on or off, etc.). This works very well for gambling, but not so well for the stock market. However, with a little adapting, its principles are applicable to the stock market also. The Kelly System assumes that you are going to bet a fixed percentage of your bankroll on each item. If you are making money, your bets will grow in size as your bankroll does. On the other hand, if you hit a bad streak and are losing, the Kelly System automatically reduces your actual bet size as the value of your bankroll decreases.

Here is the original Kelly formula in its simplest form:

$$\text{Amount of bet} = (W + L) \times p - L$$

where W = amount you could win
L = amount you could lose
p = probability of winning

For example, in a situation where you risk one "unit" and pay a 10 percent "commission," the amount you could win (W) would be 1.0, while the amount that you could lose (L) would be 1.1. This reflects the 10 percent commission, which is typical in sports betting. With these values for the variable, the Kelly formula would read:

$$\text{Amount to bet} = 2.1p - 1.1$$

So, in order to use the system, you would only need to know what your probability of predicting winners is. For example, if you can predict winners at a 60 percent rate, the Kelly System would tell you to bet $2.1 \times 0.60 - 1.1 = 0.16$, or 16 percent of your total bankroll on this one bet.

This formula also tells you that, if p is less than about 52 percent, the Kelly System would tell you not to bet at all ($2.1 \times 0.52 - 1.1 = -0.01$). That is, if you are paying a 10 percent commission and can't predict 52 percent winners, then find another line of work. Of course, it's often hard to admit that you can't predict sporting event winners, or day-trade the S&P futures, or whatever. Sometimes it's hard to admit the results yourself, as the following anecdote relates.

A basketball bettor was having a particularly poor season and was lamenting to his friend that he had lost a good deal of money. The concerned friend said, "Well, why don't you try something else? Like betting hockey." The bettor's reply: "Hockey?! I don't know anything about hockey!"

At least with the Kelly criteria, this poor guy could have plugged his winning percentage into the formula and seen, mathematically, that he should have given up basketball betting.

The Kelly formula can't be directly applied to the stock market, because results are more complicated. Each trade doesn't produce a complete loss or a 100 percent profit, less commissions, as sports or casino betting does. A stock, futures, or option trade can have an infinite number of outcomes. Therefore, we have to adapt a little in order to use the Kelly formula. We not only have to gauge the probability of having a winning trade, but also have to take into account how big the wins and losses are. That is, we have to factor the average return into the Kelly formula. In this case, the Kelly formula becomes:

$$\text{Amount to risk} = \frac{\left((r+1) \times p - 1\right)}{r}$$

where p = probability of winning and r = average win/average loss under this strategy (where the average win and loss are computed, assuming an equal investment in each trade).

Alternatively stated, r is also the average rate of return on a trade for whatever system you are using. If you use the average rate of return, then you don't have to enforce the requirement that your historical statistical data are based on an equal investment in each trade. However, the average win and average loss statistics are often readily available for trading system summaries. For example, if you are analyzing an S&P futures day-trading system, most system designers will give you the percent of winning trades and the average win and average loss. This information can then be plugged directly into the Kelly formula.

Suppose that we have the historical results of a trading system, and that it has produced 35 winners and 45 losers, or a probability of winning of 44 percent. In addition, we know that the average winning trade produced a profit of $1,000, and the average losing trade lost $500. This is all the information we need in order to use the Kelly formula (p = 44 percent and r = 2).

$$\text{Amount to risk} = \frac{\left((2+1)\times 0.44 - 1\right)}{2}$$

$$= 0.16$$

Thus, the Kelly criteria say that we should invest 16 percent of our total funds in each trade, when using this strategy.

This is very useful information, as it allows us to increase the size of our trades when our account size is increasing, and forces us to cut back on the size of our trades when the system is losing. Despite that benefit, the Kelly criteria have some problems in that they assume that you are investing sequentially. That is, you are using the system for one trade at a time.

However, most investors are trading several things at a time. For example, suppose you are trading option volume alerts, watching for increasing option volume and then buying stock in anticipation of corporate news events, as described in Chapter 4. At times, there may only be a few of these situations, but at other times there may be many of them. If the Kelly criteria told us to invest 20 percent of our funds in each one trade, what would we do if there were more than five trades that needed to be positioned at one time? One solution might be to trade on margin, but a more conservative approach would be to use what is called the *risk-adjusted* method. In this method, the amount invested in a trade is the Kelly percentage of the *available* equity in the account.

Suppose that we computed the Kelly criteria, and they say to invest 20 percent of our capital in each trade. Then, incorporating the risk-adjusted method into the trading would result in the following amount of capital being invested in each trade.

Trade Number	Available Capital Before This Trade (%)	Capital Invested in This Trade (%)	Available Capital After This Trade (%)
1	100	20	80
2	80	16	64
3	64	12.8	51.2
etc.			

Thus, if Kelly says to invest 20 percent, then the first trade would consume 20 percent of your whole equity. That leaves 80 percent of your equity to be invested. The next trade would then be 20 percent of the available equity—or 20 percent of 80 percent (16 percent) of the entire account. In terms of the whole account, 20 percent would be invested in the first trade and 16 percent in the second trade, leaving 64 percent of the account as available equity. The third trade would require 20 percent of 64 percent, and so forth.

The main problem with this sequence of money management is that the first trade is bigger than the rest, but it is the only way to guarantee that you don't overinvest and still adhere to the Kelly criteria. Moreover, if a lot of trades are going into the account at one time, and all might be negatively affected by the same event (news or volatility, for example), this method automatically scales back the size of each new position. This reduces the tendency to overtrade a particular system at any one time. In addition, as time passes and trades are opened and closed, the sizes of the trades will tend to even out.

Using the risk-adjusted method will even allow you to combine different strategies (which presumably would have different Kelly percentages). For each new investment, you merely use the apropriate Kelly percentage and apply it against the remaining equity in the account, in order to determine how much to invest in any particular trade.

In summary, then, the Kelly criteria can be coupled with the risk-adjusted method to produce a useful and impartial way to help you manage your money as you establish each new position.

Speculative Trading Procedures

In this book, many of the trading opportunities identified are speculative in nature. If you are using option volume, option premiums, or the put–call ratio as a predictive indicator, you are most likely going to take an outright position as opposed to a hedged strategy. Therefore, it would be pertinent to discuss the general philosophy of trading an outright position.

In a broad sense, outright speculative positions are the easiest to manage—you are generally long a security (stock, futures, calls, or puts) and all you have to do for followup action is to adhere to some sort of a stop loss. In reality, though, an outright trading position needs more management than that—from initial selection to final sale. In some cases there is no underlying—sector index options, for example, so options are then the only choice. However, when there is a choice, the only way to logically make it is to evaluate the options with a mathematical model. *You must know the relative price of an option before you trade it.* If the options are too expensive, you may then decide to trade the underlying instead.

In order to decide if the options are "too expensive," you must have some gauge against which to measure the current option price. That gauge, of course, is volatility. You should compare the current implied volatility of the options to the recent historical volatility of the underlying. In addition, you should also compare the current implied volatility with recent implied volatilities. An example should help in understanding this procedure.

A trader is going to buy "the market." He can either buy OEX options or buy S&P 500 futures. With OEX at 550, these are the relevant statistics:

OEX: 550

Option	Implied Volatility (%)
545 call	13
550 call	12
555 call	11

Historical volatility: 9

Given this information, it appears as if the options are overpriced, and so the trader might opt to buy the S&P 500 futures instead of any of these options. However, a little more investigation reveals that the OEX options *always* seem to have an implied volatility that is higher than the historical volatility. In fact, over the past few months, OEX implied volatility has ranged between 11 and 18 percent. Thus, implied volatility is currently near the lower end of that range.

Moreover, looking at historical volatility in the same context, the trader finds that over the past few months, historical volatility has ranged between 6 and 13 percent, so it is currently near the center of that range.

Given this additional information—that implied volatility is near the lower end of its normal range, and that it is normally higher than historical volatility—the trader would opt to buy the calls instead of the futures.

Another decision that must then be made is which option to buy. As mentioned earlier in this chapter, buying the short-term in-the-money option is usually the best choice. The trader obtains leverage because he owns an option, but he does not spend a lot for time value premium. The number one reason that option buyers lose money is that they buy options that are too far out-of-the-money. These options also may have too little time remaining. This mistake can cause the trader to lose money even though the underlying may move in his favor. Whereas, with the in-the-money option, he will almost assuredly make money if the underlying has a favorable move.

As for actually buying the position, be careful about using market orders in options unless (1) you are trading a very liquid option, such as OEX or IBM, or (2) you are placing a small order of 10 contracts or less. Otherwise, limit orders would serve you better in the long run. You may find that you can often "split" a market (i.e., buy between the bid and offer), especially in a moderately active option. Don't be stubborn about using limits, though. If you are attempting to buy a very thin (illiquid) option, the market makers may just raise their offer when they see your bid, for they don't really want to take a position.

Risk management, through stops, of an existing position is another important factor, especially in speculative trading. Not only must you adhere to a stop loss of some sort, but you should also have a plan for taking partial profits at times along the way. I generally prefer to set my stops based on technical support and resistance levels in the chart of the underlying security. Some traders who buy options set stops based on the *option* price; this can mean that time will stop them out or that they sell their options when the underlying is sitting right on a support level—*not* a good idea. However, when they are trading in-the-money options, they don't have to worry about time decay so much, so they can use the underlying's technical levels to place their stops.

If you are trading options, use a *mental* stop; if you are trading stock or futures, you can use an *actual* stop. A mental stop means that you don't actually have a stop-loss order on the floor of an exchange, but when the underlying hits your mental stop price, you can evaluate the situation at that time. If it seems that the position should be sold, then you can decide on a market or limit order. In general, if your mental stop has been violated, and the stock or futures contract seems to be headed in the wrong direction, a market order is best. However, if the stock or futures seem stable, you might try to use a limit order to exit the position.

Perhaps even more important than limiting losses is managing profits. Everyone wants to follow the conventional wisdom to "limit your losses and let your profits run." But actually doing it is more difficult than it might appear. Most traders know the anguish of seeing a position move in their favor, thereby generating an unrealized gain, only to have it fall back and stop them out. To me, this is far more devastating than taking a profit too early, although we can attempt to get the best of both worlds. There are two ways to do this: (1) take partial profits, and (2) use a trailing stop.

Some traders take partial profits on a strict basis. For example, if they own options, they may sell a part of the position if they get a 25 percent profit. Then they would sell a similar portion if they get a 50 percent profit. Then they would attempt to hold the remainder with a mental stop. Other traders prefer to take profits based on the underlying's action—if it hits resistance or spurts ahead too fast, they take partial profits on their position. In either case, this is the correct approach, for it allows them to take some realized gains but still lets their profits run.

The other technique that protects profits is the trailing stop. Once a position begins to move in your favor, raise your stop price, whether it be a mental or an actual stop. Initially, you use a fairly tight stop in a trading position. But, if you are taking partial profits along the way, you might not want to keep the trailing stop as tight when you raise it. That is, when things are going your way, leave some extra room for a small correction to take place without stopping you out.

Actual Trading Examples

On the following pages, there are some rather extraordinary historical examples of actual positions that I have been involved in at one time or another; some of you may call these "war stories." These examples will help to illustrate some of the points regarding judgment, timing, and luck in the stock and options market. I once heard Jack Schwager (author of *Market Wizards*) say that no one ever gives bad examples of their theories or systems, just good ones. That's a good point, so some of these examples are of losing trades as well as winning ones. Even experienced traders might enjoy these examples, perhaps because they had similar positions themselves.

The previous section discussed the usage of stops. Of course, no matter how carefully you plan to set stops, there is very little that you can do if no trading takes place. One of the most severe trading gaps that I personally experienced was in the stock of Cities Service Company, back in 1982. All during 1981 and 1982, there had been a myriad of oil company takeovers, many at very inflated prices. Two of the biggest were Conoco (which was eventually acquired by Dupont after outbidding both Seagrams and Mobil) and Marathon Oil (which was acquired by U.S. Steel).

In 1982, Gulf Oil made a bid for Cities Service at $63 per share. As head of the arbitrage department for Thomson McKinnon, I began to acquire a position. Not only was the stock selling at a wide discount to the eventual tender price—it was selling in the mid-50s—but out-of-the-money puts were expensive as well. So we sold puts naked and bought stock. Most of the arbitrage departments on Wall Street did the same, and then we all tendered our stock to Gulf Oil. After that, one could only sit and wait until the appropriate date, when Gulf would take in the stock and pay out cash.

Unfortunately, that day never came. For reasons that were never specified, Gulf decided to back out. Rumors had begun to spread that something was amiss, but no one could really sell their Cities Service stock because virtually all of the shares in existence had been tendered to Gulf. That made matters worse; the only thing that traders could do was buy puts for protection, but those quickly became so expensive as to be prohibitive. A few Cities Service shares were trading in the cash market, but they were few and far between. By and large, though, most arbs still felt the deal was going to go through.

It was as if Gulf Oil was out to exact the maximum amount of pain, as they waited until a Friday afternoon to make it official—they were, in fact, withdrawing their offer and were releasing all shares that had been tendered to them. Trading halted in Cities Service and didn't reopen until the following Wednesday because of order imbalances (not a very good showing by the NYSE's specialist system). When it finally opened, it opened at 30, down 22 from the last trade!

The aftermath of this Cities Service blown deal was, at the time, one of the biggest single disasters that Wall Street trading firms had ever suffered in their own accounts. Some smaller trading houses went out of business; even Ivan Boesky's firm was in dire straits, needing to borrow money to stay afloat until somebody could rescue the stock.

Cities Service executives, who were basically as much in the dark as anyone else during Gulf's nefarious internal board meetings, set about to find another suitor. They did, in Occidental Petroleum, who bought the company a few months later for about $50 per share. This prevented disaster for any arbs who had the staying power to hold onto their stock during the worst of the mess. Even though we lost money, our loss was only about a tenth of what it might have been had OXY not rescued us all. To this day, I refuse to buy Gulf Oil products.

The preceding story illustrates how unexpected losses can occur when a stock gaps. Not only that, it shows that the unexpected can strike any position. No matter how careful your planning and analysis, and no matter how many others doing independent analysis agree with your position, there are just no guarantees, period. However, life does have its strange twists, and you must keep alert for opportunities at all times. It does no good to mope and become mentally weakened by such a loss as the Cities Service deal inflicted. Time and again, I have seen a very good opportunity follow right on the heels of a major loss.

The Cities Service deal blew apart in early August 1982. By late August, another deal was formulating for the stock of Martin-Marietta. There was a vague bid for the company that not many arbs were taking seriously. However, Martin-Marietta stock traded up to near 40 and options were very expensive. At the time, our independent floor broker on the PHLX (which is where Martin-Marietta options were traded) called to show us a seemingly very attractive trade: we could buy the stock at 40 and sell the September 35 calls for 8. This was a huge premium for an option that had less than a month of life remaining, so we took the trade in size. The downside breakeven for this trade was thus 32 at September expiration.

As the next few weeks progressed, the chances of a real bid for Martin-Marietta seemed to weaken, and the stock fell to the 33–34 area. This was perilously close to the breakeven point, but since we were approaching this from a risk arb point of view, the position was held in its original form. The premiums remained large on the options. Even with the stock at about 33½ on Wednesday of expiration week, the Sep 35 calls were trading at a price of more than a dollar.

At that point, option volume increased significantly and option premiums picked up even more, although the stock itself didn't move much at all. After a series of internal meetings with the executive vice president overseeing the arbitrage, who encouraged us to play the situation aggressively if we really liked it, we covered the Sep 35 calls that we were short. This was theoretically illogical, of course, since the options were so expensive; moreover, it left us completely exposed on the downside.

The next day, Bendix Corporation emerged as a major factor and bid $45 for Martin-Marietta. Within a matter of two weeks, they had purchased the stock and the arbs received their cash.

The point of the Martin-Marietta story is a subtle one, in terms of trading. The actual strategy employed was extremely risky, but that's the game we had elected to play in risk arbitrage. The example is not meant to demonstrate that you should unhedge your hedged positions, but rather to show that you should operate your strategies consistently. Both Cities Service and Martin-Marietta were aggressive positions. To have changed strategies after the Cities Service deal blew would have been a mistake.

Of course, you don't *always* get such a great chance to recover from major losses. I was once asked at a seminar to describe my best trade and my worst trade. I chose the following as my worst trade, not only because of the result, but because of the trading mistakes that were made.

Nineteen eighty-six had been a pretty good year for risk arbitrage, even for those of us who were operating without access to Drexel Burnham's Mike Milken's deals. That was the heyday of leveraged buyouts, and many deals were consummated via that method. For those needing a definition, a leveraged buyout occurs when an entity interested in taking over a company uses the company's own assets as collateral for the buyout of the company. The collateral often took the form of "junk bonds," which were marketed by Mr. Milken's group at Drexel. For those wanting a more in-depth description, see the movie *Wall Street* or read the books, *Den of Thieves*, by James Stewart, or *Barbarians at the Gate*, by Borrough and Helyar.

One week in late November, there was a rumor that Gillette was going to be taken over. The stock traded up to 60 on the rumor and options got very expensive, as volume increased in both the stock and the options. The person who did the research for our arbitrage department liked the prospects and I liked the opportunity to sell some of the expensive put premium. Thus, we wound up both buying the stock and selling the puts. After the close of trading on Friday, I realized that we had accidentally doubled our purchase of stock. I was working the order, and the research director was also working the same order, through another broker. This wasn't a crisis, though, as we usually added to a position for several days if we continued to like it.

Saturday morning, I picked up a copy of the *New York Times* and saw the headline "Ivan Boesky Arrested." Uh oh. Over the remainder of the weekend, arbs everywhere speculated on the severity of the beating that the market, and arb stocks in particular, would take on Monday. As it turned out, the market was actually quite calm on Monday, so it appeared that nothing untoward was going to happen.

However, by Tuesday, the attitude had changed and there was nothing but scrambling going on to exit from as much inventory as possible, all over the street. Heavy losses were taken by most arbs in the next week or two, reducing a good year to a less than average one. We eventually exited the last of our Gillette at prices under $50 per share.

There were several reasons that this Gillette trade ranks in my mind as my worst trade, and none of them really have to do with the bad timing of Ivan Boesky's arrest occurring right after we had taken the position. First, there was the matter of the double purchase of stock. Second, we didn't sell much stock on Monday, while the market was stable. I might argue, by the way, that I don't always feel that I know how the market will react to a certain piece of news. I normally let the market show *me* which direction it will take (this has kept me from some bad guesses over the years). However, in this particular case, the market seemed to take a whole trading day to make up its mind, an almost unheard-of occurrence in the volatile markets of the 1980s and 1990s. In any case, there was a chance to sell Gillette stock at a small loss on Monday and lessen risk in the face of the Boesky news. The fact that no one else was selling, either, should not have been a real consideration, but it was. The third mistake was a more personal one, and is not necessarily related to the management of a trading position, but it was in taking a large risk near the end of the year when our compensation was based on profits for the total year.

On top of all those problems, there was the fact that the random event—Boesky's arrest could and did occur at just the wrong time, and it blew the position out of the water. I believe that's what's called Murphy's Law, to a large degree. Moreover, there was no *one* trade—à la the Martin-Marietta deal—that allowed traders to bounce back from the losses of December 1986, although the first half of 1987 was generally very profitable for arbs and traders alike.

When I didn't sell the Gillette on Monday, it was the same as saying, in effect, that I didn't believe in my own analysis (which was that the Boesky arrest would be bad for arb stocks). It wasn't the same as having researched a company's prospects and having a definitive, statistical or mathematical opinion to go by—it was more of a gut feeling, which can be wrong at times. However, if you *do* have a well-researched opinion, you should stand your ground. That is the point of the next section.

An important aspect of trading is believing in your own methodology, if you are convinced that you have adequately researched it. You need to have enough conviction in your own ideas and methods so that you can profit from them. It *is* possible to discover something that the majority of the investment community has overlooked or has chosen to ignore. I don't mean some small stock that no one knows about—that kind of information is generally of an "inside" nature. Nor am I talking about deciding that some patently obvious fact will make a stock move. I mean a public fact that, for one reason or another, is just not being acted upon by the majority of traders. The next two examples demonstrate the wrong approach and the right approach.

In 1973, Disney began to rerelease some of its classics for the first time in years. My neighbor went to see whatever the current release was—perhaps *Cinderella*, I really don't remember. He was so convinced that this was a superior strategy on Disney's part that he went out and bought the stock. Over the next year, which encompassed one of the century's worst bear markets, the stock fell over 50 percent. Now, that's not bad luck, that's poor analysis. Didn't the entire world have the chance to evaluate the impact of Disney's releases and factor that into the stock price? Of course they did, so there was no advantage in his "information."

This was clearly an "obvious" analysis, poorly researched; on the other hand, the next example is about information that is not readily apparent to the average trader. If you have taken the time and effort to thoroughly analyze a position, you should check your research with someone who is knowledgeable and you can trust. If your analysis holds up under that scrutiny, then do not be afraid to act on it. You must realize that most useful technical indicators were invented by individuals; had they not had the conviction to act on their research, they might have missed out on a golden opportunity. Such ideas might involve buying or selling volatility when no one else seems to think it is the right time to do so, or it may involve a more intricate, but no less obvious, thing such as a hedged opportunity. We look for them in our newsletter all the time. Here is an example from several years ago.

In 1980, gold stocks were very popular and the price of gold was near its all-time high. It came to my attention—rather luckily—that the South African gold stocks were all paying unusually high dividends in the summer of 1980. The only reason that I even noticed these dividend increases was that I had bought a few of these stocks for my children, and I saw the dividends hitting their accounts.

Now, ASA Limited (at the time known as American South African) is a closed-end mutual fund of South African gold stocks, that trades on the NYSE. ASA would collect dividends from the stocks it owned all year. However, it would pay a "normal," small dividend in February, May, and August. Then, if there was any excess dividend income, it would pay it out in the form of a special dividend in November. For several years, the special dividend had been 50 cents each year. However, by getting the report of ASA's holdings, and calculating how much they were receiving in dividends, it appeared that they would have to pay a special dividend in excess of $2.50 in order to pay out most of the unusual dividend income they were receiving that year.

I checked this information with a small research firm, with whom we had a friendly working relationship, and they concurred with my analysis. However, the option market had not factored this information in at all. If you know there is going to be a special dividend, then the puts should be expensive and the calls cheap, to reflect the fact that the stock will go ex-dividend with no corresponding benefit to the option holders. In reality, the options were priced exactly as if the special dividend was going to be 50 cents, as usual.

Trading the arbitrage account for Thomson McKinnon, we established risk-free conversions by buying stock, buying puts, and selling calls. We were paying only 50 cents for the special dividend portion of the conversion, however. As we established these conversions, market makers and others taking the other side made it quite obvious that they thought we were fools for overpaying for the arbitrage. If you have a truly original idea, this is the point where you must gather yourself and ignore the "traditional" information. By the time we had set up 100,000 shares, the markets adjusted, and some of the bigger market makers had come to see our point of view.

Eventually, the big day came. ASA Limited held their dividend meeting in New York on a Thursday morning, and did indeed decide to declare a $2.50 special dividend. However, they only made a brief press release and headed out for lunch. Reuters News Service picked up the release and issued a one-line message, but Dow Jones would not publish the news because they needed confirmation (a company policy) and no one was at the ASA offices—they were all at lunch! This caused us consternation because, in those days, very few people—not us—had Reuters News; Dow Jones was the news "king." So we had to wait through the lunch hour in order to be sure that we were going to officially make our profits. We succeeded.

What was especially amazing was that this strategy worked for the next several years, but never to the same degree. It only "disappeared" when the price of gold got into a real bear market and the South African stocks stopped paying large dividends in the mid-1980s. In retrospect, it appears that the reason that this strategy worked was twofold: (1) not many people were interested in it, and (2) the information regarding the South African dividends was not widely published, although it was certainly available to anyone who bothered to look for it.

You can see the difference between the Disney example and the ASA example: one was an obvious fact that everyone knew, while the other was a public fact that no one was paying any attention to. When we refer to serious research that you must stand behind, even if no one else is believing it or acting upon it, we are referring to something akin to the ASA example.

Lest you feel that those sorts of things only happened in the early days of options, when people were less sophisticated, I want to describe the potential available in two-tiered tender offers. The similarities between the St. Joe Minerals takeover in 1981 and the Chiron takeover in 1994 are striking.

Both takeovers involved partial-tender offers, with a residual stock trading after the partial tender. This is sometimes referred to as a "two-tier" deal. Before getting into the actual historical examples, a general one explaining two-tier deals and how options can be used with them might be useful.

In a two-tier deal, the company doing the buyout usually makes a cash tender offer for a percentage of the company to be acquired, something like 50 percent or so; this initial tender is called *the front end*, while whatever happens afterwards is called *the back end*. After the front-end tender is completed, the remainder of the company to be acquired, called *the stub*, trades freely in the marketplace, sometimes with a different name. In the 1980s, the acquiring company could then make a tender offer for the stub as well, but laws were changed, so currently the stub has to trade as stock.

While the first part of the two-tier deal—the cash tender offer—is taking place, the stock being acquired will trade at a price that reflects the *total* value of both parts of the deal. Suppose that ABC is going to buy XYZ in a two-tier deal. It is going to offer $100 a share for 50 percent of the company; after that, the remaining stub, which represents 50 percent of the original XYZ, will trade freely in the marketplace. Furthermore, suppose that analysts place the value of the stub at $60 per share.

We would then see XYZ trading at about 77 per share, for if you bought 100 shares of XYZ and tendered them, you would get 100 for 50 shares, and the other 50 shares would be worth 60 (if the analysts' estimates are correct), which you could sell in the open market. Thus, you would sell the XYZ for an average of $80 per share (half at 100 and half at 60). The reason that XYZ sells for slightly less than 80 is that some carrying cost is built into the current price, since it takes time for the tender to be completed, and for the stub to begin trading. As the actual date of the cash tender approaches, XYZ will drift upwards toward 80.

Before reading on, with XYZ at 77, what price would you expect a put with a striking price of 80 to sell for in the preceding example? The answer is at the end of the next paragraph.

In-the-money calls on XYZ in the example would be trading at parity prior to the first part of the deal, the cash tender offer. They wouldn't have any time value premium because the stock will drop 20 points (from 80 to 60) as soon as the first part of the deal is over. If you owned calls on XYZ in this example, you could always exercise them and tender the stock you got via the exercise. If you didn't, your calls would lose a tremendous amount of value (you can't tender calls, only stock). Puts, on the other hand, reflect the value of the stub. So, since the stub is supposedly going to be trading at 60, a put with a striking price of 80 would have to sell for at least 20 points. This is an important concept that is not readily understood by the average option trader.

The two-tier deal just described was not new to Wall Street in 1981, when Fluor Corporation decided to bid for St. Joe Minerals. However, since puts had only been listed for a short while at that time (they were first listed in 1977), this may have been the first two-tier deal in which the company to be acquired—St. Joe Minerals—had listed puts available.

Fluor Corporation made a two-tiered bid for St. Joe Minerals in 1981. The front end was for 60 percent at a price of 60. The back end was also scheduled to be a tender offer—at an unspecified price in the high 40s. As I recall, the cash tender in the front end was to expire in early February, so we were buying February puts to hedge the stock being purchased.

For reasons that I never quite understood, the marketplace was offering a virtually free arbitrage. With St. Joe trading at 53, the Feb 55 puts were selling at about nine. These are rough numbers, as a lot of years have passed since this arbitrage was executed, but they are indicative of what happened. Consider this trade:

Buy 1,000 St. Joe at 53	$53,000 debit
Buy 4 Feb 55 puts at 9	3,600 debit
Sell 600 St. Joe at 60 via tender	36,000 credit
Sell 400 St. Joe at 55 via put exercise	22,000 credit
Net credit:	1,400 credit

As long as the front end of the deal went through, this was guaranteed money. Apparently, most institutional money managers and many other arbitrageurs were skeptical about the back end of the deal, and thus weren't willing to pay too much for St. Joe—they kept the price around 53. The relative newness of put options meant that they either didn't realize puts were available for trading, or they didn't visualize being able to lock in the back end by buying the puts. In any case, we made a very nice profit.

You might think that situations like that would have disappeared as the years went by. To a certain extent, you would be right. However, these two-tier deals are rather rare, and whenever one appears, there seems to be opportunity for the buyer of stock who also hedges himself with puts. This was true as recently as the end of 1994, when Chiron was involved in one of these two-tier deals.

This was the "deal" for Chiron (symbol, CHIR): a partial tender offer was being made for 40 percent of the company at $117 per share. The remainder of the company was then to exist in the open market, trading as its own stock once again. The partial tender was probably going to happen before January option expiration, but there was a chance that a second request for information by the government could delay the payout until after January expiration.

Here were the current prices at the beginning of December with CHIR at 75:

Dec 70 call: $5\frac{1}{4}$ Dec 70 put: $\frac{1}{4}$
Jan 70 call: 6   Jan 70 put: $7\frac{1}{2}$
April 70 call: 7   April 70 put: 18

Anyone with any understanding of option prices at all, would have to know that the Jan 70 and April 70 puts look very expensive—but why? The novice often views such puts as an attractive sale. Moreover, the novice would probably not understand why Chiron was only trading at $75. Note that the calls are trading near parity, only reflecting enough time value premium to account for the time until the front-end tender actually occurred.

Now, I didn't have the wherewithal to analyze what the back-end stub would be worth, but I didn't need to. Apparently, analysts had looked at what the remaining company would contain and had decided that it would be worth something in the low 50s. I knew this, even without talking to one of these analysts. Why? Because we have to assume that the arbitrageurs are not stupid, and have priced the stock properly, where "properly" means that they could make about a three-point profit or so if the deal goes through and their analysis is correct. Since a Chiron shareholder would sell 40 percent of his stock at 117, then the total value of his stock would be: $0.40 \times \$117 + 0.60 \times \text{stub} = \$78$. With Chiron currently at 75, leaving a little room for arbitrage profit (78 − 75, or 3 points) on the total deal, is about right for carrying costs, and so on. Solving this equation, we find that the stub is projected to be worth 52.

Now, admittedly, there could be some conjecture over whether the back end (the part of Chiron that is going to trade after the partial-tender offer) is worth more or less than 52. However, given that the current price of Chiron ($75) is "predicting," arithmetically, a price of 52, the put options had to be priced as if Chiron were going to be there when the tender ended. Thus, if Chiron were 52, an April 70 put should be worth about

18, which is exactly where it was trading. As in the two previous examples, the puts' prices are only related to where Chiron would be trading *after* the tender; put holders or sellers would not participate in the partial tender offer at 117.

Okay, so why were the Jan 70 puts only selling for 7? Weren't they a steal? Actually, the Jan puts were a huge speculation, because it wasn't known whether they would be worth zero (if the tender were not completed before January expiration) or 18 (if the tender were finished before January expiration). Only people who had some specific feeling on the timing for the deal should have traded the January puts.

The strategy that we established was to buy Chiron stock at these levels and to buy the *April* puts against the remaining 60 percent position. For example, buy 1,000 CHIR and buy 6 April 60 puts. Then, as long as the partial tender at 117 takes place, the downside risk is limited by the presence of the long puts.

If, for some reason, CHIR traded at a higher price than 52, then we might be able to generate additional profits for we would, in effect, own the stub and the April 60 puts—which is equivalent to owning an April 60 call. So if the stub really took off, we would own free calls.

The risk, of course, is that something happens to "break" the deal, and the partial tender never takes place. In that case, CHIR would collapse and large losses would occur on the 1,000 long shares of stock, despite the presence of the six long puts.

The way things worked out, that was an unnecessary worry. As the tender date approached (which turned out to be *before* January expiration), Chiron stock rose slightly to just over 80. This rise, however, reflected more optimistic estimates for the back end of the deal. In fact, the stub opened for trading at 61 (much higher than the original estimate of 52) and eventually traded all the way up to 67. The "equivalent" calls that were bought for a fractional price, eventually became worth $7. Thus, the two-tier strategy paid off, just by observing what was happening in the arbitrage and by constructing the appropriate hedge using the puts.

Why didn't everybody set up this hedge? I don't really know. Although one logical reason is probably *size*. The positions held by aribtrageurs and money managers in Chiron were so huge that there just weren't enough puts available for purchase to hedge the positions. Thus, a smaller trader can sometimes have a safer trade than the "big boys."

OPTION TRADING PHILOSOPHY

In this final section of the book, we discuss some of the aspects of trading that are specific to options. These are not all-encompassing, nor do they guarantee a profit, but if you follow these guidelines, you will have the best chance of being successful with your option trading. These guidelines are *not* the path to easy riches, but following them will generally keep you out of trouble, increase your efficiency of capital, and hopefully improve your chances of making money with options. If you are an experienced option trader, you probably follow a lot of these guidelines subconsciously, not even bothering to think about them. However, if you're new to option trading, then these might prove to be things that you'd want to check as you establish a new position. Some of these have been mentioned in earlier sections of the book, but they are important enough to stress again.

Trade in accordance with your comfort level.

There is a myriad of strategies that option traders can employ. Some will be more in line with your risk and reward levels than others. For example, some traders don't like to buy options. In fairly stagnant markets, the daily wearing away of the option due to time decay is more than they can handle. If this is the way that *you* feel, then you may want to specialize in spread trading and volatility selling.

On the other hand, if you are not comfortable selling naked options, then don't. Even though such strategies are nicely profitable for some traders, they should not be used if they cause you sleepless nights or other consternation.

A friend of mine was an option trader on the floor of the AMEX. As was the custom in the mid-1980s, he was a rather large seller of naked options. However, somewhere along the way, he stopped selling options. I asked him why, and he replied, "I was wishing my life away. I always wished it was next month so that the options would expire."

My favorite story regarding an aversion to selling naked options, though, goes back to someone you would least expect—a very risk-oriented individual, who was head of an arbitrage department.

In the 1970s and 1980s, it was common for most of the equity risktaking of a firm—even one as large as Paine Webber—to be done by one department. Thus, the department would trade risk arbitrage, convertible arbitrage, index arbitrage, reversal and conversion arbitrage, and also would take a certain number of risk-oriented positions. These risk-oriented positions might be some outright long or short positions in stock, some option strategies, and so forth.

A good friend of mine was trading convertible arbitrage and also setting up option strategies. The head of the department was a well-known arbitrageur who didn't blink at positions of several hundred thousand shares in a risk arbitrage position. However, he didn't really understand options too well, so one day, in 1974, he asked my friend to explain his position in IBM options. Apparently the position had been marking to market at a small loss, and the head of the department wanted to know why. The reason was that IBM had been rallying in October and November, coming out of its oversold bottom of the 1973–1974 bear market.

The position was a 1-by-2 ratio call spread—the specific details are forgotten, but it was on the order of being long 100 IBM Jan 240 calls and short 200 Jan 270 calls. The spread had an upside breakeven point of about 300. Thus, it was net naked short about 100 IBM calls and IBM was trading around 210 or 220.

So the trader explained that the position was good for another 80 points or so on the upside over the next three months, and that it could make about $300,000 if IBM got to 270 at expiration. However, the head of the department wanted to know what the result would be if IBM were at 350. When told that this would be a loss of $500,000, he said "What if the Arabs take over IBM at 350? We're screwed. Take off the position."

Now that's paranoia. What were the odds of the Arabs (who were extremely powerful with their OPEC cartel in those days) even *wanting* a computer company? Probably something way less than one-tenth of one percent. Still, it was too much risk for this otherwise heavy risktaker. At the least, the department head, an experienced trader, knew what made him uncomfortable, and he didn't want to pursue that strategy any longer.

Your comfort level extends beyond just deciding whether to trade options strictly from the long side or the short side. It goes deeper—more toward your approach to the overall market. Some people prefer hedging, some prefer speculating. Hedgers generally limit their overall profit, but also have less risk than speculators do. If hedged positions drive you crazy because you know you'll have a losing side as well as a winning side, then perhaps you should trade options more as a speculator, forming opinions and acting on them accordingly.

One friend of mine, back in the early 1970s, was trading the house account for one of the major grain companies. That is, he was risking their money in the futures market. After a successful career doing that, he decided that he could do better as a floor trader, and he moved to Chicago and bought a seat on the CBOT to primarily trade corn.

His first major position was a very large intramarket spread in corn, something like long May, short March, perhaps. He had always approached the market as a speculator, so this position was a little foreign to him, but he felt that the safety of the spread was a good idea. It turned out to be a bad idea. No matter which way the price of corn went—up, down, or sideways—the spread continued to go against him and cost him money. Eventually, the losses wiped out all the equity in his account.

He later became one of the biggest and most successful corn speculators, but he never traded a hedged position again.

The important thing to realize is that it is much easier to make money if you are "in tune" with your strategies, whatever they may be. No one strategy is right for all traders due to their individual risk and reward characteristics, and accompanying psychological demands.

Many traders don't like speculating, preferring a more conservative tack. If that is your philosophy, that's fine. You should look for hedged positions with a statistical edge, and not attempt to day trade or engage in other forms of short-term speculation.

There's an interesting footnote to the previous story about the grain trader. He did go broke from that corn spread, but was able to borrow money and get started again. Eventually, after he had made his fortune, he told me that there's a saying: "You're never broke until you go broke twice." What he meant was that many successful traders went broke once, but bounced back to make large profits. The first time was a learning experience.

Now, I'm not sure that everyone needs to go broke before becoming successful, but it happens to a lot of traders. Those who learn from their initial mistakes can recover to become successful traders.

Always use a model.

We have, throughout the book, referred to the necessity of employing a model to evaluate options. The biggest mistake that option traders make is failing to check the fair value of the option before it is bought or sold. It may seem like a nuisance—especially if you or your broker don't have real-time evaluation capability—but this is the basis of all option investments, whether they be strategic or speculative. You need to know whether you're getting a bargain or paying too much for the option.

Don't always use options—the underlying may be better (if options are overpriced or markets are too wide).

This statement is related to the previous tenet of using a model. Sometimes it's better to trade the underlying stock or futures contract rather than the options, especially if you're looking for a quick trade. Over a short time period, an overpriced option may significantly underperform the movement by the underlying instrument. There are other advantages to trading the underlying. For one thing, there is more liquidity and markets are therefore tighter. Also, you can more readily use stop orders (I don't recommend using stop orders on options themselves). On the other hand, the advantages to trading options are leverage, limited dollar risk, and a possible theoretical advantage if the options are cheap.

Avoid buying out-of-the-money options.

In Chapter 4, we stressed the importance of buying in-the-money options as a substitute for the underlying stock. So this is a related statement. In reality, there are some rare occasions on which you might benefit from buying out-of-the-money options, but it would generally be to limit your risk to a fixed amount in a highly volatile situation. We discussed the Federal Paperboard (FBO) bull spread as an example of that. Another example is Sybase.

In Chapter 4, we related the story of how Sybase (SYBS) had heavy put volume, and then the stock collapsed when the company forecast poor earnings. This was an extremely volatile stock, so that even the in-the-money options had a good deal of time value premium. With the stock at 42, and the negative rumors being very rampant, the following option prices existed (April was the near-term month) for SYBS: 42:

> April 50 put: 9½
> April 45 put: 5½
> April 40 put: 2
> April 35 put: none available for trading

These all had ridiculously high implied volatilities, which would have collapsed had the negative rumor proved to be false. If there had been an April 35 put listed, I would probably have bought a bear spread (buying the April 40 or 45 put and selling the April 35). But, since there wasn't, I was faced with the choice of buying an expensive in-the-money put, or buying the out-of-the-money April 40 put. The April 40 was, of course, the most expensive in terms of implied volatility, but it also offered the least dollar risk. Therefore, I decided on the amount of money that I was willing to lose in this issue and bought the April 40 puts. It was the only out-of-the-money option that I bought all year.

This example is atypical in that the in-the-money options were so expensive. In that case, and that case only, would I consider buying an out-of-the-money option.

Don't buy more time than you need.

The longer-term options often appear, to the naked eye, to be better buys. For example, suppose XYZ is 50, the Jan 50 call costs 2, and the April 50 call costs 2¾. You might feel that the April 50 is the better buy, even if both have the same implied volatility (i.e., neither one is more expensive than the other). This could be a mistake, especially if you're looking for a short-term trade. The excess time value premium that you pay for the April call, and the resultant lower delta that it has, both combine to limit the profits of the April 50 call vis-à-vis the Jan 50 call. On the other hand, if you're looking for the stock or futures contract to move on fundamentals—perhaps better earnings or a crop yield—then you need to buy more time because you don't know for sure when the improving fundamentals will reflect themselves in the price of the underlying.

> Know what strategies are equivalent and use the optimum one at all times.

Equivalent strategies have the same profit potential. For example, owning a call is equivalent to owning both a put and the underlying instrument. However, be aware that the capital requirements of two equivalent strategies (and their concomitant rates of return) can vary widely. The purchase of the call will only cost a fraction of the amount needed to purchase the put and the underlying stock, for example. However, the call purchase has a much larger probability of losing 100 percent of that investment.

The option positions that are equivalent to long stock (or long futures) and to short stock (or short futures) are perhaps the most important ones.

Buying a call and selling a put, both with the same terms (strike price and expiration date) produces a position that is equivalent to being long the underlying instrument. Similarly, buying a put and selling a call with the same terms is equivalent to being short the underlying instrument. The next three guidelines deal with these equivalences. It was shown in Chapter 3 that the equivalent option strategy may be better than owning the underlying stock itself. Also, the equivalent option strategy is better than selling stock short, and of course is the only way to completely short an index. Not only that, it doesn't require a plus tick to establish the short position. Finally, the equivalent option strategy is mandatory knowledge for futures traders, for it allows you to extricate yourself from a position that is locked limit against you.

Trade all markets.

There are strategic option opportunities in all markets—equities, indices, and futures. To ignore one or two of these just doesn't make sense. The same principles of option evaluation needed to construct a statistically attractive strategy apply equally well to all three markets. Furthermore, there are often intermarket hedges that are extremely reliable, but in order to take advantage of them, you have to trade all of the markets.

Have a little humility.

The market has a way of exacting a toll on braggarts. Whenever I meet someone at a social function and he starts telling me about his winning trades, I know I'm not talking to a professional trader. Professional traders, if they want to tell you about their trading *at all*, will more likely tell you about their losses (those are often better stories, anyway). Also, *remember not to confuse brains with a bull market*. That is, if you got lucky in a position because the market moved your way, don't feel that you are of superior intellect; you might get stung the next time.

The Biggest Mistake

I'm often asked what is the biggest mistake that novice option traders make. There are a lot of good answers to this question: not trading with volatility (or, alternatively stated, not using a model) is a good answer. So is failing to use good money management, both in terms of stops as well as taking partial profits. But the one that seems to me to be the most applicable, is that most novice traders—and some not so novice ones, too—put too much *hope* in a position. They buy options with too little time remaining and that are too far out-of-the-money. They are too optimistic. So, use a model, manage your positions well, and take a realistic view of the position's prospects.

SUMMARY

The information included in this chapter was less specific in nature than the trading systems, strategies, and methods described in earlier chapters. However, since trading is more of an art than a science, this information is extremely important. First, there were suggestions on basic brokerage and data gathering. We also described techniques to help with money management. The historic examples illustrated some of the good and bad points of speculation and option trading. Finally, we laid out some general guidelines on the philosophy of trading

Appendix A

Listed Sector and Index Options

The following list contains all the available broad-based and sector indices that were trading at the time of publication. An ^{L} indicates that LEAPS trade on this index.

Airline Index: PLN (PHLX), XAL (AMEX)
Automotive: AUX
Big Cap Index: MKT
Biotech Stock Subindex: BGX^L (CBOE) and BTK^L (AMEX)
Banking Stock Subindex: BKX (PHLX) and BIX (CBOE)
Broker Dealer Subindex: XBD
Chemical Stock Subindex: CEX
Computer and Technology Stock Subindex: XCI
Computer Software Stock Subindex: CWX
Consumer Stock Subindex: CMR
Cyclical Stock Subindex: CYC
Drug Stock Subindex: DRG^L
Eurotop 100 Index: EUR
Environmental Stock Subindex: EVX
Forest and Paper Products: FPP
FTSE-100 (London) Index: FSX
Gaming Subindex: GAX
Global Telecommunications: GTX
Gold and Silver Stock Subindex: XAU^L
Health Care Stock Subindex: HCX
Hong Kong Option Index: HKO
Insurance Stock Subindex: IUX
Institutional Index: XII^L
Interest Rate Indices:
   Short-Term Interest Rates: IRX^L
   5-year Treasury Note: FVX^L
   10-year Treasury Note: TNX^L
   30-year Treasury Bond: TYX^L
Internet: IIX (AMEX) and INX (CBOE)

Israel Index: ISX
Japan Index: JPN[L]
Latin Index: LTX
London Stock Index: see FTSE-100
Major Market Index: XMI[L]
Mexico Index: MEX[L] (CBOE), MXY[L] (AMEX)
Mid-Cap 400 Index: MID[L]
Morgan High-Tech: MSH
Nasdaq-100 Index: NDX
Natural Gas Subindex: XNG
Nikkei 300: NIK[L]
NYSE Composite Index: NYA
Oil Stock Subindex: XOI
Over-the-Counter Stock Index: XOC[L]
Pharmaceuticals: see Drug Stock
Phone Index: PNX
REITs Index: RIX
Retail Stock Subindex: RLX
Russell 2000 Index: RUT[L]
S&P 100 Index: OEX[L], CPO(Caps)
S&P 500 Index: SPX[L], NSX, CPS(Caps)
Semiconductor Index: SOX
Small Cap 600 Index: SML
Supercap: HFX
Technology: TXX (CBOE) and PSE (PSE)
Telecommunications: XTC (AMEX), TCX (CBOE)
Top 100 Index: TPX[L]
Transportation Stock Subindex: TRX
Utility Stock Subindex: UTY[L]
Value Line Index: XVL[L]
Volatility Index: VIX
Wilshire Small Cap Index: WSX

Futures Options Terms and Expirations

Underlying	$ / Point of Movement	Expiration Date
British Pound	$625 (150.00–151.00)	Second Friday before third Wednesday
Canadian Dollar	$1,000 (72.00–73.00)	Second Friday before third Wednesday
Cattle, Feeder	$500 (80.00–81.00)	Last Thursday that's not a holiday
Cattle, Live	$400 (72.00–73.00)	First Friday
Cocoa	$10 (1,100–1,101)	First Friday of preceding month
Coffee	$375 (82.00–83.00)	First Friday of preceding month
Copper	$250 (87.00–88.00)	Fourth day preceding LBD of preceding month
Corn	$50 (260–261)	Friday preceding LBD of preceding month by $\geqq 5$ business days
Cotton	$500 (80.00–81.00)	Third business day of month
Crude Oil	$1,000 (16.00–17.00)	(See a calendar)
Deutsche mark	$1,250 (58.00–59.00)	Second Friday before third Wednesday
Eurodollar	$2,500 (94.00–95.00)	Second London business day before third Wednesday
Gasoline (unleaded)	$420 (48.00–49.00)	(See a calendar)
Gold	$100 (381.0–382.0)	Second Friday of preceding month
Heating Oil	$420 (46.00–47.00)	(See a calendar)
Hogs, Live	$400 (45.00–46.00)	First Friday
Japanese Yen	$1,250 (97.00–98.00)	Second Friday before third Wednesday
Lumber	$160 (326.00–327.00)	Last Friday of preceding month)
Muni Bonds	$1,000 (90-00 to 91-00)	Eighth to last business day

(continues)

Underlying	$ / Point of Movement	Expiration Date
Nikkei Stock Average	$500 (201.00–202.00)	Third Friday; second Friday in Mar, Jun, Sep, Dec)
Orange Juice	$150 (100.00–101.00)	First Friday of preceding month
Platinum	$50 (388.0–389.0)	Second Friday of preceding month
Pork Bellies	$400 (54.00–55.00)	(See a calendar)
Silver (COMEX)	$50 (525.0–526.0)	Second Friday of preceding month
Soybeans	$50 (653–654)	Friday preceding LBD of preceding month by $\geq$ 5 business days
Soybean Meal	$100 (187.0–188.0)	Friday preceding LBD of preceding month by $\geq$ 5 business days
Soybean Oil	$600 (25.00–26.00)	Friday preceding LBD of preceding month by $\geq$ 5 business days
S&P 500 Index	$500 (443.00–444.00)	Third Friday
Sugar (#11)	$1,120 (11.00–12.00)	Second Friday of preceding month (Dec: 2nd Friday of Dec.)
Swiss Franc	$1,250 (69.00–70.00)	Second Friday before third Wednesday
T-Bills	$2,500 (95.00–96.00)	(See a calendar)
T-Bonds	$1,000 (105-00 to 106-00)	Friday preceding LBD of preceding month by $\geq$ 5 business days
T-Notes	Same as T-Bonds	Same as T-Bonds
Wheat	$50 (314–315)	Friday preceding LBD of preceding month by $\geq$ 5 business days

Notes: LBD: last business day. If no month is specified, *option* contract month is assumed; "preceding month" refers to month preceding *option* contract month.

Appendix C

Option Models

Black–Scholes Model

$$\text{Value} = pN(d_1) - se^{-rt}N(D_2)$$

where

$$d_1 = \frac{\ln(p/s) + (r + v^2/2)t}{v\sqrt{t}}$$

and

$$d_2 = d_1 - v\sqrt{t}$$

The variables are:

p	stock price
s	striking price
t	time remaining, in years
r	current risk-free interest rate, usually the 90-day T-bill rate
$\ln$	natural logarithm
$N(d)$	normal density function

The normal density function can be approximated with the following polynomial. First, calculate the values for x, y, and z. To find $N(\sigma)$:

$$z = 0.3989423e^{-\sigma/2}$$

$$y = 1/(1 + 0.2316419\,|\sigma|)$$

$$x = 1 - z(1.330274y^5 - 1.821256y^4 + 1.781478y^3 - 0.356538y^2 + 0.3193815y)$$

The Greeks can be computed by taking partial derivatives of the model's formula. For example,

$$\text{Delta} = N(d_1)$$

$$\text{Gamma} = \frac{e^{-x/2}\big/\sqrt{(2\pi)}}{pv\sqrt{t}}$$

where

$$x = \ln\left(p\big/\left(s(1+r)^{-t}\right)\big/\left(v\sqrt{t}\right)\right) + v\sqrt{t}/2$$

Binomial Model

Believed by some to be more accurate because it gives the modeler the ability to define his own distribution of prices, the binomial model involves more calculations than the Black–Scholes model does. However, with today's faster computers, that's less of a consideration than it once was. The model is also known as the Cox–Ross–Rubinstein (C-R-R) binomial model.

To begin, construct a lattice as shown in Figure C.1. The left side of the lattice represents the current stock price. The defined probabilities are then used to determine the stock prices all along the lattice. The width of the lattice represents the time periods that a trader might be willing to consider from the current time until expiration (in actual practice, up to 50 time periods may be used to value an option).

In the example lattice shown here, it is assumed that the stock can make only two movements: either up 20 percent or down 20 percent for each time period. Furthermore, assume that we are only onsidering three time periods. In this simple example, the stock must be either at 172.8, 115.2, 76.8, or 51.2 after three time periods. Note that each up node is 1.2 times the previous node, while each down node is 0.8 times the previous node.

Once this process is completed, the intrinsic value of an option at the right-hand side of the lattice is easily determined. For example, if we were trying to evaluate a call with striking price 100 that expired after three periods, then we can see that the options would be worth the following at expiration:

Stock Price	Option Value at Expiration
172.80	72.80
115.20	15.20
76.80	0
51.20	0

Now, we'd like to also know with what probability these moves occur. The C-R-R formula gives us a formula to determine this:

$$p = (R - d) / (u - d)$$

where p = probability of an up move
  $R = e^{rt}$
  r = risk-free interest rate
  t = years remaining until expiration
  u = size of an up move
  d = size of a down move

Figure C.1
BINOMIAL MODEL LATTICE

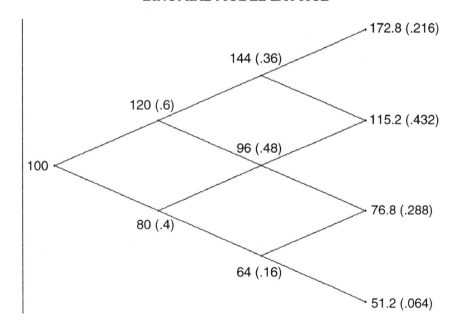

In our simple example, the size of an up move, u, is 1.2 (a 20 percent increase), while the size of a down move is 0.8 (a 20 percent decrease). Furthermore, for simplicity's sake, assume R = 1.04. Then we can calculate:

$$p = (1.04 - 0.8) / (1.2 - 0.8) = 0.6$$

Thus, p = 0.60, so there is a 60 percent chance that the stock will rise during time period, and, of course, that means that there is a 40 percent chance that it will decline. This is something like the log-normal distribution in that there is a larger chance that the stock will rise than that it will decline.

All of this information is summarized in Figure C.1. The stock prices at each node are shown, as well as the probability of each of them occuring—the number in parentheses. Note that a node that has *two* inputs (one from above and one from below) has a probability equal to the sum of the probabilities from the previous node.

Finally, we can use this information to determine the theoretical value of a call today at the initial node. We merely calculate the intrinsic value at expiration times the probability of being at that node, for each node, and sum them. In this example, the call value is

$$C = 0.216 \ (172.80 - 100) + 0.432 \ (115.20 - 100) +$$
$$0.288 \ (0) + 0.064 \ (0)$$
$$= 15.72 + 6.57 + 0 + 0 = 22.29$$

Thus, the theoretical value of a three-period call with striking price 100, with the stock at 100, under these assumptions, is 22.29.

In general, the C-R-R model gives us the following formula for determining the value of a call at any node. All that is required is to know the call value at the *succeeding* node. Thus, in actual application, we evaluate the lattice *from right to left* in order to determine the value of the call at the initial node.

The way we do this is to use the C-R-R formula to determine the theoretical call value, C:

$$C = \frac{pC_{up} + (1 - p)C_{down}}{R}$$

where p and R are defined as before; C_{up} is the value of the call if the underlying moves up by u; and C_{down} is the value of the call if the underlying moves down by d. If we are evaluating the tree *from right to left*, we always know C_{up} and C_{down}, so this is a quick computation.

To summarize, then, we first establish the lattice from left to right, using the assumptions about stock price movement. Then, we work from right to left, using the formula just given to arrive at a theoretical value for the call itself.

For further information on the use of the C-R-R model, you should read *Options Markets*, by John C. Cox and Mark Rubinstein (Prentice-Hall, 1985).

Index

SPECIAL OFFER
TO BOOK OWNERS

Trial subscriptions to either or both of these two services, written by Lawrence G. McMillan, author of two best-selling books on options, are available to book owners. *The Option Strategist* is a twice-monthly newsletter that concentrates on strategies using equity, index, and futures options. It also contains educational articles. **The Daily Volume Alert** is a fax service (also available by e-mail) that uses equity option volume to pinpoint stocks that are going to move (see "The Predictive Power of Options"—Chapter 4).

The Option Strategist features:

- Specific recommendations for equity, index, and futures options, including follow-up action.
- FREE telephone HOTLINE (toll call required outside of 201 area code).
- Ideas to improve your trading and hedging; articles on timely topics.

The Daily Volume Alert fax service features:

- Specific entry and exit points for short-term trading of stocks and stock options.
- Occasional OEX recommendations, based on our proprietary indicator.
- *Every business day,* analysis of issues with unusual option activity.

YES! Sign me up for the following trial subscriptions:

☐ 3 months of *The Option Strategist* (6 issues) for $19

☐ 1 month of **Daily Volume Alert Service** for $60 (regularly $95)

MasterCard **1-800-724-1817** **VISA®**

Name _____ Charge to MC __ VISA__ Exp. Date _____

Address _____ Card # _____

City _____ State ___ Zip _____ Signature _____

McMILLAN ANALYSIS CORPORATION

Publishers of **Daily Volume Alert** and *The Option Strategist*
P.O. Box 1323, Morristown, NJ 07962-1323
e-mail: mac19@ix.netcom.com